Charles E. Hambrick-Stowe

The Practice of Piety

Puritan Devotional Disciplines in

Seventeenth-Century New England

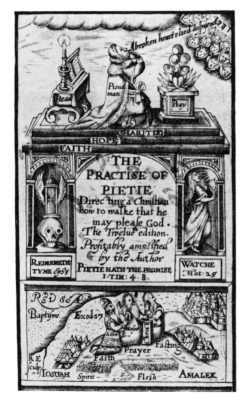

Published for the Institute of

Early American History and Culture

Williamsburg, Virginia

by The University of North Carolina Press

Chapel Hill

The Institute of
Early American History and Culture
is sponsored jointly by
The College of William and Mary
and The Colonial Williamsburg Foundation.

This book was the winner of the Jamestown Manuscript Prize for 1980.

Library of Congress Cataloging in Publication Data

ISBN 0-8078-1518-7

An early form of chapter 1 appeared in
the *Journal of Presbyterian History*, LVII (1980);
and parts of chapter 4 are in the Dublin Seminar for
New England Folklife, *Annual Proceedings*, IV (1979).

For

John von Rohr and David D. Hall

and for

Elizabeth A. Hambrick-Stowe

Preface

Historians have long treated New England Puritanism as an intellectual and a social movement. At its heart, however, Puritanism was a devotional movement, rooted in religious experience. This book deals with the form, content, and spiritual impact of the worship and private devotional activity of seventeenth-century New Englanders.

In this study I am attempting to write what Catherine Albanese has recently called, though perhaps with a different method in mind, "inner history." The history of religious experience is related to traditional intellectual and social history, to the study of literature, and to church history. It is kin to a great tradition in Roman Catholic historiography, exemplified by Pierre Pourrat's four-volume *Christian Spirituality*. At the same time, my study of New England spirituality attempts to honor recent demands, arising out of the American Studies approach to interdisciplinary research, that historians should write not only of elites but also of common folk and popular mentality.

The history of personal experience at the popular level is obviously more difficult to write than conventional institutional or even social history. We are dependent on diaries, spiritual autobiographies, meditative poetry, and other private writings. These are primarily (though not exclusively) the product of social elites. But evidence suggests that in seventeenth-century New England the gap between elite and popular culture was not wide. In many areas of religious life, clergy and populace inhabited the same cultural world. The private writing that survives pertinent to devotional practice is, I have good reason to believe, broadly reflective of common experience. Glimpses into the religious experience of folk, as recorded, for example, in the confessions of faith of individuals joining the Cambridge Church, show it to be of a piece with the personal religious experience of their pastor, Thomas Shepard himself, or of Anne Bradstreet and Cotton Mather.

Historians of Puritanism have relied heavily on the ministry's published sermons for insight into the religious beliefs of the movement. I have read these again with an eye to the neglected area of their devotional content and advice. But another genre altogether has been much less studied and opens a window into the nature of Puritanism.

Devotional manuals were an important part of the Puritan movement from the late sixteenth century onward, a product of the demand for pious reading matter that widespread Protestant literacy created. Such manuals were brought to New England with the immigration, were imported continually thereafter, and by the second half of the seventeenth century were being published in Cambridge and Boston. Social historians with an interest in counting will ask certain questions: Precisely how many households owned these manuals? How many of the individuals who owned them actually used them? I have not attempted this research. Even if we knew the answer to the first question, the second, I am sure, is unanswerable. Still, the manuals can be trusted as revelations of popular experience for two reasons. First, the model forms of meditation and prayer contained in the manuals correspond closely with surviving records of private experience. Second, the manuals were written in a popular style, were published in large and numerous editions, and were widely disseminated. From diary references to their use and from the shabby condition of the rare extant copies, we may infer they were heavily used. Taken together, the private writings and the printed devotional manuals provide a fuller picture of personal and religious experience at a popular level than one might expect. Evidence from other types of popular publications, such as captivity narratives and almanacs, sheds further light on the themes of devotional practice that emerge from the historical study of manuals, private writing, and sermons.

This book seeks to supplement certain commonly held ideas about New England religion in the seventeenth century and to correct others. Puritanism was as affective as it was rational, and Puritans were as wont to withdraw into contemplative solitude as they were to be active in the marketplace. Indeed, the particular forms of public worship and the characteristic private devotional exercises were what made a Puritan a Puritan.

My interest in these exercises is a new departure in that scholars have usually maintained that early seventeenth-century New Englanders were especially hostile to "technique," because they were rationalists, were chained by an inordinate doctrine of Original Sin, or were passively dependent on the unmanipulatable will of God. But Puritans did engage in devotional exercises quite similar to those of their Catholic forebears, contemporaries, and adversaries. Devotional methods were not, as Perry Miller believed, desperate late-century innovations. Rather, they were integral to Puritan spirituality throughout the century. And formal meditation on the sublime joys of heaven, with the resulting ecstasy, was not, contrary to Louis Martz's thesis, introduced only in the second half of the century; it was part of Puritan practice from the start. I have found that despite extensive social change in the seventeenth century, devotional practice remained essentially the same. The changes that were introduced in the second half of the century were no more than minor modifications of existing practice, intended to secure continuity by revitalizing traditional methods and themes.

Conversion, which has rightly commanded much scholarly attention, was only one part, the onset, of the devotional life. Most of my discussion focuses on post-conversion experience. The order of redemption, heretofore associated only with conversion, characterized the more advanced exercises and experiences as well. The major metaphor of the pilgrimage of the soul through ascending stages to heaven provided an interpretive framework for the ongoing life of worship, meditation, and prayer. In the state of grace progress on the pilgrimage was more important than spiritual rest, suggesting a dynamic understanding of devotional activity as preparation for salvation. Salvation in Puritan spirituality was not a fully achieved state but always a journey and a goal: Resurrection from the world in union with Christ after death. I interpret the important topic of preparationism more broadly than has usually been the case in the debate over human ability in the first stages of conversion.

This book is the result of my dual calling as a historian and a pastor. In colonial New England it was the scholar-pastor—Thomas Prince and Cotton Mather were only the most notable—who took upon himself the task of recording and interpreting his people's history. Conscious of the high quality of their work and that twentieth-century historians rely upon it to a remarkable extent, in humility I follow in their steps. That I write in service to both the Church and the secular community of historians is partly a reflection of my own interests. It is also indicative of the breakdown of the academic monopoly on scholarship that has prevailed since the late nineteenth century. As universities find they are less and less able to contain the flood of graduates from their own doctoral programs, we can look forward hopefully to a reintegration of learning with the community outside the walls of academe.

I am indebted to many people, three of whom are named in the dedication, and to several institutions. John von Rohr excited me about church history, introduced me to Thomas Hooker and the Puritans, and stimulated my first research at the Holbrook Library, Pacific School of Religion, a decade ago. Fr. James Hennesey wanted to know what the differences were between Puritan and Roman Catholic spirituality. At Boston University, where I completed an earlier version of this book as a doctoral dissertation, Norman Pettit, Cecelia Tichi, Ellen Smith, and Susan Geib shared insight, encouragement, and support. The primary influence of David Hall is, I am sure, evident throughout. I can hardly overstate my appreciation and respect for him as a teacher and advisor. Harold Worthley helped make the Congregational Library in Boston a most congenial place for research. I appreciate the help I received at the Massachusetts Historical Society, the Boston University Libraries, the New England Historic Genealogical Society, the American Antiquarian Society, the Union Theological Seminary, and the Folger Shakespeare Library. I am enormously grateful to the Jamestown Prize Committee of the Institute of Early American History and Culture for its 1980 award, and to Norman Fiering and his staff for vigorous and wise editing. The Consistory and people of St. Paul's United Church of Christ, Westminster, Maryland, have been very supportive of this work over the past two years.

Elizabeth is the one without whose constant presence at each stage along the way this book could not have been written, and whose loving companionship on the "parfit glorious pilgrimage" makes the journey exciting.

Contents

Illustrations

FIGURE 10.
Emblematic pictures and didactic verse from *The New England Primer*.
220–221

FIGURE 11.
Emblems of death and resurrection on seventeenth-century
New England gravestones.
232–233

FIGURE 12.
Frontispiece to Thomas Williamson, *The Sword of the Spirit*.
235

FIGURE 13.
Emblematic printer's ornament from Increase Mather,
Returning unto God the Great Concernment of a Covenant People.
252

FIGURE 14.
Title page of Lewis Bayly, *Manitowompae Pomantamoonk*,
translated and abridged by John Eliot.
269

The illustrations at the beginning of each chapter
are from Francis Quarles, *Emblemes, Divine and Moral . . .* ,
first published in 1635.
The scriptural references that accompanied each emblematic
illustration are cited below.

Preface: Book V, Emblem 5 (Canticles 5:6)
Chapter 1: Book V, Emblem 15 (Canticles 8:14)
Chapter 2: Book III, Emblem 15 (Psalm 31:10)
Chapter 3: Book IV, Emblem 7 (Canticles 7:11)
Chapter 4: Book III, Emblem 11 (Psalm 69:15)
Chapter 5: Book V, Emblem 10 (Psalm 142:7)
Chapter 6: Book III, Emblem 12 (Job 14:13)
Chapter 7: Book V, Emblem 8 (Romans 7:24)
Chapter 8: Book IV, Emblem 2 (Psalm 119:5)
Chapter 9: Book V, Emblem 13 (Psalm 55:6)

"Behold," said he, "the ancient and excellent character of a true Christian; 'tis that which Peter calls 'holiness in all manner of conversation' [1 Peter 1:15]; you shall not find a Christian out of the way of godly conversation.

"For, first, a seventh part of our time is all spent in heaven, when we are duly zealous for, and zealous on the Sabbath of God. Besides, God has written on the head of the Sabbath, REMEMBER, which looks both forwards and backwards, and thus a good part of the week will be spent in sabbatizing.

"Well, but for the rest of our time! Why, we shall have that spent in heaven, ere we have done. For, secondly, we have many days for both fasting and thanksgiving in our pilgrimage; and here are so many Sabbaths more. Moreover, thirdly, we have our lectures every week; and pious people won't miss them, if they can help it.

"Furthermore, fourthly, we have our private meetings, wherein we pray and sing, and repeat sermons, and confer together about the things of God; and being now come thus far, we are in heaven almost every day.

"But a little farther, fifthly, we perform family-duties every day; we have our morning and evening sacrifices, wherein having read the Scriptures to our families, we call upon the Name of God, and ever now and then carefully catechise those that are under our charge.

"Sixthly, we shall also have our daily devotions in our closets; wherein unto supplication before the Lord, we shall add some serious meditation upon his word: a David will be at this work no less than thrice a day. Seventhly, we have likewise many scores of ejaculations in a day; and these we have, like Nehemiah, in whatever place we come into.

"Eighthly we have our occasional thoughts and our occasional talks upon spiritual matters; and we have our occasional acts of charity, wherein we do like the inhabitants of heaven every day. Ninthly, in our callings, in our civil callings, we keep up heavenly frames; we buy and sell, and toil; yea, we eat and drink, with some eye both to the command and honour of God in all.

"Behold, I have not now left an inch of time to be carnal; it is all engrossed for heaven. And yet, lest here should not be enough, lastly, we have our spiritual warfare. We are always encountring the enemies of our souls, which continually raises our hearts unto our Helper and Leader in the heavens.

"Let no man say, ' 'Tis impossible to live at this rate'; for we have known some live thus; and others that have written of such a life have but spun a web out of their own blessed experiences. New-England has examples of this life: though, alas! 'tis to be lamented that the distractions of the world, in too many professors, do becloud the beauty of an heavenly conversation.

"In fine, our employment lies in heaven. In the morning, if we ask, 'Where am I to be to day?' our souls must answer, 'In heaven.' In the evening, if we ask, 'Where have I been to-day?' our souls may answer, 'In heaven.' If thou art a believer, thou art no stranger to heaven while thou livest; and when thou diest, heaven will be no strange place to thee; no, thou hast been there a thousand times before."

—From a sermon by John Eliot,
recorded by Cotton Mather

PART I

Puritanism Considered as a Devotional Movement

By Reading . . . in a Book called The Practice of Piety
I found some Description, of the Misery of Men
in Hell & of Happiness of the Godly which
somewhat stirred me.

JOHN BROCK
"Autobiographical Memoranda, 1636–1659"

Chapter One

New England Devotional Practice
Four Vignettes

 The study of Puritan devotion is first of all the study of people, not ideas. To be sure, seventeenth-century New Englanders were men and women whose lives were guided by a system of religious belief. But the theology is inseparable from those who believed in it. Further, Puritan theology was designedly experiential in nature. The Reverend John Eliot, in the portion of a sermon I have quoted in the epigraph to this book, was not primarily preaching dogma. He was exhorting all to practice the spiritual exercises he and others regularly engaged in. Cotton Mather used the sermon quotation to portray Eliot himself: "Indeed, I cannot give a fuller Description of him, than what was in a Paraphrase that I have heard himself to make upon that Scripture, 'Our Conversation is in Heaven' . . . and he did what he said." Puritan theology emphasized religious practice and was intended to promote the experience of God and His grace individually and in social groups. It was a popular theology, communicated through plain preaching and straightforward devotional manuals, poetry, and almanacs, and stated in themes and metaphors rooted deep in the religious traditions of common English men and women. The proper study of Puritanism begins with the spiritual experiences of Puritans.[1]

Captain Roger Clap, the Reverend Thomas Shepard, the Honorable Samuel Sewall, and Mistress Anne Bradstreet all qualify as representative "Puritans" under any definition of the term. In the episodes from their lives that I describe below, each of these figures is intended

---

1. Cotton Mather, ed., *The Life and Death of the Renown'd Mr. J. Eliot . . .* , 2d ed. (London, 1691), 19–21. The fundamental contribution of Perry Miller, especially in *The New England Mind: The Seventeenth Century* (Cambridge, Mass., 1954 [orig. publ. New York, 1939]), was to rescue from oblivion the intricate grandeur of Puritan theology. The result has been, in the words of Philip Greven, a bias toward "thought rather than feelings . . . theology rather than piety" (Philip Greven, *The Protestant*

to serve as an exemplar, almost in the same sense as Cotton Mather's biographies in *Magnalia Christi Americana* were intended. Yet even though all four lived in seventeenth-century New England, they were a diverse group. Puritanism was not simply a clerical movement; of the four only Shepard was a clergyman. Puritanism changed in the course of the century, and the story of each of these persons reveals something of the decades in which he or she lived and worked. Individuals also change over time, and the accounts illustrate different stages on life's way. In the lives of these four, the Puritan as young adult in the throes of conversion searching for assurance of grace, as mature adult preparing for Sabbath worship, as parent struggling with the death of a child, and as older person preparing for death all stand revealed. We also have examples of the Puritan as male and female. Finally, although none of the four was poor at the time of writing, the experience that Roger Clap recounted took place when Clap was young and unestablished. It is my contention that popular piety infused the experience of nearly everyone in New England society, though obviously in varying degrees, and that in matters of devotion, lines of class were inconsequential. The four are held to-

---

Temperament: Patterns of Child-Rearing, Religious Experience, and the Self in Early America [New York, 1977], 5). Puritan spirituality has not been totally ignored by scholars, however, and Greven's picture of Miller is overdrawn. See especially: Geoffrey Fillingham Nuttall, *The Holy Spirit in Puritan Faith and Experience* (Oxford, 1946); Horton Davies, *The Worship of the English Puritans* (London, 1948); Alan Simpson, *Puritanism in Old and New England* (Chicago, 1955); Gordon S. Wakefield, *Puritan Devotion: Its Place in the Development of Christian Piety* (London, 1957); Norman Pettit, *The Heart Prepared: Grace and Conversion in Puritan Spiritual Life* (New Haven, Conn., 1966); U. Milo Kaufmann, *The Pilgrim's Progress and Traditions in Puritan Meditation* (New Haven, Conn., 1966); Owen C. Watkins, *The Puritan Experience: Studies in Spiritual Autobiography* (New York, 1972); Michael McGiffert, ed., *God's Plot: The Paradoxes of Puritan Piety, Being the Autobiography & Journal of Thomas Shepard* (Amherst, Mass., 1972), Introduction, 3–32; Irvonwy Morgan, *Puritan Spirituality: Illustrated from the Life and Times of the Rev. Dr. John Preston* . . . (London, 1973); Robert S. Paul, "The Accidence and the Essence of Puritan Piety," *Austin Seminary Bulletin*, XCIII, no. 8 (May 1978). Works dealing with the broader religious spectrum include: Joseph B. Collins, *Christian Mysticism in the Elizabethan Age: With Its Background in Mystical Methodology* (Baltimore, 1940); Helen C. White, *English Devotional Literature (Prose), 1600–1640* (Madison, Wis., 1931); Louis L. Martz, *The Poetry of Meditation: A Study in English Religious Literature of the Seventeenth Century* (New Haven, Conn., 1954); Horton Davies, *Worship and Theology in England*, I: *From Cranmer to Hooker, 1534–1603* (Princeton, N.J., 1970), II: *From Andrewes to Baxter and Fox, 1603–1690* (Princeton, N.J., 1975). Many of these works deal primarily with English religious history and treat theology far more than experience. The idea of the primacy of "intellect" in Puritan psychology is effectively corrected by Norman S. Fiering, "Will and Intellect in the New England Mind," *William and Mary Quarterly*, 3d Ser., XXIX (1972), 515–558.

gether by the practice of devotion, and they exemplify well-developed patterns, themes, and techniques. Further, all four wrote about their spiritual experiences, since diary keeping and spiritual autobiography were key practices of Puritan devotion. In their personal writings New Englanders wrestled with God over the state of their souls. They recorded in their journals, diaries, poems, and confessions their devotional practices and the resulting heights and depths of religious experience.[2]

ROGER CLAP

Alone in the dark Roger Clap lay lost in meditation.

Barely twenty-one and already a member of the Dorchester Church, he now felt a wave of uncertainty and insecurity rush over him. "In my saddest Troubles for want of a clear Evidence of my good Estate," he wrote years later in his *Memoirs*, "I did . . . Examine my self upon my Bed in the Night, concerning my spiritual Estate."[3]

Why did these doubts persist? His recent immigration in the spring of 1630 had, after all, been a spiritual experience for him—a personal exodus from the bondage of apprenticeship, from servitude to parental consent, and from the limited future of a youngest son. "It was

---

2. The idea of the exemplar in New England Puritanism is treated by Sacvan Bercovitch, *The Puritan Origins of the American Self* (New Haven, Conn., 1975). One wishes, of course, that there had been more women like Anne Bradstreet who left personal spiritual and autobiographical writings. Much of what is available comes from the pens of men, and especially clergymen. William D. Andrews has pointed out that the majority of published funeral sermons memorialized women and that a large proportion of funeral poems were dedicated to women of extraordinary piety ("The Printed Funeral Sermons of Cotton Mather," *Early American Literature*, V [Fall 1970], 24–44). One excellent spiritual autobiography by a 17th-century woman, Elizabeth White, which has been assumed to be the product of New England, is in fact not American. Daniel B. Shea, Jr., in *Spiritual Autobiography in Early America* (Princeton, N.J., 1968), included a major discussion of White's *The Experiences of God's Gracious Dealing* . . . on the basis of its publication in Boston in 1741. *The Experiences* was originally published in Glasgow in 1696, however, with a second edition there in 1698. For a suggestive beginning toward an understanding of "collective mentality," see David D. Hall, "The World of Print and Collective Mentality in Seventeenth-Century New England," in John Higham and Paul K. Conkin, eds., *New Directions in American Intellectual History* (Baltimore, 1979), 166–180.

3. *Memoirs of Capt. Roger Clap. Relating Some of God's Remarkable Providences to Him . . .* (Dorchester Antiquarian and Historical Society, *Collections*, I [Boston, 1854 (orig. publ. 1731)]), 17–25, hereafter cited as *Clap's Memoirs*. (Subsequent quotations in the text are taken from this source.) Shea discusses Clap's *Memoirs* in *Spiritual Autobiography*, 118–125, emphasizing Clap's conflation of his own and New England's salvation.

God that did draw me by his Providence out of my Father's family" and guided the journey into the "Wilderness" of New England, on the road to the Promised Land of heaven. The physical hunger of the first year in the Massachusetts Bay Colony was more than offset by the spiritual nourishment gained through the ministers' preaching. "The Lord Jesus Christ was so plainly held out in the Preaching of the Gospel unto poor lost Sinners, and the absolute Necessity of the New Birth, and God's holy Spirit in those Days was pleased to accompany the Word with such Efficacy upon the Hearts of many" that the number of conversions soared. The vast majority of the population entered the churches as covenanted members. Unlike their Old Testament prototypes, Clap reported, these children of New Israel were not tempted to turn back. "The Discourse, not only of the Aged, but of the Youth also, was not, 'How shall we go to England?' (tho' some few did not only so Discourse, but also went back again) but 'How shall we go to Heaven?'" Clap himself was among the convicted and, he had hoped, soundly converted. His faith centered especially on his yearning for fellowship with believers, and after a thorough self-examination based on 1 John 3:14 ("We know that we have passed from death unto life, because we love the brethren") he entered into the church covenant by the end of 1630.

Young Clap's joy at being on the right path diminished, however, as he listened to the conversion narratives of others as they joined the saints. He was aware of Christ's having saved him from sin, and the psychological order of his experience was the same as that testified to by others. After all, "the way of coming to [Christ] by Believing was plainly shown forth" by the ministers in their sermons. But the intensity of experience seemed so much greater in others. "Many in their Relations spake of their great Terrors and deep Shame of their lost Condition." Clap's experience of salvation had not been at all dramatic. Worse, his account of his conversion experience and of God's involvement in each stage was not nearly as precise as the accounts of others whose stories he now heard. "I could not so find as others did, the Time when God wrought the Work of Conversion in my Soul, nor in many respects the Manner thereof." Perhaps his own experience had been a delusion and not the work of God after all. "It caused in me much Sadness of Heart, and Doubtings how it was with me, Whether the Work of Grace were ever savingly wrought in my Heart or no?" He refused to believe the worst, "yet how to be in some measure assured thereof was my great Concern."

In this anguished search for assurance of his divine election Clap now turned inward, meditating once again on the central issues of his

own sinfulness. Late at night he put himself "upon . . . Trial." Following established methods of self-examination, he focused his thoughts
on the secret sin most difficult to resist. He put the question "to my
very Heart and Soul" whether he would willingly commit that sin
again after receiving assurance of salvation. Suddenly he found the
resolution welling up within not to commit that sin again. And this
then led to a deeper experience. "At that Time my conscience did witness to me that my State was good: And God's holy Spirit did witness
(I do believe) together with my Spirit, that I was a Child of God; and
did fill my Heart and Soul with such a full Assurance that Christ was
mine, that it did so transport me as to make me cry out upon my Bed
with a loud Voice, 'He is come, He is come.' And God did melt my
Heart."

The intensity of the experience is vividly expressed in Clap's ecstatic
cry in the darkness, echoing the mystically erotic Song of Songs ("Behold, he cometh," 2:8) and Jesus' parable of the ten virgins ("And at
midnight there was a cry made, Behold the bridegroom cometh,"
Matthew 25:6). The inner reconciliation of sin and assurance, and of
New England's experiential standard and an individual's yearning for
religious experience, yielded a moment of spiritual power. It was an
intensity Roger Clap never recaptured, although he practiced the disciplines of meditation and prayer throughout his life. In the external
world Clap pursued a successful career as a merchant and a militia
officer. In his spiritual life he had found the breakthrough he so
desperately needed.

THOMAS SHEPARD

The Reverend Thomas Shepard, pastor of the Cambridge Church,
sat writing in his study by candlelight. It was a Saturday night in the
depths of the winter of 1640/1641, and the end of a long day. The
morning had been taken up with finishing his sermon and with the
usual visitors. The afternoon was given mostly to family devotions in
preparation for the Sabbath. The late evening now found him in
secret meditation and prayer. Shepard was preaching the next day
on Isaiah 32:1–2: "Behold, a king shall reign in righteousness, and
princes shall rule in judgment. And a man shall be as an hiding place
from the wind, and a covert from the tempest; as rivers of water in a
dry place, as the shadow of a great rock in a weary land." In meditation Shepard moved through the text, doctrines, and arguments of
his sermon. It is likely that the wording of the Geneva Bible, the popu-

lar early Puritan translation, persisted in his mind (and perhaps he had that, rather than the 1611 version, open before him), for his thoughts began to center on the phrase "a King shal reigne in *justice*."[4]

Shepard recorded the experience in his journal. "January 9. As I was walking in my study musing on my sermon in Q. 10, that God's mercy was as near as his justice also was, the one to men that come to Christ, and that are out of Christ, the other." He followed the meditative technique of applying the question to his own experience. "Hence I considered when I come to Christ there is no wrath, justice to devour, but sweet love." And who will inherit God's justice? Who are those who are "out of Christ"? Shepard wrote the answer that came to him: "Wrath there is for refusing him, not else." What then of the Calvinist doctrine, shared by Puritans, of predestination and the damnation of the nonelect? How did that square with the hint of freedom in the action of coming to Christ or refusing to come? These theological issues were inappropriate to meditation: "The Lord let me then see I had nothing to do with that."

Shepard returned to the Scriptures. He clearly knew to whom the man in his text referred. The Geneva Bible translation reads, "And *that* man shal be as an hiding place," thus identifying the king of justice with the man of mercy. The marginal note (New England pastors continued to use the Geneva Bible's annotations throughout the century) makes the connection explicitly: "This prophecie is of Hezekiah who is a figure of Christ, and therefore ought chiefly to be referred to him." The king, the man, the hiding place, the rivers, and the rock: they were all Christ. In his pilgrimage through the wilderness, in tempest or in barrenness, Shepard found salvation only in Christ. If New England was "a weary land," God in His mercy had provided Christ as a rock for shade.

In his meditation, religious experience now flowed freely from the scriptural fountain. The Bible was for Puritans above all a devotional book. Shepard had begun by studying his text, moved quickly to the memory of his own past experience of "sweet love," and then focused his meditation on the theme of the wilderness pilgrimage. He wrote that when he considered that "to them that come to him, that he would stand as a rock between that scorching sun and their souls"—borrowing a phrase from Song of Songs 4:9—"my heart was sweetly ravished."

The passage has a millennialist thrust as well, and this finally drew

4. Thomas Shepard, "Journal," in McGiffert, ed., *God's Plot*, 85–86. (Subsequent quotations in the text are taken from this source.) Geneva Bible references are to *The Geneva Bible: Facsimile of the 1560 Edition* (Madison, Wis., 1969).

Shepard's meditation out beyond even present spiritual delight. The king was yet to come. Christ's heavenly kingdom would soon be established on earth. But Shepard's thoughts turned to that other sense in which saints would enter the kingdom, immediately after death. "Hence my heart was sweetly ravished," he wrote, "and began to long to die and think of being with him." Here Shepard reached the heights of his evening meditation, in preparation not only for the Sabbath, but for the eternal Sabbath of full union with Christ in glory.

Completing his journal entry, Shepard recalled the denouement of his meditation, a sermonic application to his own life. "And my heart said, to comfort yourself thus when you lie on your sick-bed, to lie under this rock as in a hot day." Spiritually refreshed, fully prepared for the Lord's Day, Thomas Shepard lay down his pen and went to bed.

SAMUEL SEWALL

Samuel and Hannah Sewall's son Henry, only three weeks old, was dying. He was not their first child. They had been married ten years earlier, in February 1676, and had produced one offspring at least every two years. Nor was Henry the first to die in infancy. Their first child, John, had died in the summer of 1677 at two months. Of the four others now living, the youngest, Hull (Hannah's maiden name), at seventeen months suffered from chronic convulsions.[5]

Sewall was thirty-three in 1685 and was fast becoming one of the most prominent men in the Massachusetts Bay Colony. Hannah's father, in whose home the Sewalls lived, was one of Boston's foremost merchants. Perhaps better than any other late seventeenth-century Puritan, Samuel Sewall combined worldly success and piety. But now and throughout his life he felt himself oppressed with the sorrow and spiritual uncertainty of the deaths of his children. Why was God dealing with him so? When Henry was born on December 7, 1685, the Reverend Samuel Willard baptized him in church the very next Sabbath. It seemed important to bring the child officially into the covenant as quickly as possible. Only a week later Henry fell seriously ill, and for four days and nights the Sewalls strove mightily with God in prayer for the life of their child.

5. M. Halsey Thomas, ed., *The Diary of Samuel Sewall, 1674–1729* (New York, 1973), I, 87–90. (Subsequent quotations in the text are taken from this source.) See David E. Stannard, *The Puritan Way of Death: A Study in Religion, Culture, and Social Change* (New York, 1977), 56, on the anguish of Sewall and his contemporary Cotton Mather.

Serious illness was both a church and a family concern. The first indication of trouble appeared in Sewall's diary entry for Saturday, December 19. Samuel Willard called at their home, probably at Sewall's request. The diary reads simply, "Mr. Willard Prayes with my little Henry, being very ill." Hannah and Samuel, like most New Englanders, believed in the efficacy of prayer for well-being in this life and for salvation in the life to come. A model prayer for a sick child, similar in words and tone to those poured out at Henry's cradle side, is found in the popular Puritan devotional manual, John Downame's *A Guide to Godlynesse:*

> We humbly intreat thee, to extend thy grace and favour unto this thy sick servant; and seeing thou art not onely the God of the faithfull, but also of their seed, and lovest and tendrest not onely the sheepe of Christ, but even the tender lambes; wee earnestly beseech thee, make good thy gracious Covenant with this thy weake and sick servant. And because hee is not capable of outward meanes, supply graciously the defect of them by thine holy Spirit. Unite him thereby unto Jesus Christ, that becoming a lively member of his body, he may be partaker of his righteousnesse, death and obedience, for his justification, and so hee may stand righteous in thy sight. Free him from the guilt and punishment of all his sinnes, and sanctifie him in his soule and body, that either hee may be fit to glorifie thee on earth, or to be glorified by thee in heaven. If it be thy blessed will, restore him. . . . But if thou art purposed to put an end to his days, so fit and prepare him for thy Kingdome, as that he may live with thee in glory and immortality, through Jesus Christ our Lord. Amen.[6]

On the morning of the Sabbath the child was no better and Samuel hurriedly sent off "Notes to Mr. Willard and Mr. Moodey to pray for my Child Henry." Great concern for the life of the child would be expressed at church, and Samuel probably attended at least one of the services. Hannah, only three weeks after delivery, was obliged to remain at home.

The child still did not improve. "Monday, about four in the Morn the faint and moaning noise of my child forces me up to pray for it." Neighboring women and the child's midwife, Mrs. Weeden, came to help minister to the infant, and so the prayer circle enlarged. The Reverend Mr. Moodey came on Monday night and Sewall wrote, "I get him to go up and Pray with my extream sick Son."

6. John Downame, *A Guide to Godlynesse, or a Treatise of a Christian Life* . . . (London, [1622]), 958–959.

Very early Tuesday morning the end was clearly near. "Child makes no noise save by a kind of snoaring as it breathed, and as it were slept." Before even the first dim light of dawn the Sewall family gathered for devotions. The reading from the Old Testament for the morning (following the general custom of families and individuals to work through both testaments sequentially) was the sixteenth chapter of the First Book of Chronicles. Around the fire in the cold morning Sewall read the words that undergirded the entire Puritan family and social structure: "Be ye mindful always of his covenant; the word which he commanded to a thousand generations" (16:15). The family was in covenant with their Lord; they all knew that. The covenant extended even to Henry in his cradle. Sewall turned to the New Testament reading, from the Gospel of John. "The fourteenth Chapter fell now in course, which I read and went to prayer." The utter sadness of the morning, resting still on confidence in God's purpose, found perfect expression as Sewall read the words of Jesus: "Let not your heart be troubled: ye believe in God, believe also in me. In my Father's house are many mansions: if it were not so, I would have told you. I go to prepare a place for you" (14:1–2). The prayers of the family, spoken aloud by Samuel and perhaps silently by Hannah, Nurse Hill, and the children, revolved around those "many mansions" prepared on the other side of death for those in covenant.

The prayers drew to a close just before sunrise. From the cradle the family "could hear little Breathing." Finally, as Nurse Hill held the child in her lap, "about Sun-rise, or a little after, he fell asleep, I hope in Jesus." The prayer returned to their hearts that "a Mansion was ready for him in the Father's House."

Sewall recorded the details then attended to, all part of the devotional ritual surrounding the death and burial of a family member. "Nurse Hill washes and layes him out: because our private Meeting hath a day of Prayer tomorrow, Thorsday Mr. Willard's Lecture, and the Child dying after Sun-rise (wether cloudy), have determined to bury on Thursday after Lecture." Events conspired to make a great impact on Sewall. He prayed that through the experience God might "prepare me and mine for the coming of our Lord, in whatsoever way it be."

The biblical metaphor of "fruit" strangely began appearing in Samuel Sewall's devotions. His exercises on Tuesday evening with Hannah and Nurse Hill centered on the fifteenth chapter of John. Just as the reading of John 14 had been providential, so now it seemed foreordained that the next chapter should come up this particular evening, since it was the chapter "out of which Mr. Willard took his

Text the day Henry was baptized." Afterward, with the entire family gathered, they read the third chapter of Matthew. The two passages preached a common theme to Samuel and Hannah, "both requiring fruit" from them in the sense of outward lives of godliness. "Herein is my Father glorified," they read in John, "that ye bear much fruit" (15:8). And in Matthew, "Bring forth therefore fruits meet for repentance. . . . Every tree which bringeth not forth good fruit is hewn down, and cast into the fire" (3:8 10). For the Sewalls, Scripture suggested, life must go on. Henry was in the Lord's hands; they had no fear for his soul. They had to look now that their own souls continued to grow in grace. Wednesday Samuel went as he always did to his "private Meeting," or neighborhood devotional group, which was holding a "privat Fast" at one of the member's home. The reasons for the fast included concerns larger than the Sewalls' grief, but sincere words of consolation were certainly spoken. Even Sewall's seemingly dissolute brother-in-law from Newbury, William Longfellow, appeared near the end of the meeting. When his presence angered Samuel momentarily—"he being so ill conditioned and outwardly shabby"—he felt immediately repentant. Had he so quickly forgotten the message of Matthew 3? "The Lord humble me. As I remember, he came so before; either upon the funeral of my Father or Johnny."

The most stunning experience for Sewall occurred at the Thursday lecture, just before the funeral. There, he recorded, "the 21. Psalm was Sung from the 8th to the end." The psalm warns that the Lord would "finde out" and punish all His enemies and "swallow them in's wrath." But the words of the tenth verse are what leapt out at Samuel from the page of the *Bay Psalm Book.* That key word "fruit" appeared again, now used in a distressingly different sense. Sewall surely forced himself to sing:

> Thou wilt destroy the fruit,
>   that doth proceed of them,
> out of the earth: & their seed from
>   among the Sonnes of men.[7]

Was God destroying Sewall's "fruit"—his children—as punishment for his own sinfulness? "The Lord humble me kindly in respect of all my Enmity against Him, and let his breaking my Image in my Son be a means of it."

With these heavy thoughts pressing upon him, and accompanied by an impressive array of ministers and magistrates, Sewall wrote, "We

7. *The Whole Booke of Psalmes Faithfully Translated into English Metre* ([Cambridge, Mass.], 1640), Psalm 21.

follow Little Henry to his Grave. . . . I led Sam., then Cous. Savage led Mother, and Cousin Dummer led Cous. Quinsey's wife, he not well. Midwife Weeden and Nurse Hill carried the Corps by turns, and so by Men in its Chestnut Coffin 'twas set into a Grave (The Tomb full of Water) between 4 and 5."

That night there was "considerable snow" and "little Hull had a sore Convulsion Fit." The convulsions continued "Wave upon Wave" Friday morning. The visiting minister from Rowley called at the Sewalls' home. With the snow accumulating outside, Samuel Sewall recorded in his diary, "Mr. Phillips Prayes with Hullie."

ANNE BRADSTREET

On August 31, 1669, Anne Bradstreet meditated, as she and others in New England often did, on the course of her life and her hope for the life to come. Preparation for death and eternity was a central theme in Puritan devotional practice. Aging quickly at sixty, suffering from a painful disease, her longing for heaven became acute.

Anne Bradstreet wrote a poem that gave outward expression to her contemplation, or was perhaps (as with the New England poet Edward Taylor) itself the means of meditation. Employing a devotional convention long and well used by Puritans and their spiritual ancestors since the time of Christ, and by contemporary European poets, she likened her life to a journey. She began to write: "As weary pilgrim. . . ."[8]

Christ had said of himself, "The foxes have holes, and the birds of the air have nests; but the Son of man hath not where to lay his head" (Matthew 8:20). Bradstreet followed this lead. Her voyage from England on the *Arbella* in 1630 was a formative experience, especially for an eighteen-year-old newlywed leaving all behind for an uncertain, somewhat utopian future. As Robert Cushman of Plymouth had written in a widely read tract that appeared in the 1622 *Mourt's Relation:* "But now we are all in all places strangers and pilgrims, travelers and sojourners, most properly, having no dwelling but in this earthen

8. Anne Bradstreet, "As Weary Pilgrim, Now at Rest," in Robert Hutchinson, ed., *Poems of Anne Bradstreet* (New York, 1969), 77–78. (Subsequent quotations are from the same source.) I have edited the punctuation to clarify the reading of the poem. Josephine K. Piercy, *Anne Bradstreet* (New York, 1965), 123 n. 28, suggests lines in Philip Sidney's *Arcadia* and Robert Herrick's *Hesperides* similar to Bradstreet's opening line. See also Ann Stanford, "Anne Bradstreet As a Meditative Writer," *California English Journal*, II (Winter 1966), 24–31, and her *Anne Bradstreet, the Worldly Puritan: An Introduction to Her Poetry* (New York, 1974).

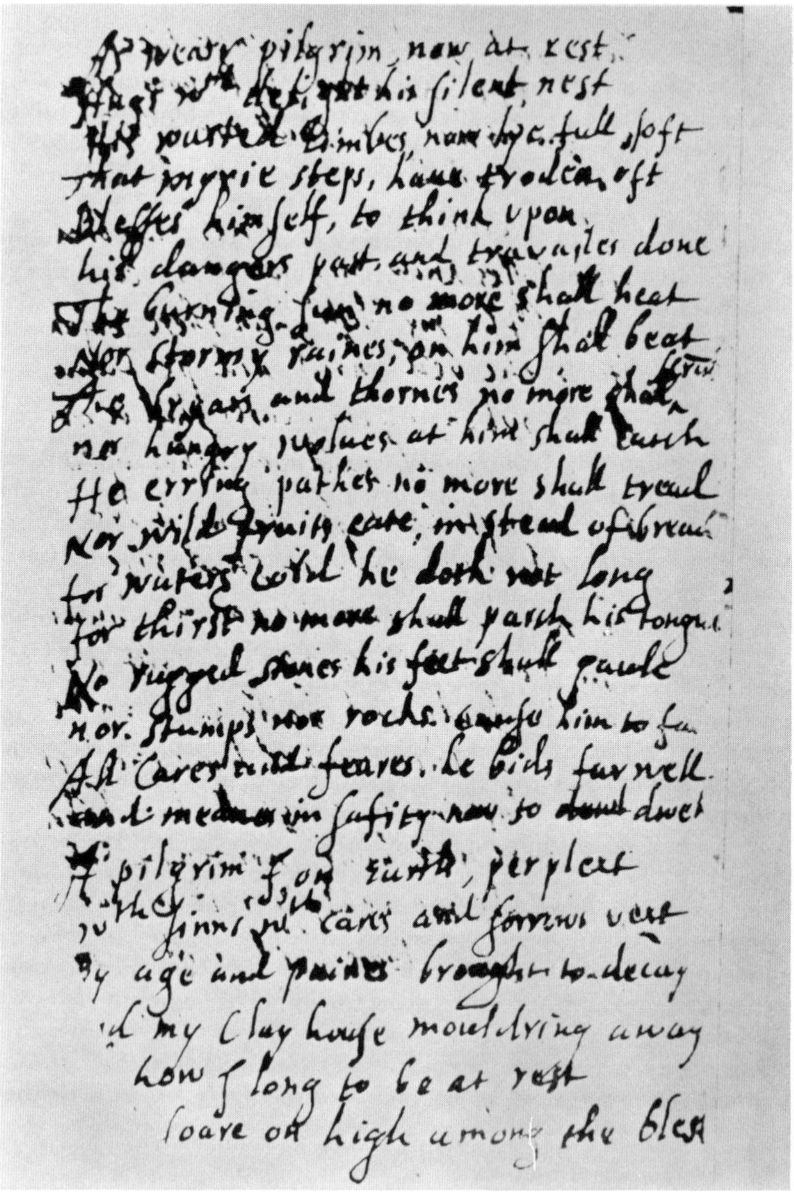
As weary pilgrim, now at rest,
Hugs with delight his silent nest
His wasted limbes, now lye full soft
That myrie steps, haue troden oft
Blesses himself, to think vpon
his dangers past, and travailes done
The burning sun no more shall heat
Nor stormy raines, on him shall beat.
The bryars and thornes no more shall scratch
nor hungry wolues at him shall catch
He erring pathes no more shall tread
nor wild fruits eate, instead of bread,
for waters cold he doth not long
for thirst no more shall parch his tongue
No rugged stones his feet shall gaule
nor stumps nor rocks cause him to fall
All cares and feares, he bids farwell
and meanes in safity now to dwell.
A pilgrim I, on earth, perplext
with sinns with cares and sorrows vext
By age and paines brought to decay
and my Clay house mouldring away
Oh how I long to be at rest
and soare on high among the blest

Figure 1. Anne Bradstreet's manuscript of her poem "As Weary Pilgrim," dated August 31, 1669, the only poem extant in her own hand. Her use of an uppercase "C" in the word "Come" supports my reading of the last line ("Come

This body shall in silence sleep,
Mine eyes no more shall weep,
No fainting fits shall me assail
nor grinding paines my body fraile
...
...
...
...
...
...
...
...
...
...
...
...
Lord make me ready for that day
then come deare bridgrome Come
away

Aug 31

deare bridgrome Come away"). *Courtesy the Stevens Memorial Library, North Andover, Massachusetts.*

tabernacle. Our dwelling is but a wandering, and our abiding but as a fleeting, and in a word our home is nowhere but in the heavens—in that house not made with hands, whose maker and builder is God, and to which all ascend that love the coming of our Lord Jesus." The biblical reference is to one of Puritanism's favorite texts, Hebrews 11:10–16, "They were strangers and pilgrims on the earth . . . they desire a better country, that is, an heavenly." Anne Bradstreet had heard the phrases intoned in countless sermons. Even settled in New England the Bradstreets' abiding was "but as a fleeting," as they moved from Cambridge to Ipswich to North Andover. Their beloved North Andover home burned to the ground in 1666. In the poem she wrote on that occasion, Anne Bradstreet recounted how she tenderly surveyed the damage after watching "the flame consume my dwelling-place." "My pleasant things in ashes lye." The scene became for her no less than a painful reminder of the Christian's transiency in this world and an emblem of that "house on high erect/Fram'd by that mighty Architect." Meanwhile, her constant battle with physical infirmity had already twelve years earlier caused her to refer in her diary to her life as "my weary Pilgrimage."[9]

A pilgrimage always has a destination, the "Celestial City" of John Bunyan's Christian, and it was to this place that Anne Bradstreet's meditation turned. In the 1657 diary entry in which she first used the phrase that now opened her meditative poem she thanked God that on her pilgrimage she had had "many a refreshment . . . in this valley of Baca many pools of water." Psalm 84, to which this is an allusion, evidently played a role in evoking the "weary pilgrim" image for her. Verse three of the psalm, in fact, contains an Old Testament analog of Jesus' "birds of the air" saying: "Yea, the sparrow hath found an house, and the swallow a nest for herself, where she may lay her young, even thine altars, O Lord of hosts, my King, and my God." The image of the swallow's nest came to mind as she wrote her poem. The twist, not lost on Mrs. Bradstreet, was that the pilgrim can have a home even in this life if her heart is in heaven. But she could never be fully *at* home in this life. To be fully at home one must rest completely at the altar of the King, and this would not come until the end of the journey. The psalm, and the pilgrimage motif itself, pulled her toward

9. Robert Cushman, "Reasons and Considerations Touching the Lawfulness of Removing out of England into the Parts of America (London, 1622)," in John Demos, ed., *Remarkable Providences, 1600–1760* (New York, 1972), 27. Anne Bradstreet, "Upon the Burning of Our House, July 10th, 1666," in Hutchinson, ed., *Poems of Bradstreet*, 54–56. "Autobiographical Passages in the Bradstreet Manuscript," entry for May 11, 1657, *ibid.*, 184–185.

that final fulfillment in God's Kingdom. Now in meditation she could feel glorious rest coming very close.

As weary pilgrim, now at rest,
  Hugs with delight his silent nest;
His wasted limbes now lye full soft
  That myrie steps have troden oft;
Blesses himself to think upon
  his dangers past and travailes done.

Exploring the pilgrimage metaphor further, she found the image of wilderness filling her thoughts. The difficult physical and spiritual journey is frequently connected in the Bible with the idea of wilderness (as, for example, in the Exodus or in Jesus' temptations). In the history of Christian devotional and mystical writing pilgrimage and wilderness are two great themes that often converge. Less than a decade later John Bunyan would begin his narrative of another pilgrim with the words, "As I walk'd through the wilderness of this world." For New Englanders in the seventeenth century the idea of wilderness was irresistible whenever a pen touched paper. But perhaps most significantly, there is an eschatological element in the concept of wilderness, just as there is in the concept of pilgrimage. The satisfaction and overturning of wilderness deprivation, hardship, and violence commonly formed part of the vision of biblical prophets. Isaiah 35, for example, begins: "The wilderness and the solitary place shall be glad for them; and the desert shall rejoice, and blossom as the rose."[10] Anne Bradstreet's words flowed from these traditions.

The burning sun no more shall heat,
  Nor stormy raines on him shall beat.
The bryars and thornes no more shall scratch,
  nor hungry wolves at him shall catch.
He erring pathes no more shall tread,
  nor wild fruits eate in stead of bread;
for waters cold he doth not long,
  for thirst no more shall parch his tongue.
No rugged stones his feet shall gaule,
  nor stumps, nor rocks cause him to fall.

10. John Bunyan, *The Pilgrim's Progress from This World to That Which Is to Come . . .* (1678), ed. James Blanton Wharey and Roger Sharrock, 2d ed. (Oxford, 1960), 8. See generally, Collins, *Christian Mysticism*, and George H. Williams, *Wilderness and Paradise in Christian Thought: The Biblical Experience of the Desert in the History of Christianity & the Paradise Theme in the Theological Idea of the University* (New York, 1962).

> All cares and feares he bids farwell,
>   and meanes in safity now to dwell.

Mrs. Bradstreet's meditation here reached its crucial moment. Having established in her mind the vision of the pilgrim arriving home, she now focused her gaze on her own condition. She herself was a pilgrim, but she had not yet completed her journey. Each step, in fact, now seemed more difficult.

> A pilgrim I, on earth, perplext
>   with sinns, with cares and sorrows vext;
> By age and pains brought to decay,
>   and my Clay house mouldring away.

But her vision of the arriving pilgrim filled her with anticipation and yearning.

> Oh how I long to be at rest
>   and soare on high among the blest.

She longed immediately for death, for the silence of the grave. Meditation on the body's decay brought solace, not fear. All the ailments that would soon no longer plague her rushed to mind in an instant of jubilation.

> This body shall in silence sleep.
>   Mine eyes no more shall ever weep.
> No fainting fits shall me assaile,
>   nor grinding paines; my body fraile
> With cares and feares ne'r cumbred be,
>   Nor losses know, nor sorrowes see.

Comfort came with the thought that Christ too had rested in a tomb.

> What tho my flesh shall there consume,
>   it is the bed Christ did perfume.

Perfect rest was not to be found in a tomb, however. Christ's resurrection from the grave was the sign of even greater glory to come in the resurrection of the dead at the last day. She recalled phrases and images from St. Paul's grand vision in 1 Corinthians 15. The day was both real and imminent.

> And when a few yeares shall be gone,
>   this mortall shall be cloth'd upon.
> A Corrupt Carcasse downe it lyes,
>   a glorious body it shall rise.

In weaknes and dishonour sowne,
in power 'tis rais'd by Christ alone.

The doctrine of the reunion of soul and body and the thought of her residence in heaven filled Bradstreet with joy in the anticipation of it.

Then soule and body shall unite
and of their maker have the sight.
Such lasting joyes shall there behold
as eare ne'r heard nor tongue e'er told.

The most wonderful joy came last, and here her meditation reached its zenith. The consummation of the saint's personal union with Christ would occur after her death, with the coming of Christ in glory at the end of time. The day of her death and the Day of the Lord were coming on quickly. They were so near that in the intensity of her devotions Anne Bradstreet could feel them as present reality. She could only use words inspired by Jesus' parable of the ten virgins (Matthew 25:6) conjoined in a startling way with a phrase from the Song of Songs ("Rise up, my love, my fair one, and come away." 2:10) to express the ecstasy of her own mystical union with Christ:

Lord make me ready for that day;
then, Come deare bridgrome. Come away.

Her meditative cry of longing, "Come deare bridgrome," transported her soul. The last two words—"Come away"—were spoken *to* Anne Bradstreet by Christ.[11]

In each of the cases described in these vignettes, Puritans called upon certain specific spiritual exercises from their devotional tradition to progress through life crises and daily duties. The reading of Scripture and the practice of meditation and prayer had a spiritual

11. My reading of Bradstreet's final line is, as far as I know, unique. See the discussion of the poem in Piercy, *Anne Bradstreet*; Stanford, *Anne Bradstreet*, 115–120; and Amanda Porterfield, *Feminine Spirituality in America: From Sarah Edwards to Martha Graham* (Philadelphia, 1980), 36–37. Stanford develops the interesting idea that the poem must be read in the tradition of the wedding song. She concludes, however, by suggesting that "a characteristic call to the bridegroom occurs in the final address to Christ: 'then Come deare bridgrome Come away.'" In fact, the line only makes sense when read with a period after "Come deare bridgrome." Mrs. Bradstreet calls upon Christ to come to her, and Christ answers with his own invitation. The two phrases, "Come deare bridgrome" and "Come away," are from two distinct scriptural sources. In the Song of Songs the invitation to "Come away" is spoken not by the bride but by the "beloved," the bridegroom himself. Mrs. Bradstreet's use of capitalization reinforces this reading.

and psychological impact of great power. The experiences of Clap, Sewall, and Bradstreet were stirred by crises in which each felt religious anxiety, and even in the case of Shepard anxiety played its role as he prepared to preach the Word of God. To a great degree, anxiety was a motivating force in the daily devotional practice of New Englanders throughout their lives. Sewall, Shepard, and Bradstreet were all in some way preparing for death, though Mrs. Bradstreet was the most explicit in this regard. Shepard and Bradstreet in their exercises were self-consciously and purposefully preparing for the Sabbath. Shepard began by preparing only for the morrow's worship, but both he and Mrs. Bradstreet ended by preparing joyfully for the eternal Sabbath of heaven. All but Sewall, whom we left in the midst of anxiety and spiritual humiliation, experienced an ecstatic resolution and release of the tension that attended the onset of their devotions. Surprisingly, the words all spontaneously used to express outwardly the fire that burned within came from the poetry of the Song of Songs and the associated bridegroom imagery used by Jesus. The feeling of being ravished by Christ, the Great Lover of the mystical tradition, the Bridegroom, was clearly not unique to Edward Taylor, whose poetry seemed so un-Puritan to scholars only a few years ago. The devotions of these four were characteristic of common practice. If their intensity occurred only occasionally in the life of any one individual (though for some it came weekly), the patterns, techniques, and themes of worship, meditation, and prayer were widely shared.[12]

The major themes in Puritan devotional practices are incapsulated in these vignettes and in the epigraph to this book by John Eliot and Cotton Mather. A grand devotional and theological scheme begins to suggest itself, that of the spiritual life as a journey or pilgrimage from sin to salvation and glory. Joseph B. Collins has identified this way of thinking as "the allegory of the Pilgrimage of Life" and has traced its development from the medieval mystics through Elizabethan England. The sense of being on pilgrimage structured Puritan religious experience from the first stages of conversion on through the saint's growth in God's grace, and it strongly colored the daily and weekly disciplines of devotional activity.[13]

12. For discussions of the role of anxiety in Puritan spirituality from varying viewpoints, see McGiffert, ed., *God's Plot*, Introduction, 3–32; William K. B. Stoever, *'A Faire and Easie Way to Heaven': Covenant Theology and Antinomianism in Early Massachusetts* (Middletown, Conn., 1978), esp. 147–155; and David Leverenz, *The Language of Puritan Feeling: An Exploration in Literature, Psychology, and Social History* (New Brunswick, N.J., 1980).

13. Collins, *Christian Mysticism*, esp. 64–70.

Scholars have commonly limited their discussions of Puritan religious life to the issue of conversion. New Englanders, admittedly,
made much of this experience as a personal milestone and credential,
but it marked only the beginning of their journey. The stages through
which the soul must pass in conversion indeed formed the core of the
preaching heard week after week, but such preaching was received
with significance by auditors who were well beyond first conversion
as well as by beginners. The spiritual dynamics of preparation and
implantation—death and resurrection, repentance for sin and subsequent salvation—described the actual experience of individuals
over the course of their spiritual lives. This was true even for those
among the laity who could never identify a precise moment of conversion. The redemptive cycle of death and resurrection was an
element in the very air New Englanders breathed, unavoidable and
ubiquitous in the rituals of public worship and the words of private
devotion. The pattern for Puritan devotion is to be found in the
Bible. God's dealings with His people, recorded in the Old Testament
—notably the covenant with Abraham, the Exodus from Egypt, and
the return from Babylonian Captivity—and in the gospel accounts of
the work of Christ, were the ground of Puritan spirituality. The biblical drama of salvation, perceived to be God's great plan for all creation, was now being played out in individual hearts and in church
and society in New England. The pilgrimage of the saints, then, had
its goal in God's eternal Kingdom. The end time was quite real for
New Englanders, both in the sense of each person's death and that of
the imminent end of the world, the chiliad, and the establishment of
the Kingdom on earth. In his sermon on "the way of godly conversation" Eliot preached, "God has written on the head of the Sabbath,
REMEMBER, which looks both forwards and backwards." In weekday devotions, Eliot suggested, individuals looked back to the Word
preached the previous Sabbath and also prepared for receiving grace
on the following Sabbath. In a larger sense, New England devotional
disciplines looked back to the Bible and the work of Christ for form
and inspiration and forward to the Kingdom for fulfillment. The
exercises were designed to prepare the soul for the final perfect glory.

"Preparation for salvation" has generally been understood only in
the context of conversion. But preparationist exercises, as William
Stoever has pointed out, were part of a far broader reality in New
England spiritual life. The disciplines of public worship and private
devotion, which we will analyze in detail, were all aimed at the preparation of the heart for heaven. Salvation was the culmination of a life
process rather than a state achieved at first conversion; the soul was in

transit from sin to salvation throughout life, and the goal could not finally be reached until after death. In this life New Englanders continually expressed the full cycle of sin and salvation in worship and devotion. The redemptive drama was enacted in daily exercises (especially in the evening and in the morning), in the private duties of meditation and prayer, in preparation for and participation in Sabbath worship, in the sacraments, in special public and private days of fasting and thanksgiving, and in the various other occasions of worship instituted in New England. Even as it was driven by anxiety, Puritan devotion was capable of producing experiences of great spiritual satisfaction. The pilgrim soul anticipated and even tasted the joy of arrival. Preparationism did not lead to futility, but commonly to progress toward the "heavenly city" and "that house not made with hands."[14]

14. Stoever, '*Faire and Easie Way*,' 192–199.

Chapter Two

"The Better Part: Heart Religion"

 A devotional revival swept Europe from the late six-
teenth through the seventeenth centuries. The aim
both of Protestantism, with its new emphasis on the
availability and authority of the Bible, and of the
Counter-Reformation, in its various fresh expressions
of spiritual discipline, was renewal of personal religious experience. In both Reformed and Roman
Catholic spirituality the seventeenth century inaugurated "the cult of
the Sacred Heart," though in different ways. Priests and pastors alike
urged a personal and well-cultivated relationship with Christ. Publication of popular religious tracts, and especially devotional manuals
advising men and women of every secular vocation how to meditate
and pray and receive the Sacrament, rose astronomically. Puritanism
in England, whatever else it accomplished in the economic, ecclesiastical, political, and social turmoil of the period, was a devotional
movement dedicated to the spiritual regeneration of individuals and
society. Although Puritans believed they were in the vanguard of the
revival and sought to distinguish themselves from other theological
parties, as a devotional movement Puritanism was part of a larger
spiritual awakening.[1]

When Puritanism is viewed as a devotional movement, the motiva-
tions behind the Puritans' migration to New England are revealed to
be continuous with those of zealous Christians since Pentecost. Not
seeking religious freedom in any modern sense, New Englanders
thought of themselves as the germ of a new order that God would
soon establish throughout Christendom and the world. More than
just the establishment of purity of worship, the essence of the new
order was individual union with Christ, achieved through participation in a whole range of private and public devotional disciplines. The
new order was to be peopled by saints who through these exercises

1. Terence C. Cave, *Devotional Poetry in France, 1570–1613* (Cambridge, 1969).
Wakefield, *Puritan Devotion*, 99–101. Louis B. Wright, *Middle Class Culture in Elizabethan
England* (Chapel Hill, N.C., 1935), chaps. 5 and 8.

were experiencing a rebirth in the Holy Spirit and progressive growth in God's grace. In a sermon preached to members of his congregation departing for New England in 1630, John Cotton interpreted the migration in these terms. His concluding biblical rationale for moving into a new country was to establish "the liberty of the Ordinances." Not legalistically concerned with correct forms, Cotton preached of personal devotion within the godly community. "You must labour to finde him in his Ordinances, in prayer and in Christian communion. These things I owe him as my Landlord, and by these I finde and enjoy him. . . . And if you knew him before, seeke him yet more, and feele after him till you finde him in his Ordinances, and in your consciences."[2]

The drive to establish pure gathered churches at the congregational level was more than a point of ecclesiastical contention. The Puritans believed that church organization in this form was most conducive to spiritual rebirth. The Reverend Thomas Welde wrote in a 1632 letter to former parishioners in England: "O how hath my heart been made glad with the comforts of His house and the spiritual days in the same wherein all things are done in the form and pattern showed in the mount, members provided, church officers elected and ordained, sacrament administered, scandals prevented, censured, fast days and holy feast days and all such things by authority commanded and performed according to the precise rule." He insisted that the task did not lead to the sin of pride, however. New Englanders were "the poorest and unworthiest of all his servants." The work was God's, while through the exercises of worship and devotion, "we desire to breathe after perfection." A young merchant, Edward Trelawny, wrote in a similar vein to his brother:

> For my part I have just cause even to bless the Lord for so high a favor in bringing me hither. . . . Oh dear brother, I now find what it is to be a Christian, a most difficult hard thing it is to bring that heart into frame and subjection that hath formerly ever drunk in iniquity like water and run the race of all licentiousness, even with greediness. A crucified Christian, what a most honorable title is it. . . . Oh Newe England, Newe England, how much

2. John Cotton, *Gods Promise to His Plantations* . . . (London, 1634 [orig. publ. 1630]), 9, 13. See also William Bradford, *Of Plymouth Plantation, 1620–1647*, ed. Samuel Eliot Morison (New York, 1952), 23; John Robinson, *A Justification of Separation from the Church of England* . . . , in Robert Ashton, ed., *The Works of John Robinson, Pastor of the Pilgrim Fathers* (Boston, 1851), II, 268; Everett Emerson, ed., *Letters from New England: The Massachusetts Bay Colony, 1629–1638* (Amherst, Mass., 1976), 42; and Edmund S. Morgan, *The Puritan Dilemma: The Story of John Winthrop* (Boston, 1958), chap. 3.

am I bound to the Lord for granting me so great a mercy as to tread on thy grounds and to enjoy and partake of these many sweet examples and holy practices as thou hast afforded me. Oh that Old England could but speak in thy language.[3]

Trelawny's prayer in the final sentence was echoed a decade later when John Cotton wrote for the benefit of revolutionary England. "Pray we, that they may see the Moone, which God hath set in the Firmament, even the true forme of a Church of the New Testament." Like the young settler, Cotton was preaching spirituality more than politics. The material of godly New Testament churches was godly individuals, "crucified Christians." "Rest you not," Cotton went on, "untill you finde Christ manifested to your spirit as yours; grow up in a Lambe-like frame of spirit and way, untill the mystery of God be finished in you." The means of such personal salvation was private prayer and corporate worship. Beginning in individual hearts and local congregations, the new order would soon be the new world order, God's Kingdom. "Though it begin in a corner of the world, it will not cease till it have shaken all Christendome."[4]

THE CONTINUITY OF THE DEVOTIONAL TRADITION

Throughout the history of Christian faith the rigorous simplicity of the spiritual life and a vision of the eschatological Kingdom have attracted the zealous. Puritans recognized their kinship with medieval Roman Catholic devotional masters and with contemporary Anglican and even Catholic writers. Despite the Puritans' strong opposition to the Roman Catholic church, they never isolated themselves from long-established devotional traditions. The rise of Puritanism and the settlement of New England ought to be understood as a significant episode in the ongoing history of Christian spirituality. In private devotional practice especially—in the disciplines of meditation and prayer—continuity with earlier traditions may be traced as clearly as may the more easily recognizable discontinuity.

Perry Miller has identified the overarching tradition of which Puri-

3. Thomas Welde to his Former Parishioners at Tarling, June/July 1632, Emerson, ed., *Letters from New England*, 97. Edward Trelawny to Robert Trelawny, Oct. 10, 1635, *ibid.*, 176.

4. John Cotton, *The Powring Out of the Seven Vials . . .* (London, 1645 [orig. publ. 1642]), 154–155. The classic expression, of course, is John Winthrop's "A Modell of Christian Charity," most readily available in Perry Miller and Thomas H. Johnson, eds., *The Puritans*, rev. ed. (New York, 1963), I, 195–199.

tanism was an expression as "the Augustinian strain of piety." Puritans
were typically Protestant in this regard. The major themes of Calvin's
theology were Augustinian, Luther himself had been an Augustinian
monk, and precursors of the Reformation such as the Brethren of the
Common Life, John Wycliffe, and John Huss were Augustinian in
their theology. A primary emphasis on personal experience, human
sinfulness, and divine initiative in salvation through grace are the
hallmarks of Augustinian spirituality. Although Miller greatly overes-
timated the number of diaries when he remarked that "there survive
hundreds of Puritan diaries and thousands of Puritan sermons," his
conclusion was undoubtedly right: "we can read the inward meaning
of them all in the *Confessions*."[5]

St. Augustine was the prototype for devout New Englanders when
he prostrated himself before the Lord: "The way back to you is
through humility and devoutness, and you cleanse us from our evil
habits and look mercifully on the sins of those who confess them to
you." Twenty-year-old William Adams, a student at Harvard College,
opened his diary with the retrospective entry: "Anno Christi 1650.
May 27. I was born a Sinner into an evil world." Augustine prayed to
the God of mercy: "Accept the sacrifice of my confessions which my
tongue sets before you." Cotton Mather threw himself on the floor
and "humbled and loathed" himself before God, for "former Iniquities, and . . . present Infirmities." "I confessed my Unworthiness of
all mercies," Mather wrote, and was then able to record, "My Spirit
was, after this, at some Ease." Augustine's meditation on God culminated in an ineffable vision of Divine Being: "What, then, is my
God? What, I ask, except the Lord *God*? . . . O highest and best, most
powerful, most all-powerful, most merciful and most just, most deeply
hidden and most nearly present, most beautiful and most strong, constant yet incomprehensible, changeless, yet changing all things, never
new, never old, making all things new. . . . And in all this what have I
said, my God, my Life, my holy sweetness?" Thomas Hooker repeated
this meditation in its essence, with remarkably similar results:

> Me a miserable sinner! To send a Son to save me, it is incom-
> parable; I could not conceive to doe so much evill against him, as
> he hath done good to me: oh the bredth of that mercie beyond all
> limits, oh the length of that mercie beyond all time, oh the depth

5. Miller, *New England Mind: Seventeenth Century*, 1–5. See John T. McNeill, *The
History and Character of Calvinism* (New York, 1954), esp. 30, 255, 393; François Wendel,
Calvin: The Origins and Development of His Religious Thought (New York, 1963); and
Harold J. Grimm, *The Reformation Era, 1500–1650*, 2d ed. (New York, 1973), 43–44,
81–82.

of that mercie below a mans miserie, oh the height of that mercie above the height of mine understanding! If mine hands were all of love, that I could worke nothing but love, and if mine eyes were able to see nothing but love, and my minde thinke nothing but love, and if I had a thousand bodies, it were all too little to love that God that hath immeasurably loved me a poore sinfull hellhound. . . . I will love thee dearely, Oh Lord my strength.

In Augustinian and in Puritan piety, contact between the humble sinner and the loving God sparked passionate experience.[6]

The Puritans were not Augustine's sole heirs in England, as Perry Miller mistakenly implied when he portrayed their Anglican opponents as "entirely" guided by the spirit of "Thomas Aquinas and scholastic tradition." A far broader stream than the Puritan or even the Reformed movement issued from the meditative and mystical tradition of the *Confessions*. Augustine had Catholic and non-Puritan Church of England heirs as well, notably among the meditative poets such as Richard Crashaw, Robert Southwell, John Donne, and George Herbert. The tradition was passed to all parties in the seventeenth century through the writings of medieval Catholic mystics, which along with the works of Augustine himself, were increasingly available in England. St. Teresa of Avila, for example, acknowledged her debt to Augustine in a passage that a Puritan could easily have penned: "Scarcely had I begun to read the *Confessions* of St. Augustine than I seemed to have discovered myself." Her reading prompted her conversion from a "frivolous and dissipated life." "When I reached his conversion, the voice which he heard in the garden, the Lord, I believe, made it ring in my ears, so keenly was my heart touched. Long I remained bathed in tears, overwhelmed with grief and regret." The methods of meditation and prayer that Teresa outlined in *The Interior Castle*, together with such other major works as Ignatius of Loyola's *Spiritual Exercises* and Francis de Sales's popular *Introduction to the Devout Life*, had tremendous impact on the seventeenth century. All of them, and the lesser works they generated, were part of the "Augustinian strain of piety" within Puritanism. Catholics and Puritans alike could be spiritless Scholastics, but the search for religious experience more truly dominated the religious movements of the period. Moreover, as Terence Cave has pointed out in his study of similar move-

---

6. St. Augustine of Hippo, *Confessions*, ed. Rex Warner (New York, 1963), 64, 90, 19. "Memoir of the Rev. William Adams, of Dedham, Mass. . . . ," Massachusetts Historical Society, *Collections*, 4th Ser., I (1852), 8. W. C. Ford, ed., *Diary of Cotton Mather* (New York, 1957), I, xxi. [Thomas Hooker], *The Soules Implantation . . .* (London, 1637), 179–180.

ments in France, it is "legitimate to speak of a Protestant devotional tradition running parallel to the Catholic one and encouraging private prayer and meditation" with "a great deal of common ground between the two traditions."[7]

Puritans knew and used classic Catholic devotional works. The most popular, judging from the number of editions, were the works of St. Augustine, St. Bernard of Clairvaux, Thomas à Kempis's perennial *The Imitation of Christ*, and the primers (anthologies of religious direction for lay use). Some of these, especially *The Imitation of Christ*, began appearing in Protestant editions. It was not unheard of for a Protestant to pirate the work of a Catholic writer and present himself as the author, as with Edmund Bunny's edition of the Jesuit Robert Parsons's *A Booke of Christian Exercise* (1584). Perhaps most important, excerpts and phrases from medieval classics and Church Fathers worked their way silently into Protestant devotional manuals, sermons, and treatises and so were passed on to the laity.[8]

To a large extent the Puritan devotional writing that blossomed in the early seventeenth century was modeled on earlier Roman Catholic devotional literature. Aware that Catholics were far ahead in this area, Protestants rushed to close the gap. They consciously copied well-established Catholic forms and frequently used similar titles. The sensual imagery of the Song of Songs nourished devotional writing among all parties, and the image of the garden particularly emerged as a metaphor for the devotional setting. As the beloved came to his

7. Miller, *New England Mind: Seventeenth Century*, 5. Martz, *Poetry of Meditation*, 112–113, and *passim*. St. Teresa of Avila, quoted in Pierre Pourrat, *Christian Spirituality* (Westminster, Md., 1953–1955), III, 128. At least five English Catholic editions of the *Confessions* were published from 1620 to 1638, though even Protestants had long worked from earlier Latin editions, and Puritans commonly cited Augustine in their sermons (Babette May Levy, *Preaching in the First Half Century of New England History* [Hartford, Conn., 1945], 20). Cave, *Devotional Poetry*, 18–23. On the English mystical tradition, exemplified by Richard Rolle, Walter Hilton and his widely read *The Scale of Perfection*, Juliana of Norwich, and the anonymous *Cloud of Unknowing*, see Collins, *Christian Mysticism*, 77–80. Collins shows "the continuity of English mysticism," especially through the metaphor of "the Pilgrimage of Life" in such Protestant works as *The Faerie Queene* and ultimately *The Pilgrim's Progress*.

8. White, *English Devotional Literature*, 75–86. Charles C. Butterworth, *The English Primers (1529–1545): Their Publication and Connection with the English Bible and the Reformation in England* (Philadelphia, 1953). Wright, *Middle Class Culture*, 244, 252. White comments on the *Imitation of Christ*: "The story of how this thoroughly medieval work of mystical devotion serenely rode all the storms of religious controversy of the three bitterest of modern Christian centuries is one of the most impressive demonstrations of the enduring authenticity of a classic to be found in the annals of literature." More than 60 editions in at least six translations of this work appeared in English before 1640, with 18 more editions before the end of the century.

spouse in the garden, so Christ came to the devout soul in meditation and prayer. "I have come into my garden, my sister, my spouse: I have gathered my myrrh with my spice; I have eaten my honey-comb with my honey; I have drunk my wine with my milk: eat, O friends; drink, yea, drink abundantly, O beloved" (5:1). The garden image evoked biblical references with strong devotional connotations— paradise, the Garden of Eden, the desert garden of the prophets, and Gethsemane. Catholic manuals used in their titles such phrases as "A Paradise of Prayers," "The Flowers of Lodowicke," "The Garden of Our Blessed Lady." Protestants followed with "The Flower of Godly Prayers," "A Garden of Spiritual Flowers," and "A Posie Gathered out of Mr. Dod's Garden." Other motifs were matched as well, especially those of warfare and pilgrimage. At least two well-known Catholic manuals bore the title *The Spiritual Combat*, while one of the most prominent of Puritan manuals was John Downame's mammoth *The Christian Warfare against the Devill World and Flesh*. Luis de Granada's title *The Sinner's Guide* was paralleled on the Puritan side by many that suggested the pilgrimage motif: Downame's *A Guide to Godlynesse*, Arthur Dent's *The Plaine Mans Pathway*, and Henry Scudder's *The Christians Daily Walke*, to name only a few.[9]

The emblem book, a new sub-genre of devotional writing, flourished in both Protestant and Catholic circles in the early seventeenth century and influenced the style of other manuals as well. Emblem books combined visual devotional aids with meditative verse, thus continuing medieval iconographic traditions in an age of increasing literacy. Devotional pictures such as those in emblem books can be traced back to picture Bibles, the Book of Hours, and stained glass. At the popular level, engravers and poets hawked emblematic pictures and verse at English fairs. The most widely used Protestant emblem books were those by George Wither and by Francis Quarles. Quarles's *Emblemes, Divine and Moral* derived directly from Jesuit sources. Quarles was no Puritan, but Puritans knew and appreciated his works. Illustrations from the book were copied on funeral broadsides and gravestones in New England and influenced the poetry of Anne Bradstreet and Edward Taylor. The emblem book style further influenced the design of other Puritan publications, especially the title pages and chapter headings of books with iconographic printers' ornaments. Through these means, in spite of their well-known hostility

9. Good bibliographies of Roman Catholic devotional manuals are found in Martz, *Poetry of Meditation*, 361–365; White, *English Devotional Literature*, 271–291; and John R. Roberts, *A Critical Anthology of English Recusant Devotional Prose, 1558–1603* (Pittsburgh, Pa., 1966).

to stained glass and other icons, Puritans carried forward the use of symbolic and biblical illustrations for devotional purposes.[10]

Puritan devotional manuals generally followed the format of the earlier Catholic manuals, but with important differences. The Puritan manuals tended to have more sermonic and theological material. The true manual (as distinct from the treatise or the collection of sermons) offered meditations and prayers ready for use, in addition to exhortations to a life of the spirit. The meditations and prayers were intended as models or samples for the novice, who would gradually abandon them as he or she became more adept at the disciplines. Puritan manuals only rarely provided a set of daily exercises for a specific period of weeks, whereas Catholic manuals commonly did so, as exemplified by the Ignatian *Exercises*. Catholics typically underwent such a rigorous program while on special spiritual retreat; Puritans were expected to apply themselves to the exercises daily, as saints in the world. The Puritan manuals were therefore usually organized topically: meditation on the misery of sin, on death, on reconciliation with God in Christ, on heaven; meditation and prayer for morning, evening, and at mealtime in families and privately; preparatory devotions for receiving the Lord's Supper; Sabbath day devotions; prayers for the sick; and so on.

Even the publication of manuals specifically for lay readers was not exclusively a Puritan practice. The idea of preparing a manual for men and women in the world rather than in the cloister was actually introduced by St. Francis de Sales. De Sales's aim was to make the kind of disciplines systematized in the Ignatian *Exercises* available to the laity. The Puritan devotional manual similarly provided a means by which all believers might engage in regular meditation and prayer while pursuing their secular callings.

In the area of technique, as well, continuity existed between Roman

10. Cave, *Devotional Poetry*, 276, 303. Rosemary Freeman, *English Emblem Books* (London, 1948), 117. Allan I. Ludwig, *Graven Images: New England Stonecarving and Its Symbols, 1650–1815* (Middletown, Conn., 1966), 88–89, 216, 240, 274–283, 295. Stanford, "Bradstreet As a Meditative Writer," *Calif. English Jour.*, II (Winter 1966), 24–31. Jeff Hammond and Thomas M. Davis, "Edward Taylor: A Note on Visual Imagery," *Early Am. Lit.*, VIII (1973), 126–131. Elaborate title pages are found in Downame, *Guide to Godlynesse*; John Downame, *The Christian Warfare* . . . (London, 1604); Johann Gerhard, *The Soules Watch: or, a Day-Booke for the Devout Soule* . . . , 3d ed. (London, 1621); and Lewis Bayly, *The Practice of Piety: Directing a Christian How to Walke, That He May Please God* (London, 1669 [orig. publ. ca. 1610]). Iconographic printers' ornaments are well used in John Dod, *A Plaine and Familiar Exposition on the Lords Prayer* . . . , 2d ed. (London, 1635), and J[ohn] Dod and R[obert] Cleaver, *Ten Sermons Tending Chiefely to the Fitting of Men for the Worthy Receiving of the Lords Supper* . . . (London, 1609).

Catholic and Puritan practice. Most important was the use of the imagination and the senses in the exercise known as composition of place, the usual point of departure in Catholic meditation. A passage from de Sales's *Introduction to the Devout Life* illustrates the method: "When you kneel before your spiritual father, imagine that you are on Mount Calvary, at the feet of Jesus Christ crucified, whose Precious Blood drops down on all sides to wash and cleanse you from your iniquities. For though it be not the very blood of the Saviour, yet it is the merit of the Blood He shed for us that waters abundantly the penitent in the confessional." Puritan manuals and sermons were equally vivid in attempting to put the believer into the spiritual and biblical setting upon which he or she was meditating. Arthur Dent, in the widely read manual *The Plaine Mans Pathway to Heaven*, advised meditation on the Cross in conjunction with his model "prayer to be used in private families." "Nail down all our sinnes and iniquities to the crosse of Christ, burie them in his death, bathe them in his bloud, hide them in his wounds, let them never rise up in judgement against us." John Downame, in his directions for the stages of meditation, advised saints to let "our hearts [be] affected with a lively taste, sense, and feeling of the things whereon wee meditate."[11]

Using the methodology of composition of place, New England ministers included sensual meditation on biblical scenes in their sermons and devotional writings. John Cotton led his congregation through an extended meditation on the death of Christ in *The Way of Life*, concluding by imagining the experience of His atoning death. The Pauline formula, "I am crucified with Christ, nevertheless I live," was Cotton's vivid conclusion. Thomas Hooker, supposedly the New England pastor least prone to using the meditative imagination, both advocated and introduced it to his congregation in sermons. He advised his people to "make and keep the evil of sin really present in thine apprehension." In his meditation on the person of Judas he then employed the technique of composition of place effectively:

> Follow him into the High-Priests Hall, see his pale face, his ghastly looks, and shaking hands; hear him yelling out of the horror of his heart, *I have sinned.* See him flinging his money away and follow him thence, and behold him putting the halter about his neck, sighing out, the blood of Jesus, the innocent blood, the blood of Jesus; let me not be, rather than be thus

11. St. Francis de Sales, *Introduction to the Devout Life* (1608), trans. and ed. John K. Ryan, 2d ed. (New York, 1952), 31. Arthur Dent, *The Plaine Mans Pathway to Heaven . . .* (London, 1629 [orig. publ. 1601]), sig. Dd2. Downame, *Guide to Godlynesse*, 578.

miserable, and with that he flings himself head-long and his bowels gush out, and his soul departs his body, and the Devils they lay hold upon it: Send thy thoughts post to Hell after him, hear him there.

Puritan devotion, like that practiced by Roman Catholics and by other non-Puritans in England, depended upon the use of the imagination for putting oneself into the biblical drama of redemption.[12]

It is certainly incorrect to distinguish between Puritan and Catholic meditation on the grounds that Puritans were in "grim" bondage to "rigorous self-examination" for the discovery of sin while Catholics soared in "formal meditation on the joys of Heaven." Puritan meditation throughout the century indeed began with meditation on one's own sinfulness. But it advanced to later stages of meditation on the work of Christ, remission of sins, the blessings of the saints, and glorification at the end of the world. Catholic practice, meanwhile, also depended on confession of sin. Ignatius wrote, "While one is going through the Spiritual Exercises, a far deeper insight into his sins and their malice is acquired than at a time when he is not so engaged with what concerns his inner life. Since at this time he attains to a deeper knowledge and sorrow for his sins, there will be greater profit and merit than he would otherwise have had." The entire first week of the Ignatian *Exercises* is devoted to meditation on one's own sinfulness, and shorter meditations on sin are repeated daily throughout the cycle, usually in the morning. In his "Method of Making the General Examination of Conscience" Ignatius advised confession even more frequently than his system required. St. Francis de Sales also strongly recommended meditation on sin at the beginning of each meditative cycle. Similarly, as Terence Cave has stated, "the fountain of all penitential meditation is the self-examination recommended by Granada for the first day's reflection." Self-examination and meditation on one's sinfulness can no longer be construed as uniquely Puritan. Puritans engaged in penitential meditation were part of a broader devotional tradition.[13]

Preparatory meditations for the Lord's Supper that have survived in New England personal writing, most dramatically in Edward Taylor's poetry, suggest that believers of all religious parties practiced

12. John Cotton, *The Way of Life* . . . (London, 1641), 255. Thomas Hooker, *The Application of Redemption, . . . the Ninth and Tenth Books* (London, 1656), 189. Kaufmann, *Pilgrim's Progress and Meditation*, 126.

13. Louis L. Martz, Foreword to Donald E. Stanford, ed., *The Poems of Edward Taylor* (New Haven, Conn., 1960), xxiii–xxvii. For advanced stages of meditation in an early manual, see Downame, *Guide to Godlynesse*, 565. St. Ignatius of Loyola, *The Spiritual Exercises of St. Ignatius* . . . (1522), ed. and trans. Louis J. Puhl (Chicago, [1951]), 23–24.

sacramental meditation in a similar manner. Though theological differences existed, and Protestants of every stripe rejected the doctrine of transubstantiation, Puritans did hold a doctrine of the real presence. Resistance to the iconoclastic, anti-sacramentalist tendency in Puritanism—embodied in New England in the Antinomian, Quaker, Gortonist, and Anabaptist movements—was so bitter partly because of orthodox Puritans' interest in the possibilities of eucharistic devotion and the experience of Christ in the Sacrament. "When I can see something beyond bread, and something beyond pouring out, and something beyond taking, and see as certainly the Spirit of God communicating the spirituall comfort unto my soule, as the outward elements would do to my body," Hooker preached, then "the Spirit of God doth . . . communicate assurance." Lewis Bayly in *The Practice of Piety* gave even more explicit advice to the communicant: "When the Minister bringeth towards thee the Bread thus blessed and broken; and offering it unto thee, bids thee Take, Eat, etc. then meditate that Christ himself cometh unto thee." Meditation ought to attend the action of partaking, so when receiving the bread, he advised, "rowze up thy soul to apprehend Christ by Faith, and apply his merits to heal thy miseries; Embrace him sweetly with thy faith in the Sacrament, as ever Simeon hugged him with his arms in his swadling clouts." When eating the bread, "imagine that thou seest Christ hanging upon the Cross, and by his unspeakable torments, full satisfying Gods justice for thy sins." While drinking the wine focus on the realization that "thy sins are as verily forgiven, as thou has now drunk this Sacramental Wine, and hast it in thy Stomack." "In the instant of thy drinking," Bayly urged, "settle thy meditation upon Christ, as he hanged upon the Cross, as if like Mary and John, thou didst see him nayled." Finally, the sensation of the wine "warming thy cold stomack" was the means of feeling "the Holy Ghost cherishing thy soul." Clearly, use of the senses and imagination was a common characteristic of Puritan sacramental devotion.[14]

Protestants and Catholics not only followed many of the same de-

---

St. Francis de Sales, *Introduction to the Devout Life*, trans. and ed. Ryan. Cave, *Devotional Poetry*, 40.

14. See Philip F. Gura, "The Radical Ideology of Samuel Gorton: New Light on the Relation of English to American Puritanism," *WMQ*, 3d Ser., XXXVI (1979), 78–100; James Fulton Maclear, "'The Heart of New England Rent': The Mystical Element in Early Puritan History," *Mississippi Valley Historical Review*, XLII (1955–1956), 621–652; and E. Brooks Holifield, *The Covenant Sealed: The Development of Puritan Sacramental Theology in Old and New England, 1570–1720* (New Haven, Conn., 1974). Thomas Hooker, *The Paterne of Perfection* . . . (London, 1640), 375–376. Bayly, *Practice of Piety*, 349–351.

votional forms, they also used the same verbal images. These were rooted in a long tradition of Christian spirituality, and ultimately in Scripture. An example, useful because of its association with just one New Englander, Cotton Mather, is the "dust" and "prostration" imagery of confession and meditation on sin. The beginning of all devotion was penitence and humility—or, to use the stronger Puritan term, humiliation—with the confessor on his knees before the throne of God's mercy.

Perry Miller chided Cotton Mather for regularly prostrating himself in the dust of his study floor, but the significance of Mather's physical posture comes from its power as a biblical and traditional metaphor. One such episode occurred during a secret fast in January 1685 as Mather struggled with the question of whether or not to marry. "This Day, with Anguish of Soul, in the Sense of my own Sinfulness, and Filthiness, I cast myself prostrate, on my Study-floor with my mouth in the Dust. Here, I lamented unto the Lord, my Follies, which might have an Influence to deprive mee of the Blessing which I was now pursuing. I judg'd, I loath'd, I hated myself, because of those accursed Things and besought the Forgiveness thereof, thro' the Blood of the Covenant." If the passage is taken out of context, Mather indeed appears to be engaged in aberrant and neurotic behavior, as Miller claimed. But Mather was enacting advice long given by Puritans and non-Puritans alike and using terminology that dated back thousands of years. Mather's description drew from a typological use of Old Testament instances of humiliation, as when after the defeat of Israel at Ai, "Joshua rent his clothes, and fell to the earth upon his face before the ark of the Lord until the eventide, he and the elders of Israel, and put dust upon their heads" (Joshua 7:6). Mather interpreted personally the description of the penitent Israelite in Lamentations: "He putteth his mouth in the dust; if so be there may be hope" (3:29). In other places in the Bible dust is a symbol of human mortality (Genesis 3:19, 18:27; Psalm 103:13–14), and therefore of the grave (Psalm 22:15), and, together with ashes, of mourning (Esther 4:1). Death and mourning are integral to the experience of repentance, as one laments one's own death in sin before God. Mather's cry was thus forecast by Job's final repentance before God: "I abhor myself, and repent in dust and ashes" (42:6).[15]

15. Ford, ed., *Diary of Cotton Mather*, I, 109. Miller flippantly remarked: "This peculiar visitation frequently invigorated Cotton Mather, usually, he tells us, when he was prostrate in the dust of his study floor. Whether this signifies that the housekeeping of his various Mesdames Mather was remiss, or that they were not allowed to invade the study with so vulgar an object as the broom, is unknown; possibly it means that the

The biblical passages alluded to in Mather's meditation have always been important in Christian devotional practice. St. Augustine wrote in his *Confessions,* "Lord cleanse me from my secret faults. . . . I am only dust and ashes, but allow me to speak, since, see, it is to your mercy that I am speaking." In *The Imitation of Christ* Thomas à Kempis advised "The Disciple" to seek "Self-abasement in the sight of God" in words that echo Abraham and anticipate Mather: "I will speak to my Lord, I who am but dust and ashes. If I consider myself anything more than this, behold You stand against me, and my sins bear witness to the truth which I cannot contradict. If I abase myself, however, if I humble myself to nothingness, if I shrink from all self-esteem and account myself as the dust which I am, Your grace will favor me, Your light will enshroud my heart." St. Ignatius's *Spiritual Exercises,* in the disciplines of meditation on sin and hell, also advocated the posture of lying prostrate on the ground.[16]

Mather was not just relying on Catholic precedent. Early Puritans wrote of meditative techniques for self-abasement of the soul that were similar to those of Ignatius. John Downame in *A Guide to Godly-nesse* recommended "Gestures of the body" that the devout should adopt to "further the inward humility, reverence, and fervency of devotion," specifically suggesting "standing, kneeling, uncovering the head, lifting up the eyes and hands; and in extraordinary and greater humiliation, prostrating our selves upon the ground, casting down our eyes, as being ashamed to looke towards heaven, and knocking of the brest, as bewayling the sinfull corruption therein contained." But Downame also cautioned that the penitent's "chiefest endeavour must be, that the inward affection and disposition of the heart, do answer unto the outward gestures of the body, without which they are but hypocritical shewes." Thomas Hooker preached that in humiliation the penitent "falls downe before the Lord" and "freely acknowledgeth that it is in Gods power to doe with him and to dispose of him as he will; and therefore he lies and lickes the dust, and cries mercy, mercy Lord." John Cotton advised, "Meditate on what you are. . . . Dust you are, and to dust you return, you have no dependance but on God; shall we then be full of ourselves?" And Thomas Shepard preached, "Be exhorted therefore to lie down in the dust before the Lord, and under the Lord; nay intreat the Lord that he would put thee upon his

experience was so ecstatic as to be expressed only in hyperbole." *The New England Mind: From Colony to Province* (Cambridge, Mass., 1953), 403.

16. St. Augustine, *Confessions,* ed. Warner, 20. Thomas à Kempis, *The Imitation of Christ* (Milwaukee, Wis., 1940), 100. St. Ignatius, *Spiritual Exercises,* ed. and trans. Puhl, 36.

wheel, and mould thy heart to his will." John Winthrop, much earlier
in the century than Mather, had meditated in the same manner. "O
my God, my Kinge, what am I but dust! a worme, a rebell, and thine
enemie." In short, the practice of prostration and the use of the imagery of "dust" formed part of Christian devotional tradition reaching
back to Scripture and across theological party lines.[17]

In traditional Catholic programs of spiritual exercise, meditation
on the joys of heaven followed the rigors of confession and self-
abasement. The same was true in the Puritan practice of the disciplines. Cotton Mather recorded in his diary that four days after his
private fast he kept "a Day of secret THANKSGIVING." "In these
Exercises," Mather wrote, "my Heart was rapt into these heavenly
Frames, which would have turned a Dungeon into a Paradise." The
language of spiritual ecstasy, as the vignettes in the first chapter have
shown, was that of sensual love and rapture. Here, too, Puritans were
well within the mainstream of the Christian devotional tradition. Bernard of Clairvaux was only the most notable Catholic predecessor who
mediated the tradition for them. His *On Loving God* and *The Twelve
Degrees* were well known and often quoted in Puritan sermons.[18]

The Augustinian devotional tradition, so firmly rooted in Scripture, bound Puritan spirituality to the practices of other parties in
seventeenth-century England. While raging theological and ecclesio-
logical conflicts divided Christians, religious experience in the practice
of the devotional life was remarkably similar. The manuals, for example, frequently rode above the storm of controversy and were used
by a wide range of believers. The clearest instance of this was *The
Imitation of Christ*. On the Protestant side, Lewis Bayly's *The Practice of
Piety* had a tremendous impact on the personal religious lives of con-
formists and nonconformists alike for almost two hundred years.
Bayly himself intended his manual to have this irenic effect. He
wanted "to extract (out of the Chaos of endless controversies) the old
Practice of true Piety, which flourished before these controversies
were hatched." The belief that theological differences were rending

17. Downame, *Guide to Godlynesse*, 230. [Thomas Hooker], *The Soules Humiliation*
(London, 1637), 117. John Cotton, *A Practical Commentary, or an Exposition . . . upon the
First Epistle Generall of John* (London, 1656), 135. See also his *Christ the Fountaine of Life
. . .* (London, 1651), 14. Thomas Shepard, *The Sound Beleever . . .* (London, 1645), 125,
146. John Winthrop, "Experientia," *Winthrop Papers* (Boston, 1929), I, 204.

18. Ford, ed., *Diary of Cotton Mather*, I, 110. Levy, *Preaching in New England History*,
20. See Étienne Gilson, *The Mystical Theology of Saint Bernard*, trans. A.H.C. Downes, 2d
ed. (New York, 1955); St. Bernard of Clairvaux, *On Loving God and Selections from
Sermons*, ed. Hugh Martin (London, 1959); and *St. Bernard on Consideration*, trans.
George Lewis (Oxford, 1908).

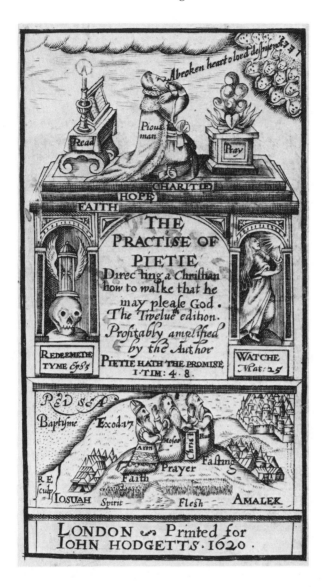

Figure 2. Title page of an early edition of Lewis Bayly's The Practise of
Pietie *(London, 1620). Iconographic title pages and printer's ornaments were
common in supposedly iconoclastic Puritan devotional manuals and tracts.
The emblems shown here illustrate the major devotional disciplines and,
notably, the theme of preparation for death. Courtesy the Folger Shakespeare
Library, Washington, D.C.*

the Body of Christ led Richard Baxter to eschew controversialism and embrace devotionalism, and his position had an effect on New England. Baxter's works, especially *The Saints Everlasting Rest* (London, 1652), and those of Bishop Joseph Hall on methods of meditation and prayer, were widely read in New England in the second half of the seventeenth century.[19]

Puritanism was from the start a devotional movement, and traditional practices such as meditation and prayer were integral to its formation and persistence. Louis Martz was mistaken, therefore, when he argued that Puritans began to engage in systematic meditation only after Richard Baxter published *Saints Rest*. According to Martz, Puritans generally denounced devotional methods as mere human invention. What good was a technique when only the Spirit could bring a soul to Christ? "Devotion waited on the operations of the Spirit. . . . The Spirit would provide its own Method, and who would presume to 'co-operate' with it, or to explain how its mysterious workings could be 'provoked.'" The best the Puritan could attempt was self-examination, a far cry from the flights of the spirit possible with Ignatian disciplines. Horton Davies followed Martz when he emphasized Baxter's uniqueness in using the composition of place methodology. "Employing the senses," Davies stated, was "usually regarded as inimical by Protestants to true spirituality." Even U. Milo Kaufmann, who pushed back the use of "sensual" and "affective" methods to Richard Sibbes, retained Martz's framework by presenting Puritan homiletical method as bound to "a literal hermeneutics" that excluded sense and imagination. We have seen, however, that it is incorrect to dichotomize Puritanism into devotional camps in this manner. In fact, Martz's case rests heavily on nothing more than Baxter's use of a phrase on the title page of the famous fourth part of his book. Meditation, Baxter said, is an "Excellent unknown Duty." Martz failed to recognize that Baxter's title was hortatory rather than descriptive. Puritans from the beginning followed the practices of regular and systematic meditation and prayer. They used traditional methods such

19. Bayly, *Practice of Piety*, sig. A4. C. J. Stranks, *Anglican Devotion: Studies in the Spiritual Life of the Church of England between the Reformation and the Oxford Movement* (London, 1961), chap. 2. Richard Baxter, *Gildas Salvianus . . . The Reformed Pastor* (London, 1657 [orig. publ. 1656]), 183–205. For Baxter's ties with New England, see F. J. Powicke, "Some Unpublished Correspondence of the Rev. Richard Baxter and the Rev. John Eliot, 'The Apostle of American Indians,' 1656–1682," John Rylands Library, *Bulletin*, XV (1931), 138–176, 442–466, and Raymond Phineas Stearns, "Correspondence of John Woodbridge, Jr., and Richard Baxter," *New England Quarterly*, X (1937), 557–583. See Worthington Chauncey Ford, *The Boston Book Market, 1679–1700* (Boston, 1917), for imports of books written by Baxter, Hall, and other English devotional writers.

as composition of place and did not avoid the exercise of sense and imagination. They were not limited to self-examination but soared with the best of their contemporaries into the ecstasy of union with Christ.[20]

DEVOTION AS SEPARATION

How, then, can we speak of Puritanism as a distinct movement within English religious life when we have defined it as a devotional movement in continuity with other parties? A qualification is needed. Devotionalism tended to unite all persons and groups inclined toward the practice of piety. When confronted with worldliness or religious legalism, however, it tended to fuel antagonisms. In meditation and prayer, one consciously separates oneself from the world. Devotional practice exacerbated conflict because its locus was not entirely the privacy of the individual heart; it extended as well to the community of believers. The individual Puritan and the communal Puritan were inseparable components of the same person, "new men, newly created in Christ" gathering for worship and to form a new society. When religion infuses the dominant culture, forms of religion perceived as corrupt must be rejected. In the early seventeenth century, individual and communal Puritan devotion expressed itself in opposition to the ungodliness commonly found outside the walls of the fellowship.[21]

Puritan spirituality employed a matrix of negative referents in contrast to which believers defined, in the words of Hebrews, their own "new and living way" (10:20). Reaction against the perceived ribald irreligion of Stuart England is clear in the artless autobiographical narrative of the tailor John Dane, who immigrated to Massachusetts Bay in 1637 against his father's wishes. On his pilgrimage through temptation Dane encountered one snare after another. Many were of a sexual nature, as when he returned to an inn after work, and "the ostis sat in a chare by the fyer, in hur naked shift, houlding her brests open. She said to me, a chare being by hur, she houlding out hur hand, Cum let us drink a pot." Dane marveled time and again at the "wonderfull, unspekable, unsarchabl marseys of a god that taketh care of us when we take no Care of ourselvese." In the end he experienced a conversion of sorts and departed from England in revulsion.

20. Martz, *Poetry of Meditation*, 157. Davies, *Worship and Theology*, II, 118. Kaufmann, *Pilgrim's Progress and Meditation*, 23, 120, 147.
21. Geoffrey Fillingham Nuttall, *Visible Saints: The Congregational Way, 1640–1660* (Oxford, 1957), 161–164.

The same antipathy is evident in Arthur Dent's satire of "merry England" in *The Plaine Mans Pathway to Heaven*, which presents a hilarious and didactic conversation among four stock characters. The villain, Antilegon, is identified as "a Caviller"—that is, a cavalier who cavils at Puritan preoccupation with religion. He is a member in good standing in the Church of England, but his outward respectability masks the "Beelzebubs of the world": whoredom, covetousness, contempt of the Gospel, swearing, lying, drunkenness, idleness, and oppression. The Puritan alternative is represented by the godly divine, Theologus. The same opposition was depicted iconographically on the elaborate title page of John Downame's *A Guide to Godlynesse*. Under the twin female figures of "Charitie" (a maternal figure seated with children on her lap) and "Humilitie" (a seated woman with long hair hanging loose) stand two chief virtues: "Faith," in nunlike habit with book in hand, and "Repentance," a woman in penitent pose, head down. At the feet of Repentance lie the emblems of sin: playing cards, a mirror, and a theatrical mask.[22]

New England's participation in this moral system is well known and persisted through the century even as the society itself changed. John Hull complained of the rise of the cavalier vices of "pride in long hair, new fashions in apparel, drinking, gaming, idleness, worldliness, etc." Samuel Sewall's hostility to the wearing of periwigs—the emblem of luxury—stems from the same desire for spiritual purity. Cotton Mather stunned Sewall in 1691 by saying in a sermon that wigs were "an innocent fashion," and Mather soon wore one himself but retained the essence of Puritan asceticism. In his eucharistic manual he denounced "all those Massing Furnitures and Fooleries, of Tapers, Candlesticks, Basons, Crosses, Rich Altar-Clothes, clasped Books, with Crosses instead of Books, and Crimson and scarlet Cushions" associated with Rome.[23]

Episcopal ecclesiology identified the Church of England with the nation, but in the Puritan analysis Stuart culture was coterminous not with the Kingdom of God but with the "world," in the New Testament sense. The Puritan said with Paul, "Now we have received, not the

22. John Dane, "A Declaration of Remarkabell Prouedenses in the Corse of My Lyfe," *New England Historical and Genealogical Register*, VIII (1854), 150–151. For a discussion of the Dane narrative, see Shea, *Spiritual Autobiography*, 126–138. Dent, *Plaine Mans Pathway*, 25, 30–32. Downame, *Guide to Godlynesse*, title page. See Leverenz, *Language of Puritan Feeling*, 23–40.

23. John Hull, *The Diaries of John Hull, Mint-Master and Treasurer of the Colony of Massachusetts Bay* (Boston, 1857), 212. Thomas, ed., *Diary of Samuel Sewall*, I, 82. Cotton Mather, *A Companion for Communicants. Discourses upon . . . the Lords Supper . . .* (Boston, 1690), 19.

Figure 3. Title page of John Downame's A Guide to Godlynesse *(London, 1622 edition). The symbolic figures depict the devotional virtues and the social antipathies of Puritanism. Courtesy the Folger Shakespeare Library, Washington, D.C.*

spirit of the world, but the spirit which is of God" (1 Corinthians 2:12). When the Puritan said, "A visible segregation from the world, and a visible aggregation to Christ, is necessary to Church union and communion," he could not help but mean segregation from the official church. "The scorching flame, which hinders all things in the Church of England, is the prelacy," John Robinson wrote, including papist liturgics among his objects of complaint. Thomas Hooker prophesied upon his 1631 escape to Amsterdam: "God forsook Shiloh because his ordinances were not purely kept there. When the people left the Ark, viz., his pure worship, then God left the people. . . . And hence it is that the saints are so urgent for God's ordinances in the purity of them. But the wicked say: 'Once a Sabbath is enough and once a week is too much.' By this we may see that England is ripe." Hooker preached, "God is packing up his gospel, because none will buy his wares." Separation as understood by immigrants to New England was a spiritual and devotional necessity. Though other motives may certainly be discerned and cannot be ignored, it was the devotional impulse to separate from the world that most basically underlay the movement. "We have here the true Religion and holy Ordinances of Almightie God taught amongst us," Francis Higginson wrote. "Thankes be to God, wee have here plenty of Preaching, and diligent Catechizing, with strict and carefull exercise and good and commendable orders." The founding of New England was a devotional act in that it was an act of separation from the world in order to worship. The Great Migration was in essence a communal mirror of the individual separating himself from the world in order to meditate and pray.[24]

The close connection between public worship and private devotion,

---

24. Nuttall, *Visible Saints*, 53. Robinson, *Justification of Separation*, in Ashton, ed., *Works of Robinson*, II, 68. Thomas Hooker, "The Danger of Desertion," in George H. Williams et al., eds., *Thomas Hooker: Writings in England and Holland, 1626–1633* (Cambridge, Mass., 1975), 236–237, 242, 246. Francis Higginson, *New-Englands Plantation* (1630), in [Robert Stewart Mitchell], ed., *The Founding of Massachusetts: Selections from the Sources of the History of the Settlement, 1628–1631* (Boston, 1930), 93–94. See also [John White], *The Planters Plea . . .* (London, 1630), in Peter Force, ed., *Tracts and Other Papers . . .* , II (Washington, D.C., 1838), 36; Hull, *Diaries*, 168; Edward Johnson, *Wonder-Working Providence of Sions Saviour in New-England* (London, 1654), ed. William Frederick Poole (Andover, Mass., 1867), 1–2. This is not to say, of course, that New England Puritans intended to separate organically from the Church of England. Perry Miller made this classic distinction in *Orthodoxy in Massachusetts, 1630–1650: A Genetic Study* (Cambridge, Mass., 1933). For Thomas Hooker's nonseparatist position, see *The Christians Two Chiefe Lessons . . .* (London, 1640), 204, and Cotton Mather, *Magnalia Christi Americana; or, the Ecclesiastical History of New England . . .* (London, 1702), ed. Thomas Robbins (Hartford, Conn., 1853–1855), I, 339.

and the unusual vehemence of the Puritans' discrimination between godly and ungodly worship, are important to understand. These relationships are evident in Thomas Hooker's 1633 letter to John Cotton from Holland: "The state of these Providences to my weak eye seems wonderfully ticklish and miserable. For the better part [with respect to] heart religion they [the Dutch] content themselves with very forms though much blemished; but the power of godliness [see 2 Timothy 3:2], for aught I can see or hear, they know not. And if it [heart religion, as distinguished from the form thereof] were thoroughly pressed, I fear lest it will be fiercely opposed." The Puritan mind perceived a fundamental distinction between religion that affirmed the primacy of piety and experience and religion that emphasized established liturgical forms. Liturgical worship that treated form as paramount would stifle experience, resulting in the loss of "the power of godliness." The biblical reference of Hooker's phrase "the better part, heart religion" further elucidates his meaning. In Luke 10:38–42 Jesus looked favorably on Mary's posture of devotion rather than Martha's busy activity. "Martha, Martha, thou art careful and troubled about many things: But one thing is needful: and Mary hath chosen that good part, which shall not be taken away from her." Mary and Martha have always been interpreted as classic types of the contemplative and the active life, respectively. Hooker now identified the busy show of activity in the liturgy with Martha and the devotional life of "heart religion" with Mary.[25]

The decadence of church and society could not be separated from the official liturgy. Thomas Shepard insisted that even though many of the prayers included in "the Popish Formes of Masse, Matten, and Evensong, etc." were inoffensive, the godly should still "refuse the whole Forme." The Book of Common Prayer, "this corrupt Servicebooke," he wrote, has "stunk above ground twice 40 yeeres, in the nostrills of many godly, who breathed in the pure ayre of the holy Scriptures." Liturgical worship was nothing more than empty ritual, a routine made up of external gestures without deep inner commitment. By contrast, simplified worship that used the words of Scripture for its content promoted "heart religion." The Puritan form of worship gave the worshiper the sense of going directly to the true Source, of finding God in His own Word and rooting all words of sermon and prayer in the Word itself. At the same time, the worshiper had the stirring sense of righteous zeal that comes from opposing official

25. Thomas Hooker to John Cotton from Rotterdam, c. Apr. 1633, Williams *et al.*, eds., *Hooker: Writings*, 297.

norms. Puritanism, based on spiritual separation from the world for
worship and devotion, was above all a religion of the heart.[26]
Certain theological differences that bore on spirituality also separated Puritans from other groups. The crucial doctrinal issues of the
century concerned questions about human nature and God's grace.
In what manner did God communicate redemption? How might an
individual transcend sin and find salvation? How did God elevate a
soul into union with Himself? Protestants from the beginning rejected
Catholic teaching concerning a "divine spark" that survived the Fall
and remained unblemished by Original Sin. Catholic (and Arminian)
spirituality was based partly on the assumption that a person has the
ability to activate that spark. A sinner might thus find within himself
or herself the means of salvation. Even St. Augustine, who took Original Sin as seriously as anyone until the Reformation, expressed this
view of human nature: "I was admonished by all this to return to my
own self, and, with you to guide me, I entered into the innermost part
of myself, and I was able to do this because you were my helper. I
entered and I saw with my soul's eye (such as it was) an unchangeable
light shining above this eye of my soul and above my mind." Augustine
knew that he was unable to find that light and that it was "entirely different" from any created light. But the medieval mystics believed that
the created and unfallen "spark" or "eye" was capable of attaining the
light. The Reformers utterly rejected this spirit/flesh dualism, with its
Gnostic overtones, asserting that the entire person is flesh in the Pauline sense: sinful to the core, and perhaps especially sinful in the very
center of the heart. Shepard stated it clearly: "Every man is born stark
dead in sin, Eph. 2. 1. he is born empty of every inward principle of
life, void of all graces, and hath no more good in him (whatsoever he
thinks) than a dead carrion hath. . . . Their bodies are living coffins to
carry a dead soul up and down." Nothing one could do would have

26. Thomas Shepard, *A Treatise of Liturgies, Power of the Keyes, and of Matter of the
Visible Church* . . . (London, 1653), 37, 61. See also John Cotton, *An Exposition upon the
Thirteenth Chapter of the Revelation* (London, 1655), 67; "Articles Objected by His
Majesty's Commissioners for Causes Ecclesiastical against Charles Chauncey, Clerk,
Vicar of Ware in the County of Hertford and Diocese of London," in Demos, ed., *Remarkable Providences*, 32–36; and Isabel MacBeath Calder, ed., *Letters of John Davenport,
Puritan Divine* (New Haven, Conn., 1937), 39–41. Mary Douglas takes issue with this
devaluation of ritual, carried into the modern academic world by sociologists: "Ritual,
defined as a routinised act diverted from its normal function, subtly becomes a de-
spised form of communication. . . . The ritualist becomes one who performs external
gestures which imply commitment to a particular set of values, but he is inwardly with-
drawn, dried out and uncommitted." *Natural Symbols: Explorations in Cosmology* (New
York, 1970), 2.

any influence on God's will. The Holy Spirit would come wholly from outside the realm of human activity and ability. "Bring a dead man to the fire, and chafe him, and rub him, you may produce some heat by this external working upon him: but take him from the fire again, and he is soon cold."[27]

The Holy Spirit would nevertheless enter the soul through the means of well-established forms of devotion and worship. It is important to understand that in Puritan spirituality God did not come *because* someone engaged in a certain exercise; but if God was going to come, He would do so through the means of that exercise. For Puritans, God provided both the content of the exercise (in Scripture) and the will to undertake it (through grace); human ability thus played no role. Although the methods of Puritans and Catholics were similar, a very real difference between the two groups emerges on the issue of human ability. The Puritan's goal was always to know God's will for the soul: Am I among the elect or not? Am I experiencing the benefits of that election in union with Christ? The Catholic's goal was to elect God. St. Francis de Sales wrote, "Promise them [i.e., the Virgin and the saints] that you will press forward. . . . Encourage your soul to make this choice." Similarly, one goal of the Ignatian *Spiritual Exercises* was to enable the practicer to "make an election"—to choose a vocation within the Church. The Puritan doctrine of election was more radical and always referred to God's election of the person. It also encouraged Puritan devotional iconoclasm, since it devalued the forms of worship. The difference, often fine and difficult to discern (and one that the orthodox were accused of obliterating in the Antinomian controversy), served to fuel hostility and harden party lines.[28]

The Puritan drive to separate from the world of official English worship was frequently expressed in devotional and liturgical iconoclasm. Here the relation of even moderate Puritanism to the radical

27. St. Augustine, *Confessions*, ed. Warner, 149. Evelyn Underhill, *Mysticism: A Study in the Nature and Development of a Man's Spiritual Consciousness* (New York, 1961 [orig. publ. 1911]), 74. Underhill notes that "this spark or 'part of the soul'" is "the fountain . . . of mystic life." Steven Ozment, "Luther and the Late Middle Ages: The Formation of Reformation Thought," in Robert M. Kingdon, ed., *Transition and Revolution: Problems and Issues of European Renaissance and Reformation History* (Minneapolis, Minn., 1974), 109–152. Heiko A. Oberman, "*Simul Gemitus et Raptus:* Luther and Mysticism," in Steven E. Ozment, ed., *The Reformation in Medieval Perspective* (Chicago, 1971), 219–251. Thomas Shepard, *The Sincere Convert . . .* (London, 1648), 47. See also William Perkins, *A Reformed Catholike . . .*, in *The Whole Works of . . . William Perkins* (London, 1623–1631), I, 559.
28. St. Francis de Sales, *Introduction to the Devout Life*, trans. and ed. Ryan, 28. St. Ignatius, *Spiritual Exercises*, ed. and trans. Puhl, 71–78.

wing of the Reformation is evident. Horton Davies has written that in the late sixteenth century, "in some measure in Anglican worship, and altogether in Puritan worship, the iconoclasts won the arguments with the iconophiles. The result was the almost complete smashing of the figures on the roodscreen and the ending of the making of religious sculptures in wood, as well as the almost total elimination of painting on walls or windows." A common thread of iconoclasm runs through an entire century: the smashing of images in Germany while Luther preached on free grace; the action in London of "individual icono-clasts" incited by John Hooper's Lenten Sermon in 1550 "to turn the altars into tables"; the destruction of the stained-glass windows, cross, and ornaments of John Cotton's church in Boston, England, before the bishop's visitation sermon in 1621.[29]

In New England, though the orthodox magistracy and clergy re-sisted extremism, iconoclasm continued to break out almost unavoid-ably. The famous incident of John Endicott and the flag at Salem is one example. Israel Stoughton, in a letter to his brother, explained that "the greatest part" of the magistrates, ministers, and people dis-approved of Endicott's rash excision of the cross. Still, "some of the magistrates with some ministers and divers of the people do appre-hend it an idol, unlawful to be continued in so honorable a place and time to be abolished." Governor Winthrop opposed Endicott's "in-discreet zeal" but agreed the cross came from the pope and was "so a superstitious thing, a relique of antichrist." When Thomas Shepard received reports of revolutionary iconoclasm in England he noted: "In hearing news of the destroying of the cross in Cheapside and those on steeples in England, I saw how good a thing it was, because in opposing such small evils we resemble God in his holiness the more." The Antinomian controversy ought to be seen not as an aber-ration but as an inevitable expression of radical Puritan spirituality.[30]

Iconoclasm was indicative of other aspects of Puritan spirituality that set the movement apart from its opponents. Puritanism was an uprising of the laity, and although in devotional activity they tem-

29. Davies, *Worship and Theology*, I, 354, 363–364. Steven E. Ozment, *The Reformation in the Cities: The Appeal of Protestantism to Sixteenth-Century Germany and Switzerland* (New Haven, Conn., 1975). Larzer Ziff, *The Career of John Cotton: Puritanism and the American Experience* (Princeton, N.J., 1962), 51.

30. Israel Stoughton to John Stoughton, 1635, Emerson, ed., *Letters from New England*, 144–145. John Winthrop to John Winthrop, Jr., Nov. 6, 1634, *ibid.*, 125. John Winthrop, *Winthrop's Journal: "History of New England," 1630–1649*, ed. James Kendall Hosmer (New York, 1908), I, 137. Shepard, "Journal," in McGiffert, ed., *God's Plot*, 220. See Stoever, 'Faire and Easie Way,' which shows Antinomianism as a distortion of orthodox Puritan spirituality and Reformed theology.

porarily separated from the world, Puritans denied the validity of monastic separation. Puritan devotion was lay devotion, devised for people "in the world," engaged in secular pursuits. The manuals, the advice given in sermons, the rules for meditation and prayer in diaries and other personal writing that one generation left for the benefit of the next, were all typically written for the lay person who must carry on in the world of business. Catholics also wrote manuals and primers for the laity, as already noted, but not nearly as many as did Protestants. Further, the Catholic practicer was rarely encouraged to assume individual responsibility for his or her own spiritual development. Catholic manuals often bound the laity to repetition of forms, such as the Rosary. Puritan manuals, on the contrary, located responsibility for devotional practice in heads of households and ultimately in individuals. The clergy produced a great deal of the devotional material and wrote most of the significant spiritual diaries. But they directed their public writings to lay people, and their private devotions separated them only from the world of sin, not from the laity. Although Puritanism is frequently understood as a movement of clerical scholars, educated and organized primarily at Cambridge, the activities of this "Spiritual Brotherhood" are only half the story. The other source of Puritanism was the lay piety of the countryside of southern England and East Anglia. Puritanism was in effect a marriage of the academic and the rustic. The union produced congregational polity (in which clergy were not a separate class or estate) and a popular culture of personal and social reform based on spiritual regeneration through worship and devotion.[31]

Puritanism was not only a lay movement; like radical religious movements in Europe generally, it was also a women's movement. Women formed the "front line in defense of their preachers" under persecution in England, and women emerged as leaders and "prophets" among radical groups throughout the Civil War. Even among moderate Puritans women played key roles. When Thomas Hooker acted as chaplain in the home of Mrs. Joan Drake and spent much time counseling her, she "being visited with such distresses of soul, as Mr. Hooker himself had passed through," he was performing a service typical of Puritan clerics. John Davenport had a similar pastoral relationship with a wealthy patroness, Mary, Lady Vere, with whom

---

31. Stranks, *Anglican Devotion*, 35. William Haller, *The Rise of Puritanism: Or, the Way to the New Jerusalem as Set Forth in Pulpit and Press from Thomas Cartwright to John Lilburne and John Milton, 1570–1643* (New York, 1938), chap. 2. See A. G. Dickens, *The English Reformation* (New York, 1964), chaps. 1 and 2, and Patrick Collinson, *The Elizabethan Puritan Movement* (Berkeley and Los Angeles, Calif., 1967), e.g., 88–89.

he continued an active correspondence. Puritanism tended to elevate the status of women, although New England society was obviously patriarchal. Puritan ministers wielded little authority of their own and did not have the support of an ecclesiastical hierarchy. They depended for their existence simply on the support of men and women who shared their beliefs.[32]

The major themes that colored the content of Puritan prayers had long been at the heart of popular piety. Traditional and popular lay religion in England was closely related to the Puritan movement. Chaucer's Parson, the piety of Everyman, Piers Plowman, and the tradition of biblical devotion and anticlericalism handed down by Wycliffe and Lollardy are well-known landmarks of this tradition. Popular piety celebrated the life of the pilgrim over that of the self-satisfied, decency over degeneracy, frugality over liberality, asceticism over luxury, simplicity over pomp and prelacy, holiness over formalities. If Puritanism was an effort to reform popular culture, it was an effort to reform it from within. Reform was not led by elites, nor was it carried out through the structures of the Church of England. It was initiated within the context of the lives of ordinary men and women. Puritanism sought social reform that began with and was instigated by groups of already regenerate individuals within popular culture.[33]

Puritan iconoclasm stemmed from its deeper mythoclasm. The Puritan vanguard was dedicated to the destruction of an entire world view, a whole system of values and meaning woven from Roman liturgical forms and pagan religious traditions in their English manifestations. The clearest illustration of this "purification" process was the Puritan renunciation of the ecclesiastical year, ordered according to saint's days and local agricultural legends, a renunciation that one

32. Collinson, *Elizabethan Puritan Movement*, 93. Keith Thomas, *Religion and the Decline of Magic* (New York, 1971), 138. See, more generally, Norman Cohn, *The Pursuit of the Millennium: Revolutionary Millenarians and Mystical Anarchists of the Middle Ages*, rev. ed. (New York, 1970), 160. C. Mather, *Magnalia Christi Americana*, I, 334. Calder, ed., *Letters of Davenport, passim*. Laurel Thatcher Ulrich, "Vertuous Women Found: New England Ministerial Literature, 1668–1735," in Alden T. Vaughan and Francis J. Bremer, eds., *Puritan New England: Essays on Religion, Society, and Culture* (New York, 1977), 215–231.

33. Dickens, *English Reformation*, chap. 2. Peter Burke, *Popular Culture in Early Modern Europe* (New York, 1978), esp. chap. 8, "The Triumph of Lent: The Reform of Popular Culture," 207–243. Burke is incorrect to stress so strongly that Puritanism stood over and against popular culture, attempting to reform it from outside. For example, Burke one moment presents John Bunyan as an "'enthusiastic' sectarian lay preacher" sprung from popular culture and later subsumes him into an elite clerical caste above that culture, the product of university scholarship.

scholar referred to as "Puritan calendar iconoclasm." Economic and social as well as religious reasons motivated the shift to a weekly Sabbath and the attack on the paganism of the maypole and the sports of holy days and Sabbaths. The result, however, was a major devotional disjunction with the Roman system of special days, which had been carried into the practice of the Church of England. Not a single saint's day survived the voyage to New England. Entirely new temporal patterns and rhythms emerged as Puritan spirituality developed and matured.[34]

Puritan emphasis on literacy, based on the Protestant insistence that individuals must be able to read their own Bibles, was a further iconoclastic and socially divisive element in Puritan devotion. The ready availability of Bibles and other religious books, especially devotional manuals, destroyed the exclusive spiritual authority and efficacy of the priest. Although the Puritan pastor retained the role of counselor, the printed manual took over some of the functions of the spiritual director of Roman Catholic monastic devotion. English Catholic publishing of devotional materials was by no means small either, but it was characteristically aimed at an upper-class market and was, of course, carried out clandestinely. Protestant publications reached a more popular market, the same market that otherwise might have been tempted by the ribald romances and jest books that Arthur Dent's "caviller" adored. Sermons and other devotional works had long been standard material for the English press. This literature was not elitist but popular. *The Plaine Mans Pathway* went through twenty-five editions by 1640 and more after that. *The Practice of Piety* had appeared in almost sixty editions by the end of the seventeenth century. Thomas Shepard's pirated sermons, published as the enormously popular *The Sincere Convert*, came out in nineteen editions between 1641 and 1692. His more proper *The Sound Beleever* was printed in at least ten editions between 1645 and 1671. In New England the number of printed copies of religious publications was remarkably high in proportion to the population, even when exports are taken into account. The first printing of the *Bay Psalm Book* was seventeen hundred copies; the 1651 edition was increased to two thousand. Michael Wigglesworth's vivid epic poem, *The Day of Doom*, which touched the popular imagination in New England more successfully than any other seventeenth-century publication, sold out its initial printing of eighteen hundred copies in the first year. *The Day of Doom* was successful, as David Hall has suggested, because "all the basic themes of the 'traditional' [book-

---

34. Davies, *Worship and Theology*, II, 240–241. Christopher Hill, *Society and Puritanism in Pre-Revolutionary England* (New York, 1964), 146, 151–152, 168.

selling] marketplace converged in a single text." Most Puritan publications were, in fact, intended for a wide and popular audience. The
survival of the Cambridge press in New England indicates the extent
to which the writings of the clergy reflected, indeed were bound up
with, the popular religious culture and reading tastes of the population.[35]

Puritanism encouraged believers to read, meditate, and pray on
their own. Meditation focused on personal experience, and prayers
expressed personal hopes and concerns. Both meditation and prayer
were to be lifted up to God in the individual's own words. Puritanism
encouraged believers along the path of free spiritual expression and
initiative, which could be achieved only in separation from the corrupt forms of the world's church. It was incumbent upon the minister
to be exemplary in his prayers, thereby providing a new model for the
laity. The minister was expected to demonstrate that he was himself
able to approach God personally and independently of "set forms" of
prayer and also to show others how they might become able. The
demand for plain preaching and for zealous prayer not read from a
book but "conceived" in the heart of the minister in response to the
requirements of the moment was unequivocal. "Set" prayer in public
worship was not only "an humane invention" that rested on tradition
rather than Scripture, but it was also an infraction of the Second Com-
mandment, an "image." When Puritans separated from the world for
worship and for private devotion it was to approach God in words
"indited by the Spirit of God in the heart of him that prayeth."[36]

A NEW ORDER

The devotional impulse to separate from the world was not simply
iconoclastic or concerned only with destruction of the traditional
medieval *mythos*. Orthodox Puritans attended also to the constructive

35. Kenneth Lockridge, *Literacy in Colonial New England: An Enquiry into the Social Context of Literacy in the Early Modern West* (New York, 1974). Lockridge concludes that in the 17th century "Protestantism was perhaps the sole force which could rapidly in- crease literacy to high levels or bring the level of this skill to universality" (p. 5). Davies, *Worship and Theology*, I, 408–410. Hall, "World of Print," in Higham and Conkin, eds., *New Directions in American Intellectual History*, 174–175. H. S. Bennett, *English Books & Readers, 1475–1557: Being a Study in the History of the Book Trade from Caxton to the Incor- poration of the Stationers' Company* (Cambridge, 1952), 57. George Parker Winship, *The Cambridge Press, 1638–1692: A Reexamination of the Evidence concerning* The Bay Psalm Book *and the* Eliot Indian Bible (Philadelphia, 1945), 34.
36. John Cotton, *A Modest and Cleare Answer to Mr. Balls Discourse of Set Formes of Prayer* ... (London, 1642), 16.

task of re-forming the world. They were iconopoietic and mythopoi-
etic as well as iconoclastic and mythoclastic. In England, and decisively
in New England, they consciously set about building a new society that
anticipated the Kingdom of God. Their constructive work led them
back into the realm of ritual and image. Even seeming anti-ritualists
cannot live without ritual, and iconoclasts cannot survive without
images that give meaning to their lives. Ritual may be taken to mean
activity that a society establishes to celebrate and renew commonly
held perceptions, to be repeated at specified times by members of
the society, either corporately or individually. Ritual activity thus expresses a society's understanding of itself. In New England the Puritans re-ritualized religious experience.[37]

Freedom was indeed one pole of the Puritan axis, but order was the
other. The new order was to be rooted in biblical authority and precedent. If any people ever were, Puritans were people of the Book.
The new order they created, and the world view that undergirded it,
was meticulously scriptural in nature. Puritans rejected liturgical traditions, no matter how venerable, that had no discernible basis in the
Bible, replacing them with worship and devotional practices seen as
more soundly scriptural. At the same time, as we have seen, some
devotional themes and methods with slight scriptural foundation
were so strong that they were able to survive the transition from
medieval Catholicism to New England Puritanism.[38]

The Puritan program for social reform was to a large extent
founded on the reform of English worship and devotion along scriptural lines. Basic to the reform program was the reconstruction of the
Sabbath. Gone were the Mass, the vestments, the processions of the
hierarchy. Gone was the festival and sportive atmosphere among the
populace. The new Sabbath, beginning in biblical fashion on the
evening before the day itself, was built around family devotions, the
hearing of God's Word read and preached both morning and afternoon, and rest from secular work and play. Puritans understood their
Sabbath not as a new invention but as a reinstitution of God's original
intent, which had become hidden by layer after layer of pagan and
papist adulterations. As Thomas Shepard wrote, "It cannot be denied
but that the Sabbath (like many other precious appointments and
truths of God) did shake off her dust, and put on her comely and

37. On ritual, see Douglas, *Natural Symbols*; Victor W. Turner, *The Ritual Process: Structure and Anti-Structure* (Chicago, 1969); and James D. Shaughnessy, ed., *The Roots of Ritual* (Grand Rapids, Mich., 1973).

38. David Little, *Religion, Order, and Law: A Study in Pre-Revolutionary England* (New York, 1969). David D. Hall, *The Faithful Shepherd: A History of the New England Ministry in the Seventeenth Century* (Chapel Hill, N.C., 1972).

beautiful garments, and hath been much honoured and magnified since the times of the Reformation on; the doctrine and darkness of Popery... obscured this of the Sabbath." Shepard defended the movement against the charge that a weekly Sabbath was "but a late Novelty" and "a superstitious seething over of the hot or whining simplicity of an over-rigid, crabbed, precise, crack-brain'd Puritanicall party." Puritans produced biblical precedents for every detail of their program of worship and devotion. As John Eliot punned, the"Novangles are not New Fangles but No Fangles (in respect to worship)."[39]

Orthodox Puritans had to defend the Sabbath not only against Anglicans but also against the radical wing of their own movement. In their iconoclastic spiritualism the radicals tended to rise even above the letter of Scripture, accusing the Puritans of "a phanatick Judaizing," a falling short of the Spirit by settling for external forms. Shepard responded that the radicals "have spiritualized [the Sabbath] out of the Decalogue, yea out of all the Churches in the world" and urged that the Sabbath be understood as a spiritual sense within each person rather than as a day of the week. "They hereby abolish a seventh dayes Sabbath, and make every day equally a Sabbath to a Christian man." Shepard warned that such extremism could only lead back to an otherworldly monasticism that Protestantism had begun by rejecting. "The times are now come, wherein by the refined mysticall divinity of the old *Monks*, not only the Sabbath, but also all the Ordinances of Christ in the New Testament are allegorized and spiritualized out of the world." Shepard and his New England colleagues clung to their reading of the Bible, and to the religious order it sanctioned, and never let go.[40]

Even in the matter of "set prayers" the iconoclasm of Puritanism was limited by practical considerations. Orthodox Puritans allowed printed aids for private devotional practice while rejecting them for public worship. The devotional manuals that Puritans consulted contained guidelines and advice on how to meditate and pray, and also sample meditations and prayers that could actually be used. If "set prayers" were ungodly for public worship, how did the use of printed models for individuals avoid idolatry? John Cotton drew a distinction between "set prayers" and "devised prayers." The first oppressed spirituality because they were forced upon a congregation by external authority. But "devised prayers" in a published manual might be the

39. Thomas Shepard, *Theses Sabbaticae: Or the Doctrine of the Sabbath* ... (London, 1650 [orig. publ. 1649]), sig. A3. The Eliot quote is in Williams, *Wilderness and Paradise*, 101.

40. *Ibid.*, sig. A4–A7.

means of true spirituality if they were voluntarily taken up. Cotton rejected the possibility of using them in public worship. God's people, and especially His ministers, must be able to pray publicly in exemplary extemporaneous fashion. The "distinction of voluntary and necessary helps, may not be stretched so farre, as to justifie devised and set formes of prayer, to supply the defects of sinfully ignorant, or carelessly bashfull people, as cannot pray (especially before a company) without a Booke: For, first, God would not have such persons (so sinfully ignorant and bashfull) to be called forth into publique Ministry . . . nor may such ignorant and lame Christians be admitted to come into the publike place in the Church." John Preston, whom Cotton had converted in 1611, wrote that "the end of a set forme of prayer is to be a helpe for the private, . . . a helpe that one may use that is yet exceeding weake." Cotton argued similarly: "Wee grant that a man may make use of another mans penned prayers read in private, not onely for an example, or instruction how to pray; but also occasionally for his present prayer; If he finde the Petitions sutable to his present occasions."[41]

The Puritan's goal in preaching and in producing and using manuals with devotional aids was always to promote the individual practice of piety, which ultimately relied on no printed work save the Bible. The entire pastoral work of the clergy, and the most basic thrust of the Puritan movement itself, were aimed at the spiritual regeneration of sinners through the means of worship and devotional activity. Personal religious experience was at the heart of Puritanism. Everything in church and state was intended to serve this primary end. And this end, in turn, was the means of establishing the new order, which was the vanguard of God's Kingdom itself. Puritans engaged in many activities other than worship and devotion, and they have frequently been described as rationalists, capitalists, political revolutionaries, and members of a new and upwardly mobile middle class. But whatever else it may have been, and whatever social changes it may have brought in its wake, Puritanism must first be considered as a devotional movement. As such, its continuity with the much broader devotional revival of the post-Reformation years and with the general history of Christian spirituality emerges. But this approach also enables us to understand more precisely the distinctive character of the Puritan way.

41. Cotton, *Modest and Cleare Answer*, 18–20. John Preston, *The Saints Daily Exercise: A Treatise Unfolding the Whole Dutie of Prayer . . .* , 3d ed. (London, 1629), 80–84.

Chapter Three

Puritan as Pilgrim

The principal metaphor running through Puritan spirituality and devotional practice was the pilgrimage. Pilgrimage was already a common concept in the Middle Ages. The term had long been used to connote not only a geographical pilgrimage to a shrine but also, on a deeper level, the journey of the soul to God. Puritans in the seventeenth century used the metaphor to structure their understanding and experience of the life of the spirit. Of the four vignettes in the first chapter, the idea of a journey from sin through the wilderness to final glory is stated specifically in two of them, the narratives of Thomas Shepard and Anne Bradstreet. It is implicitly present in the other two, in the literal journey from England and in the stages along life's way.[1]

The spiritual pilgrimage to heaven was a concept that Puritans inherited from medieval mystical writers who had fully employed "the allegory of the Pilgrimage of Life." All the images of sainthood and sin, all the literary conceits, all the spiritual adversaries so brilliantly displayed by John Bunyan in his classic expression of the tradition, *The Pilgrim's Progress*, were present at least in germ form in the work of Prudentius, St. Bernard of Clairvaux, St. Bonaventure, the Abbot of St. Victor, Jean Gerson, and Walter Hilton. The Roman Catholic origins of the Puritan devotional structure are undeniable. Yet the source that evoked the image most vividly for Puritans was the Epistle to the Hebrews. In the eleventh chapter of that book the Puritans' progenitors in the faith—Abraham and Sarah, Isaac, Jacob, Joseph, Moses, and Rahab—are all described as men and women on a journey. Puritans likened themselves to Abraham, who was "called to go out

---

1. The pervasive importance of the pilgrimage theme in early America is discussed in Cyclone Covey, *The American Pilgrimage: The Roots of American History, Religion and Culture* (New York, 1961). Josephine K. Piercy, following Anne Bradstreet's own use of the term, has discussed the poet's life as a "Christian Pilgrimage" in chap. 2 of her *Anne Bradstreet*. See also Cecelia Tichi, "Spiritual Biography and the 'Lords Remembrancers,'" *WMQ*, 3d Ser., XXVIII (1971), 64–85.

into a place which he should after receive for an inheritance; and he went out, not knowing whither he went." True saints, according to Hebrews, "confessed that they were strangers and pilgrims on the earth" seeking "a better country, that is, an heavenly" (11:8, 13, 16).[2]

In Puritan devotional manuals the term "pilgrimage" described the spiritual life. John Downame, in *The Christian Warfare*, pointed to the need to feel "contempt of the World, and love of Heaven, grounded upon the consideration of our lives short and momentary continuance." He concluded, "We are Pilgrims here ... we shall rest (as it were) but one night, and then be gone." The world was "to be used as a place of passage, and not as a place of habitation." Paul Bayne wrote in the same vein in his *Briefe Directions unto a Godly Life*. The basis of the spiritual journey was the "holy and earnest desire to have more communion with God; even to enjoy his blessed presence, and to see his glory, 2 Corinthians 5.1 ['For we know that, if our earthly house of this tabernacle were dissolved, we have a building of God, a house not made with hands, eternal in the heavens.']." He wrote, "The former grace maketh [the believer] to forsake this World, to become a stranger and a pilgrime here, and so to have no more to doe in this World than hee needs most."[3]

Despite the Puritans' debt to the earlier Catholic tradition, their concept of the pilgrimage was significantly different from that of the cloistered Catholic mystic. Bayne explained that devotional pilgrimage was to take place within the context of the saint's secular calling. "Not that he leave the necessary duties or forsake his calling, but that hee is not so tied to these things, but that he could willingly leave them, and so being ready to die, is made fit to live."[4]

The emblematic meditative verse found in some manuals also utilized the pilgrimage metaphor. Some simply restated the theme from Hebrews 11:

The saints are pilgrims here below
And tow'rds their countrey heaven go.

Others, such as Francis Quarles's *Emblemes, Divine and Moral*, elaborated on the theme in ways that anticipated Bunyan's vision later in the century. The engraving that accompanies Quarles's meditation

2. Collins, *Christian Mysticism*, 64–76.

3. Downame, *Christian Warfare*, 627, 693. Downame reiterated, "We should not set our hearts on the World and worldly things, because we are but pilgrims and strangers on the earth" (p. 691). Paul Bayne, *Briefe Directions unto a Godly Life* (London, 1637 [orig. publ. 1618]), 21.

4. Bayne, *Briefe Directions*, 21.

Oh that my wayes were Directed to keepe thy Statutes. Ps·119·5.
W·Simpson Sculp:

Come my beloued, let vs goe forth into ye fields, let vs remaine in ye Villages. Cant·7·ij
W·Simpson·Sculp:

Figure 4. Four selections from Francis Quarles, Emblemes, Divine and Moral . . . *(London, 1635 edition) illustrating the devotional themes of the*

on Psalm 119:5 ("O that my ways were directed to keep thy statutes") shows the soul as pilgrim wearing the traditional hat and carrying a staff. He is heading into a labyrinth but holds a guideline that leads directly up to Christ, in a tower outside the maze. The epigrammatic verse reads:

> Pilgrim, trudge on: what makes my soul complain,
> Crowns thy complaint? the way to rest is pain:
> The road to resolution lies by doubt:
> The next way home's the farthest way about.

The emblematic poem itself is filled with phrases and images long associated with the pilgrimage tradition, including the themes of weariness and renunciation of the world's values.

My Soule melted, when my beloved spake. Cant: 5.6.
Will: Simpson scul:

O wretched Man that I am; who shall deliver me from the body of this Death?
Rom: 7.24.
Will: simpson sculp:

spiritual pilgrimage, the preparation for death, and the "melted soule."
Courtesy the Folger Shakespeare Library, Washington, D.C.

Thus I, the object of the world's disdain
With pilgrim face surround the weary earth;
I only relish what the world counts vain;
Her mirth's my grief; her sullen grief my mirth;
Her light my darkness; and her truth my error,
Her freedom is my gaol; and her delight my terror.

Like Christian in Vanity Fair, the spiritual pilgrim lived according to a standard that was the exact reverse of the world's.[5]

5. Johann Gerhard, *Ger[h]ards Prayers: Or, a Daily Practise of Pietie*, 5th ed. (London, 1638), 290. The verse is from Meditation XLVII, "Of the beatificall vision of God, in heaven," according to traditional scholarship a distinctly un-Puritan theme. Francis Quarles, *Emblems, Divine and Moral; the School of the Heart; and Hieroglyphics of the Life of Man* (1634–1635), ed. W[illiam] W[ilkins] (London, 1866), 145–147.

New Englanders followed the manuals in using the pilgrimage metaphor, as the cases of Shepard and Bradstreet illustrate. Their personal writings suggest that New Englanders truly considered themselves to be descendants of the pilgrim stock of Israel celebrated in Hebrews. Richard Mather in his 1661 will praised God, who "by his good Providence preserved the being and comfort of my life all the dayes of my Pilgrimage until now, even for the space of these Sixty five years." Increase Mather followed his father's lead when he wrote the older man's biography, reverently recounting "the time of his Pilgrimage in New-England." Rustic John Dane organized his autobiographical narrative around the adventures of his travels and used the word "pilgrimage" to describe his transiency. In an autobiographical sketch John Higginson cited "things I desire to leave upon Record as a thankful Remembrance of the gracious dealings of God with me, in the midst of all the changes of times that have passed over me, in this my Pilgrimage upon Earth." Jonathan Mitchel wrote in a pastoral letter to a friend that "whatsoever may happen to you here, yet hereafter it shall be well with you, and in your wearisome pilgrimage it may be for a Consolation to you, that you shall rejoice in time to come." Edward Taylor referred in a poem to "this pilgrim life of mine."[6]

When New Englanders wrote elegiac poetry, the image again came naturally to mind, as in John Fiske's poem in memory of Ipswich pastor Nathaniel Rogers.

> The Sabbath is a Day of Rest all know
> How many Sabbaths did He heere enjoy
> The feeling-sweets of that Sabbath I trow
> which now to him a Rest most sweet is aye
>
> This weary pilgrime glad of shady-Tree
> (Under the which heere oft a Rest he made
> That Tree of Life, his Right, his food, his Cure
> still heere.) now Rests for aye under its shade.
>
> In this worlds wildernes no Rest He found
> But heavenly Canaans Rest his hope it was
> His weary Travells now dispatcht hath He
> and by our Josua that Rest He has.

6. [Increase Mather], *The Life and Death of That Reverend Man of God, Mr. Richard Mather* . . . (Cambridge, Mass., 1670), 34, 25. Dane, "Declaration of Remarkabell Prouedenses," *NEHGR*, VIII (1854), 152. John Higginson, "To the Reader," in Higginson, *Our Dying Saviour's Legacy of Peace to His Disciples in a Troublesome World* . . . (Boston,

Fiske's phrases are very similar to Anne Bradstreet's a few years later when she contemplated her own death. The idea of life as a spiritual pilgrimage clearly took on special power when New Englanders wrote about death, the actual completion of the journey. Bradstreet referred to her frustrated desire for more "constant Joy in my Pilgrimage" as early as 1656 when she wrote a short account of her life for the benefit of her children. But it was her meditative poem written as she faced death that allows us to discern the metaphor as a major theme that permeated her whole spiritual life.[7]

New England ministers used the pilgrimage theme in their preaching in several different ways. The metaphor described their separation as Reformed Christians from the perceived corruption and static hierarchy of Roman Catholicism and of papist vestiges in the Church of England. The church must be ever reforming, must never settle uncritically "in any outward estate," they preached. The saints must follow Christ, the original pilgrim, who does not rest in the complacency of a status quo. John Cotton proclaimed: "Notwithstanding the reformation of religion, Christ may be pleased rather to live abroad in the fields, then at home, where the people would willingly assemble. . . . Rome hath long doted on Peters Chair, and Jerusalem might as well have bragged of her Priviledges as any other place, but Christ leaves them. . . . The Palatinate hath been as reformed as any Church for Doctrine, and though they might say, their bed was greene, and their beames were of cedar, and their rafters of firre, yet God hath left them." Cotton asserted that "notwithstanding the purity and simplicity" of a church's worship, "yet Christ is not bound to any place." The etymology of the word "pilgrim" suggests a journey through a field. Thus, Cotton preached, Christ is "abroad in the fields" as a pilgrim, in the vanguard of the Reformation. The relation of New England to this movement is clear, and diaries suggest that believers prayed not only for their own part in God's plan but for other fronts in the war against the papacy as well.[8]

1686). Jonathan Mitchel, "A Letter Written by the Author to His Friend in New England," appended to Mitchel, *A Discourse of the Glory to Which God Hath Called Believers by Jesus Christ . . .*, 2d ed. (Boston, 1721), 291. Edward Taylor, "Preparatory Meditations," II, 45, l. 52, in Stanford, ed., *Poems of Taylor*, 164.

7. Harold S. Jantz, ed., *The First Century of New England Verse* (Worcester, Mass., 1944), 127. See also Samuel Danforth's anagrammatic elegy for William Tompson, "William Tompson, Anagram 2: now i am slipt home," in Kenneth B. Murdock, ed., *Handkerchiefs from Paul: Being Pious and Consolatory Verses of Puritan Massachusetts . . .* (Cambridge, Mass., 1927), 19–20. Bradstreet, "Autobiographical Passages," in Hutchinson, ed., *Poems of Bradstreet*, 181.

8. John Cotton, *A Briefe Exposition of the Whole Book of Canticles, or, Song of Solomon . . .*

The ministers also applied the metaphor of the pilgrimage to the individual soul. Thomas Hooker described human life generally as "this vale of teares, this pilgrimage of ours." More specifically, they considered the soul to be a pilgrim on its journey first through the conversion process and then on the long road to full union with Christ. John Cotton preached that "so soon as ever the Lord hath given this self-denying spirit unto the soul" God made the penitent into a pilgrim. The person became "like a Traveller that is out of his way, and willing to take any man by the hand that will lead him into his way again." It was God, the Father of all pilgrims, who would take him by the hand and lead him to salvation.[9]

Beyond conversion, the preachers applied the theme to progress toward union with Christ in glory, especially through meditations on death and eternity. These devotions were not limited to the elderly. Ministers continually urged even young people to meditate on their mortality as a means of recognizing their need for the eternal God. Without regard to age, Cotton would "exhort to the remembrance of our Creatour and to prepare for a change. Here we have no abiding City, we seeke one to come, Heb. 13. 14."[10]

Thomas Shepard brought together all these usages of the pilgrim metaphor in one of his most famous sermon series, *The Sound Beleever*. After elaborating on what saints might look for in the life to come, Shepard assured his auditors that they were approaching the end of the journey. His description of dangers and afflictions, including the common image of the "weary pilgrim," was much like John Bun-

---

(London, 1648 [orig. publ. 1642]), 60–61. Cotton's work is an example of the variety of ways Puritans read the Song of Songs. Not only was it used in private devotion as a mystical love song between the soul and Christ, but also Cotton treated it (following another exegetical tradition) as an ecclesiastical textbook and as a guide to eschatology. See also Cotton, *Thirteenth Chapter of Revelation*, 21, 45; Cotton, *Powring Out of the Seven Vials*, 154–156; Cotton, *The Covenant of God's Free Grace* (London, 1645), 8. *Oxford English Dictionary*, s.v. "pilgrim." Shepard, "Journal," in McGiffert, ed., *God's Plot*, 129–130, 208. Clifford K. Shipton, ed., "The Autobiographical Memoranda of John Brock, 1636–1659," American Antiquarian Society, *Proceedings*, N.S., LIII (1943), 103–104." Hull, *Diaries*, 173, 200–201, 228. Ford, ed., *Diary of Cotton Mather*, I, 41–42.

9. Thomas H[ooker], *The Soules Vocation or Effectual Calling to Christ* (London, 1638), 61. John Cotton, *A Treatise of the Covenant of Grace . . .* , 3d ed. (London, 1671), 124. The relationship of the pilgrim theme to the conversion experience receives special attention later in this chapter.

10. John Cotton, *A Briefe Exposition with Practicall Observations upon the Whole Book of Ecclesiastes*, 2d ed. (London, 1657), 244. The various forms of preparatory devotions by which the believer advanced toward the goal are the subject of chap. 7, below.

yan's imaginative vision a little later. We can reappropriate some of the passage's full rhetorical effect—and therefore its impact for the worshiper—by resetting Shepard's phrases in poetic form.

This is therefore the great glory
　　of all those whom God hath called
　　to the fellowship of his deare Son;

and which is yet more, blessed be God the time is not long,
　　but that we shall feel what now we doe but heare of,
　　and see but a little of,
　　as we use to doe of things afar off:

We are here but strangers, and have no abiding city,
　　we look for this that hath foundations;

and therefore let sinne presse us downe;
　　and weary us out with wrastling with it;

let Satan tempt,
　　and cast his darts at us;

let our drink be our teares day and night,
　　and our meat gall and wormwood;

let us be shut up in choaking prisons,
　　and cast out for dead in the streets,
　　nay upon dung-hils, and none to bury us;

let us live alone as Pelicans in the wildernesse,
　　and be driven among wild beasts into deserts;

let us be scourged, and disgraced,
　　stoned, sawn asunder, and burned;

let us live in sheep-skins, and goat-skins,
　　destitute, afflicted, tormented
　　(as who looks not for such days shortly?)

yet oh brethren, the time is not long,
　　but when we are at the worst,
　　and death ready to swallow us up;
　　we shall cry out,
　　Oh glory, glory,
　　oh welcome glory.[11]

11. Shepard, *Sound Beleever*, 316–317.

The extravagance of this passage, powerful as it is homiletically, seems at first to bear little relationship to the fairly comfortable life New Englanders enjoyed soon after settlement. Shepard's meaning becomes evident, however, when it is understood that these words were no rhetorical flight of his own invention, but a rhapsodic conflation of phrases from the agonized Psalm 102 and the "strangers and pilgrims" passage in Hebrews 11. God's pilgrim people had suffered at the hands of the world in the past; Puritans understood the people of the Bible as ancestors and prototypes. More recently Queen Mary had exiled and executed English reformers. In the days of the Great Migration Archbishop Laud was moving against Puritans; some were again being "shut up in choaking prisons." If Psalm 102 gave poignant voice to the experience of persecution—"Mine enemies reproach me all the day. . . . I have eaten ashes like bread, and mingled my drink with weeping"—it also expressed hope of divine vindication in the Kingdom, "when the people are gathered together, and the kingdoms, to serve the Lord" (vv. 8–9, 22).

Shepard exhorted the saints to continue on the painful journey to the Kingdom. They must not stop, contented, before reaching the goal. Shepard, it seems, almost longed for the day when suffering would once again descend upon the saints. His words ring as a call to asceticism and strife. His repetition of "let," meaning "no matter that," was also an exhortation: "Let our drink be teares day and night. . . . Let us live alone as Pelicans in the wildernesse." Even when conditions were relatively comfortable and stable, as they were in New England, saints must not define their homes in earthly terms.

The terrors Shepard enumerated were not outlandish when applied to events in Europe, and he prophesied that the wars of religion would shortly spread to engulf New England. The conflict, Shepard believed, would ultimately escalate into the complete destruction that was to precede the Second Coming of Christ. He again anticipated Bunyan and echoed Genesis 19 and Revelation 6–9 as he cried:

> Away to the mountaines,
> > and hasten from the towns and cities of your habitation,
> > where the grace of Christ is published, but universally despised,
> > you blessed called ones of the Lord Jesus;
>
> for the dayes are coming,
> > wherein for this sin, the heavens and earth shall shake,
> > the sunne shall be turned into darknesse,
> > and the moone into blood,

and mens hearts failing for feare of the horrible plagues
which are comming upon the face of the earth.

Dreame not of faire weather,
 expect not better days,
 till you heare men say,
 Blessed is he that cometh in the name of the Lord.[12]

The Puritan spiritual pilgrimage was the journey from the city of sin
through the wilderness of humiliation and mortification to the heavenly city of God's Kingdom.

Puritans found in the pilgrimage metaphor a powerful instrument
for interpreting their individual and communal lives. Certainly no
Puritan was ever seen on the road to Canterbury with hat, beads, and
staff. But the extent to which this ancient style was carried over into
Puritan spirituality is suggested by the illustration of John Bunyan's
dream ("The Sleeping Portrait" by Robert White) included in the
third (1679) and fourth (1680) editions of *The Pilgrim's Progress* and
by the thirteen "copper cuts" of key scenes of the journey from the
fifth (1680) edition on. In all of these engravings the pilgrim is garbed
in the traditional medieval and Roman Catholic trappings. Puritans
appropriated the devotional tradition of the spiritual pilgrimage for
their own use. Its prevalent and powerful use by preachers, writers of
manuals, diarists, and poets indicates that it was a controlling theme,
even the main current within which other elements of Puritan piety
found their direction.[13]

An example of how the idea of the spiritual pilgrimage could serve
as a device for organizing personal experience may be found in John
Winthrop's account of his "Christian Experience," written in January
1636/1637. Winthrop did not coincidentally examine the course of
his life at this particular time. It was his forty-ninth birthday, and he
seems to have been plunged into spiritual uncertainty as he faced the
last quarter of his life. He had just been voted out of the office of governor, thereby losing control of the colony he had organized. Thus
personal and social crises converged. His personal faith had ebbed to
the point that he felt spiritually "drowsy." Where was the zeal of 1630?
Yet all around him Winthrop observed religious excitement and renewal, though of a kind he disapproved. The revival that attended

12. *Ibid.*, 318–319.
13. John Bunyan, *Pilgrim's Progress*, ed. Wharey and Sharrock, Introduction, xxxviii–
xxxix, li; Appendix, 353–354.

Figure 5. John Bunyan's dream, the frontispiece to the fourth edition of
The Pilgrim's Progress *(London, 1680). The author is reclining on a lion's*
den, symbolic of his imprisonment ("As I walk'd through the wilderness of this
world, I lighted on a certain place, where was a Denn; And I laid me down in
that place to sleep" [Bunyan, The Pilgrim's Progress . . . , *ed. James*
Blanton Wharey and Roger Sharrock, 2d ed. (Oxford, 1960), 11]), while the
open prison bars suggest Bunyan's spiritual freedom (see Daniel 6) as he
envisions Christian on his journey from sin to glory. Courtesy the Folger
Shakespeare Library, Washington, D.C.

John Cotton's arrival at the Boston Church saw large numbers convert and covenant. Most of these new members tended toward spiritual radicalism, the iconoclastic wing of Puritanism. Enthusiasm centered in study and prayer meetings in private homes, notably at the home of Anne Hutchinson, where the immediacy of the Holy Spirit's presence in the believer's heart was emphasized over adherence to the outward aspects of the covenant. Hutchinson and her zealous followers condemned moderate orthodoxy as lukewarm, concerned only with external conformity to the Law, and even unregenerate. Winthrop, who symbolized the founding principles of the colony, was one of those attacked.

John Winthrop's external, political reaction to the threat of the radicals, whom he and the ministers perceived as antinomians, was to stamp out the movement and banish its leaders. This he proceeded to do when he returned to the office of governor in 1637. But his internal, spiritual reaction to the crisis was quite different; he put *himself* on trial. Winthrop perceived painfully that the Hutchinsonians were able to testify to a livelier experience of Christ than he was able to do at the time. "The Doctrine of free justification lately taught here," he wrote, "took mee in as drowsy a condition, as I had been in (to my remembrance) these twenty yeares, and brought me as low (in my owne apprehension) as if the whole work had been to begin anew." While outwardly duty impelled him to indict others, inwardly Winthrop felt himself indicted by God for his lack of feeling. Perhaps by reviewing his earlier experiences, including his conversion and early growth in grace, he could recapture what he knew he once had. It was clearly time to take stock.[14]

Winthrop's account of his experience followed the pattern long established as the Puritan norm. He began with a formal statement, "In my youth I was very lewdly disposed," progressed to his early movements in the direction of faith, his early marriage, his still tentative interest in religion through his twenties, the influence of a prominent minister, his conversion (rather late) at thirty, and his spiritual vicissitudes over the twenty years that culminated in his "drowsy" state at the onset of his self-examination. He concluded with the prayer, "The Lord Jesus who (of his own free grace) hath washed my soule in the blood of the everlasting Covenant, wash away all those spots also in his good time. Amen even so doe Lord Jesus." His use of the phrase "free grace"—the Antinomian slogan—to describe his own earlier

14. John Winthrop, "Christian Experience," *Winthrop Papers*, I, 154–161. (Subsequent quotations are from the same source.) Shea, *Spiritual Autobiography*, 102. See the study of English Puritan spiritual autobiography, Watkins's *Puritan Experience*.

experience with God indicates his final resolution that he was every bit as saved as Anne Hutchinson and the others thought themselves to be.

The pilgrim theme is inconspicuous in Winthrop's narrative, but once recognized it gives cohesion, structure, and hope to his words. It first appears in obvious phrases, such as his thanksgiving that the Lord did not leave him on account of his "stubbornesse, and unkind rejections of mercy" in young adulthood but continued to work on his heart until he could "bid farewell to all the world." On his journey, then, he found "some peace and comfort in God" but still slipped repeatedly into sin. Fear that having continually to repent was no repentance at all made it "like hell" for him to meditate on a passage from Hebrews (the book that puts forth the "strangers and pilgrims" paradigm) that warned against such backsliding. Further, his account contains the traditional and common biblical phrases about "walking more close with God," which lend themselves to the pilgrimage theme.

More subtle use of pilgrim phraseology is a seemingly offhand phrase, "up and down." Winthrop wrote of an illness during his youth in which "I went up and down mourning with myself; and being deprived of my youthfull joyes, I betook my self to God." Later, just before his conversion the phrase appears again: "While I wandred up and downe in this sad and doubtful estate" of less than complete faith in Christ. The phrase was habitually connected in the seventeenth-century English mind with life as pilgrimage. Two quite diverse sources demonstrate this connection. John Dane recorded in his autobiographical narrative how as a youthful convert he decided, "I would goe and work Jurney work thorow all the Countries in ingland, and so walk as a pilgrim up and doune on the earth." In an unusually sophisticated play on words, Dane was referring to his journeywork as a journeyman tailor, to his geographical journeyings as a newly independent young man, and to his spiritual travels as a saint on his way to heaven. In all three senses life was a pilgrimage for John Dane, which the phrase "up and doune on the earth" expresses in well-worn words from the popular vocabulary. Thomas Shepard, a university graduate trained in the use of language, echoed the phrase when he warned against false self-reliance on the outward means of grace, that is, on "duties" such as prayer, fasting, and pilgrimage. "Mourn in some wildernesse till dooms day . . . walk up and down the world like a distressed Pilgrim going to another countrey," he challenged, "these cannot deliver thee, for they are not the blood of Christ." Pilgrimage was a mere wandering unless the journey was to Christ and by the grace of Christ. The phrase "up and down like a pilgrim" apparently was a traditional folk image that continued to find currency among Puritans. Clergy and laity, learned and unlearned, employed it. Winthrop's use of the phrase indicates that the idea of pilgrimage was present in his mind as he wrote.[15]

After Winthrop's conversion the theme of the journey continued to appear in his account. As a new man in Christ, "If I went abroad hee went with mee, when I returned hee came home with mee. I talked with him upon the way, hee lay down with mee and usually I did awake with him." We often find a dream in conjunction with the pilgrimage metaphor (as in Bunyan's *Pilgrim's Progress*), and Winthrop reflects this tradition. When he slipped into sin after his conversion, he wrote, it was never for long: "But in such a condition hee would not long leave mee, but would still recall mee by some word or affliction or in a prayer or meditation, and I should then bee as a man awakened out of a dream or as if I had been another man." Once Winthrop's work is recognized as essentially a pilgrimage narrative, the resemblances to Bunyan's later work become increasingly apparent. "Many falls I have had" along the way, Winthrop wrote. "But still when I have been put to it by any suddaine danger or fearfull temptation, the good spirit of the Lord hath not fayled to beare witnesse to mee, giveing mee comfort, and courage in the very pinch, when of my self I have been very fearefull, and dismayed."

John Winthrop's use of the pilgrimage metaphor to order his self-examination allowed him to find a sense of hope. His spiritual failings did not lead to despair because he was able to find that he had indeed made great progress. If his condition was "drowsy" at the time of the Antinomian controversy, the charges of the Hutchinsonians, when he applied them to his own soul, became the basis of new assurance. The conversion process began with contrition and humiliation, and within this framework he had meditated on his own past experience. Finally, "when the voice of peace came, I knew it to bee the same that I had been acquainted with before, though it did not speak so loud nor in that measure of joy that I had felt sometimes." John Winthrop was still on the path that led up to the "city which hath foundations, whose builder and maker is God" (Hebrews 11:10).

15. Dane, "Declaration of Remarkabell Prouedenses," *NEHGR*, VIII (1854), 152. *OED*, s.v. "Journey-work." Shepard, *Sincere Convert*, 108. See Covey, *American Pilgrimage*, 18, for other pilgrimage references in Winthrop's writings.

THE STAGES OF THE JOURNEY:
THE ORDER OF REDEMPTION

The Puritan spiritual journey followed many traditional patterns of the medieval pilgrimage to holy places. The fourteenth-century proto-Puritan, Chaucer's Parson, before preaching his sermon asked,

> Jesu in his grace wit me sende
> To shewe you the way in this viage
> Of thilke parfit glorious pilgrimage
> That highte Jerusalem celestial.

The way of the journey, both geographically and spiritually, led the pilgrim through a series of stages. Scholars have discussed the "stages" of the conversion experience and of the order of redemption without realizing that the word "stage" was derived from the language of pilgrimage. "Stage" connoted not simply a degree of movement through a process, or even ascending levels of platforms, but also an established resting place or station on a well-marked road. Just as the king's highway between, say, London and Cambridge was dotted with official stops where horses were watered or changed and where inns and taverns provided weary travelers with food and drink, so the ancient routes of pilgrimage to the shrines at Glastonbury, Canterbury, Westminster, and St. Albans had traditional stops along the way for devotion and sustenance. Puritans went beyond Chaucer's Parson and banned geographical pilgrimages to holy places altogether. But they clearly did not ban the metaphor of the spiritual pilgrimage. Puritans transmuted the journey into a purely spiritual one, retaining the key idea of progress through set stages to a holy destination.[16]

The Puritans' sense of spiritual order and their celebrated sense of purpose and orientation toward goals stem in some measure from their inheritance of the pilgrimage tradition. In an ironic inversion, Puritans ridiculed as aimless wanderers their contemporaries who continued to tread the paths to shrines. The phraseology of Dane, Shepard, and Winthrop reflects this. To "wander up and down" implies a futility that the saint overcame when he set out on the truly spiritual path to the heavenly city. Indeed, to be on any road other than the King's Highway, "the plaine mans pathway to heaven," was to be a spiritual vagabond. Not that progress was always steady. It was easy to lose one's way between stages. But even this wandering fit into

---

16. *The Norton Anthology of English Literature*, I (New York, 1962), 174. *OED*, s.v. "stage." Thomas, *Religion and the Decline of Magic*, 26.

the overall pattern as it might be understood farther down the road. The road was well established, after all, and help was readily available from other saints who knew the landmarks. Ultimately a would-be pilgrim had no excuse if he failed to find his way again. Puritans defined themselves against those who wandered and never learned, or even cared to learn, the way.

Spiritual vagabonds were commonly geographical ones as well, and Puritans opposed the self-seeking men and women who wandered England's country roads and city streets in search of a handout or sailed newly charted seas for easy wealth. England itself, emigrating Puritans charged, had become a self-seeking rather than a God-seeking nation. "Assuredly God can be God without England's prosperity," Thomas Hooker preached upon his departure. England had become "a vagabond people."[17]

Just as the medieval geographical pilgrimages were inadequate as a means of grace, however, so mere migration to the New World did not itself confer holiness. Not all immigrants were on the pilgrim way. From the beginning of settlement, orthodox New Englanders were quick to ferret out the self-seekers and send them packing. Perhaps most notorious was Thomas Morton of Merrymount, Massachusetts, whose values ran completely counter to those of the Puritan colonies. If the Puritan social ideal was of saints "knitt together . . . as one man," Morton was an individualist with essentially hedonistic impulses. The leaders judged Anne Hutchinson and her followers as being on a different road because the Antinomians rejected the very idea of an order of redemption with stages. Why trudge on an arduous journey when it is possible to be swept up by Christ immediately? The saint who "had a calling upon just grounds to come hither" to New England would find rest on the journey to heaven, John Cotton wrote, for he would "sit down under the Ordinances, under the shadow of the Almighty." The spiritual vagabond had a restless spirit, however, and chafed under the "ordinances." In geographical terms this meant he quickly desired to move on "to a new plantation" and more land. "Therefore the Lord sees it not meet to give us rest, no not in Sion, because in heart we are not returned from Babell." Whether land hungry settlers, against the wishes of the elders, moved on of their own accord or whether spiritual anarchists were banished for their threat to the spiritual and social order, the principle at stake was the same: whether or not New England was to be a true resting place, or stage, on the way to the heavenly city. The archetypal wanderer was

17. Hooker, "Danger of Desertion," in Williams *et al.*, eds., *Hooker: Writings*, 234.

the arch-sinner Cain, of whom Anne Bradstreet wrote, "A Vagabond to Land of Nod he goes."[18]

Puritans did have a certain rootlessness in common with English vagabonds, but it was a rootlessness tempered by their sense of religious purpose. Thomas Dudley wrote of New England that "if any come hither for worldly ends that can live well at home, he commits an error, of which he will soon repent him. But if for spiritual and that no particular obstacle hinder his removal, he may find here what may well content him." Dudley called not for "the poorer sort" but for settlers with some resources and great ambition who would come "out of religious ends." Among these saints, certitude at being on the King's Highway created at least a tendency to see geographical separation from England as equal to spiritual separation from sin. When Roger Williams accused the orthodox of falling into this trap, John Cotton felt constrained to insist that no one in Massachusetts ever held that the voyage itself purified a soul and made one a child of God. "It is not locall remooval from former pollutions . . . that fitteth us for fellowship with Christ, and his Church: but that it is necessary also, that we doe repent of such former Pollutions, wherewith we have been defiled and enthralled." And, more decisively, "I did not think that any in Old-England, or New, had been so ignorant, or uncharitable, as to think, the Pen-man of the Answer to these Questions had conceived, that either the voyage by Sea, or the change in aire from Old-England to New, could change the judgements or Consciences of men." The geographical journey to New England was not an end in itself, as though it were a new pilgrimage to a holy place in the old sense. To the extent that the realm of geography and the realm of the spirit coincide, New England was at most a resting place along the way.[19]

In spiritualizing the pilgrimage tradition Puritans did not altogether abandon geography, but they transformed it. Although the old

18. Winthrop, "Modell of Christian Charity," in Miller and Johnson, eds., *The Puritans*, I, 198. Cotton, *Thirteenth Chapter of Revelation*, 240–241. Anne Bradstreet, "Contemplations: 15," in Hutchinson, ed., *Poems of Bradstreet*, 82. See Carl Bridenbaugh, *Vexed and Troubled Englishmen, 1590–1642* (New York, 1968); Christopher Hill, *The World Turned Upside Down: Radical Ideas during the English Revolution* (New York, 1972), 32; Larzer Ziff, *Puritanism in America: New Culture in a New World* (New York, 1973), chap. 3; and Michael Zuckerman, "Pilgrims in the Wilderness: Community, Modernity, and the Maypole at Merry Mount," *NEQ*, L (1977), 255–277.

19. Thomas Dudley to the Lady Bridget, countess of Lincoln, Mar. 12, 28, 1630/1631, Emerson, ed., *Letters from New England*, 75. John Cotton, *A Reply to Mr. Williams His Examination* . . . , bound with *The Bloudy Tenent, Washed, and Made White in the Bloud of the Lambe* . . . (London, 1647), 61. Cotton, *Bloudy Tenent*, 185.

holy places were banned, and pilgrimage to them rejected as pagan and vain, the New Englander was still a geographical as well as a spiritual traveler. The stages of the physical journey often corresponded with the stages of the spiritual pilgrimage. For the first generation of New England Puritans actual travel, and especially the ocean passage, provided a context for understanding spiritual progress. Thomas Shepard, for example, wrote that as pressure against Puritan preaching mounted in England he took to the road. He preached (in that important phrase) "up and down in the country and at last privately in Mr. Fenwick's house." He rested there "till Mr. Cotton, Mr. Hooker, Stone, Weld went to New England, and hereupon most of the godly in England were awakened and intended much to go to New England. And so, seeing I had been tossed from the south to the north of England and could go no farther, I then began to listen to a call to New England." "I saw the Lord departing from England when Mr. Hooker and Mr. Cotton were gone," Shepard noted.[20]

Other migrating Puritans saw the work of redemption in their lives and the move to New England as two aspects of the same divine handiwork. Roger Clap testified that "it was God put it into my Heart to incline to Live abroad"; it was God who made each step possible and "landed me in Health at Nantasket"; it was God who caused New England to prosper and wrought conversion in his soul. For Clap the spiritual map was perfectly superimposed on the geographical. Francis Higginson pointed to the same confluence, one evidence of which was his improved physical health. "I have great cause to give God praise that he hath made my coming to be a method to cure me of a wonderful weak stomach and continual pain of melancholy wind from the spleen." As reasons for such grace he identified the "pious and Christian-like passage," during which passengers and seamen alike "constantly served God morning and evening by reading and expounding a chapter, singing, and prayer. And the Sabbath was solemnly kept by adding to the former preaching twice and catechizing. And in our great need we kept two solemn fasts and found a gracious effect." The tailor Anthony Thacher's account of shipwreck on the final leg of his voyage, the short trip from Boston to Marblehead, reprinted later in the century by Increase Mather, was at once the narrative of a geographical and a spiritual journey. Through the danger of the voyage God worked on his soul. When he and three others "by that wave were clean swept away from off the rock also into the sea," it was God's doing, "the Lord in one instant of time disposing

20. Shepard, "Autobiography," in McGiffert, ed., *God's Plot*, 54–55.

of the souls of us to his good pleasure and will." Battered by the storm, Thacher wrote, "My legs was much bruised and so was my heart." "Cast upon an unknown land in a wilderness," his sins severely oppressed him. But in the lowness of his condition God brought his wife and him to safety. Thacher's final prayer was that "The Lord in his mercy direct me that I may so lead the new life which he hath given me as may be most to his own glory." For the first generation in New England, emigration was the physical counter of the spiritual pilgrimage.[21]

The Puritan spiritual pilgrimage, besides being undertaken in the context of geographical movement, was also preeminently biblical in nature. Recent scholarship investigating Puritan use of typology in biblical hermeneutics has greatly deepened our understanding of how the Puritans might have understood their own pilgrimage in the light of a series of uprootings undertaken at God's command in the Bible. The earlier, scriptural pilgrimages were vital because they were identifiably salvific journeys in which God fulfilled His promises to His people. The Hebrews 11 text, which christocentrically summarizes the entire Old Testament, focused on Abraham, whom Puritans revered as their first ancestor in the covenant of grace. Genesis records that "Now the Lord had said unto Abram, Get thee out of thy country, and from thy kindred, and from thy father's house, unto a land that I will shew thee" (12:1). Hebrews emphasized that it was "by faith" that "he went out, not knowing whither he went" (11:8). The other key Old Testament figure was Moses as he led the Exodus from bondage in Egypt. For Puritans the entire drama of God's guiding His people through the Red Sea, through the wilderness, and finally into the Promised Land was typical of the divine process by which God still led souls out of slavery to sin toward the new land of heaven.

New Englanders applied the biblical types to the soul's journey in countless sermons, but nowhere so clearly as in Richard Mather's "Farewel-Exhortation" to his Dorchester congregation in his old age. Mather presented the scheme of salvation in absolutely biblical terms:

> But what should I speak of comming to heaven? the truth is,
> without Compunction of heart & sorrow of soul for a mans sinns,
> he is never like to attain to any truth of saving grace upon earth.
> For can a child be born, where there never was any travailing

21. *Clap's Memoirs*, 19. Francis Higginson to His Friends in England, July 24, 1629, Emerson, ed., *Letters from New England*, 23–24. Anthony Thacher to Peter Thacher, Sept. 1635, *ibid.*, 168–174. Increase Mather included the account in *An Essay for the Recording of Illustrious Providences* . . . (Boston, 1684).

paines? can there be a crop of corn at harvest, where the ground was never plowed, nor broken up? Is not the way to Canaan through the wilderness? doubtless through the wilderness you must go, if ever you will come to Canaan[.] And what was that wilderness? a terrible place surely, yea a place wherein were fiery flying Serpents, and Scorpions, and drought, *Deut.* 8. 15. a land of desarts, and of pits, and of the shaddow of death, *Jer.* 2. 6. and yet through this wilderness must Israel go, before they could enter into the good land. In like sort, a soul must go through a wilderness-like condition, that is, he must be afflicted with sight and sense of spiritual misery & sin, before he can attain to any state of saving rest & grace in Christ Jesus[.] For the Scripture tell us that they to whom Christ Jesus is sent, are poor, broken hearted, captives, prisoners, blind, and bruised creatures, *Luk* 4. 18.[22]

Thomas Hooker preached in identical terms, explicitly linking the wilderness experience of Israel with the stages of spiritual preparation for grace, contrition and humiliation. The journey he was speaking of was intensely personal. The soul traversed its stages not on a geographical but on the spiritual road. "There must be Contrition and Humiliation before the Lord comes to take possession," Hooker preached. "This was typified in the passage of the Children towards the promised Land. They must come and go through a vast and roaring Wilderness, where they must be bruised with many pressures, humbled under many overbearing difficulties, before they could possess that good land which abounded with all prosperity, flowed with Milk and Honey." The flight from England to the New World was an obvious emblem of the biblical message of salvation. But preachers were most vehement in proclaiming that Scripture's truest antitype was the interior and spiritual pilgrimage of the soul to God.[23]

22. Richard Mather, *A Farewel-Exhortation to the Church and People of Dorchester in New-England* (Cambridge, Mass., 1657), 3.

23. Hooker, *Application of Redemption, Ninth and Tenth Books,* 5–7, cited in Bercovitch, *Puritan Origins,* 31–32. See Sacvan Bercovitch, ed., *Typology and Early American Literature* (Amherst, Mass., 1972); Ursula Brumm, *American Thought and Religious Typology,* [trans. John Hoaglund] (New Brunswick, N.J., 1970); John Cotton, *The New Covenant . . .* (London, 1654); Bradford, *Of Plymouth Plantation,* ed. Morison, 61–63; D. G. Hill, ed., *The Record of Baptisms, Marriages, and Deaths, and Admissions to the Church and Dismissals therefrom, . . . Dedham, 1638–1845 . . .* (Dedham, Mass., 1888), 3, hereafter cited as *Dedham Church Records*; and Jesper Rosenmeier, " 'With My Owne Eyes': William Bradford's Of Plymouth Plantation," in Bercovitch, ed., *Typology and Early American Literature,* 75–77.

Figure 6. Illustration on the title page of the 1560 Geneva Bible, a version popularly used in New England long after the availability of the 1611 edition. The exodus of Israel from Egyptian bondage was considered a type of Christ's death and resurrection, of devotional practice and of the experience of grace, and of migration from old to New England. From The Geneva Bible: A Facsimile of the 1560 Edition *(Madison, Wis., 1969). Courtesy the University of Wisconsin Press.*

Other elements of the Old Testament pilgrimage came into play as well. Sacvan Bercovitch has shown how Cotton Mather applied the figure of Nehemiah, leading the Jews back into Israel after the Babylonian Captivity, to John Winthrop. The significance of Winthrop's political achievement in New England, Mather insisted, could only be understood within the context of Nehemiah's rebuilding of the Temple in Jerusalem. Puritan exegetes, however, never simply identified any single biblical episode with events and people in New England. Although typology always had concrete historical referents, it also operated on a level above history. More than one early leader in New England could identify with and be identified as "Moses." Passage to New England, which every saint undertook, evoked Abraham, Exodus, Exile, and Restoration all at once. Logical consistency was possible because the central act of God in the history of salvation was located in none of these but in the person of Jesus Christ. Old Testament figures did not relate directly to Puritan experience; rather, they were projected onto it through the prism of Christ's death and resurrection. And it was the cycle of death and resurrection that most fully gave form and content to the Puritan spiritual pilgrimage. Through God's grace, individuals converted from sin became children of God and thus heirs of the Promised Land toward which all the Old Testament types were oriented. In their journey toward the New Jerusalem these latter-day pilgrims interpreted their lives according to Old Testament patterns, but always in light of the fulfillment of those patterns by the work of Christ.[24]

Various elements of Jesus' life are reminiscent of Old Testament soteriological themes and also look forward to the Puritan order of redemption. Chief among these was Jesus' own time in the wilderness. His forty days of temptation at the hands of Satan after baptism by John echoed Israel's forty-year-long wanderings through the wilderness after liberation from Egypt and prefigured the wilderness experience in New England, especially the initial trying stages of Puritan conversion. Jesus' journey to Jerusalem in order to die was followed by every penitent sinner who would die to sin (1 Peter 2:24). In a preliminary way in baptism, but especially in conversion, the person followed Christ into death (Romans 6:3–4). The penitent became "dead with Christ from the rudiments of the world" (Colossians 2:20) in order to become a "new creature" (2 Corinthians 5:17) by means of Christ's resurrection. As John Cotton preached, "It is the very Spirit of Christ that makes you to dye with Christ, as well as Christ to dye for you; he may dye for many men, but he only dyes with those that are brought on to the fellowship of his grace; if a Spirit of Christ so knit you together, that he is yours, and you are his, then you have the Sonne, because you have the spirit of the Sonne; because you are sonnes, God hath sent forth the Spirit of the Sonne into your hearts." John Brock used the same death and resurrection imagery when, as an older student at Harvard College in 1644, he noted a small student revival: "Young People begin to awaken from the Dead." Participation

24. Bercovitch, *Puritan Origins*, 1. Joseph A. Gladon, S.J., *Typology and Seventeenth-Century Literature* (Paris, 1975), 58–63.

in this sequence of, as Thomas Shepard put it, mortification and vivification made spiritual progress possible.[25]

The pilgrimage brought the person into a cosmic drama of salvation, which God had from Adam on been enacting with those in covenant with Him. The drama was enacted and reenacted in personal experience and in historical events such as the Great Migration. Its power derived from its source in the work of Christ, in which the forces of evil and death were defeated. Christ won the decisive battle against Satan at the Resurrection, but until the chiliad, His Second Coming, and the establishment of the Kingdom Satan is still loose in the world. Each individual triumph for the Lord, each step of spiritual progress, presaged God's ultimate and, Puritans believed, imminent triumph.

The stages of the spiritual pilgrimage found classic expression for Puritans in conversion and in the theological order of redemption. The two are not the same thing, as William Stoever has shown, but they are related. Much scholarly discussion has been mistaken in its emphasis on conversion as an isolated and distinct moment in a person's life. Conversion was but one part, albeit with its own stages, of a larger pilgrimage. Just as God continually dealt with His people in Scripture—He did not simply on one occasion bring them out of Egypt—so He continually dealt with His saints in New England. Just as the Exodus was part of a larger journey for the people of Israel, a journey that repeatedly required God's aid to bring them out of bondage, so the individual repeatedly required God's aid. The stages of conversion were indeed important to go through once, decisively, Exodus-like. But the saint would inevitably fall into captivity and require renewed salvation in the future. The case of John Winthrop on his forty-ninth birthday during the Antinomian controversy is illustrative. Bruce C. Woolley has shown in his study of the spiritual relations of persons joining the Cambridge Church, recorded by Thomas Shepard in a notebook, that few saints pointed to a single change of heart as the basis for their membership. Rather, their narratives, much like John Dane's "Declaration of Remarkabell Prouedenses," describe an ongoing process, marked by spiritual highs and lows, whereby God gradually brought souls into closer communion with Himself. The experience of New Englanders—gradual growth in the grace of sanctification and in union with Christ, and uneven progress toward an ultimate glorification—demands that conversion be

25. Cotton, *Christ the Fountaine*, 72–73. Shipton, ed., "Autobiographical Memoranda of Brock," Am. Antiq. Soc., *Procs.*, N.S., LIII (1943), 100.

viewed as only one key event in the course of a life-long pilgrimage.[26]

That conversion and the subsequent stages of growth in grace are related to the concept of pilgrimage is brought out clearly, even startlingly, when we compare the schemes of William Perkins and John Bunyan. Perkins's enumeration of ten "actions" of God was an attempt to join a description of God's order of redemption (in which He elects, calls, justifies, adopts, sanctifies, and glorifies the soul) with a psychology of conversion and new birth. Perkins's ten actions of grace are remarkably similar to the ten stages that John Bunyan's Christian traversed in *The Pilgrim's Progress.* Just as in Perkins's first action "God gives man the outward meanes of salvation, specially the ministrie of the Word: and with it hee sends some outward or inward crosse, to breake and subdue the stubbornnesse of our nature," so in the first stage Bunyan presents Evangelist as the instigator of Christian's taking to the road. As in Perkins's fourth action, "upon the sight of sin" God "smites the heart with a legall feare, whereby when man seeth his sins, he makes him to feare punishment and hell, and to despair of salvation, in regard to any thing in himselfe," so in the fourth stage Bunyan's pilgrim suffers in the Valley of Humiliation. In Perkins's seventh action there is a "combat" with "doubting, despaire, and distrust"; in the seventh stage Bunyan has Christian and Hopeful cast into Doubting Castle by the Giant Despair. Perkins states that in the eighth action "mercie quiets and settles" the soul, and in Bunyan's eighth stage the pilgrims find rest at the Delectable Mountains. The "new obedience" of Perkins's tenth action is reflected in Christian's final ability to cross the river. The correspondence between the two presentations is so close that it may be surmised that Bunyan was consciously working from Perkins's earlier scheme.[27]

Besides indelibly linking the order of redemption with the stages of spiritual pilgrimage, the resemblance between Bunyan and Perkins further shows that the various lists of stages in spiritual growth did not apply solely to conversion. Perkins's ten actions of God in the soul were indeed first known in conversion, but that was only the begin-

26. Stoever, 'Faire and Easie Way,' 124. The traditional emphasis on conversion is seen in Miller, *New England Mind: Seventeenth Century*, esp. chaps. 9–12; Edmund S. Morgan, *Visible Saints: The History of a Puritan Idea* (New York, 1963), 66–73; Pettit, *Heart Prepared*; and Pettit, "The Order of Salvation in Thomas Hooker's Thought," in Williams et al., eds., *Hooker: Writings*, 124–139. Bruce Chapman Woolley, "Reverend Thomas Shepard's Cambridge Church Members, 1636–1649: A Socio-Economic Analysis" (Ph.D. diss., University of Rochester, 1973), 63–64.

27. William Perkins, *The Whole Treatise of the Cases of Conscience . . .* , in *Works*, II, 13. Bunyan, *Pilgrim's Progress*.

ning of God's work in salvation. Conversion, according to Perkins, was God's "giving of the first grace," the ability to "beleeve and repent." In "the giving of the second grace," the ability "to persevere and continue in faith and repentance to the end," God continually acted in the soul according to the same ten-part scheme. *The Pilgrim's Progress* can be understood in a variety of ways—and this is part of the genius of the allegory—but it cannot be read as the story of Christian's conversion. Christian was already converted, already bore the name Christian, when he set out for the Celestial City. Christian and Hopeful gave each other mutual support along the way by retelling for one another their conversion narratives. *The Pilgrim's Progress* recounts the journey of the soul to union with Christ *after* conversion. It is the story, in Perkins's terms, of "the giving of the second grace." In the phrase most commonly used by New England divines in their presentation of the order of redemption, Bunyan's is the story of "growth in grace." [28]

The Pilgrim's Progress and (in part) *The Whole Treatise of the Cases of Conscience* were devotional manuals. As such these books could be used by penitents and believers both during and after conversion. The spiritual dynamics followed the same progression in first conversion and in subsequent spiritual growth. The only difference, Perkins suggested, is that the journey through the ten stages in one's first conversion is wholly the product of God's regenerative work in the soul, whereas after conversion the soul, already sanctified in some measure, is active together with God in the pilgrimage. [29]

Puritan divines put forth many elaborations of the order of redemption, all greatly resembling one another. Such consensus was possible because all writers drew from the biblical pattern of bondage and redemption, wilderness and promised land, death and resurrection. The pattern was, in fact, as old as Christianity, mediated by centuries of devotional tradition. "Penance and mortification" first freed the person from sin, making possible the awakening of the soul and advancement toward union with God. Almost every version of the regenerative experience included a dynamic two-part cycle of emptying and filling. Thomas Shepard summarized, "Faith empties the Soul, and looks upon it as dead, and sees its life laid up in Christ; and hence forsakes itself, and embraceth the Lord of Glory. Secondly, the Spirit comes and possesseth a forsaken empty House, and there lives and dwells." John Cotton espoused the same basic scheme:

28. Perkins, *Cases of Conscience*, 13. Bunyan, *Pilgrim's Progress*.
29. See Stoever, *'Faire and Easie Way,'* 196.

Thus when it cometh unto saving work, the will and soule of a man is so cast downe, that a man cannot tell what to make of himselfe, but there he lieth to see what the Lord will doe with him, whether he will reach forth the hand of salvation unto him or no. In this case the soule is left utterly void, and hath in himself neither root nor branch, but seeth how unable he is to himselfe to beleeve or waite; nor can he tell whether Jesus Christ be his possession, and now doth the Lord take possession, and fill the empty soule.

This cycle was ubiquitous in Puritan spirituality. It was the rhythm dominating first conversion, the pattern of devotional activity after conversion, the preaching of the ministers, and the tenor of public ritual. The cycle played a formative role in the life of every man and woman in New England.[30]

The psychological stages of the pilgrimage of conversion and of progression in the spiritual life were described in detail by Thomas Shepard and Thomas Hooker, two of the greatest New England preachers of the first generation. In the writings of these men the order of redemption set forth is the same, both in general thrust and in most details. Further, the stages delineated by Shepard and Hooker correspond closely to versions by other New England pastors. In addition to the language of death and resurrection and of emptying and filling, both men generally used horticultural terminology based on Romans 11:23–24. Like Perkins, Shepard and Hooker divided the process of redemption into two major parts, each made up of a series of stages. The first act was that of preparation, the "cutting off of the Soul from the old Adam, or the wild Olive-Tree." The second act was that of implantation, "putting or ingrafting the Soule into the second Adam, Christ Jesus." Hooker and Shepard identified the stages of contrition and humiliation (and the subsidiary stages within each) as the way of preparation. Through implantation, then, the soul became aware of its vocation, that it was both called and carried into Christ by "the irresistable power of the Spirit in the call." The justified saint continued to grow in grace through the stages of implantation until sanctification was perfected in full union with Christ in heaven.[31]

It must be emphasized that in the eyes of all Puritans, despite

30. Pourrat, *Christian Spirituality*, I, v. Thomas Shepard, *The Parable of the Ten Virgins Opened and Applied* . . . (London, 1695 [orig. publ. 1660]), 182. Cotton, *New Covenant*, 188.

31. Thomas Shepard, *The First Principles of the Oracles of God* (London, 1650), 70–80. [Hooker], *Soules Humiliation*, 9. [Hooker], *Soules Implantation*, 88, 138. Hooker, *The*

charges during the Antinomian controversy that the orthodoxy had lapsed into Arminianism, the entire journey to heaven was the result of God's work in the soul. Though God did not undertake the work except through human participation (participation that increased as the individual progressed through the stages), the journey was begun in Christ and completed in Christ. New Englanders consistently rejected the idea that an unregenerate sinner could achieve preparation for conversion. They understood preparation for conversion to be *of* a sinner *by* Christ. They regarded the soul as incapable of any saving action until it was made capable by God in the preparation of the heart. As a woman succinctly stated in her spiritual relation upon joining the Cambridge Church: "hearing of souls' preparation for Christ, I was stirred up to seek." She did not bestir herself but, she testified, was stirred by God. To the question, "But must I receive Christ with my own strength?" her pastor Thomas Shepard answered definitively: "No, you cannot, nor ought not; but if the Lord puts strength in thee, put it forth."[32]

That preparation within the conversion experience was understood as preparation of and not by the sinner is clear from the horticultural metaphor that many Puritans used to describe the process. "As it is with the graft," Hooker wrote, first the heart is "cut off from the old stock" and then "it must be pared" with the knife to be "made fit for the implantation into another. Soe the soule being cut off from sinne: then humiliation pares it, and makes it for the ingrafting into Christ." The plant does not pare itself for the graft; only "the Gardners knife" is sharp and sure enough for that task. God was the gardener of Puri-

---

Application of Redemption, . . . The First Eight Books . . . (London, 1656), 157. See also John Davenport, "A Profession of Faith, Made by the Reverend Divine, Mr. John Davenport, at His Admission into One of the Churches of God in New-England," bound with Cotton, *Covenant of God's Free Grace,* 37; Cotton, *Way of Life,* 12; Cotton, *New Covenant,* 19–28; R. Mather, *Farewel-Exhortation,* 2; and Shepard, *Sound Beleever,* 4, 247, and *passim.*

32. Perry Miller was incorrect in his original analysis of preparationism, both in limiting his discussion to preparation for conversion and in stating that "Hooker and Shepard shamelessly improve the concept of preparation to mean that every man can perform the requisite actions" for salvation while yet unregenerate (*New England Mind: From Colony to Province,* 64–65). The original essay, " 'Preparation for Salvation in Seventeenth-Century New England,' " appears in *Nature's Nation* (Cambridge, Mass., 1967), 50–77. Norman Pettit has carried Miller's erroneous position forward in *Heart Prepared,* and in "Order of Salvation in Hooker's Thought," in Williams *et al.,* eds., *Hooker: Writings,* 124–139. Woolley, "Shepard's Cambridge Church Members," 159. Shepard, *Ten Virgins,* 82. The means of grace, those acts of devotion through which God reached a soul and elicited its participation, will be the subject of the next three chapters.

tan preparationism. In the course of the main stages of this preparation, contrition and humiliation, the Spirit first "loosens a man from his sin, makes him see an absolute necessity to be another man," and then "loosens a man from himself, makes him see an utter insufficiency in what he hath or doth, for to procure the least spiritual relief unto his soul." Conviction and compunction for sin were followed by complete "self-abasement." Only when God had fully emptied the penitent in this way could faith be wrought in the heart.[33]

Hooker preached that this "sorrow of preparation" was unlike the later sanctified acts of contrition and humiliation that formed an important part of devotional practice. "The one [is] wrought upon us, wherein we are patients of the work of the Spirit bringing of us unto Christ; the other is wrought by us through the Spirit given to us and dwelling in us when we have received Christ." His position, which was orthodox in New England, assumed the existence of "a double repentance. The first of preparation, wrought by the almighty and irresistible power of the Spirit, causing the sinner to go out of himself (and sin) in humiliation before he can go to God in Christ by faith in vocation; and this goes before faith and I conceive it to be nothing but the stroke of the Spirit in the very first work of conversion wherein the soul make itself merely passive as our divines used to speak, and in the true nature of it, cannot be in any reprobate. Second, there is a repentance in sanctification, that word being strictly so taken; and it comes after faith." The second kind of repentance was tremendously important in the ongoing spiritual life of the saint and was marked by the same cycle of emptying and filling as the first. But first repentance, though it came by means of meditation on one's own sins and listening to sermons, was properly the work of God.[34]

Implantation into Christ consisted of vocation, or effectual calling, followed by stages of continued "growth in grace" toward full union with Him. The effects of God's call were repulsion from sin, awakened fear of evil and disgust at sinfulness, and, simultaneously, attraction to the good. Hope and desire were stirred as the person "embraced"

---

33. [Hooker], *Soules Humiliation*, 9. Shepard, *Sound Beleever*, 99. Hooker, *Application of Redemption, Ninth and Tenth Books*, 15. Technically, Hooker defined contrition as "that Preparative Dispensation of the Heart, whereby the sight of sin, and the punishment due to the same, the soul is brought to sound sorrow for it, and so brought to detest it, and to sequester it self from it" (*ibid.*, 16). Humiliation then "pares away all self-sufficiency . . . confidence . . . good performances . . . by which [a person] is ready to shelter himself." *Soules Humiliation*, 8.

34. Thomas Hooker, "To the Reader," in John Rogers, *The Doctrine of Faith*, in Williams *et al.*, eds., *Hooker: Writings*, 145. "John Paget's XX Questions and Thomas Hooker's Answers," *ibid.*, 290. Shepard, *Sound Beleever*, 98.

the Gospel and engaged in acts of devotion at new spiritual depths. New grounds for hope arose, a "saving desire by which God causeth both grace to breed, and faith to spring in the soule." Finally, God awakened love and joy, which Hooker described as "spawns and seeds of faith," and transformed the soul. The mind had seen Christ, the affections (hope, desire, love, joy) had longed for and received Him, and now "the will saith Amen to the business." A bounty of spiritual graces then began to flow into the soul, a "conveyance of sap, or sweet-nesse," from God. Through devotional activity thereafter "the power of the Spirit on God's part" and "the power of faith on the beleevers part" worked together. "The spirit of God workes upon a beleever, and the beleever goes out againe to God by faith." Hooker summarized the whole adventure by paraphrasing Romans 8:30: "Christ by the vertue of his Resurrection, and by the power of his Spirit, he doth rescue the soul, and humble him, and call him, and justifie him, and sanctifie him, and glorifie him, and then deliver him up to the Father at the great day."[35]

The spiritual pilgrimage through established stages was not simply an invention based on spiritual ideals. It described inner movements that many New Englanders experienced directly. The scheme the ministers preached was a map based on biblical soteriology and the tradition of centuries of devotional practice and religious experience. It was a scheme both evoked by and, in turn, evoking deep spirituality. Robert Middlekauff has perhaps not unfairly stated that Puritans "transmuted raw feelings into feelings sanctioned by their code," but it would be more accurate to point out that this was a system capable of producing as well as interpreting the growth of faith. The vividness with which preachers and printed word related the conversions and faith of the ministers themselves continually reinforced its availability. The stages of redemption we have outlined were preached in New England because they came together as a good map of what actually happened.

The scheme presented in sermons and manuals was an accurate representation, first of all, because it described the experience of the ministers themselves. That first-generation New England ministers were often converted while studying at Cambridge University, where the analysis of spirituality was a serious task, contributed to the unity of theory and practice among the leaders. When Thomas Hooker, for example, finally underwent "the experience of true regeneration" as a fellow at Emmanuel College, in the words of Cotton Mather, "it

35. H[ooker], *Soules Vocation*, 203, 283. H[ooker], *The Soules Exaltation . . .* (London, 1638), 2, 26. Hooker, *Application of Redemption, First Eight Books*, 124.

pleased the spirit of God very powerfully to break into [his] soul . . . with such a sense of his being exposed unto the just wrath of heaven . . . [that it] broke not only his rest, but his heart." Mather judged that Hooker wandered "a considerable while in this spirit of bondage" in order "to fit him for the great services and enjoyments which God intended him." That is, Hooker's conversion not only prepared him for Christ but also enabled him to lead others to Him. "At length he received the spirit of adoption, with well-grounded perswasions of his interest in the new covenant." The delineation of the stages of the pilgrimage, on which Hooker was himself embarked, became the major theme of his preaching throughout his career.[36]

Thomas Shepard wrote that it was "when I was most vile" that "the Lord began to call me home to the fellowship of his grace." Having fallen in with a group of "loose scholars of other colleges" Shepard was finally brought low when

> I drank so much one day that I was dead drunk, and that upon a Saturday night, and so was carried from the place I had drink at and did feast at unto a scholar's chamber, one Basset of Christ's College, and knew not where I was until I awakened late on that Sabbath and sick with my beastly carriage. And when I awakened I went from him in shame and confusion, and went out into the fields and there spent that Sabbath lying hid in the cornfields where the Lord, who might justly have cut me off in the midst of my sin, did meet me with much sadness of heart and troubled my soul for this and other my sins which then I had cause and leisure to think of.

God led Shepard to the practive of regular devotions and made him "resolve to set upon a course of daily meditation about the evil of sin and [his] own ways." He meditated in the fields, "sometimes every morning but constantly every evening before supper," chiefly on sin and "the terror of God's wrath." He wrote that "I did see God like a consuming fire and an everlasting burning, and myself like a poor prisoner leading to that fire. . . . And so I fell down in prayer, and being in prayer I saw myself so unholy and God so holy that my spirits began to sink, yet the Lord recovered me and poured out a spirit of prayer upon me for free mercy and pity . . . and so my heart was humbled."[37]

---

36. Robert Middlekauff, "Piety and Intellect in Puritanism," *WMQ*, 3d Ser., XXII (1965), 470. C. Mather, *Magnalia Christi Americana*, I, 333–334. Frank Shuffelton, *Thomas Hooker, 1586–1647* (Princeton, N.J., 1977), 77–98.

37. Shepard, "Autobiography," in McGiffert, ed., *God's Plot*, 40–41.

In another place Shepard portrayed in biblical terms God's new creation of his soul: "Gods Spirit moved upon the Chaos of those horrible thoughts" of unbelief. He cited a contemplated suicide as the turning point. At that moment, "the Lord came between the bridge and the water" and led Shepard in "anguish of spirit . . . to pray unto him for light in the midst of so great darkness; In which time he revealed himselfe, manifested his love, stilled all those raging thoughts, gave returne in great measure of them; so that though I could not read Scripture without blasphemous thoughts before, now I saw a glory, a majesty, a mistery, a depth in it, which fully perswaded, and which light . . . is not wholly put out, but remaines while I desire to walk closely with him." Shepard concluded in his autobiography that just as the Gospel of John promised "that so many as receive him, he gives power to be sons of God" (1:12), so "I saw the Lord give me a heart to receive Christ with a naked hand, even a naked Christ, and so the Lord gave me peace."[38]

Although the second generation of ministers in New England, those who were educated for the most part at Harvard rather than Cambridge, came to maturity in a very different environment than had the first generation, the inner dynamics of spiritual death and resurrection, emptying and filling, remained in essence unchanged. Increase Mather was unable to confess to the episodes of riotous sin that led to Shepard's contrition, but this did not prevent him, as a fourteen-year-old penitent, from undergoing a similar anguish. The first stroke came through an illness that caused him to reform "many vain, wild, courses, and extravagancies." He began to study more seriously. But at the death of his beloved mother, "who had so often prayed for me," he was again in a state of forgetfulness of God. In the first three months of 1655 his conscience was stricken by "terrible convictions and awakenings," and he plunged into the "extremity of anguish and horror in my soul." He dealt with his situation in the manner recommended in sermons and in books—through devotional exercises. When his father was away for a few days, he shut himself up in his study, and "there wrote down all the sins which I could remember I had bin guilty of." He laid them before God, cried for mercy, and burned the paper. "Everyone observed I was strangely changed," and a few fellow boarders at the home of John Norton accused him of being too precise with his conscience. The next op-

---

38. Thomas Shepard, *Certain Select Cases Resolved* . . . (1648), bound with second edition of *Theses Sabbaticae*, first published in 1649 (London, 1650), 44–45. Shepard, "Autobiography," in McGiffert, ed., *God's Plot*, 46.

portunity for intense exercises sealed his faith when on election day, with everyone away, Mather secreted himself for a day of fasting and prayer. "[I] poured out my soul in complaints before God that day, and cryed to God that Hee would shew me mercy. At the close of the day, as I was praying, I gave my selfe up to Jesus Christ, declaring that I was now resolved to be his Servant, and his only, and his forever, and humbly professed to him, that if I did perish, I would perish at his feet. Upon this I had ease and inward peace in my perplexed soul immediately." In his autobiography Mather goes on to make clear, however, that this was simply the beginning of his journey. Conversion was not an end in itself but the first major stage of the pilgrimage.[39]

For those destined to become clergymen, conversion was frequently a vocational (career) crisis as well as a crisis concerning the vocation of the soul. For the laity, the condition of the soul was tied directly to the possibility of church membership. New England Congregationalists specifically made evidence of conversion the cornerstone of church membership, and a public relation of one's spiritual experience was the test by which admission decisions were made. As one would expect, records of these confessions of faith correspond to the broad outlines laid out by the preachers.[40]

Conversion could be gradual, sudden, violent, mild, or scarcely perceptible. In his diary John Hull moves so quickly over the events of conversion and church membership that they appear to flow almost naturally out of the course of his life. "1647. It pleased God not to let me run on always in my sinful way, the end of which is hell: but, as he brought me to this good land, so he planted me under choice means, —viz., in Boston, under the ministry of Mr. John Cotton,—and, in the end, did make his ministry effectual (by the breathings of his own good Spirit) to beget me to God, and in some measure to build me up in holy fellowship with him. Through his abundant grace, he gave me room in the hearts of his people, so that I was accepted to fellowship with his church, about the 15th of October, 1648." By contrast, John Winthrop told of the conversion of "a youth fourteen years of age (being the son of one of the magistrates)"—probably his own son Deane—who was "so wrought upon by the ministry of the word, as, for divers months, he was held under such affliction of mind, as he could not be brought to apprehend any comfort in God, being much humbled and broken for his sins . . . yet, attending to the means, and

39. M. G. Hall, ed., "The Autobiography of Increase Mather," Am. Antiq. Soc., *Procs.*, N.S., LXXI (1961), 279–280.

40. Morgan, *Visible Saints*, chap. 2. Hall, *Faithful Shepherd*, 26, 97–100.

not giving over prayer, and seeking counsel, etc., he came at length to be freed from his temptations, and to find comfort in God's promises, and so, being received into the congregation, upon good proof of his understanding of the things of God, he went on cheerfully in a Christian course, falling daily to labor, as a servant." Although the two cases differ in their attributes, in essence they both follow the inner dynamics of the stages that the ministers preached. The same may be said to be true of the surviving spiritual relations of persons who joined the church at Malden, Massachusetts. Those of Harvard graduate and minister-to-be John Collins, Michael Wigglesworth's wife, Mary, John Green, Joseph Champney, and an unnamed former seaman—though dissimilar in detail, strength, and degree of spiritual resolution—all conform to the redemptive cycle of humiliation and grace, of being emptied and then filled.[41]

One of the finest sources for glimpsing the religious experience of lay New Englanders preparatory to church membership is the notebook that Thomas Shepard kept of the spiritual relations of fifty-one young men and women (twenty-two of the men and nineteen of the women were between the ages of eighteen and thirty-five) who joined the Cambridge Church between 1638 and 1645. It is unclear how many others joined, for Shepard simply titled his notes, "The Confessions of Divers Propounded to Be Received and Were Entertayned as Members."[42]

Shepard encouraged his congregation to interpret their spiritual journey within the framework of the stages of redemption. The "Confessions" indicate that his people were generally able to do so. Elsewhere he emphasized that he detested as "not fit" for public religious ceremony long "Relations and groundless joyes," or the simple listing of "all the particular passages of their lives, wherein they have got any good." Shepard believed the relations ought to have didactic value; they should exhibit the actual results of God's application of redemption in the hearts of local people. They ought to include "such [accounts] as may be of special use unto the people of God, such things as tend to shew, Thus I was humbled, then thus I was called, then thus I have walked, though with many weaknesses since, and such special providences of God I have seen, temptations gone through, and thus

41. Hull, *Diaries*, 144–145. Winthrop, *Journal*, ed. Hosmer, I, 120–121. Edmund S. Morgan, ed., *The Diary of Michael Wigglesworth, 1653–1657: The Conscience of a Puritan* (New York, 1965), 107–125. The spiritual relations are bound with Wigglesworth's manuscript diary.

42. Woolley, "Shepard's Cambridge Church Members," 96.

the Lord hath delivered me, blessed be his Name, etc." The intense interrogation of a few individuals also suggests that the ceremony was not perfunctory.[43]

Few of these narratives point to a single moment of conversion. They reveal the spiritual life to be an ongoing journey from sin, through the ups and downs of temptation, assurance and new doubts, toward a gradually increased knowledge of being in Christ. The cycle of mortification and vivification is repeated many times in most of the narratives. As Shepard concluded the lengthy and detailed account by John Sill, "By degrees the Lord hath let him see something." The question of why applicants were allowed to join the church without being able to report a once-for-all transformation is resolved when we understand the lifelong nature of the Puritan pilgrimage. Membership in the church signified that one was truly on the road, not that one had already arrived at the destination. The criterion for membership that comes out in most of the confessions is full repentance for sin. The narratives tend to reach their climax at this point, and hope for future growth in the joy of grace was founded on such preparation. The relations do not, therefore, record the advanced devotional life of mature saints. Rather, they tell of its initial stages.[44]

Even the eleven individuals who pointed to their pious parents' influence on them were aware of the sinful nature of their souls from an early age. Goodman Shepard opened his narrative, "The Lord brought me into a family where I saw what a vile creature I was." Goodman Fessington confessed, "In the days of my youth living in my father's house I lived in sin and lying and excused one lie by telling another." A large number of the applicants confessed to breaking the Sabbath (a sin instrumental in their pastor's own conversion). Goodwife Usher told how "The Lord first convinced me of the breach of the Sabbath and how I had done nothing else but dishonour Him." The narratives commonly relate an early remorse for sin and a realization of the importance of repentance, though this may still have left them far from true repentance. Still, progress was thus made. "The hidden corruption of my own heart" revealed itself in "Sabbath breaking and company keeping," Nathaniel Eaton reported, and "my conscience was convinced that my ways were of death." Goodwife Grizzell confessed, "I heard God was all sufficient and so might support me but yet I knew I was vile." Such an awareness was the beginning of

43. Shepard, *Ten Virgins*, II, 200, cited in Morgan, *Visible Saints*, 92. Woolley, "Shepard's Cambridge Church Members," 24.
44. Woolley, "Shepard's Cambridge Church Members," 96.

humiliation. The confessions tell the often tortuous tale of the soul's journey through the depths of this stage.[45]

Sinners who knew they must be humbled prayed for the onset of that dark time. Brother Parish's wife "sought the Lord to humble" her. When Fessington "was cast down because I was not humbled," that was itself the start of true humiliation. Mrs. Sparhawk, who "came to the ship thinking to get God," found in New England that her heart had not changed. She "saw herself far from humiliation and thought it was a shame." A neighbor woman pressed her on her diligence in private devotions, and she confessed she had not "sought God in private . . . for some weeks." She grew worse, she said, until the reading of Scripture "brought me to submit to the Lord." In full repentance "she saw her own emptiness and Christ's fullness." Penitents commonly saw "an emptiness" in themselves, which led to a recognition of hope only in God's mercy. As "Brother Jackson's Man Richard Eagle" put it, after finding "more and more light to see into my lost estate every day," finally "the Lord broke my heart in the consideration of my own vileness and so I saw a necessity of Christ." Brother Moore's wife, while still in England, "hearing Christ came to save sinners," had felt her heart "somewhat quickened," but in New England lapsed into "hardness of heart." She cried for "mercy to be free from depths" and finally experienced grace. "I found Lord had filled my soul with glorious apprehensions of Himself."[46]

The "Confessions" demonstrate that an awareness of the stages of redemption was not the property of the clerical elite alone. Although the ministers' expectations certainly influenced the laity in their confessions, the ideas were part of popular religious culture, at least in rough form. One young man told in his relation of going for advice to "a youth [who] used to keep cattle" and was "oft keeping of catechism." The farmhand advised that "the Lord doth break off soul from sin by contrition and self by humiliation and . . . leaves the soul to be wearied in itself and each was to bring off soul from self." Another individual, at the end of his account, found that "all repentance would not satisfy justice. And Lord brought that to mind—come all ye weary and heavy laden and I'll refresh—hence I came to them for justification and sanctification." John Stedman's wife felt that in New England, while hearing John Cotton preach on Revelation 10, "afresh . . . the Lord had begun to humble and subdue and quicken and sanctify." When a person who was aware of the spiritual stages could

45. *Ibid.*, 186, 188, 193, 99, 195–196.
46. *Ibid.*, 162, 188, 110–113, 102, 149, 161–162.

say, "then I saw Lord had begun," the doors to church membership opened.[47]

None of the narratives concludes, therefore, with a sense that the work of redemption was complete. They all look forward to the journey still ahead. Francis Moore confessed, "The spirit of God did seal to his soul that he was truly humbled, not only broken for, but from, sin with detestation of it and hence was a new creature and hence was received to mercy." But he continued to sin and repent, with "the Lord recalling him usually back again." When he joined the church he believed he was making progress, for God enabled him "to walk more humbly." William Hamlet said explicitly that "the way whereby I came to know I was united to Christ was the fruits of it as mortification." He concluded with the words, "I desire to walk under the feet of God and His people and all men, being more vile than any." Few of the new members were able yet to attest to a soul-ravishing union with Christ. All of them were able to speak of their humiliation in their sins, their repentance, and their hope that they were in Christ.[48]

Faithful New Englanders were men and women spiritually driven toward the goal of union with Christ. This inner drive was an essential force in their devotional practice. The nature of conversion was in part responsible for the sustained power of the yearning for union. Even when conversion was a decisive personal event, it left many questions unanswered and opened new doors of spirituality. The questions centered around the search for assurance that God was indeed imparting grace. Although much has been written about the anxiety that accompanied the Puritan's inner quest for assurance, it is significant that the quest led to an ever-deepening relationship with the God of salvation. Diaries indicate that a spiraling effect commonly marked Puritan experience. The intensity of each crisis contributed to an ever greater intensity of assurance. Ongoing anxiety served a beneficial purpose and was one way that Puritans felt God leading them on to the ultimate end of their pilgrimage. New doors opened, too, because the entire process called the application of redemption, of which conversion was one moment, was one of progressive stages. After the preparation of the heart and the implantation of the soul into Christ came many precious moments in which the saint was nourished in God's grace.

The pattern of spiritual stages first established in conversion continued to mark the journey to heaven. The devotional life of the

47. *Ibid.*, 206, 189–190, 142.
48. *Ibid.*, 87–88, 155–158.

saints, the means by which they progressed on the pilgrimage, was a system of ritual self-emptying in preparation for the renewed experience of being filled by God with His grace. The redemptive cycle of Christ's death and resurrection was translated into a set of spiritual exercises, devotional acts that became the path of renewed repentance and fulfillment. It is to the means of grace that we now turn.

PART II

"The Way of Godly Conversation"

And truly when I am most near God,
I have no greater request than this
for my self and you, that God would use
any means to make us see things really as they are,
and pound our hearts all to pieces,
and make indeed sin most bitter,
and Christ most sweet, that we might be
both humbled and Comforted to purpose!
JONATHAN MITCHEL
"A Letter . . . to His Friend" (1649)

Chapter Four

The Ordinances of Public Worship

The Puritan devotional pilgrimage was a mystical journey in Christ, frequently leading to experiences of union with Him. But New Englanders were not mystics if that term implies abandoning life in society or earthly, historical means for reaching God. Puritans clung to the traditional "means of grace," including ecclesiastical "ordinances," and to the concept of "the Church," through which God mediated Himself. Thomas Shepard preached that "the visible Church of God . . . is the kingdom of Heaven upon earth." The people of New England were led to find their salvation in the rituals performed in and endorsed by the Church. And whereas most of the seven Roman Catholic sacraments constituted rites de passage, Puritan believers employed ordinances continually.[1]

The means of grace were technically divided into two groups, ordinances of public worship and private devotions. Puritan theologians never canonized a precise number of approved ordinances; so any listing of them remains informal and flexible. By every account they included the sacraments of Baptism and the Lord's Supper, plus other scripturally founded acts of worship. Early manuals generally set forth three public means through which God was expected to act: the ministry of the Word (reading of and preaching on the Bible), the sacraments, and prayer. Sometimes the list included fasting.[2]

New Englanders built upon this foundation through the seventeenth century. One enumeration gave five "principal" public ordinances: Prayer, "the Apostles Doctrine" (Bible reading and the sermon), the sacraments, "Mutual Communion," and "Discipline." At its gathering in 1638 the Dedham Church identified the following as official ordinances: preaching of the Word, administration of Baptism and the Lord's Supper, application of discipline among members,

---

1. Shepard, *Ten Virgins*, 4.
2. Downame, *Guide to Godlynesse*, 479. Bayne, *Briefe Directions*, 113. Dod and Cleaver, *Ten Sermons*, 123. Hooker, *Paterne of Perfection*, 3. [Hooker], *Soules Humiliation*, 82.

excommunication and absolution, collection for the poor, prophecy by members with "speciall guifts" (exercised when "approved by the Church as fitt for publike edification"), singing of psalms, and Sabbath worship itself. Even this was a preliminary list. Nothing was said about the rituals of covenant making and renewal, key liturgical actions throughout the seventeenth century. Nor did the Dedham Church mention lecture days, fast days, and thanksgivings. These, together with the weekly cycle of Sabbaths, formed the outward religious practice of the inhabitants. New Englanders also understood certain civil events, notably elections and militia training days, as occasions for special worship.[3]

The private devotional life of New Englanders, meanwhile, consisted of exercises that took various forms: "private" prayer meeting, "conference" with another believer, family prayer time, and individual, or "secret," devotion. A complete view of worship and devotional practice in New England must include this wide range of activities and settings.

The maintenance of outward means of grace ran counter to the iconoclastic spiritualizing thrust within Puritanism that renounced sacrament, Scripture, and ministry. The cry of "Christ alone" was heard on the lips of Antinomians, Gortonists, Quakers, and early Baptists. All Puritans, of course, denied the Catholic doctrine of the efficacy of forms in themselves and the Arminian doctrine of human capability of salvation through self-willed use of forms. The spiritualizing impulse in all Puritans was apparent in John Cotton's warning that "it is not the liberty of Gods Ordinances, and the dispensation of them that can secure us; and therefore trust not in them, trust not in this, that you are diligent Hearers, or that you can pray powerfully; trust not in this, though you were Preachers of the Word of God, but trust on him only for life, and salvation, and he will never deceive you." But orthodoxy went on: "There is no life in them further than [God] puts in them." Cotton broke finally with Anne Hutchinson on the matter of immediate revelation and her negation of the need for Scripture and ministry. The New England clergy denied that the "emptiness" of forms mandated their abandonment. They were empty in themselves, but full of grace when God employed them. New England continued to insist that the way to God was through outward forms and exercises.[4]

---

3. Cotton, *Practical Commentary upon the First Epistle Generall of John*, 337. *Dedham Church Records*, 4.

4. Hooker, *Application of Redemption, First Eight Books*, 415. Hooker, *Application of Redemption, Ninth and Tenth Books*, 34, 299–300. Cotton, *Christ the Fountaine*, 22. Cotton,

Orthodox Puritan spirituality would not endorse the mysticism of the fourteenth-century author of *The Cloud of Unknowing*. For him, and for his New England descendants Anne Hutchinson and Samuel Gorton, "creatures" like bread and wine, scriptural Word, and baptismal water came "between you and your God" as a barrier. It was "far better to think about His naked being." Gorton in this spirit denounced sacramental wine as "the juice of a poor, silly grape" and even the simplified liturgical apparatus of New England as a set of "idols." To the orthodox this was unscriptural and unrealistic. Thomas Shepard could long for and experience "Christ with a naked hand, even a naked Christ," but never would he presume to approach the deity except through the scriptural means of grace. Thomas Hooker's diatribe against mystical antinomianism was highly graphic. He warned, "We must not looke for revelations and dreames, as a company of phantastical braines doe; but in common course Gods Spirit goes with the Gospell."[5]

The phrase "in common course" is important. Union with Christ, ecstatic as it might be, always resulted from an orderly set of exercises that centered on the devotional use of the Bible. The Puritan God, Perry Miller proved, was the God of order, and the divine order corresponded with "the order of nature," manifested in the faculty psychology of the day and in the stages of conversion. Just as Bunyan's Christian made his way in orderly (nonetheless suspenseful and dangerous) fashion through Perkins's ten stages, so the New England pilgrim progressed beyond conversion along an orderly devotional way marked by Sabbath worship, personal and family devotions, and pious counsel of clergy and other saints. God could, of course, save without the means of grace but He did not "ordinarily" do so. In Puritan theology the word "ordinarily" carried a stronger meaning than modern usage conveys, for the Puritans believed that since the close of the apostolic age God had ceased to work in "extraordinary" ways. He continued to work in remarkable ways (and the recording of one's own "remarkable providences" was an important part of Puritan de-

―――――
Thirteenth Chapter of Revelation, 240. David D. Hall, ed., *The Antinomian Controversy, 1636–1638: A Documentary History* (Middletown, Conn., 1968), 14–20.

5. Ira Progoff, trans., *The Cloud of Unknowing: A New Translation of a Classic Guide to Spiritual Experience* (New York, 1957), 71. Samuel Gorton, *Simplicity's Defence against Seven-Headed Policy*, ed. William R. Staples (Rhode Island Historical Society, *Collections*, II [1835]), 263–270, cited in Gura, "Radical Ideology of Gorton," *WMQ*, 3d Ser., XXXVI (1979), 89. Shepard, "Autobiography," in McGiffert, ed., *God's Plot*, 46. Shepard, *Ten Virgins*, 31. H[ooker], *Soules Vocation*, 63. T[homas] H[ooker], *The Unbeleevers Preparing for Christ* (London, 1638), 160.

votion), but not in extraordinary ways that defied the order of nature. It was "not that God is tyed to any means, but he tyeth himself to this means." The Lord will indeed eventually come "as a Theefe" in the night, Cotton preached, but in the meantime the believer will find Him "at Supper, he shall finde him at the Ordinances, at every spirituall dutie he shall finde him." The phrases "in ordinary course" and "in common course" were used in conjunction with the practice of devotion to describe both the regularity of devotional exercises and their importance as God's "conduits to convey [the] water of life." As expressed in one popular manual, the godly life was "upholden by means."[6]

PUBLIC WORSHIP

Worship in New England revolved around the Sabbath. Much of private devotion during the week was preparation for that special day on which the greatest concentration of spiritual activity occurred. Use of the Sabbath as the devotional point of reference was a major Puritan innovation within Christianity. The Puritans replaced an annual, irregular cycle with a weekly, regular one, a celebration of the salvation drama in which "the mighty acts of God in the creation, redemption and sanctification of man, through the life, death, and resurrection of Christ" were each week completely re-presented and reexperienced. The Puritan Sabbath voiced Old Testament Sabbatarian ideas—especially God's rest on the seventh day of Creation and the Sabbath proclaimed in the Law by Moses—transformed by the Christian revelation of God's new creation at Easter. The Puritan Sabbath was thus a "little Easter" or "a sort of weekly Pascha," the day of Christ's resurrection and the day of believers' redemption.[7]

The nature of the rest prescribed for the Sabbath in New England

6. The orderliness of the Puritan universe is a major thesis of Miller's *New England Mind: Seventeenth Century.* See Hall, *Faithful Shepherd,* 59; Stoever, *'Faire and Easie Way,'* 74, 124, 148–150. Hooker, *Application of Redemption, First Eight Books,* 133–134. H[ooker], *Soules Vocation,* 64. [Hooker], *Soules Humiliation,* 82. Cotton, *Seven Vials,* 128. Shepard, *Theses Sabbaticae,* sig. B3. Thomas, ed., *Diary of Samuel Sewall,* I, 89. Bayne, *Briefe Directions,* 113.

7. See generally, Winton U. Solberg, *Redeem the Time: The Puritan Sabbath in Early America* (Cambridge, Mass., 1977). Davies, *Worship of the English Puritans,* 75–76. Dom Gregory Dix, *The Shape of the Liturgy* (London, 1945), 7n. Dix was clearly not thinking of Reformed liturgics when he wrote of "this idea of Sunday as a little weekly Easter" that "in practice there is no evidence that it has ever made very much appeal to popular piety in any part of christendom" (p. 359). Shepard, *Theses Sabbaticae,* 5–6.

was not identical with that of traditional England. Winton U. Solberg has suggested that in the Church of England's "ecclesiastical," or "dominical," view, the Sabbath was not based on God's eternal moral law in creation but on Mosaic Law and Jewish ceremonial, which expired with Christ. Sabbath activity was thus to be based on ecclesiastical tradition, rather than directly on biblical injunction. The Church of England "recognized man's compound nature and provided for body as well as the soul," thereby opening the way for merriment and sports. Rest became at least partly human rest and the day a time for recreation as well as worship. Puritans insisted that the Sabbath was a day to attend solely to spiritual realities. "The word Sabbath properly signifies not common, but sacred and holy rest," Shepard wrote. In the same vein *The Practice of Piety* posited two necessary elements for Sabbath keeping: first, "resting from all servile and common business pertaining to our natural life"; and second, "consecrating that rest wholly to the service of God, and the use of those holy means which belong to our spiritual life." It was a day of rest from all secular work and a day for the spiritual work whereby the soul could find rest. The Sabbath was a day for the re-creation of the soul, not the recreation of the body.[8]

The Sabbath was a means of grace. Shepard rejected the radical view that the external Sabbath was abolished with Christ and now existed as a nontemporal element within the individual soul. The best way to achieve a daily personal communion with Christ, Shepard believed, was to assign "a special day" for spiritual things, which would be "a most powerful means to Sabbatize every day." He argued that a spiritualized everyday Sabbath, which the radicals proposed, would soon have the effect of de-sabbatizing every day, including the first day of the week. Shepard's argument encompassed much of the theological and psychological basis for Puritan ritual. Special days, special observances, special things properly used according to biblical precedent, could foster the religious experience Puritans sought. The Sabbath was "the special season of grace" in the cycle of time. "If a mans heart be lost in the necessary cumbers of the weeke, (upon the Sabbath) the Lord is wont to recall it again to him; if any feare that the time of Grace is past, the continuation of the Sabbaths . . . confutes him; if a mans soul be wearied with daily griefs and outward troubles, the bosome of Jesus Christ (which is in speciall wise opened every Lords day) may refresh him." On the Sabbath the Lord again called

---

8. Solberg, *Redeem the Time*, 2. Shepard, *Theses Sabbaticae*, 77. Bayly, *Practice of Piety*, 222.

New Englanders "off from all occasions" with the words "Come to me my people, and rest in my bosome of sweetest mercy all this day."[9]

Beyond looking back to the Resurrection, Puritans on the Sabbath looked forward to the perfection of the work of redemption at the Second Coming. Since Old Testament times the Sabbath's dynamic qualities have stemmed from its eschatology; the Lord's Day pointed to the terrible approaching Day of the Lord. Thomas Shepard wrote at the end of his *Theses Sabbaticae* that devotional preparation for the Sabbath each week was a part and a miniature version of the saint's lifelong preparation for glory and eternal rest. "And as the rest of the Day is for the holinesse of it, so is all the labour of the Week for this holy rest; that as the end of all the labour of our lives is for our rest with Christ in Heaven, so also of the six daies of every weeke for the holy Rest of the Sabbath, the twilight and dawning of Heaven." The vignette of Shepard in chapter one shows something of what pre-Sabbath exercises entailed; in chapter seven we will go into more detail. The forward-looking nature of the Sabbath suited the progressive qualities of Puritan devotion. The sequence of Sabbath after Sabbath in earthly time marked off stages toward eternity, each one a resting place on the journey. The spiritual pilgrim set himself within the context of just this progress through stages established by God and leading to His heavenly Kingdom.[10]

Sabbath neglect, which Puritan diarists and church membership applicants almost invariably confessed as an early sin, was abominable because of the eschatological nature of the day. When John Dane was stung by a wasp on his finger not once but on two separate occasions as he shunned worship, he knew his heart had actually been pierced. The sting forced him to recall the redemption that should have been applied to his soul that day. As with the piercing of Christ on the cross, remarkably, "watter and blod cam out of it!" He recalled his mother's parting words as he embarked on his journeys: "Goe whare you will, god he will finde you out." Her warning referred not only to small judgments such as the stings but to the great and final judgment of which they were emblematic. Thomas Shepard warned that while "the Lord Jesus certainly hath great blessings in his hand to poure out upon his people in giving them better dayes, and brighter and more beautiful Sabbaths, and glorious appearances," neglect of the day would bring God's Judgment on soon. New England had better attend to the means of grace, Shepard preached, "lest the Lord make quick

9. Shepard, *Theses Sabbaticae*, 65, sig. B1.
10. *Ibid.*, 79. Davies, *Worship and Theology*, II, 245.

work, and give those things to a remnant to enjoy, which others had no hearts to prize."[11]

New Englanders worshiped publicly in both the morning and the afternoon of the Lord's Day. Services were long, about three hours each, so in effect the day was spent in church. Appraisals of individuals' emotional involvement in worship range from the unsympathetic description by the Labadist Jasper Danckaerts of Boston in 1680 —"There was no more devotion than in other churches, and even less than at New York; no respect, no reverence; in a word, nothing but the name of Independents; and that was all"—to the sanguine picture in ministerial and pious lay diaries. Since church members and nonmembers alike throughout the century were required by law to attend worship, it is not surprising that attitudes varied. But however one felt about being present, Sabbath worship constituted a common experience of the populace. And it seems likely, as Sacvan Bercovitch has suggested, that the themes of public worship infused the entire culture. By granting six hours on the first day of every week for the clergy to rehearse the drama of sin and salvation before the people, New England put the Sabbath at the center of its temporal existence.[12]

Nor was public worship limited to the Sabbath. "Every week in most of our Churches," John Cotton wrote in his survey of New England's worship practices, "lectures are kept on some or other of the weeke days." Boston's lecture, the first established, was held on Thursday throughout the century. Cotton noted that "such as whose hearts God maketh willing, and his hand doth not detaine by bodily infirmitie, or other necessary imployments, (if they dwell in the heart of the Bay) may have opportunitie to heare the Word almost every day of the weeke in one Church or other, not farre distant from them." The emphasis on lecture day was ostensibly on doctrinal teaching complementary to the Sabbath's evangelical preaching; in churches with both a pastor and a teacher, the teacher usually gave the lecture. But this distinction broke down quickly (most churches soon had only one minister in any case), and the faint line between preaching and teaching all but vanished. For the parishioner lecture day was a weekday worship service, with the same type of prayers, psalm singing, and

11. Dane, "Declaration of Remarkabell Prouedenses," *NEHGR*, VIII (1854), 149–155. Shepard, *Theses Sabbaticae*, 98.

12. Bartlett Burleigh James and J. Franklin Jameson, eds., *Journal of Jasper Danckaerts, 1679–1680* (New York, 1913), 261–262. Sacvan Bercovitch, *The American Jeremiad* (Madison, Wis., 1978).

sermons as on the Sabbath, and one could legitimately take time away from work to attend.[13]

Other, more occasional, days of public worship were proclaimed as well. Upon "extraordinary occasions," such as when "notable judgments" and "speciall mercies" from God were evident, days of humiliation and thanksgiving, respectively, were set aside. As John Eliot put it, these "were so many Sabbaths more" in the calendar of New England worship. Such days were sometimes proclaimed by civil authority for the entire populace and sometimes by churches for members. Horton Davies has remarked that in England days of humiliation and thanksgiving differed from previous national special days in two ways: first in their "great solemnity, intensity, and length, . . . with only a minimal concession to the needs of the body"; and second, such days of special providence were observed within the Puritan family as well as in public ceremony. The unity of public and private devotion was indeed characteristic of Puritan spirituality and is seen in the Puritans' approach to fasting and giving thanks. One manual noted that in both private and public fasts the participant "voluntarily undertakes, to make his body and soul the fitter to pray more fervently to God upon some extraordinary occasion." The aim was "more devoutly [to] contemplate Gods holy will, and fervently pour forth our soule unto him by prayer," so that "by our serious humiliation, and judging of our selves, we may escape the judgment of the Lord."[14]

Public fast days were held in response to dire agricultural and meteorological conditions, ecclesiastical, military, political, and social crises both in New England and in Europe, and in preparation for important events such as the ordination of a minister or the militia's embarkation on a campaign. Thanksgiving days, similarly, were proclaimed after a good harvest, military success, or some other evidence of the Lord's favor and mercy. William DeLoss Love cataloged many of these days in a classic work and showed that both fast and thanksgiving days grew in importance in New England over the course of the century. The fast especially became a standard weapon in the arsenal of public rituals available in time of trouble. It was employed regularly in the

13. J[ohn] Cotton, *The Way of the Churches of Christ in New England* . . . (London, 1645), 70. Ministers frequently took the opportunity to hear colleagues preach on neighboring lecture days. Peter Thacher, "Diary," MS and typescript, Massachusetts Historical Society, Boston, *passim.*

14. Cotton, *Way of the Churches*, 70. John Eliot, "Sermon," in C. Mather, ed., *Life and Death of J. Eliot* . . . , 20. Davies, *Worship and Theology*, II, 246. Bayly, *Practice of Piety*, 288–301. For the impact of fast days on experience, see Woolley, "Shepard's Cambridge Church Members," 106–107, 138.

wake of the major crises of the second half of the century, from general declension in piety to witchcraft. The distinctively American Puritan sermonic style, the jeremiad, which Perry Miller first identified, was based on the mood of the fast.[15]

Love also indicated that a shift occurred in New England's declarations of special days of worship. Originally, the Puritans set aside "occasional days" as events dictated. But a regular pattern of annual spring fasts and autumn thanksgivings soon developed. Diaries indicate that Love's analysis is essentially correct, although irregularly and spontaneously proclaimed special days also continued throughout the century. Given that the Puritans rejected the annual ecclesiastical cycle of saints' and holy days in favor of a more "modern" and "industrious" weekly cycle, one may ask, Why did this regular pattern develop? It seems the Puritans retained, perhaps almost involuntarily, a sense of the annual cycle. The yearly rhythms of life were too deeply ingrained to shake off. Puritans objected to the Catholic calendar, with its roots in pagan agricultural rites, but their annual cycle of special days followed the same traditional seasonal pattern.[16]

Spring has commonly been viewed as the time of new life following the winter of death. In chapter seven we will find that elements of this particular death-rebirth cycle persisted in Puritan devotion even as they rejected the springtime celebration of Easter. But spring is also the time of planting in the agricultural year. In biblical thought seedtime is a time of death. The seed, like the dead Christ and the dead saint, is buried in the ground. And death is the prerequisite of resurrection. "Except a corn of wheat fall into the ground and die, it abideth alone: but if it die, it bringeth forth much fruit" (John 12:24). Puritans, like Paul, insisted that the "old man" of sin must die before the "new man" may be born in Christ (Romans 6:6, Ephesians 4:22–24, Colossians 3:9–12). The old stock of Adam must be cut off and pre-pared before it can be grafted onto the new stock of Christ. New Englanders enacted these themes daily, weekly, and annually. They received special attention in the spring, when seeds were buried in the ground and whole days of humiliation and self-examination seemed natural. Experience reinforced biblical images: quite practi-

15. W. DeLoss Love, Jr., *The Fast and Thanksgiving Days of New England* (Boston, 1895). Horton Davies's belief that these days "were occasional and rare, and were no more than the foothills of their corporate devotion" may have been correct for England but the situation in New England was far different (*Worship and Theology*, I, 268). Miller, *New England Mind: From Colony to Province*, chap. 2.

16. Love, *Fast and Thanksgiving Days*, 79, 239–255. Peter Thacher's "Diary" lists a thanksgiving almost invariably in November.

cally, spring was a time of death, not new life, in that it was a time of hunger as the winter larder was depleted. Although they would never have acknowledged the relationship, the New Englanders' pattern of fasting corresponded with the Catholic observance of Lent. The gradual regularizing of the calendar in New England is a good example of Puritan re-ritualization.[17]

New England most often proclaimed thanksgiving days in the autumn, in association with the harvest. The mythic "First Thanksgiving" at Plymouth was actually a week-long harvest festival, yet before many years had passed, a single day of worship was observed annually in November. John Hull noted in his diary that November 8, 1665 (an unexceptional year), was "kept as a day of solemn thanksgiving that the Lord was pleased to spare so much of the fruits of the earth; that we had not want, but were able to supply other countries; and likewise the continuance of our health and present peace." Ministers connected the autumn thanksgiving not with any ecclesiastical tradition but with the Old Testament Feast of Tabernacles, the final great festival of the Hebrew calendar, when grapes and olives, the fruit of the earth, were offered to God (Exodus 23:16). New Englanders also made use of other harvest references in the Bible. Jesus connected the harvest with conversion when He sent out the seventy as "laborers" and called God "the Lord of the harvest" (Luke 10:2). And the Old Testament prophets and Revelation associated the harvest with the eschaton: "Thrust in thy sickle, and reap; for the time is come for thee to reap; for the harvest of the earth is ripe . . . and the earth was reaped" (Revelation 14:15–16). John Eliot used the theme in this manner in his celebrative tract *New Englands First Fruits* (1643). Although on public days of thanksgiving New Englanders expressed joy for divine favors recently granted—thus giving the occasions concrete historical referents—their joy looked forward to God's Kingdom in the same way the Sabbath did. New Englanders thought of themselves as firstfruits and as recipients of the firstfruits of the Holy Spirit, as converted saints and citizens of the Kingdom. As Paul had written, "Ourselves also, which have the firstfruits of the Spirit, even we ourselves groan within ourselves, waiting for the adoption, to wit, the redemption of our body" (Romans 8:23).[18]

The annual appointment of a day of fasting and humiliation in the spring, the time when seeds were buried and larders were empty,

17. I am indebted to Ellen Smith of the American and New England Studies program, Boston University, for the insight of spring as the time of the empty larder and hence as symbolic of death.

18. Love, *Fast and Thanksgiving Days*, 68–77. Hull, *Diaries*, 219.

and of a day of thanksgiving in the autumn, when the harvest was gathered in, demonstrates the Puritans' re-ritualizing activity. They persisted within the traditional cycle of the agricultural and religious calendar even as they abandoned the saints' and holy days of the Old World. They reconstructed the annual cycle through the use of biblical imagery and Old Testament cultus.

Our understanding of the ways New Englanders worshiped must take in the full scope of their activities: the regularity of the Sabbath as each week the cycle of the salvation drama was re-presented and reexperienced; the supplementary instruction and worship of the weekday lecture; the seasonally regular days of fasting and thanksgiving; and the occasional days of worship designated in connection with special events. Implicit in all these instances was the psychological and spiritual cycle of death and resurrection, or new birth—as in the humiliation and contrition of the soul in preparation for salvation and the soul's implantation into Christ. If the soul truly humbled itself in preparation for the Sabbath or in the fast, occasion for thanksgiving would surely follow in course.

THE HOLY ORDINANCES

Two extant contemporary sources illuminate for us exactly what happened in the meetinghouse during worship. One of these was written by the vehement anti-Puritan Anglican Thomas Lechford; the other is from the pen of the arch-Puritan John Cotton. Both men published their descriptions in London in the early 1640s with the intention of influencing official and popular opinion in their respective directions. Lechford's *Plain Dealing, or, News from New England* (1641) is a dispassionate, fair, and highly critical account of the civil and ecclesiastical practices of a society from which he was an outcast. Cotton's *The True Constitution of a Particular Visible Church* (1642) and *The Way of the Churches of Christ in New England* (1645) were paeans of the New England way. The two men agreed remarkably—almost exactly—on the framework of public worship. As outlined by Cotton and Lechford and corroborated by entries in clerical diaries, the order of worship was as follows for both morning and afternoon Sabbath services:

Opening prayer
Scripture reading
Exposition of Scripture
Psalm singing

Sermon
Prayer
Psalm singing
Sacraments, Lord's Supper ideally monthly or
bimonthly in the morning,
Baptism in the afternoon
Collection for needy saints, occasionally, in the afternoon
Admission of new members, occasionally, in the afternoon
Blessing

This general outline describes the activities at public days of fasting
and thanksgiving and lecture days as well. Each element of the service
was considered an ordinance, a public means of grace, a religious act
through which God might work in the worshiper's heart.[19]

Public Prayer

After the people had gathered in the meetinghouse, "men with their
heads uncovered the women covered," the pastor opened worship
with prayer, which lasted "about a quarter of an houre." This opening
prayer was generally based on themes from 1 Timothy 2:1: "prayers
and intercessions and thanksgivings for our selves and for all men,
not in any prescribed forme of prayer, or studied Liturgie," but freely
and extemporaneously. Other prayers during the service were equally
spontaneous, though with varying focuses. Before the sermon the
preacher prayed briefly for inspiration and power from the Holy
Spirit for himself and for the congregation to listen for God's Word.
The major prayer of both morning and afternoon services usually
came after the sermon, although in some churches it came before.
Ministers held it to be almost as important as the sermon itself. Peter
Thacher in his diary typically linked the two ordinances as the crux of
his work for the Sabbath: "The Lord did much to in large my heart
both in prayer and preaching, and draw it forth to himself," and "God
did graciously warme my heart in praying and preaching."[20]

The major prayer was also about equal to the sermon in length.
Thacher wrote on one occasion that he "stood about three hours in
prayer and preaching." On another: "God was pleased graciously to

19. Thomas Lechford, *Plain Dealing, or, News from New England* (London, 1641), ed.
J. Hammond Trumbull (Boston, 1867), 43–50. John Cotton, *The True Constitution of a
Particular Visible Church, Proved by Scripture* (London, 1642), 5–8. Cotton, *Way of the
Churches*, 66–70. See also, Love, *Fast and Thanksgiving Days*, 88.

20. Cotton, *True Constitution*, 5. Cotton, *Way of the Churches*, 66–67. Lechford, *Plain
Dealing*, ed. Trumbull, 44–45. Thacher, "Diary," MS, I, 37, 42, and *passim*.

assist mee much beyond my Expectation. Blessed be his holy name for it. I was near an hour and halfe in my first prayer and my heart much drawne out in it and an hour in the sermon." Jasper Danckaerts likewise attested to the length of the prayers. "We went to church, but there was only one minister in the pulpit, who made a prayer an hour long, and preached the same length of time, when some verses were sung. We expected something particular in the afternoon, but there was nothing more than usual." On a fast day he even reported that "a minister made a prayer in the pulpit, of full two hours in length." In the afternoon "three or four hours were consumed with nothing except prayers, three ministers relieving each other alternately." The norm on a common Sabbath seems to have been a major prayer of sixty to ninety minutes, with the sermon about the same.[21]

John Cotton implied that the custom for public prayer may not have been always to bow, though for prayers of confession this penitential posture was assumed. Arguing against the use of a prayer book, he said, "nor will it stand with the holy gesture of Prayer, which is to lift up our eyes to Heaven, to cast downe our eyes upon a Booke." Cotton cited two instances where Jesus "lifted up his eyes" when He prayed. In any case, kneeling in public worship was generally proscribed as papist invention (even though it was recommended for private prayer).[22]

Prayer in New England's public worship was "free" or "conceived" because in the Puritan perception Scripture offered no grounds for "a stinted Liturgie . . . by vertue of any Divine precept." Rather, "the primitive patterns of all the Churches of God in their best times" was spontaneous prayer conceived and spoken extemporaneously. Indeed, since the saints had experienced grace and had received the Holy Spirit, why did they need set prayers? God imparted "a spirit of prayer," and of all people ministers, as exemplars of sainthood, must be able to pray freely. In the primitive Church, Thomas Shepard wrote, "they prayed without a Promptour, because from the heart. . . . Their persecutions and dayes of afflictions preserved them from formalitie in prayer, and taught them how to finde their hearts and knees, and tongues, to poure out their soules to God, while under the Altar they were pouring out their blood." Could New Englanders in their pilgrimage through the wilderness do otherwise? Besides, prayer must be responsive to the congregation's immediate situation. Ministers prayed for the conversion of people present, for the spiritual con-

21. Thacher, "Diary," MS, I, 121–122, 79. James and Jameson, eds., *Journal of Jasper Danckaerts*, 261–262.

22. Cotton, *True Constitution*, 6. John 11:41, 17:1.

dition of the town and the political situation of the commonwealth, and for the welfare of other spiritual armies on other fronts of the Reformation.[23]

Styles of public prayer varied because they were conceived in the heart of the minister. Thomas Hooker was reputedly more succinct and, as the prayer reached its climax, more emotional than most ministers. As Cotton Mather remarked, "He affected Strength, rather than Length; and though he had not so much variety in Publick Praying, as in his Publick Preaching, yet he always had a seasonable Respect unto Present Conditions. And it was Observed, that his Prayer was usually like Jacobs Ladder, wherein the nearer he came to an End, the nearer he drew towards Heaven; and he grew into such Rapturous Pleadings with God, and Praysings of God, as made some to say, That Like the Master of the Feast, he Reserved the best Wine until the Last." Mather pointed to John Norton as one whose style of relevant and well-organized public prayer younger ministers emulated. Ministers who followed his example prayed "with more Pertinent, more Affecting, more Expanded Enlargements, than any Form could Afford unto them." Mather went on to comment on the state of public prayer at the end of the century. "New England can show, even Young Ministers, who never did in all Things Repeat One Prayer twice over, in that part of their Ministry wherein we are First of All, to make Supplications, Prayers, Intercessions, and Thanksgivings; and yet sometimes, for much more than an Hour together, they pour out their Soules unto the Almighty God in such Fervent, Copious, and yet Proper Manner, that their most Critical Auditors, can complain of Nothing Disagreeable, but profess themselves extreamly Edifyed."[24]

Despite the individuality and the extemporaneity of ministers' prayers, none was entirely unique or distinct in language from those that had gone before. The clergy worked with a common biblical vocabulary and adhered to a formal pattern that followed the stages of the order of redemption. Remnants of public prayers are, of course, exceedingly rare because prayers were delivered orally, without notes. In a few cases, however, ministers copied down what they could remember of their prayers after the service. From these notations we can discover something of the content and form of the prayers. The

23. [Richard Mather], *Church-Government and Church-Covenant Discussed* . . . (London, 1643), 56–57. Shepard, *Treatise of Liturgies*, 64.

24. Cotton Mather, "Piscator Evangelicus," in *Johannes in Eremo. Memoirs Relating to the Lives, of the Ever-Memorable, Mr. John Cotton, . . . Mr. John Wilson, . . . Mr. John Davenport, . . . and Mr. Thomas Hooker* . . . (Boston, 1695), 27–28. C. Mather, "Nortonus Honoratus," *ibid.*, 38.

best examples are portions of particularly efficacious eucharistic prayers by Increase Mather, recorded in his diary and transcribed in his autobiography. Mather's rhetorical style emerges when the prayers are transposed into poetic form. On March 30, 1673, Mather was "much affected in administring the Lords supper, especially in the last prayer."

> Now dearest Lord,
>   If ever there were poor creatures in this world,
>   that had cause to love and bless the Lord,
>   we are they.
>
> Wee have done thee Infinite wrong,
>   but you hast forgiven us all those wrongs,
>   and dealest with us as with thi friends this day.
>
> How can wee but mourn for the wrong wee have done thee?
>
> If wee had wronged though an enemy,
>   and that in a small matter,
>   wee should grieve for it.
>
> But wee have wronged the son of God our Saviour;
>   yea wee have killed him.
>
> Hee had never come to the cross,
>   had it not bin for our sins
>   as wee are the elect of God.
>
> But this blood which wee have shed has procured our pardon,
>   as it did for the Jewes that killed him,
>   so many of them as belonged to election.
>
> Also Christ prayed for them, saying,
>   Father forgive them,
>   And so you knowest hee has done for us.
>
> Christ has sayd before thee concerning us,
>   Father, forgive them.
>
> If children offend their Father much,
>   yet if any of them come and say,
>   I am sory for what I have done,
>   I'll do so no more,
>   Father be reconciled to me,
>   will not a Father then forgive them?

> O! our Father, wee have sinned against thee,
>   but wee are sory for it,
>   and would do iniquity no more;
>   Father forgive us.
>
> You knowest our Hearts,
>   you knowest that wee could be glad
>   if wee might never have so much as one sinfull thought in our
>   hearts,
>   nor speake so much as one unprofitable word more whilest wee
>   live.
>
> And there is another thing which wee would beg of thee,
>   if ever you wilt hear the cries of poor creatures,
>   deny us not that request,
>   It is O Lord, that you wouldst sanctify us by thy spirit.

Another prayer during which Mather was "much affected" soared by means of the eschatological imagery of the Sacrament:

> Lord, wee shall never perish.
>
> They that beleeve on Christ shall never perish;
>   And you knowest that we beleeve on him.
>
> You hast brought us to the blood of sprinkling,
>   and therefore you wilt bring us to Jesus
>   the Mediator of the new Covenant,
>   and wee shall behold his glory.
>
> Wee shall see our Joseph,
>   our Jesus in all his glory.
>
> Wee shall behold King Solomon in all his glory.
>
> Yea, Solomon in all his glory
>   was not arayed as Christ is;
>   wee shall see that glory,
>   and shall sit with him on thrones of glory.

A third focused on the hope of those in the Covenant:

> O Heavenly Father and our God in Jesus Christ,
>   wee have avouched thee to be our God,
>   and now wee know that you hast avouched us to be thi people,
>   because you hast given us thi son,
>   and you wilt with him give us all things.

Father, wee humbly expect from thee,
    that according to thi Covenant, even the new Covenant,
    you wilt forgive us our iniquities.

Such is the grace of thi Covenant
    as that you wilt not impute our infirmities to us,
    if they be our burden,
    and you knowest that they are so.

Wee put the Answer of our prayers upon that,
    and are willing to be denied if it be not so.

But you that searchest hearts,
    knowest that you hast created such a spirit within us.

Wee are willing to be delivered from all sin,
    and wee are willing to yeild Holy perfect obedience to all thi
        commands,
    tho' how to perform wee find not.

Father Father, deal with us as with thi children![25]

Mather's preeminently biblical phrases tumble over one another in an orderly fashion, according to syllogistic logic, through the stages of the salvific cycle. The first prayer begins in humiliation and confession of sin, moves to forgiveness of sin, and concludes with a prayer for sanctification. The second portion demonstrates how closely bound ministers were to a biblical language. Mather used three passages of Scripture as stepping-stones: John 3:16 ("whosoever believeth in him should not perish"), Hebrews 12:22 and 24 ("ye are come unto mount Sion . . . And to Jesus the mediator of the new covenant, and to the blood of sprinkling"), and Luke 12:27 ("Consider the lilies. . . . Solomon in all his glory was not arrayed like one of these").

When New Englanders went to prayer, without notes or books, their heads were stocked with a whole Bible full of devotional resources. Puritans relinquished the set phrases of the Book of Common Prayer, as Robert Paul has noted, in exchange for language flowing straight from Scripture, language "now made personal and immediate through the experience and eloquence of the individual pastor." The language of public prayer was formulary even while Puritans rejected printed forms.[26]

25. Hall, ed., "Autobiography of Increase Mather," Am. Antiq. Soc., *Procs.*, N.S., LXXI (1961), 316–317.

26. Paul, "Accidence and Essence of Puritan Piety," *Austin Seminary Bulletin*, XCIII, no. 8 (May 1978), 15.

The Reading of Scripture

After the opening prayer, the pastor read a biblical passage that established the theme of the entire service. The reading was generally of a chapter chosen by the preacher and containing the text that served as the basis of his sermon. In the case of a sermon series, the same chapter was used for morning and afternoon services, and even for several weeks running. It does not appear that both Old and New Testaments were necessarily included in a given service, as they were in Church of England worship. One reason may have been the Puritan typological reading of Scripture, in which they followed St. Augustine: "What else is the Old Testament but the New foreshadowed? And what other the New than the Old revealed?" The Christian revelation, specifically the work of Christ in redemption, was the prism through which Puritans received the Old Testament. Indeed, both testaments shone through the prism of Christ onto the lives of New Englanders. A second reason for the adequacy of a single reading was that sermons were studded with dozens of direct references to both testaments. Cotton Mather wrote of Samuel Danforth, for example, "The sermons with which he fed his flock were elaborate and substantial; he was a notable text-man, and one who had more than forty or fifty scriptures distinctly quoted in one discourse." And hundreds of indirect references formed the vocabulary of every sermon and prayer. Old Testament types and New Testament antitypes played off one another, and ministers pressed every possible parallel, supporting, and proof text into service. By the end of the day the congregation had heard the equivalent of the "twelve or thirteen chapters and psalms" that Lechford said typified Church of England worship.[27]

The Bible was the Word of God, a means of grace in itself. The Holy Spirit could affect the heart simply through the impact of the words. But simple reading, or "dumb reading," was deemed inadequate for a service of worship. The congregation must be well prepared and listen actively, and the pastor must give a thorough explication after the reading. William Perkins advised, "To the profitable hearing of Gods Word three things are required: Preparation before we heare, a right Disposition in hearing, and Duties to be practised afterward." In preparation individuals must first "disburden" themselves of all "impediments which may hinder the effectuall hearing of the Word" (typically "presumption," arrogance, "troubled affections" such as anger, and "superfluity of maliciousnesse, that is, the abundance of

---

27. Bercovitch, *Typology and Early American Literature*, 2. C. Mather, *Magnalia Christi Americana*, II, 61. Lechford's letter is cited in *Plain Dealing*, ed. Trumbull, 45n.

evill corruptions and sinnes"). They must "lift up" their hearts "in prayer to God." A "hearing eare" did not come naturally but was "a gift of God, enabling the heart" to understand and submit. And as the worshipers were thus enabled they must "labour to be affected with the Word," so it might "dwell plenteously" in them. Finally, the Spirit continued working through the "opening" of the passage by a skilled exegete. After the minister read the chapter, Cotton wrote, he "expoundeth it, giving the sense, to cause the people to understand the reading." Phrases from the chapter then resounded for more than two hours in the prayer and sermon and carried through the week in the private devotions of the congregation.[28]

The Singing of Psalms

"As wee are to make melody in our hearts, so with our voyces also," wrote John Cotton in his important work *Singing of Psalmes a Gospel-Ordinance*. The congregation sang psalms and sometimes other "spiritual Songs recorded in Scripture" in services both "before [the] Sermon and many times after" as well. A psalm was sung in conjunction with the administration of the Lord's Supper and with other occasional ordinances. The early versions used in New England were those by Sternhold and Hopkins (1562) and Henry Ainsworth (1612). Plymouth continued to use the Ainsworth psalter through most of the century, as did Salem until about 1667. After its publication in 1640 the translation, or more properly the versification, used most commonly, however, was the product of the Massachusetts Bay clergy, *The Whole Booke of Psalmes*, popularly called the *Bay Psalm Book*.[29]

Why should the clergy have toiled to produce a new psalter, the first book to issue from the Cambridge press? At one level, Zoltán Haraszti has suggested, the Ainsworth version was unacceptable because of its association with separatism. But the primary reason was that New England ministers deemed earlier versions linguistically inadequate. "The former translation of the Psalmes," Cotton observed, "doth in many things vary from the originall, and many times paraphraseth

28. Perkins, *Cases of Conscience*, in *Works*, II, 70–71. Cotton, *True Constitution*, 6. Cotton's description of the reading of Scripture is tied to the wording of Nehemiah 8. In John Davenport's New Haven church, and perhaps others, it seems that, following this text and ancient custom, the people stood for the reading. See Thomas Hooker's 1640 letter to Thomas Shepard, cited in Lechford, *Plain Dealing*, ed. Trumbull, 45n.

29. John Cotton, *Singing of Psalmes a Gospel-Ordinance* . . . (London, 1650 [orig. publ. 1647]), 2. Cotton, *Way of the Churches*, 67, 69. J. H. Dorenkamp, "The *Bay Psalm Book* and the Ainsworth Psalter," *Early Am. Lit.*, VII (1972), 7.

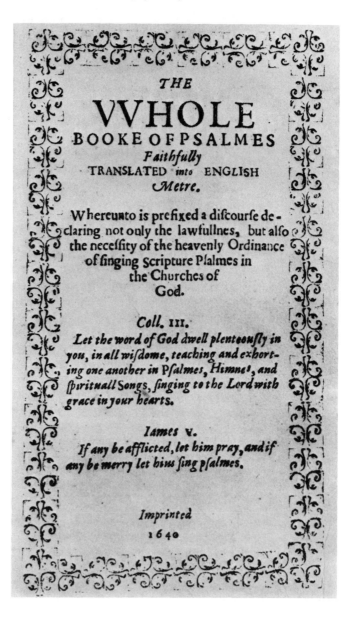

Figure 7. Title page of The Whole Booke of Psalmes (Bay Psalm Book), *published in Cambridge, Massachusetts, a decade after settlement. This and other versions of the psalter were used in public worship and private devotion. Courtesy the Trustees of the Boston Public Library.*

rather than translateth." Haraszti has demonstrated that in addition to Sternhold-Hopkins, Ainsworth, and the Geneva Bible, the 1611 version of the Bible exerted considerable influence on the New England translators. The clergy, all of whom read Hebrew, could choose what they considered the best translation of each word and line for English metric verse. The *Bay Psalm Book* was the result of accomplished biblical scholarship. Cotton explained, "Wee have endeavoured a new translation of the Psalmes into English meetre, as neere the originall as wee could expresse it in our English tongue, so farre as for the present the Lord hath been pleased to helpe us, and those Psalmes wee sing, both in our publike Churches, and in private." New England clerical leaders produced a new translation because the advances in Hebrew scholarship evident in the 1611 version of the Bible had left all previous psalters behind. New Englanders wanted the praises they sang to their Lord to be accurate and understandable renderings of Scripture.[30]

The massive undertaking of completing the *Bay Psalm Book* within the first ten years of settlement makes sense only if we recognize Puritanism as a popular devotional movement. Singing was a means of grace, a well-established way that one might communicate with God. As with all means of grace, singing was a natural phenomenon, a human activity through which God chooses to work. Cotton wrote that whereas "singing with Instruments was typicall, and so ceremoniall worship, and therefore ceased . . . , singing with heart and voyce is morall worship, such as is written in the hearts of all men by nature." That is, all persons have within them the duty and the means to sing praises. The act of singing, then, could bring a soul into harmony with God. "The end of singing is not onely to instruct, admonish, and comfort the Church" but also to help those who "are godly, though out of the Church. . . . Nay further, the end of singing is . . . to instruct, and convince, and reprove [the] wicked, as hath been shewed, Deut. 31.19." Singing was what Puritans called a converting ordinance.[31]

Devotional singing, like other means of grace, had to be biblically grounded. Puritans were more cautious about public worship than with private devotion in this regard. "Any private Christian, who hath a gift to frame a spirituall song, may both frame it, and sing it privately, for his own private comfort, and remembrance of some speciall

30. Zoltán Haraszti, *The Enigma of the Bay Psalm Book* (Chicago, 1956), 8, chap. 6. *Whole Booke of Psalmes*, sig. **2. Dorenkamp pointed out the many incidences of identical wording with Ainsworth, in "*Bay Psalm Book* and the Ainsworth Psalter," *Early Am. Lit.*, VII (1972), 9–15. Cotton, *Way of the Churches*, 67.

31. Cotton, *Singing of Psalmes*, 5–6, 48.

benefit, or deliverance." Saints could even use "an Instrument of Musick therewithall," so long as they did not thereby subordinate the devotional intent to the art of music. But in public worship songs had to be from the Bible and unaccompanied.[32]

Congregational singing was popular singing. Horton Davies has identified the great Puritan contributions to English worship as "firstly, the restoration of the people's rights to sing the Davidic Psalms in the vernacular; secondly, the versification of the psalms, that they might the easier be memorized by congregations and set to repetitive melodies." Everyone was familiar with the ballad cadences of the *Bay Psalm Book.* Everyone sang from it. Women were exempted from the rule of silence, since several scriptural precedents (for example, Miriam in Exodus 15:20–21) sufficiently justified "the lawfull practise of women in singing together with men the Praises of the Lord." The size of the printings of the *Bay Psalm Book* indicates that a large percentage of families owned a copy, but even men and women who could not read were exposed to it weekly. The self-understanding and spiritual lives of few New Englanders would have remained unaffected by the constant use of this worship book.[33]

The poetic style and method of singing furthered the likelihood of memorization. The singsong quality of the *Bay Psalm Book* is as notorious as are some of its grammatical infelicities. But whatever the aesthetic appeal of a given passage, it is evident that this type of versification made memorization easy and even unavoidable.

> The Lord to mee a shepherd is,
>   want therefore shall not I,
> Hee in the fold of tender-grasse
>   doth cause mee downe to lie . . .

The method of singing also drove the lines home. Since not all churchgoers had books or could read, "one of the ruling Elders" dictated the words "before hand, line after line, or two lines together."[34]

John Cotton defended the regular meter of the version both in

---

32. Cotton went so far as to say a gifted person could compose a song and "sing it before the Church, and the rest hearing it, approving it, may goe along with him in Spirit, and say Amen to it." *Ibid.,* 15.

33. Davies, *Worship of the English Puritans,* 162. Cotton, *Singing of Psalmes,* 42–43. Winship, *Cambridge Press,* 34. Harrison T. Meserole, ed., *Seventeenth-Century American Poetry* (New York, 1968), xxiv.

34. Meserole, ed., *Seventeenth-Century American Poetry,* 353. Haraszti, however, has shown the generally high literary quality of the *Bay Psalm Book* (*Enigma of the Bay Psalm Book,* chap. 6). *Whole Booke of Psalmes,* Psalm 23. Lechford, *Plain Dealing,* ed. Trumbull,

his preface to the *Bay Psalm Book* and in his larger work on spiritual singing. He argued that "as all Verses in all Poems doe consist of a certaine number, and measure of Syllables; so doe our English Verses . . . which make the Verses more easie for memory, and fit for melody." The poetic form of the original Hebrew warranted that psalms be translated into English poetry "soe wee may sing Lords songs." The ministers followed popular taste: "In our english tongue . . . such verses as are familiar to an english eare . . . are commonly metricall." Further, since "the Tunes of the Temple are lost and hidden from us, . . . therefore we must sing such other Tunes, as are suitable to the matter, though invented by men."[35]

All Puritan devotion was ultimately preparation for glory, and this may be said of the public singing of psalms. In the conclusion to his preface Cotton put forth the reason for the new translation. Acts of worship in the "Sion" of New England were not an end in themselves. New England was a resting place on the pilgrim way to the perfect Zion. And Zion, as envisioned by the author of Revelation and almost as clearly by New England Puritans, would be a place of singing.

> And I looked, and, lo, a Lamb stood on the mount Sion,
> and with him an hundred forty and four thousand, having his
> Father's name written in their foreheads. And I heard a voice
> from heaven, as the voice of many waters, and as the voice of a
> great thunder: and I heard the voice of harpers harping with
> their harps: And they sung as it were a new song before the
> throne, and before the four beasts, and the elders: and no man
> could learn that song but the hundred and forty and four thou-
> sand, which were redeemed from the earth (Revelation 14:1–3).

By singing in their churches now (together with the unredeemed, for the final separation of wheat from tares would not come until Judgment Day), saints hoped to glimpse that coming glory. In the meanwhile, the Church was called to be God's Kingdom on earth. It embodied in germ form the Kingdom's glory. And when the Kingdom comes, as Isaiah had seen, "the redeemed of the Lord shall return, and come with singing into Zion; and everlasting joy shall be upon their head . . . and sorrow and mourning shall flee away" (51:11). John Cotton wrote that the *Bay Psalm Book* was composed

---

45. Significant work on New England's sacred music has been done by Barbara Dailey, a graduate student in the history department, Boston University. Her group has re-searched and performed the psalms and spiritual songs of meetinghouse and home.

35. Cotton, *Singing of Psalmes*, 55, 58, 62. *Whole Booke of Psalmes*, sig. **2.

that soe wee may sing in Sion the Lords
songs of prayse according to his owne
will; untill he take us from hence,
and wipe away all our teares, &
bid us enter into our masters
joye to sing eternall
Halleluiahs.[36]

The Sermon

The preaching and hearing of the sermon were the central acts in the
New England worship service. The minister had spent several days in
its preparation, and the congregation, in return, was composed of
generally active listeners. In the early years people were so hungry for
preaching that they flocked to every possible service. The midweek
lectures were added to accommodate popular demand. Newcomers
such as young John Brock wrote excitedly in their diaries, "We came
all safe to Land, and our first Sermon was by Mr. Shepard," as though
that were the reason for their voyage. Roger Clap and others were
swept into the enthusiasm of faith as "the Lord Jesus Christ was so
plainly held out in the Preaching of the Gospel unto poor lost Sinners." As the years progressed and zeal waned, people often seemed
to become "quite sermon-proof," but the sermon retained its central place in worship and in the culture. Ministers found themselves
preaching to "larger, less enthusiastic" congregations from the 1640s
on, which suggests that the sermon had become an established element in the everyday life of the populace. Preachers continued to
place confidence in the sermon. The development of increasingly
"jeremiad" characteristics demonstrates not the decline but the vitality
of the genre. As the civil law in Connecticut stated, "The preaching of
the word by those whom God doth send, is the chiefe ordinary means
ordained by God, for the converting, edifying, and saving of the
soules of the elect."[37]

   The gathering wave of printed sermons from the Cambridge and
then Boston presses attests to the popularity of preaching. That many

36. *Whole Booke of Psalmes*, Introduction, sig. **4.
37. Shipton, ed., "Autobiographical Memoranda of John Brock," Am. Antiq. Soc.,
Procs., N.S., LIII (1943), 98. *Clap's Memoirs*, 20. Hall, *Faithful Shepherd*, 156–157. See
generally, Bercovitch, *American Jeremiad*. *The Code of 1650, Being a Compilation of the
Earliest Laws and Orders of the General Court of Connecticut . . .* , cited in David Kobrin,
"The Expansion of the Visible Church in New England: 1629–1650," *Church History*,
XXXVI (1967), 194.

of these sermons were edited for publication from listeners' notes indicates an active auditory. It was not uncommon for New Englanders to keep a personal book of sermon notes. Samuel Sewall used such a notebook in his secret devotions. In clerical diaries and in public relations of faith we see instances of the conversion process being set in motion by sermons. Evangelism fell behind the growth rate of the population but did not cease. As Perry Miller wrote, "Puritan life, in the New England theory, was centered upon a corporate and communal ceremony, upon the oral delivery of a lecture." Miller misunderstood the private devotion that complemented the public gathering, and he underestimated the emotional quality of the sermons, but he was right in placing the sermon at the center of it all.[38]

Recent scholarship employs the idea of "myth," the "cosmic redemptive drama" undergirding New England society, to understand the place of the sermon. Sermons on the stages of conversion linked preaching with New England's salvation history and finally with "God's great plot for humanity's redemption." The preachers, as the culture's spokesmen, "collectively shaped a narrative" that interpreted and defined the culture. A literary approach to the sermons has recently found even "the form of the doctrinal matter to be a narrative, mythic in its repetition and heroics." For modern readers to appreciate "the full impact of the sermons" they must "sound the phrases in the imagination and use the punctuation not so much for semantic clues as for rhythmic markers." Each sermon built from a doctrinal and rational beginning and progressed, in the uses or application, to rhetoric aimed at the affections and will. Typically a crescendo came at the sermon's conclusion, with the most emotionally compelling exhortations.[39]

The key to the power of the preached word in Puritan New England is that the culture, although highly literate by European standards and even bookish in its use of devotional manuals and its attachment to such works as John Foxe's *Acts and Monuments* (first published in London, 1563) was still very much oriented toward oral performance and oral communication. Information was available in print (in almanacs and broadsides), but most ideas and information were transmitted verbally. The society defined itself first of all through spoken means. The *Bay Psalm Book* comes to us as a great translating and pub-

38. Thomas, ed., *Diary of Samuel Sewall*, I, 26. Miller, *New England Mind: Seventeenth Century*, 297–298.
39. Phyllis M. Jones and Nicholas R. Jones, eds., *Salvation in New England: Selections from the Sermons of the First Preachers* (Austin, Tex., 1977), xi, xiii, 12–13.

lishing achievement, but it was published only so people could sing its verses. Sermons were printed, but none were published that had not first been preached, and a Puritan sermon was normally preached even before it was written down. Usually the sermons that had the greatest impact when preached were selected for publication. At that point, for the first time, a full text would be prepared from notes and memory. The printed sermon must become a means of recovering at least something of the originally preached sermon, opening for us the realm of religious experience.

Puritan rhetoric, known as the "plain style," was intended to produce powerful biblical preaching. Sermons were plain in the sense of being explicit, plain so the "simplest hearer" could follow. As John Cotton taught in his well-known catechism, "Milk for Babes," preaching drew the soul "towards Christ" by "bringing me to know my sin and the wrath of God against me for it," and then "by humbling me yet more and then raising me up out of this estate" by the application of personal redemption in Christ's death and resurrection. Even for children, preaching must be "plain and powerful" in its exposure of sin. "When sin and sinners are set out in their native and natural colours and carry their proper names," when "a Spade is a Spade, and a Drunkard is a Drunkard," when preachers "make sin appear truly odious, and fearful to the open view of all," God may be expected to work on the heart.[40]

The sermon was also "plain" in its strict adherence to accepted homiletical order. Every sermon began with a reading of the text, followed by the opening, or exegesis, of the text, the extraction from the text of the doctrine to be propounded, the discussion of reasons for and refutation of objections against the doctrine, and finally the application of the doctrine to the lives of the listeners. No New England sermon failed to follow this order.

For Thomas Hooker and the other ministers, "plain and powerful preaching" depended first on "soundness of argument," but sermons were not entirely rational expositions of doctrine. It was said of Samuel Danforth, for example, that "though he were a very judicious preacher, yet he was therewithal so affectionate, 'that he rarely, ef ever, ended a sermon without weeping.'" Great passages of emotional exhortation have survived transition to print, most exciting in the work of Hooker and Shepard but evident in others as well. A

---

40. The plain style is discussed by Miller, *New England Mind: Seventeenth Century*, chaps. 11 and 12, and Levy, *Preaching in New England History*, 81–97. John Cotton, "Milk for Babes," in Everett H. Emerson, *John Cotton* (New York, 1965), 128.

"spiritual heat in the heart" of the preachers bespoke a personal quality in the exhortations. "When the heart of a Minister goeth home with the words," Hooker said, "then he delivers the word powerfully and profitably to the hearers." The minister must preach "as if he were in the bosome of a man." Affective preaching "shoot[s] home into the hearts and consciences of men like an arrow" and "doth discover the very secrets of a mans soule; together with the vileness and wickedness that is in a mans heart." After the penitent had allowed the preacher to "hew . . . and hack . . . frame and fashion" the heart in preparation, he gently lifted the soul into union with Christ. The immediacy of the sermons was rooted in the doctrine of the means of grace. Now was the time for repentance; now was the season of faith. The Holy Spirit was present in the congregation in the words of the preacher. "Me thinkes your hearts begin to stirre," Hooker preached, "and say, hath the Lord engaged himself to this? *Oh then (Lord) make me humble.*" Again, "If there be a soule here present that it hath pleased God thus to move, oh know and consider that this is thy particular time." And, "God stands this day and knocks. . . . The Lord knocks this day."[41]

The conclusion to many sermons was framed in the quasi-poetic style of the chanted sermon, characterized by repetition, rhyme, alliteration, and rhythmic cadence. Peter Burke has said that the chanted sermon was "exceptional in early modern Europe, although it could be found in Britain" among radical lay preachers on the enthusiastic fringe of Puritanism. He cites late seventeenth-century Dissenters who "were said to 'think they hear a very powerful preacher, if his voice be sharp and quavering, and near to singing; if he draws out some words with a mournful accent.'" New England orthodoxy has never been suspected of such preaching, but one instance at the end of a sermon by Thomas Shepard has already been partially quoted. Shepard repeated similar sounds both at the end of successive lines:

> . . . the time is not long,
> but that we shall feel what now we doe but heare of,
> and see but a little of,
> as we use to doe of things afar off

and within lines:

---

41. Hooker, *Application of Redemption, First Eight Books*, 210–212. C. Mather, *Magnalia Christi Americana*, II, 61. Hooker, *Application of Redemption, First Eight Books*, 213, 215. [Hooker], *Soules Implantation*, 66–68, 78. [Hooker], *Soules Humiliation*, 297. H[ooker], *Unbeleevers Preparing*, 180, 27. See Leverenz, *Language of Puritan Feeling*, chap. 6.

let us be scourged, and disgraced,
     stoned, sawn asunder, and burned;
let us live in sheep-skins, and goat-skins,
     destitute, afflicted, tormented.

Here repetition of the "s" sound gradually gives way to hard "t" sounds. Meanwhile, the sequence of seven exhortations in the identical pattern—"let . . . and"—builds to a tension-filled climax broken finally by the ejaculation "Oh glory, glory,/oh welcome glory."[42]

Transposition from printed prose form into verse recaptures something of the original oral qualities of the Puritan sermon. It is possible to imagine the voice of John Cotton at the conclusion of a discourse on "prayer in the Spirit."

Goe home therefore, and call to remembrance what you have
     heard,
let it be your care to observe
and lay up daily some fit matters for your prayers,
and lay up the chiefest of these against the times
     of your greatest mournings, and thanksgivings;
Lay them not up for a day or two before,
     but from day to day;
Lay up bulkie passages of Gods waies, and your owne,
     that you may have them in readinesse against speciall occasions,
and then keep your heart in a praying frame
     pure from wronging God or your brethren or neighbours,
and be sensible of what you come before God for,
and keep your hearts in a very reverent and holy awe of God,
and pray for what is according to Gods will for matter,
and according to the Spirit for manner,
and stand upon your watch-Tower, to see what God will answer,
and use the meanes to obtaine your desires,
and come with confidence that your persons and prayers are
     accepted,
and when you are in the lowest case, and make the poorest shifts,
then looke up to God, in the name of Christ,
and then shall you finde your prayers not drosie and dull
but such life in them, as will put a life in your callings,
and in all the duties that ever you perform,
and it will be a matter of much comfort and refreshment to you.

42. Burke, *Popular Culture in Early Modern Europe*, 133. Shepard, *Sound Beleever*, 316–317. See above, p. 61.

Cotton created the power of the passage by vigorously piling phrase upon phrase, connecting them first by "lay" and then by the conjunction "and." Alliteration and near-rhyme carry the listener along. Cotton followed "heard" with "observe" and "prayers"; and "matter" with "manner," "watch-Tower," and "answer." He combined "mournings" with "thanksgivings"; "persons" with "prayers" and "accepted"; and "drosie" with "dull" and "duties." The most rhetorically effective couplet is composed, save one word, of monosyllables: "Lay them not up for a day or two before,/but from day to day." The last two words even heighten the sense of immediacy with their homonym, "today." Whole phrases repeat for cumulative effect: ". . . according to Gods will for matter/and according to the Spirit for manner." And, perhaps most compelling: "and when you are in the lowest case, and make the poorest shifts,/then looke up to God in the name of Christ." Here Cotton linked two lines with the rhyme of "when" and "then," and the mirroring of the phrases "the lowest case" and "the poorest shifts" with "the name of Christ." The phrase "then looke up to God" breaks the tension, and the final lines form the denouement, a safe and gentle landing at the end of an exciting rhetorical flight.[43]

The most dramatic exhortation to union with Christ that survives in the sermon literature comes at the conclusion of a sermon, "The Soul's Invitation unto Jesus Christ," preached by Thomas Shepard on a text from the Song of Songs. After developing the doctrine that Christ desires to be "an earnest Suitor and a real Speeder, between every poor Soul and himself," Shepard *performed a wedding* and then sternly warned those who had refused to enter the bond. Shepard joined the emotion implicit in the doctrine of mystical marriage with the affective rhetoric of the preached sermon:

> If thou consenteth to match with Christ, he doth so with thee,
> and so I pronounce Christ and you married;
> as he was an earnest suitor, now he is become a real speeder,
> and you are made for ever happy,
> happy that ever you were born,
> happy that ever you saw him in the Ordinances,
> and that ever he came to thee in the way of love,
> that your time was a time of love,
> happy that ever he took delight in thee,
> and that your heart is come unto him
> to close with him,

43. Cotton, *Way of Life*, 420–421.

and to be his for ever blessed:
Man or Woman, thou art in a Heavenly condition already,
and shall enjoy him for ever,
I say, you are happy if you have him,
but miserable, and wretched for ever if you want him.
Poor wretch your condition is lamentable,
who ever thou art that hast not Christ,
thou art in an undone condition, who can express it;
who can make thee understand it, altho' we should declare it
    unto thee?
The Lord pity thee, and bow thy heart, and ear
to attend unto the things that belong
to thy everlasting peace, *Amen.*

Shepard's techniques in this remarkable passage were again repetition, alliteration, and rhyme. He coupled "thee" with "married," "suitor" with "speeder," "born" with "Ordinances," and "the way of love" with "the time of love." The same short words play off one another in different combinations:

and you are made for ever happy,
happy that ever you were born,
happy that ever you saw him . . .

and that your heart is come unto him
to close with him,
and to be his . . .

The crucial moment comes after Shepard has escorted the soul into Christ's bedchamber. One can imagine him lingering over the words, "I say, you are happy if you have him," then suddenly raising his voice: "but miserable, and wretched for ever if you want him!" By the sudden use of terror he caught up those who failed to follow. It was not too late, however, and Shepard ends with yet another gentle plea in the form of a prayer:

The Lord pity thee, and bow thy heart, and ear
to attend unto the things that belong
to thy everlasting peace, *Amen.*[44]

Thomas Shepard's startling line "I pronounce Christ and you married" is unique in New England sermon literature. But the intention of his exhortation, with its strongly liturgical overtones, was identical

44. Thomas Shepard, "The Soul's Invitation unto Jesus Christ," in Shepard, *The Saint's Jewel Shewing How to Apply the Promise* (Boston, 1743), 38.

with that of every sermon: to lead the person through the redemptive drama to the point where the heart and will say "yes" to union with Christ. It was especially in passages such as these that the Spirit was felt to work through the preacher's words. God Himself was present in the meetinghouse as the minister opened his mouth. Then, as Hooker put it, "there is the Concurrence of all Causes putting forth themselves for the work of Conversion."[45]

The Sacraments

The "seals of the Covenant" were administered after the sermon and prayer, the Lord's Supper in the morning (ideally once a month but actually anywhere from six to twelve times annually) and Baptism in the afternoon as occasion required. A subtle but important distinction was made between the sacraments and other ordinances. Like all ordinances, sacraments were outward means through which God worked. But other ordinances were "ordinary" means of grace while the sacraments were "special." Ordinances were ordinary in that they were employed daily or weekly; they were the stuff of regular worship and devotion. They were also ordinary in that they were practiced by every member of the social covenant—all inhabitants of New England without regard to church membership. The sacraments were special because they were administered only on specially designated Sabbaths and were restricted to members of the church covenant.[46]

The sacraments were another sign that the life of faith was an ongoing pilgrimage. The redemptive cycle that pervaded Puritan spirituality was seen at work in the sacraments. Baptism was the sacrament of preparation and implantation, and the Lord's Supper was one means whereby the saint continued to grow in grace after implantation. John Cotton's catechism, "Milk for Babes," asked, "What is done for you in baptism?" The answer that came back was, "The pardon and cleansing of my sins," since I am washed not only with water but "with the blood and Spirit of Christ." Baptism led to "my ingrafting into Christ" and "my rising out of affliction, and also . . . my resurrection from the dead at the last day." Ministers advised parents to teach children that "a solemn Covenant . . . between the God of heaven and them" is sealed in Baptism. This preparatory sac-

---

45. A similar use of matrimonial language appears in Cotton Mather, *Ornaments for the Daughters of Zion: Or the Character and Happiness of a Vertuous Woman* . . . (Boston, 1741 [orig. publ. Cambridge, Mass., 1692]), 78–79. [R. Mather], *Church-Government and Church-Covenant*, 79–80. Hooker, *Application of Redemption, First Eight Books*, 432.

46. Cotton, *Way of the Churches*, 68. Lechford, *Plain Dealing*, ed. Trumbull, 45–46.

rament sustained a person through childhood and acted as part of the preparatory stage of conversion. The typological interpretation of the rite of circumcision as the Old Testament precursor of Baptism further strengthened its connection with the preparatory stage: "Hence you may see what circumcision once did, and baptism now seals unto . . . that hereupon [God] will prune, and cut, and dress, and water them." The acts associated with circumcision were precisely God's actions in cutting the soul off from sin and pre-paring it for the graft onto the stock of Christ.[47]

Cotton's reply to the same question concerning the Lord's Supper was that the broken bread and poured wine were "a sign and seal of my receiving the communion of the body of Christ broken for me, and of His blood shed for me, and thereby of my growth in Christ, of the pardon and healing of my sins, of the fellowship of His Spirit, of my strengthening and quickening in grace, and of my sitting together with Christ on His throne of glory at the Last Judgment." Thomas Shepard's adult catechism concurred: Baptism was the sacrament of "our new birth, and ingrafting into Christ," and the Lord's Supper, "given to nourish and strengthen beleevers, renewing their faith unto eternall life," was the sacrament of "our growth in Christ." The rituals of Baptism and Communion as they were performed in New England churches reminded participants and witnesses of the redemptive drama that framed their spiritual existence.[48]

The pastor or teacher performed Baptism "in the Deacons seate, the most eminent place in the Church, next under the Elders seate." In infant baptism (and most, though not all, cases were) the parents presented the child "to the Lord, and his Church." The minister, acting "in Gods roome[,] calleth upon the parent to renew his Covenant with God for himselfe and his seed and calleth upon God as the nature of the Ordinance requireth for the pardon of originall sinne, and for the sin of the parents and for a blessing upon the Sacrament and Infant." The minister "most commonly makes a speech or exhortation to the Church, and parents concerning Baptisme, and then prayeth before and after." After the prayer, "calling the childe by the name which the Parent hath given it, for his owne edification, and the Childes he baptizeth it either by dipping or sprinkling in the name of the Father, the Son, and the Holy Ghost." Sprinkling probably predominated among New England churches.[49]

---

47. Cotton, "Milk for Babes," in Emerson, *John Cotton*, 130.

48. *Ibid.* Shepard, *First Principles*, 86. Thomas Shepard, *The Church-Membership of Children, and Their Right to Baptisme* . . . (Cambridge, 1693), 8. R. Mather, *Farewel-Exhortation*, 12.

49. Lechford, *Plain Dealing*, ed. Trumbull, 48. Cotton, *True Constitution*, 7.

The Lord's Supper, as the recent work of E. Brooks Holifield and Edward Taylor scholars has shown, became the center of much devotional activity in New England. One thrust of Puritan piety led to sacramental iconoclasm; at the same time the orthodox displayed a burst of "fascination with eucharistic devotional material" and "sacramental piety." The private aspects of this devotion will be discussed in chapter seven. In their public worship New Englanders maintained a doctrine of the real presence that differed little from Calvin. "By the symbols of bread and wine," Calvin had written, "Christ, his body and blood, are truly exhibited to us . . . that being made partakers of his substance, we might feel the result of this fact in the participation of all his blessings." Yet he also warned that "the presence of Christ in the Supper we must hold to be such as neither affixes him to the element of bread, nor encloses him in bread, nor circumscribes him in any way." Thomas Hooker and others wrote in the same vein, that the bread and wine "present Christ neerly and visibly to the soule. They shew Christ's merits and obedience, inflaming our hearts with love to him." And Hooker, like Calvin, warned that we must look "beyond our outward elements, and see the spirit of Christ."[50]

An entry from Samuel Sewall's diary demonstrates the extent to which at least some New Englanders believed in Christ's real presence. Young Sewall, on account of coming to the table without a lively faith, worried that "for the abuse of Christ I should be stricken dead; yet I had some earnest desires that Christ would, before the ordinance were done, though it were *when he was just going away*, give me some glimpse of himself; but I perceived none." Sewall consoled himself with his increased desire "for the next Sacrament day, that I might do better." His startling phrase suggests popular belief in the literal presence of Jesus Christ in the meetinghouse during the Sacrament.[51]

The minister would announce the scheduled celebration two weeks in advance, to remind members to prepare themselves for the Sacrament. Thus, whether or not all worshipers engaged in extensive private preparatory exercises, if administered monthly, the Sacrament was either mentioned or administered on three weeks out of four or five. On Sacrament day, after the sermon, prayer, and psalm, the nonmembers in the congregation were dismissed with a blessing, and the members remained in their pews. The ministers and "ruling Elders" took their places at the table, in conscious reenactment of Jesus' Last

50. Holifield, *Covenant Sealed*, 74. John Calvin, *Institutes of the Christian Religion*, trans. Henry Beveridge (Grand Rapids, Mich., 1966 [orig. publ. Edinburgh, 1845]), II, 564, 571. Thomas Hooker, *An Exposition of the Principles of Religion* (London, 1645), 28. Hooker, *Paterne of Perfection*, 375.

51. Thomas, ed., *Diary of Samuel Sewall*, I, 40. Italics added.

Supper. The words of institution, or solemnization, were the traditional ones from the gospels:

> The Minister taketh the bread and blesseth it, and breaketh it, and giveth it to the brethren with this commandement once for all, to take and eate it, as the body of Christ broken for them, and this doe in remembrance of him; in like manner also he taketh the cup, and having given thanks, he powreth it forth, and giveth it to them, with a commandement to them all, to take and drink it as the bloud of Christ shed for them, and this also to do in Remembrance of him.

The minister took the elements first, then gave them "to all that sit at Table with him, and from the Table is reached by the Deacons to the people sitting in the next seates about them, the Minister sitting in his place at the Table." Deacons distributed the bread in a charger and the wine in a single cup. The elements were blessed and distributed separately, first the bread, until all had eaten, and then the wine. The people received the elements sitting in their pews, not, as in Catholic and Anglican liturgy, kneeling at a rail before an altar. Lechford pointed out, perhaps with some justice, that since all members were seated, some could not see the consecration of the elements.[52]

Through the words of institution, the eucharistic prayer, and the symbolism of the bread and wine the people were led once again through the stages of the redemptive drama revealed in the work of Christ. The Lord's Supper was occasion for renewed repentance followed by the experience of union with Christ. In a visually and verbally explicit way it reminded believers of the order of redemption that sustained their lives. Christ Himself was present offering that salvation to them. After the Sacrament was completed the people sang a psalm of thanksgiving, based on the model in Matthew 26:30, and were dismissed with a blessing.[53]

Mutual Communion

Under the heading of the ordinance of mutual communion we may discuss several communal rituals that acted as public means of grace. These include the ceremony surrounding the gathering of a new church, especially the act of covenant making; the call and ordina-

52. Lechford, *Plain Dealing*, ed. Trumbull, 46. Cotton, *Way of the Churches*, 68–69. Cotton, *True Constitution*, 7.
53. Cotton, *True Constitution*, 7.

tion of a pastor; covenant renewal; the ceremony admitting new members into the church; catechism of the young; the collection of contributions for needy saints; and the exercise of discipline, excommunication and absolution. All these were marked by the themes already established, so that the celebration of any one ordinance reinforced the whole sense of New England's part in God's plan of salvation. Worship in New England was a system of complementary parts geared to run together. When one element was in danger of malfunctioning, as was Baptism by the end of the 1660s, adjustments were made to preserve the ordinance and the integrity of the system. In the face of social change, covenant renewal, incipient from the beginning, emerged as a key ordinance in the last two decades of the century. Like the Halfway Covenant, the covenant-renewal ceremony was an adjustment, but not a failure, in the Puritan devotional system.

New Englanders were brought into the order of redemption by virtue of the covenant, and that covenant, with God and with one another, supported the ordinances of mutual communion. The making of the church covenant was the primary ordinance upon which the others were built. The gathering of a church was an act of public worship undertaken by a small number of charter members. Richard Mather noted that typically "about eight or nine" men acted as a church's founding members. At Dedham there were ten, "whome we had best hopes of for soundnes of grace and meete guifts for such a worke." These included the man who had been academically trained for the ministry, who had reached a tacit agreement with the other members concerning his pastorate. Even if the minister had been ordained in England, the church founders acted as if he were unordained or at least not fully ordained until they publicly chose and reordained him. In the second half of the century new towns were likely to be settled with fresh Harvard graduates. Managing the gathering of the church would be one of the graduate's first tasks.[54]

The charter members and the minister-to-be prepared for months by attending meetings "lovingly to discourse and consult together." They fasted and prayed among themselves, and each spent an entire day "to open every one his spirituall condicion to the rest, relating the manner of our conversion to god and the lords following proceedings in our soules with present apprehensions of gods love or

54. Perry Miller developed the Puritan idea of the covenant in all its ramifications in *New England Mind: Seventeenth Century*, chaps. 13–16. Richard Mather to William Rathband and Mr. T., June 25, 1636, Emerson, ed., *Letters from New England*, 202. *Dedham Church Records*, 1–13. See Kenneth A. Lockridge, *A New England Town, The First Hundred Years: Dedham, Massachusetts, 1636–1736* (New York, 1970), chap. 2.

want thereof." The men presented their spiritual qualifications to the town, then discussed further "the nature of the covenant" before setting a date for the ceremony.[55]

The church covenant was finally consummated on a day devoted to public professions of faith, many prayers and sermons, and the singing of psalms. Although it was a local affair, other churches were invited and gave their consent to the proceedings. The charter members signed, read, and officially "owned" the covenant document that was the product of their labors. Each step was carefully taken, since New Englanders believed that the hope of future purity rested on this "foundation work."[56]

The day for gathering a church was proclaimed "a day of solemn humiliation," of "fasting and prayer," because covenant making entailed subjection to God and thus resembled the mood of the preparatory stages of salvation. The making of a covenant, after all, was the work of preparation to be God's people. Worship began with a prayer of confession of sin. After the regular order of worship was complete, the future minister and the other founding members again related publicly their faith and experiences of grace. The covenanting ceremony then opened with visitors from other churches voicing their assent to the proceedings. Everyone said a prayer "for the presence of the Lord" and for grace to keep the covenant. The minister-to-be "publikly read the covenant whereof they had all agreed before," and the founding members owned it by "lifting up of hands." After the concluding prayer visiting clergy offered each member "the right hand of fellowship, in token of the loving acceptations of us into communion with them in the lord." The following day a thanksgiving service was held at the meetinghouse.[57]

The minister was likely to be ordained several months after the covenanting ceremony. A recent graduate called to an already-gathered church could also expect a waiting period between his arrival and his ordination. The pastor and lay leaders were officially elected "by the joint and free votes of the church," again on a day of fasting. At Dedham, even though the minister, John Allen, had guided the founding members through the making of the covenant, only after they "in ther judgments remaine satisfied" that he was "in some

55. *Dedham Church Records*, 5–10.

56. On the development of the covenant as a document, see Williston Walker, *The Creeds and Platforms of Congregationalism* (Boston, 1960 [orig. publ. New York, 1893]), 116–117, 131, 154–156.

57. R. Mather to Rathband, Emerson, ed., *Letters from New England*, 202. *Dedham Church Records*, 10–13.

measure guifted and by providence provided for that place," did they "in due time" proceed to "a sollemne election and ordination." Lay ordination with the laying on of hands by the lay "ruling Elders," or "some prime men in the name of the church," was characteristic of the early decades. Visiting clergy participated only by voicing their consent and extending the right hand of fellowship. By the second half of the century, with the rise of professionalism and in defensive response to a changing society, ordination increasingly became a ritual under clerical control. The 1672 ordination of William Adams to the Dedham pulpit represents a transitional stage: a neighboring minister gave "the charge" to Adams, two lay leaders of the church performed the laying on of hands, and another minister "gave the right hand of fellowship." By 1681, when Peter Thacher was ordained in Milton, the shift was complete. The entire cast was made up of clergy: "1 June 1681. This day I was Ordained (though most unworthy) Pastour of the Church in Milton. My Text 2. Tim. 4. 5. Mr. [Increase] Mather Called the votes, Old Mr. Eliot, Mr. Mather, Mr. Torry, Mr. Willard laid On hands. Mr. Torry gave the Charge, Mr. Willard Gave the right hand of fellowshipe. We sung the 24 ps. Then I gave the blessing." Cotton Mather's 1685 ordination before "one of the vastest Congregations that has ever been seen in these parts of the World" was identical, with Mather himself praying and preaching for three hours, and the Boston area ministerium conducting the entire ceremony. Mather commented that his ordination "produc[ed] a greater Number of moved Hearts and weeping Eyes, than perhaps have been at any Time here seen together." As the mirror image of the clergy's taking over the ordination procedure, local congregations became more reluctant to rush into the ordination of a candidate. Trial ministries were stretched out for years and were distressing experiences for young graduates. The ritual of ordination was owned by the clergy, but the call to ordination remained solely in the hands of the laity.[58]

The covenant of the church was the point of reference for other ordinances of mutual communion. The admission of new members, for example, centered not just on the owning of the covenant by the applicants but on a reaffirmation of the covenant by the entire church. Admission of new members was in effect a reenactment of the first founding of the church. Richard Mather said explicitly that "Members are admitted as the church state was first erected, viz., by solemn

58. R. Mather to Rathband, Emerson, ed., *Letters from New England*, 203. *Dedham Church Records*, 17–20. Hall, *Faithful Shepherd*, 47, 79, 106, 220–222, and chap. 8. "Memoir of the Rev. William Adams," Mass. Hist. Soc., *Colls.*, 4th Ser., I (1852), 20–21. Thacher, "Diary," MS, I, 212. Ford, ed., *Diary of Cotton Mather*, I, 98–99.

confession publicly before the whole church and by joining with the church in the covenant, in which the church was joined at her first gathering together." The same kind of preparatory discussion and prayer and confession of faith that preceded the first covenanting typified subsequent owning of the covenant. On the day of their covenanting, at the close of the afternoon service, applicants made "profession of ther faith unto the Church" by reading their spiritual relation. The pastor formally questioned them on their agreement to the terms of the covenant and on their willingness "to submitt themselves to every ordinance of Christ in that church, to walke in spirituall communion with Christ and his people therein, and in a way of Christian love to the Church according to the rule of the gospell." If found acceptable by congregational vote, they formally assented to the covenant. The minister "rehearseth the covenant, on their parts, to them, which they publiquely say, they doe promise, by the helpe of God, to performe." The minister "in the name of the Church, then promiseth the Churches part of the covenant, to the new admitted members" and gave them the right hand of fellowship.[59]

The administration of discipline, including the ultimate act of excommunication, was an occasional but established part of the afternoon service, continuing "sometimes till it be very late." This too was a celebration of the covenant. By judging one another, sometimes quite critically, on the basis of the covenant, New Englanders reaffirmed the bond that held church and society together. The taking up of collections for needy saints, also an irregular part of Sabbath worship, and the catechism of the young in the doctrine and ways of the church were ordinances that further maintained the ecclesial bond. The covenant was, in fact, implicitly renewed on these many occasions.[60]

The sacraments were more explicit renewals of the covenant. In Baptism, as an infant was brought into covenant, the members were reminded of and urged to reaffirm their part in the church covenant and the covenant of grace. Popular eucharistic manuals and Sacrament day sermons encouraged the understanding that "in receiving the Lord's Supper, we renew covenant with God." In receiving the elements the communicants would find grace "to live a new life . . . as

59. R. Mather to Rathband, Emerson, ed., *Letters from New England*, 202. *Dedham Church Records*, 20–21. Lechford, *Plain Dealing*, ed. Trumbull, 29.

60. Lechford, *Plain Dealing*, ed. Trumbull, 29–34. See Wilberforce Eames, *Early New England Catechisms: A Bibliographical Account of Some Catechisms Published before the Year 1800, for Use in New England* (New York, 1898); "Rev. John Eliot's Records of the First Church in Roxbury, Mass.," *NEHGR*, XXXIII (1879), 239; and "The Rev. John Fiske's Notebook," Mass. Hist. Soc., *Proceedings*, 2d Ser., XII (1897, 1899), 318–319.

having renewed [their] covenant with the Lord for that purpose."[61]

For the clergy, covenant making and covenant renewal were means of reformation in the church. In New England, where a truly new beginning was possible, John Allen and Thomas Shepard wrote, "Reformation is to be sought in the first Constitution" of churches. Covenant renewal was a way "corrupted Churches (such as we conceive the Congregations of England generally to be) are to be reformed." If such congregations could be "called by able Ministers unto repentance for former evills, and confessing and bewayling their sins, renew a solemn Covenant with God to reform themselves, and to submit unto the disciplines of Christ," then the English church could be reformed. Yet even newly covenanted New England churches soon adopted a ritual of covenant renewal. Just as Shepard and Allen urged covenant renewal in England as a way to reform originally pure but long since corrupt churches, the ceremony in New England became a means to recapture original purity after only a few years of perceived declension.[62]

Scholars have associated the covenant-renewal ceremony with the results of the Reforming Synod of 1679–1680 and with the worship practices of the late seventeenth century. As early as the first decade, however, church leaders feared declension and initiated the ceremony. John Winthrop noted in his journal that on February 25, 1636, at the onset of the Antinomian tensions, the Boston Church renewed its covenant. Other concerns, such as Hooker's move to Hartford and "the great scarcity of corn," also led the lay elders to proclaim "a general fast." Winthrop recorded: "The church of Boston renewed their covenant this day, and made a large explanation of that which they had first entered into, and acknowledged such failings as had fallen out, etc." The Reverend John Fiske, who served three churches over the course of his career, introduced a covenant-renewal ceremony at the beginning of his tenure in at least the first and third. At Salem in 1636 he used the ceremony to enlarge the doctrinal content of the original covenant. Salem's enlarged covenant was explicitly intended as a renewal of the first: "Wee whose names are here under written, members of the present Church of Christ in Salem, having found by

---

61. Increase Mather, *Renewal of Covenant the Great Duty Incumbent on Decaying or Distressed Churches . . .* (Boston, 1677), 6–7. Francis Roberts, *A Communicant Instructed, or, Practical Instructions for Worthy Receiving of the Lords-Supper* (London, 1651), cited in Wilfred W. Biggs, "Preparation for Communion: A Puritan Manual," *Congregational Quarterly*, XXXII (1954), 17.

62. John Allen and Thomas Shepard, "Preface to the Reader," in Shepard, *Treatise of Liturgies*, 10.

sad experience how dangerous it is to sitt loose to the Covenant wee make with our God: and how apt wee are to wander into by pathes, even to the looseing of our first aimes in entring into Church fellow-ship: Doe therefore solemnly in the presence of the Eternall God, both for our own comforts, and those which shall or maye be joyned unto us, renewe that Church Covenant we find this Church bound unto at theire first beginning." Similarly in 1656, within a year of Fiske's settling in Chelmsford, during a "publick general fast," "in the close of the day was the Church Covenant renewed, repeated, and voted by the Brethren." Fiske viewed the start of his ministry as an opportunity for a new beginning—or more correctly, a renewal of the first beginning—for the church. His motivation included a sense of declension and the need for reformation. It was, as John Winthrop said of himself in 1636, "as if the whole work had been to begin anew."[63]

Covenant renewal during the first half of the century was under-taken in conjunction with a fast day, at the end of a day of public re-pentance. This was utterly characteristic of New England spirituality and reflected the manner of original covenant making. Churches were gathered on a day not of thanksgiving but of fasting. Covenants were entered in a spirit of contrition, not jubilation. A day of thanks-giving was proclaimed later, but making a covenant was preparatory work; in contrition and humiliation believers prepared for union with God in the covenant. The act of covenant renewal thus involved preparation for renewed life in Christ. Self-examination, repentance, and all the stages of preparation that were expounded first in relation to conversion were also the marks of the day of renewal. Reformation of church and society, like the rebirth of an individual, would come only after the painful travail of preparatory contrition and humilia-tion. And as did the individual, so the congregation had to traverse these stages again and again if progress was to be made. In covenant renewal—and in all the ordinances of mutual communion—the sal-vation drama found in the Bible and heard from the pulpit was enacted once more.

63. Walker, *Creeds and Platforms*, 435. Hall, *Faithful Shepherd*, 242–244. Winthrop, *Journal*, ed. Hosmer, I, 175. "Extracts from Records Kept by the Rev. John Fiske during His Ministry at Salem, Wenham and Chelmsford," Essex Institute, *Historical Collections*, I (1859), 37. "The Rev. John Fiske's Notebook," Mass. Hist. Soc., *Procs.*, 2d Ser., XII (1897, 1899), 325.

WORSHIP IN CIVIL SOCIETY

Every inhabitant of the New England colonies was by definition a member of the social covenant and hence took part in a number of devotional acts that attended the civil year. Chief among these were election day, militia training days, and civil days of fasting and thanksgiving proclaimed by magistrates. Weddings were civil affairs, and no evidence indicates that ministers participated in them or that they carried religious significance. Funerals, however, took on more religious and ecclesiastical characteristics as the century progressed, with the clergy involved first as fellow mourners and finally as officiating preachers and pastors. Besides these, execution sermons stirred public interest from time to time. But throughout the century election day, training days, and public days of fasting and thanksgiving were regular events on the civil calendar that had spiritual impact on people's lives.[64]

In the capitals of the New England colonies a minister was invited every year on election day to preach a sermon on the general theme of the godly society and the duties of magistrates and citizenry. The sermons, especially those preached in Boston, were frequently printed, thus giving us access to a significant body of New England social thought. The perennial message was New England's special election by God. As Jonathan Mitchel preached in the most powerful of seventeenth-century election sermons, *Nehemiah on the Wall in Troublesom Times* (1667), the people of New England were "the People of the God of Israel." He advised those who had just been elected to the General Court:

> The Concernments of a People framed into a Body Politick,
> are put into your hands, . . . a part of Gods *Israel*, though but a
> part, yet no inconsiderable part of the people of God at this day
> in the world: such a part of Gods people as are retired to these
> Ends of the Earth, for known ends of Religion and Reformation.
> . . . You are betrusted with as precious an Interest as is this day
> upon the Earth, viz. with the Lives, Estates, Liberties, and Religious Enjoyments of some thousands whose Names are written in
> Heaven, and bound upon the Breast and Heart of Christ Jesus
> . . . The eyes of the whole Christian World are upon you; yea
> which is more, the eyes of God and of his holy Angels are upon
> you.

64. Stannard, *Puritan Way of Death*, chap. 5. Ford, ed., *Diary of Cotton Mather*, I, 279.

The great function of the election sermon, as Mitchel makes clear, was social integration and continuity. The power of his dramatic statement "The eyes of the whole Christian World are upon you" came less from its political realism than from its symbolic value. By echoing Winthrop's original phrase, Mitchel asserted that in spite of social change, in spite of any decline in piety, in spite of the more complex and less significant role of New England after the Restoration, New England was still New England. "The eyes of God" were still fixed on New England. Election sermons imbued civil election with the character of a covenant-renewal ceremony. Through these sermons the themes of Puritan spirituality continued to assert themselves in the culture.[65]

The third public institution (in addition to church and civil government) in which ministers led worship was the militia. Militia companies invited local pastors to pray with and preach to their members throughout the century. In the 1680s, for example, Peter Thacher regularly attended Milton training days, as in November 1681: "Being sent for I went and prayed with our Military Company, then went and dined with Sargant Badcock and Sargant Vose and the rest of the officers." Most of the officers were also leaders of the church, so that the social institutions of the New England town reinforced one another and worship was a major cohesive force in society. The annual election of local company officers called for a sermon, some of which were published. Preachers tended to take one of two approaches. They might follow Urian Oakes in his popular sermon, *The Unconquerable All-Conquering & More-Then-Conquering Souldier* (1674), and spiritualize the figure of the soldier to teach every citizen a lesson. "Every true Believer is a Souldier, and engaged in a Warfare," Oakes preached, elaborating the familiar theme of the saints' "Holy Warre" against the "Enemies of his Soul," sin and Satan. He continued, "I would it were reciprocally true, that every Souldier amongst us is a true Believer." Or the preacher could follow the path of Samuel Nowell's *Abraham in Arms*, which celebrated New England military might as the arm of the Lord. Nowell went so far as to preach that the New England militia was a means of worldly grace: "Our Military Strength is, under God, the appointed means, or in the ordinary way of Providence, is the proper and only means for our preservation;

---

65. Jonathan Mitchel, *Nehemiah on the Wall in Troublesom Times* . . . (Cambridge, Mass., 1671), 2, 18–19. See A. W. Plumstead, ed., *The Wall and the Garden: Selected Massachusetts Election Sermons, 1670–1775* (Minneapolis, Minn., 1968). Of special note is Thomas Shepard, [Jr.], *Eye-Salve, or a Watch-Word from Our Lord Jesus Christ unto His Church* . . . (Cambridge, Mass., 1673).

therefore it is a duty to encourage Souldiers." He reached millennialist heights reminiscent of Edward Johnson's *Wonder-Working Providence.* "It will not be long ere the Lord will call out Souldiers" for the final battle. The New England training day was for Nowell preparation for Armageddon.[66]

Sermons preached at public fasts and days of thanksgiving likewise served to integrate New England society along the lines of the original covenant. Public fast-day sermons, like their ecclesiastical counterparts, invariably called the people back to their beginnings, pleading that New England must continue to understand itself as God's own people. Though society was always more complex than the ideal presented in any sermon, to assert that the preaching was ineffectual or anachronistic is to ignore the continuing power of the myth of New England and the pervasiveness of the redemptive drama in the popular mentality. The myth and the drama were not the property of the clergy and a few magistrates but were rooted in the culture. The persistence of these themes in public worship in church and society, and the inhabitants' almost daily contact with them, leads us to infer that the rhythms and content of the rituals shaped ways of thinking and acting.[67]

66. Thacher, "Diary," MS, II, 237. The Boston, Cambridge, and Charlestown companies followed the same practice of hearing a sermon and prayer, with Cotton Mather as chaplain in the mid-1680s. Thomas, ed., *Diary of Samuel Sewall,* I, 79–80. Urian Oakes, *The Unconquerable All-Conquering & More-Then-Conquering Souldier . . .* (Cambridge, Mass., 1674), 4. S[amuel] N[owell], *Abraham in Arms . . .* (Boston, 1678), 11, 19. See Darrett B. Rutman, "A Militant New World, 1607–1740: America's First Generation, Its Martial Spirit, Its Militia Organization, Its Wars" (Ph.D. diss., University of Virginia, 1959). It may be significant that Oakes's almost pacifist sermon and Nowell's militarist sermon were preached just before and just after King Philip's War, respectively.

67. The best examples of fast-day sermons are John Davenport, *Gods Call to His People to Turn unto Him . . .* (Cambridge, Mass., 1669), and Thomas Thacher, *A Fast of Gods Chusing, for the Help of Those Poor in Spirit, Whose Hearts Are Set to Seek the Lord Their God in New-England . . .* (Boston, 1678). See Bercovitch, *Puritan Origins,* 132–133, and Bercovitch, *American Jeremiad,* 23–30.

Chapter Five

Private Devotion

Neighborhood, Family, Conference

 In his delineation of "the way of godly conversation" John Eliot encompassed much more than public worship. The system of formal religious exercises that constituted the private devotional life of New Englanders could also be considered as means of grace, according to Eliot. These exercises included reading of Scripture and other devotional books, various types of meditation, prayer, psalm singing, the keeping of a diary or other spiritual records, and "conference," or consultation, with a spiritual counselor. Everything believers did in their "daily walk" required what Eliot and the devotional writers called "spiritual armour." Every aspect of life's pilgrimage could be turned to devotional purposes through meditative self-examination and prayer. The term "private devotion" refers, therefore, to more than the individual or "secret" exercises that we will consider in chapter six. It served as a general descriptive term for all worship and devotional activity that occurred outside the walls of the church and other official public gatherings. New Englanders engaged in private devotion in a variety of settings throughout the day and week. In descending order in number of persons involved (and in ascending order in degree of privacy), private devotion took place in: private meetings, family devotions, private conference, and secret exercises.

From the first decades devout New Englanders complained in diaries and sermons that there was "not so much Prayer in New England" as there ought to have been—that people were "not gaining much in private duties, in Prayer, Meditation, Reading, and daily Examination of a mans own heart." In the final decades of the century this concern provided part of the impetus for calling the Reforming Synod of 1679. "As to what concerns Familyes and the Government thereof, there is much amiss. There are many Familyes that doe not pray to God constantly morning and evening, and many more wherein the Scriptures are not daily read, that so the word of Christ might dwell richly in them." But the ministers' jeremiads, which usually opened with a critical analysis of the state of private religion, always ended by celebrating its continued reality and importance. As John Eliot and Cotton Mather preached, "Let no man say, ' 'Tis impossible to live at this rate.' . . . New England has examples of this life." Increase Mather similarly extolled the devotional way: "What people under Heaven have ever had more encouragement unto Prayer, then we have had? Know it enemies to your terrour; Know it all the world, That the Lords poor New-England People, have ever found him to be a God that heareth Prayer: and therefore let's be at that work still. And truly, there is as much need now as ever. We may even say, as sometimes that blessed Martyr did, 'Pray, pray, pray, never more need than now.'" Mather's conclusion (which I have again transposed into verse form) underscored the devotional life that had from the beginning been the heart of life in New England:

> But I know
> that there are many, scores, Hundreds here this day,
> that have an Interest in Heaven,
> and know how to improve it.

> Why, then be up and doing.
> If thou hast but one tear in thy eyes,
> if thou hast but one Prayer in thy heart.
> spend it now.[1]

PRIVATE MEETING

At New England's regular weekly, biweekly, or monthly private meetings in homes, Eliot explained, "we pray, and sing, and repeat sermons, and confer together about the things of God." Believers were there given an opportunity to exercise gifts that on the Sabbath were reserved for the clergy alone. Also referred to as "conference meeting" and "society of conference," the practice was a continuation of English experience and an expression of the lay nature of the Puritan movement. During persecution the private conventicle had often

1. Eliot, "Sermon," in C. Mather, ed., *Life and Death of J. Eliot*, 19–21. Shipton, ed., "Autobiographical Memoranda of John Brock," Am. Antiq. Soc., *Procs.*, N.S., LIII (1943), 100. Thomas Shepard, *Subjection to Christ* (London, 1657 [orig. publ. 1652]), 52. "The Necessity of Reformation," in Walker, ed., *Creeds and Platforms*, 429. Increase Mather, *The Day of Trouble is Near . . .* (Cambridge, Mass., 1674), 30–31.

been the only setting for Puritan worship. In New England pastors agreed on the importance of "private members" exercising such weekday ministry "in Christian communion for men and women." Indeed, Thomas Shepard wrote, "in some cases, a private Brother may do more than a Minister." Thomas Hooker concurred: "A man that is asleepe cannot awaken himselfe, but another man, that is but new awake . . . can stirre another better than himselfe." Shepard listed six ways the private meeting could act as a channel for the Holy Spirit: (1) in such a small group Christians could more easily express "love for one another"; (2) as a community of prayer it could exercise "earnest prayer for the Church" of which it was a part; (3) by "timely Exhortation" members could apply the Gospel to others in a direct way; (4) it gave members the opportunity to engage in "instructing and teaching one another, as occasion serves"; (5) it could be a means of God's grace "in Comforting those that be sad" or in mourning; (6) it was a forum in which members, even those "fallen with a spirit of meekness," could learn to express their faith and the gifts of the Spirit more boldly. These were the churches' goals in promoting private meetings among their membership throughout the century.[2]

Private meetings were an effective means of integrating individuals into the devotional matrix of New England spirituality. John Hull, for example, noted in his diary that in August 1666 the meeting to which he belonged held a special fast day in honor of his father's death. "Our private meeting kept at our house a day of humiliation to show their sympathy with me, and to implore the Lord for his poor people here, to direct us and our rulers, etc., and for his poor suffering saints in England." Ten years later Hull's son-in-law Samuel Sewall took up residence in his home and began attending the same group, now convening every other week on Wednesday under the auspices of the Third Church. Sewall made an entry in his diary every time he attended, thereby providing us with data on the regularity and significance of the meetings. The lay character of the gatherings is evident: In January 1677 he "went to the Meeting at Mis. Macharta's, which is the 10th I have been at. The Script. spoken to was Hoseah 6. 3. . . . Capt. Henchman handled it." At the "privat Fast at Brother Williams's" in December 1685, "Capt. Scottow begins and is enlarged and fervent in praying for the Church and Christ's Witnesses: Made me conclude. Sung part 137. Ps." Sometimes ministers did preach, however, as when the meeting was held at Sewall's home in February

2. C. Mather, ed., *Life and Death of J. Eliot*, 20. Thomas, ed., *Diary of Samuel Sewall*, I, 29. Bayne, *Briefe Directions*, 113–114. Shepard, *Subjection to Christ*, 48–51. H[ooker], *Soules Vocation*, 522. Woolley, "Shepard's Cambridge Church Members," 122.

1686: "Mr. Willard preached excellently from Act. 1. 7. I had pray'd before, privatly, and he prayed at the Meeting in the very same words, that God would make our Houses Bethels." "Many People" were present. Once Sewall had joined this devotional group, nothing interfered with his attendance except travel. Not even the death of a child, as the vignette in chapter one shows, kept him away. Integral to New England devotional life, the private meeting became a significant part of mourning and of the funeral ceremony. To stay away at such a time of crisis would be to deny the efficacy of the system. If the means of grace brought pain, Sewall believed, they would in due course bring joy as well.[3]

The private meeting was a bridge between church and society. It helped usher Samuel Sewall into membership in Boston's Third Church. At the meeting, church members became acquainted with Sewall's gifts, his spiritual progress, and his quality as a prospective member. The private meetings enabled young Peter Thacher to gain experience as a still unordained pastor. A Harvard graduate seeking a call to a pulpit, he could preach only now and then on the Sabbath. But various neighborhood meetings invited him to lecture to them. For example, "Goodman Reed of the North End of the towne Came to desire mee to speak at a meeting at Br. Berrys from 4 Amos 11 [–12]." He was sometimes paid, though a truly lay member would certainly not receive remuneration for similar work. "This afternoon I spake at Mr. Haywards," the public notary, and he "gave me a Crowne for my paines, the Lord be praised for then I stood in need of it."[4]

At Harvard College, tutors and godly senior students organized private meetings "to further the Reformation of the College." In 1643–1644 John Brock discovered after much "private Conference" with younger fellow students that "some of the wild ones in the College begin to turn." He "thought to persuade to a private Meeting." Brock successfully accomplished this and began to discern clear evidence of God's work among the students. "As the Students grow better, and are acquainted with me, so I am refreshed by them." Tutors such as Michael Wigglesworth, who conducted meetings during the 1650s, believed that their responsibilities at the college included the

3. Hull, *Diaries*, 156. Thomas, ed., *Diary of Samuel Sewall*, I, 33, 89, 97. Sewall mentions the private meetings throughout his diary, virtually every two weeks. For specific references, see "private (prayer) meetings" in the index of the Thomas edition. Thomas is wrong in thinking that the meeting to which Hull and Sewall belonged originated in 1676 when Sewall himself began to attend. It began at least a decade earlier, prior even to the founding of the Third Church (p. 29n).

4. Thomas, ed., *Diary of Samuel Sewall*, I, esp. 28–90. Thacher, "Diary," MS, I, 6, 22, Mass. Hist. Soc., Boston.

promotion of such spirituality among the students. These tutors, and many of the participating students as well, went on to become pastors and carried their experiences into ministry in the churches.[5]

The enormous popularity of private meetings in the Bay Colony from the beginning of settlement was revealed during the Anne Hutchinson controversy. In her trial Governor John Winthrop demanded, "What say you to your weekly publick meetings? can you shew a warrant for them?" She answered simply that "there were such meetings in use before I came." Winthrop replied: "There were private meetings indeed, and are still in many places, of some few neighbours, but not so publick and frequent as yours, and are of use for increase of love, and mutuall edification, but yours are of another nature." In the Hutchinson home, as at all private meetings, participants read over sermon notes from previous Sabbaths "and then reason of them by searching the Scriptures." The elders charged that study of sermons had led to prideful criticism of local preaching. The court argued that Mrs. Hutchinson searched the Bible not to "confirm . . . the truths delivered" but to "open your teachers points, and declare his meaning, and correct wherein you think he hath failed."[6]

The infringement of conventional gender roles was also an issue: "Priscilla with her husband, tooke Apollo home to instruct him privately, therefore Mistris Hutchinson without her husband may teach sixty or eighty." Female leadership of mixed meetings was an innovation that the Massachusetts magistracy firmly brought to a stop after Hutchinson's expulsion. When she confessed, "Ey Sir, I shall not equivocate, there is a meeting of men and women and there is a meeting only for women," she overstepped the bounds of Scripture (1 Corinthians 14:34 and 1 Timothy 2:12). Women's prayer groups continued, though since they caused no further sedition, the record of them is meager. These meetings were, indeed, one New England institution fully under the control of women, and they no doubt provided a major opportunity for women's self-expression. Even ministers did not directly participate in, or perhaps even know much about them. Cotton Mather noted in 1706 the novelty of his involvement: "In the afternoon of this day, I visited a Society of devout Women, who were keeping this, as a Day of private and solemn Thanksgiving

5. Albert Matthews, ed., *Harvard College Records*, Pt. I, *Corporation Records, 1636–1750* (Colonial Society of Massachusetts, *Collections*, XV [Boston, 1925]), Introduction, cxxi–cxxiv. [John Eliot], *New Englands First Fruits . . .* (London, 1643), 14. Shipton, ed., "Autobiographical Memoranda of John Brock," Am. Antiq. Soc., *Procs.*, N.S., LIII (1943), 99–100. Morgan, ed., *Diary of Wigglesworth*, 29, 59.
6. Hall, ed., *Antinomian Controversy*, 267–268.

unto God. I prayed with them, and I preached to them, on 1. Sam. 2. 1. ['And Hannah prayed . . . because I rejoice in thy salvation.'] It may be, I am the only Man in the World, that has preached unto such an Auditory!" Leadership of women's groups, therefore, seems to have rested in the hands of women. Men held the leadership of mixed groups and, of course, of men's meetings. The successful resolution of the Antinomian controversy led to a tightening of clerical authority, but private meetings were not censured or abandoned. Nor did the clergy crush the essentially lay nature of the practice, although they carefully watched and controlled it.[7]

The joining of neighbors into devotional groups thrived through the final decades of the century. All the ministers encouraged neighborhood prayer, but the greatest promoter was Cotton Mather. When he found that "several religious Families there are among us, not yett joined unto any of the private Meetings in our Neighborhood," he resolved to "address them, to gett into this way of their Edification." By 1700 Mather boasted "thirteen or fourteen" neighborhood assemblies under his pastoral leadership. Ministers began developing new organizational patterns as well. The clergy in the second half of the century became increasingly concerned with youth, unmarried men, and other special social groups. At Middletown, Connecticut, for example, the Reverend Noadiah Russell started a monthly gathering in which "several young men met . . . in the evening for Religious exercises." Cotton Mather recorded in 1681 a day of "Fasting and prayer with our Young men's Meeting." In the winter of 1683 he met with "the young people of our Congregation" who "kept this as a Day of Thanksgiving, together; for the Success of the Gospel here; and for the Lives of my Father, and my wretched Self, who dispense it." With characteristic zeal, he wrote: "The Lord helped mee to preach unto them almost three Hours (tho' I had little more than one Hour's Time to prepare for it). . . . And a good Day it was!" Mather organized fortnightly private meetings of "Gentlemen belonging unto our Congregation" and their families—a class distinction—"wherein they shall . . . seek the Face and hear the Word of God." At the other end of the spectrum he brought together "a company of poor Negroes." The "Rules for the Society of Negroes" was published as a broadside in 1693.[8]

7. *Ibid.*, 268–269, 314–318. Ford, ed., *Diary of Cotton Mather*, I, 579.

8. Ford, ed., *Diary of Cotton Mather*, I, 135, 58, 197, 411, 80. *Diary of the Reverend Noadiah Russell of Ipswich, Mass. and Middletown, Conn. for the Old Style Year 1687* (Hartford, Conn., 1934), 16, hereafter cited as *Russell Diary for 1687*. [Cotton Mather], *Rules for the Society of Negroes, 1693* (Boston, 1693).

The private meetings of the ministers themselves may have spurred the formation of other groups, dividing society along lines of occupation, class, and sex, for devotional activity in the second half of the century. Williston Walker traced the ministerial meetings to the 1630s when, Winthrop wrote, "the Ministers in the bay and Saugus did meet, once a fortnight, at one of their houses by course, where some question of moment was debated." The *Body of Liberties* of 1641 granted the clergy "free libertie to meete monthly, quarterly, or otherwise, in convenient numbers and places . . . by way of brotherly conference and consultations." The ministers denied that they were succumbing to presbyterianism. Though ministerial associations were not without political significance, and though they contributed to the growth of professionalism, they were intended primarily for the devotional life of the clergy. Pastors worshiped together as theologically trained peers without the sense of being the spiritual leaders, as was the case at the lay meetings they attended. The Boston ministers' meeting introduced Peter Thacher into the profession, at least as a junior member, at a time when he was still an unemployed graduate living at home. He wrote, "Mr. Torry invited mee to come to the ministers meeting which was to be at Mr. Fisks the next weensday." During his long tenure at Milton, which began in 1680, Thacher attended the Boston ministerium every two weeks. When the group met at his house he centered the discussion on worship and devotion itself:

> 20. 10. 1681. The Ministers meeting was at my house.
> Mr. Torry, Mr. Fisk, Mr. Hobard, Mr. Whiteman, Mr. Adams,
> Mr. Danfort. Question was what are those speciall spirituall acts
> of worship whereby the soul doth set toward and upon god. 1. In
> his word, [2.] in prayer, 3. in the sacraments. God did much
> warme and inlarge my heart in prayer and in speaking and made
> it a good day, blessed be his holy name; they all stayed this night;
> Mr. Torry and Mr. Adams lodged at quarter mrs. the other four
> lay together in my bed.

After these sessions Thacher commonly recorded in his diary that "God made it a good day to my soul, drew out my heart much after himself." The devotional aim of the ministers' meetings was shared by the laity as they gathered in their neighborhoods.[9]

The essential form of the private meeting did not change, even as it

---

9. Walker, *Creeds and Platforms*, 467–471. Lechford, *Plain Dealing*, ed. Trumbull, 37. Hall, *Faithful Shepherd*, 220–222. Robert F. Scholz, "Clerical Consociation in Massachusetts Bay: Reassessing the New England Way and Its Origins," *WMQ*, 3d Ser., XXIX (1972), 391–414. Thacher, "Diary," MS, I, 22, 245, 28, and *passim*.

was adapted to meet changing needs and desires toward the end of the century. Society was becoming more specialized, stratified, diverse, and secular. As distinct social groups within the population became increasingly important, private devotional groups were created specifically for them. These supplemented but did not replace the old, more organic, neighborhood meetings. Even the ministerial meetings took on a new significance as the profession became more specialized. The Boston Association, organized in 1690, reflected the profession's need to protect its interests and identity. Within its fellowship, and within the fellowship of smaller local chapters throughout New England, ministers were able to find the spiritual and social support required to carry the old way into a changing age.[10]

FAMILY DEVOTIONS

When Roger Clap, near the end of his earthly pilgrimage, wrote his memoirs for the spiritual benefit of his offspring, he included as a private devotional manual a series of charges. One of these concerned the well-being of the family: "Worship God in your Families. Do not neglect Family Prayer, Morning and Evening. And be sure to Read some part of the Word of God every day in your Families, in ordinary Course. And be sure to Instruct your Families in the Grounds of Religion. And be yourselves Patterns, by your holy Lives and Conversations, unto your Children." Clap thought of himself as a pattern. "If you observed any Virtues in your Parents, (though they were but few) Imitate them in that which is Good, that God may be with you, as He was with your Fathers." It is impossible to say if Clap's children observed family devotions with the same strictness, but the memoirs leave the impression that he exerted his influence until his death at eighty-two in 1690.[11]

Accounts by other New Englanders exemplify the importance of family devotions. When Samuel Sewall's infant Henry died in 1685, it was the family's prayers together that gave them hope. Throughout the baby's last moments the family read and prayed. Death was not an external event to which family members reacted in prayer; it was an event within the devotional matrix. Other entries in Sewall's diary indicate the daily nature of the family's exercises. Theorizing on the importance of these prayers, John Cotton even suggested that the serious exercise of family piety was a sign of grace. "Would any man

10. On the Boston Association, see Hall, *Faithful Shepherd*, 220–222.
11. *Clap's Memoirs*, 48.

or woman know whether they have received a spirit of grace and prayer, or no? why aske thine own heart, dost thou pray with thy Family?" In his next breath Cotton warned against the dangers of hypocrisy, but he had established the importance of the exercises both in theory and in practice.[12]

Scholars writing on the New England family and on Puritan religious practices point to the family as a religious unit. The family was "a little church," with the father as priest. Edmund S. Morgan's description of the daily practices is correct in its outline. Family devotions consisted chiefly of morning and evening Scripture reading, prayer, and psalm singing, and of thanksgiving at meals. The Bible was read "in course," sequentially by chapter from beginning to end, and family members often took turns reading aloud. Morgan cites Cotton Mather's account of his grandfather's practice. John Cotton read a chapter of Scripture "with a little applicatory exposition, before and after which he made a prayer; but he was very short in all, accounting as Mr. Dod, Mr. Bains, and other great saints did before him, 'That it was a thing inconvenient many ways to be tedious in family duties.'"[13]

The Mather quote is suggestive not only in its description of the exercises but also in its mention of two well-known devotional writers. Puritans from the late sixteenth century on believed that manuals written by Dod, Bayne, and others were useful for family worship. Richard Baxter wrote fully in this tradition when he advised ministers to "see that they have some profitably moving book (besides the Bible) in each family: If they have not, perswade them to buy some of small price, and great use; such as Mr. Whatelyes New Birth, and Dod on the Commandments; or some smaller moving Sermons. . . . And engage them to read on it at nights when they have leisure and especially on the Lords day."[14]

The manuals New Englanders used were the tools of family devotion and usually gave specific guidance on how to conduct it. Models were deemed important for developing the ability to meditate and pray freely and extemporaneously, as Roger Clap's charge to his offspring shows. Cotton Mather observed: "I plainly see, that from

---

12. Thomas, ed., *Diary of Samuel Sewall*, I, 89. Cotton, *Way of Life*, 94–95.

13. Edmund S. Morgan, *The Puritan Family: Religion & Domestic Relations in Seventeenth-Century New England*, rev. ed. (New York, 1966), esp. chap. 6. John Demos, *A Little Commonwealth: Family Life in Plymouth Colony* (New York, 1970), esp. 12–13. Davies, *Worship and Theology*, I, 422–423, 429–430, II, 123–132. Greven, *Protestant Temperament*. The quote from *Magnalia Christi Americana* is cited in Morgan, *Puritan Family*, 136–137.

14. Baxter, *Gildas Salvianus*, 85–86.

the public Prayers I make in our Congregation, my Hearers take Example, for their own private Prayers. Oh! then, Lett mee therein bee so affectionate, so argumentative, so instructive, so intending to sett an Example for their Devotions." The manuals, along with the Bible and the guidance of the pastor, served the same function of determining the wording and rhetorical patterns of private devotion. In fact, the picture of daily family devotions that appears in the manuals corresponds closely with that revealed in diaries and other private writings. I believe we may therefore take the printed prayers in the manuals as models of the actual prayers said in New England families.[15]

Morning prayers in the family normally began with the confession of sin and a plea for forgiveness but quickly proceeded to an expression of thanksgiving for God's blessings. Lewis Bayly opened his "Morning Prayer for a Family" in *The Practice of Piety* with the confession that "we have been born in sin, and do daily break thy holy Laws and Commandments." George Webbe began similarly in "A Short Direction for the Daily Exercise of a Christian": "O most mighty and eternall God, who art the Creator, Guider, Governor, and preserver of all things both in Heaven and Earth; Vouchsafe wee humbly beseech thee, to looke downe with the eyes of pitty and compassion upon us miserable and wretched sinners, who at this time are prostrate here before thee, to offer up this our morning Sacrifice of Prayer and Thanksgiving unto thee." Both prayers, then, in reciting the stages of the order of redemption, proceed to give God "hearty thanks, for thou hast elected, created, redeemed, called, justified, and sanctified us in good measure in this life, and given us an assured hope that thou wilt glorifie us in thy heavenly Kingdom." Prayers commonly concluded with a repetition of the Lord's Prayer.[16]

The model "Morning prayer to be used in private families" in Arthur Dent's *The Plaine Mans Pathway* was even more clearly a prayer of thanksgiving: "O Lord our God, and heavenly Father, wee thy unworthy children do here come into thy most holy presence, to give thee praise and glory, for all thy great mercies and manifold blessings toward us." The prayer gave thanks for preservation "this night past from all the dangers and feares thereof," for the "quiet rest to our bodies," and for the hope of coming "safely to the beginning of this

15. Geo[rge] Web[be], "A Short Direction for the Daily Exercise of a Christian," in Ri[chard] Ro[gers] *et al.*, *A Garden of Spirituall Flowers* (London, 1625), 100–102. Ford, ed., *Diary of Cotton Mather*, I, 135.

16. Bayly, *Practice of Piety*, 203–205. Web[be], "Daily Exercise," in Ro[gers] *et al.*, *Spirituall Flowers*, 114–119.

day." The family prayed for God "now [to] renew all thy mercies upon us, as the Eagle renueth her bill. . . . O Lord open our eyes every day more and more, to see and consider of thy great and marvelous love to us in all these things . . . even as it were force our hearts, and compel us to come into thy most glorious presence with new songs of thanksgiving in our mouths." Dent's prayer ended on an eschatological note, entreating God "to set thy self against the Antichrist of Rome" and to "Powre down the Vials of the fulnesse of thy wrath upon the kingdome of the Beast." The same sort of conclusion would have characterized New England prayer, including prayer for the victory of Reformed churches abroad and the coming of the Kingdom of God. Progress through the order of redemption pointed invariably to the eschaton.[17]

Psalm singing was typically part of family devotion, and the psalms recommended for morning use also adhered to the theme of thanksgiving. *The Practice of Piety* recommended, among others, Psalm 22, which begins (in the *Bay Psalm Book* version) with the cry of despair—"My God, my God, wherefore hast thou forsaken me?"—but moves, through the use of childbirth imagery, to an affirmation of God's preservation of life.

> But thou are hee that me out of
>   The belly forth didst take:
> when I was on my mothers breasts,
>   to hope thou didst mee make.
>
> Unto thee from the tender-womb
>   committed been have I:
> yea thou hast been my mighty-God
>   from my mothers belly.

It concludes with a triumphant look to the future:

> With service a posterity
>   he shall attend upon;
> to God it shall accounted bee
>   a generation.
>
> Come shall they, and his righteousness
>   by them declar'd shall bee,
> unto a people yet unborn,
>   that done this thing hath hee.[18]

---

17. Dent, *Plaine Mans Pathway*, sigs. Dd–Ee4.

18. *Whole Booke of Psalmes*, Psalm 22: 1, 9, 10, 30, 31. Other psalms for morning use suggested in Bayly, *Practice of Piety*, 216–217, are 3, 5, 16, and 144.

The language of childbirth was appropriate to morning devotions. God awakened the believer from sleep to a new day in a manner reminiscent of his or her original physical birth. God delivered the person from darkness into light, from danger into life. The imagery of birth and awakening to the new day also called to mind the believer's second birth and salvation in Christ. Natural rebirth in the morning after a night's sleep thus signified and brought to mind the new birth in the Spirit. Dent's morning prayer "O Lord open our eyes every day more and more" referred to awakening in the morning but also harkened back to the opening of the eyes at birth, the spiritual sight gained in rebirth, the increased sight of growth in grace, and the future full vision of God on the other side of death. The devotional writers used the awakening of the body in the morning as an emblem of this progressive spiritual rebirth.

Devotions during the day centered on mealtime, with prayers offered before and after eating. Prayers "before Meate" commonly gave God thanks for providing sustenance but were offered in utmost humility. Puritans focused their thoughts before eating on their own weakness in requiring food and on God's omnipotence in providing it. Curiously death was a theme as believers thanked God that "beasts, fish, and fowl" were sacrificed for human survival. The consumption of animals as food taught a further lesson. Puritans humbled themselves with the thought that the bodies now being fed would be "(thou knowest not how soon) meat for worms." A typical "Thanksgiving before Meate" incorporated these themes:

> O Lord our God and heavenly Father, which of thy unspeakable mercy towards us, hast provided meate and drinke for the nourishment of our weake bodies. Grant us peace to use them reverently, as from thy hands, with thankful hearts: let thy blessing rest upon these thy good creatures, to our comfort and sustentation: and grant wee humbly beseech thee, good Lord, that as we doe hunger and thirst for this food of our bodies, so our soules may earnestly long after the food of eternall life, through Jesus Christ our Lord and Saviour, Amen.

The family ate in a spiritual manner, their food becoming a reminder of God's nourishment of the soul. The prayers lent an almost sacramental quality to daily meals. The themes of meditation and prayer in preparation for the simple act of eating are striking in their use of the religious language of preparation for salvation.[19]

19. Bayly, *Practice of Piety*, 208–212. Web[be], "Daily Exercise," in Ro[gers] *et al.*, *Spirituall Flowers*, 113.

The prayer after the meal voiced the fulfillment of the preparatory hopes. "To thee O Lord, which has created, redeemed, continually preserved, and at this time fed us, be ascribed all honor, glory, power, might, and dominion, now and evermore." The prayer concluded by looking to the eschaton: "Finish soone these daies of sin, and bring us to everlasting peace, through thy Sonne our Lord and Saviour Jesus Christ, Amen." As the family moved away from the table and back into the world they directed their eyes once more toward the Kingdom. The prayer before eating invoked the preparatory stages of redemption. Prayer afterward employed images of the second half of the order: the beginning of the fulfillment of God's work in the soul and a foretaste of perfection. Families in New England who prayed in the manner set forth in the manuals reenacted on a small scale the experience of God's salvation of their souls.[20]

Evening devotions in the family, like those in the morning, consisted of Scripture reading, perhaps an exposition of the passage, psalm singing, and prayer. Peter Thacher recorded a session that continued quite late—"This night between 11 and 12 a Clock my maid Lydia Chaffin when I was at prayer fell down on the flower in a swonde"—but family prayer was commonly conducted earlier, between the end of the meal and the start of individual secret devotions. In contrast to morning devotions, evening prayers were characterized almost entirely by repentance for sin, especially for the sins of the day. Family members were to "loke back unto thy former workes of the day; call thy soule to a scrutiny." In this way evening devotions again evoked the themes of preparation for salvation. Historians have usually interpreted the preparationism of Thomas Hooker and others in New England with reference to the conversion experience alone. But the scheme was also played out on a daily basis in private devotions. Hooker's classic definition of contrition was "that Preparative Disposition of the Heart, when by the sight of sin, and the punishment due to the same, the soul is brought to sound sorrow for it, and so brought to detest it, and to sequester it self from it." In evening devotions the penitent died to sin in contrition and humiliation in preparation for sleeping in the hands of God and in hope of being born again in the morning of God's Spirit. Sleep became a means of grace. "Commit thy selfe, both body and soule into the hands of God, who after these Exercises thus spent, will give thee an holy sanctified rest and sleep." Sleep was sanctified if it was emblematic of dying in Christ.[21]

20. Web[be], "Daily Exercise," in Ro[gers] *et al., Spirituall Flowers,* 113–114.
21. Thacher, "Diary," MS, I, 19–20. Web[be], "Daily Exercise," in Ro[gers] *et al., Spirituall Flowers,* 98. Hooker, *Application of Redemption, Ninth and Tenth Books,* 16.

In his "Evening prayer to be used in Private families" Arthur Dent petitioned God that by confessing the day's sins "we may daily die to sin, and live to righteousnesse." Lewis Bayly's prayer confessed, "Our Hearts are full of secret Pride, Anger, Impatience, Dissembling, Lying, Lust, Vanity, Prophaneness, Distrust, too much love of our-selves and the World, too little love of thee and thy Kingdom; but empty and void of Faith, Love, Patience, and every Spiritual Grace." Affirming that Christ's "bitter death and bloody passion" were "suf-fered for us," the Puritan family prayed, "O let us feel the Power of Christ's Death killing sin in our mortal Bodies." Only through such nightly "Repentance from dead works" did the hope of "his Resur-rection raising up our Souls to newness of Life" become real.[22]

When the family prepared for sleep, their thoughts turned speci-fically to death and the hope of resurrection. "Living in thy fear, and dying in thy favour," the evening prayer went, "we may in thy ap-pointed time attain to the blessed Resurrection of the just unto Eternal Life." A safe night's sleep was suggestive of sleeping eternally with Christ after death. New Englanders prayed for protection from dan-gers such as fire, robbery, and other perils that threatened their physi-cal lives; salvation from these threats gave rise to the hope of salvation for their souls. They prayed "that sleeping with thee, we may in the next morning be awakned by thee; and so being refreshed with moderate sleep, we may be the fitter to set forth thy Glory." Psalms designated for evening use contain the same theme of death. New Englanders sang from Psalm 141, for example:

> O God, my Lord, on thee I call,
>   doe thou make hast to mee . . .
> Bow not my heart to evill things;
>   to doe the wicked deed . . .
> ev'n so our bones at the graves mouth
>   are scattered abroad.
>
> But unto thee o God, the Lord
>   directed are mine eyes:
> my soule o leave not destitute,
>   on thee my hope relyes . . .[23]

The cycle of the redemptive drama of death and resurrection was therefore expressed, not as a morning-to-evening cycle, but as an evening-to-morning cycle. As Scripture states, "Evening, and morn-

22. Dent, *Plaine Mans Pathway*, sig. Dd6–Dd7. Bayly, *Practice of Piety*, 217–222.
23. Bayly, *Practice of Piety*, 217–222. *Whole Booke of Psalmes*, Psalm 141: 1, 3, 7, 8.

ing, and at noon, will I pray, and cry aloud: and he shall hear my voice" (Psalm 55:17). Saints spent the waking hours in the world, the place of sin, where they were called by Scripture to "die daily" (1 Corinthians 15:31). Evening devotions provided the setting for family members to scrutinize their carriage during the day and in the acts of psalm singing and prayer to die to their sin through renewed repentance. The entire day, then, may be seen as preparatory to lying down in the temporary grave of the bed. Morning would again (God willing) bring cause for rejoicing. Morning was the time to know and feel that God had "elected, created, redeemed, called, justified, and sanctified us."

These were the words and rhythms of family devotional exercises in the manuals used in New England, to whose authors Cotton Mather referred in connection with his grandfather's family devotions. The same pattern was set out on the Sabbath in public worship, was reinforced in the continually repeated lessons of the catechisms, and was explained by the pastor when he came to call. Believers worked through the cycle of repentance and renewal every evening and morning. On a snowy evening in the winter of 1681, after spending the day secluded in his study, Peter Thacher found family devotions a particularly powerful experience. "This night," he recorded in his diary, "I was much Inlarged in family Exercise after Catechizing, and in family prayer the Lord helped mee much in wreastleing for a blessing. I found my spirit goe out Extreordinarily god ward. I pleaded that wee could not let him goe etc. The Lord grant that what I then found (which I cannot Expresse by words) may be found really the strong workings of faith, and not a hot fit of transient passion."[24]

Family devotions should not be characterized as an emotionless routine, even though the acts were based on repetition and routine. For Puritans they were means of grace, acts through which the redemptive drama was reenacted and reexperienced, exercises in which the soul might move toward and even experience union with Christ.

PRIVATE CONFERENCE

Parents, ministers, and all saints had an obligation to watch over the spiritual welfare of their family members and neighbors. Conversely, as the manuals pointed out, believers ought to seek out "much conference, especially with Ministers and other experienced Christians."

24. Thacher, "Diary," MS, I, 247.

In Bunyan's *Pilgrim's Progress* private conference is what makes Christian's journey at all possible. Time and again as destruction is imminent the advice and comfort of a fellow pilgrim enable him to press on. Private spiritual counseling guided individuals through the conversion experience; screened church members and led them to make a public profession of faith; enabled parents to bring their children and servants to the experience of grace, and saints to help one another grow in grace. John Cotton wrote of the helpfulness of the "presence and assistance of a Christian friend in learning to pray." In "A Letter . . . to His Friend," Jonathan Mitchel urged:

> If you had a friend with whom you might now and then spend a little time, in conferring together, in opening your hearts, and presenting your unutterable groanings before God, it wou'd be of excellent use: Such an one would greatly strengthen, bestead, and further you in your way to Heaven. Spend now and then (as occasions will permit) an hour (or so) with such a friend more then ordinary (sometimes a piece of a day, sometimes a whole day of extraordinary fast, in striving and wrestling with God for everlasting mercy.) And be much in quickning Conference, giving and taking mutual encouragements and directions in the matters of Heaven! Oh! the life of God that falls into the hearts of the Godly, in and by gracious Heavenly Conference. Be open hearted one to another, and stand one for another against the Devil and all his Angels. Make it thus your business in these and such like ways, to provide for Eternity.

The private counseling and mutual support that occurred in this way was the third major setting for private devotion.[25]

Private conference among peers is illustrated by an episode recorded by William Adams, who was able to act as counselor, while yet a student, to a graduating senior at Harvard. Adams's "good friend Penom." came to him with a vocational crisis that also had serious spiritual implications. "Penom" was uncertain about whether or not his call to the pulpit of a church was from God, and this uncertainty seems to have raised the deeper question for him of whether God had called him to the ministry at all. Worse yet, "Penom" now wondered if God had even called him in election as a saint! After much consultation and prayer with Adams, the young man engaged in intense se-

---

25. John White, *A Way to the Tree of Life: Discovered in Sundry Directions for the Profitable Reading of the Scriptures . . .* (London, 1647), sig. A4. Cotton, *Modest and Cleare Answer*, 36. Mitchel, "Letter to His Friend," appended to *Discourse of the Glory*, 2d ed., 285–286.

cret prayer. "Having lost himself in the mazes of divine goodness, he applyes himselfe to the Omnipotent One; leaves himselfe with him." "Penom" presumably accepted the call to the church. Another student, John Brock, also wrote of the importance of private conference, not with peers but with mentors. "My Tutor [Henry Dunster] very loving," he wrote. "I had good experimental Conference with his Wife; and so by little and little I knew many Saints here." Thomas Shepard, pastor in Cambridge, called on Brock and "spake very lovingly to me." Brock in turn developed his own ability as a spiritual guide while at Harvard. Through preliminary exercises of private conference he was able to gather students into established private meetings. Later, as pastor at Reading, he continued to perfect his skill in counseling. When he died in 1688 his successor wrote: "He was a man who excelled most men in Faith, Prayer, and private Conference."[26]

The pastor of a church held private conference with persons who were preparing for membership and continued his spiritual counseling once they had joined. Peter Thacher recorded some of these conversations at Milton. "Good-wife Keney came to speak with mee and gave an account of much workings of spirit toward the Lord and her desire to Injoy god in all his ordinances. I went to prayer with her and soe dismissed her." On another occasion, "Father Vose came to my house and Brother Tucker soe I took them up into my study and went to prayer. Then father Vose told his Experiences and Brother Tucker and I were satisfyed and I concluded with prayer." At such pre-covenantal conferences Samuel Sewall was able to get help with his spiritual anxiety. His counselor was Peter Thacher's father, pastor of Boston's Third Church. In January 1677, Sewall wrote that he "went to Mr. Thachers, found him at home, mentioned my desire of communion with his Church, rehearsed to him some of my discouragements, as, continuance in Sin, wandering in prayer. He said 'twas thought that was the Sin Paul speaks of, Rom. VII. At my coming away said he thought I ought to be encouraged." Sewall waited several months before approaching Thacher again. In March he returned to

26. "Memoir of the Rev. William Adams," Mass. Hist. Soc., *Colls.*, 4th Ser., I (1852), 10–11. Shipton, ed., "Autobiographical Memoranda of John Brock," Am. Antiq. Soc., *Procs.*, N.S., LIII (1943), 99. "Extracts from the Diary of Rev. Jonathan Pierpont," *NEHGR*, XIII (1859), 256. For examples of private conference conducted through letter writing, see Calder, ed., *Letters of Davenport*, 27–29; Hall, ed., "Autobiography of Increase Mather," Am. Antiq. Soc., *Procs.*, N.S., LXXI (1961), 279; Samuel E. Morison, ed., "The Commonplace Book of Joseph Green (1675–1715)," Col. Soc. Mass., *Transactions*, XXXIV (1943), 226–229; Paul Bayne, *Christian Letters, of Mr. Paul Bayne . . .* (London, 1637); and Mitchel, "Letter to His Friend," appended to *Discourse of the Glory*, 2d ed.

the pastor's home intent on further conference with Thacher and Elder Rainsford. "Mr. Thacher . . . took us up into his Chamber; went to prayer, then told me I had liberty to tell what God had done for my soul. After I had spoken, prayed again. Before I came away told him my Temptations to him alone, and bad him acquaint me if he knew any thing by me that might hinder justly my coming into Church. He said he thought I ought to be encouraged, and that my stirring up to it was of God." By the end of that month, Sewall's doubts being sufficiently resolved and the church leaders' questions about his state answered, he joined in the covenant.[27]

Diaries refer to the need for private conference after covenanting as well. Pastoral calls on the sick were one important type of conference. In a typical diary entry, Peter Thacher wrote that one morning in Barnstable, "while I was at dutys Mr. Thomas Huckins came to Call me to his Mother who was very ill. . . . I prayed with her." After his visit, the next day Thacher spent the entire afternoon "at Deacon Cowpers with Mr. Hinckley, Elder Chipman and some other brethren in prayer for Mrs. Huckins. Elder began, then Brother Bearce, then Mr. Hinckley, and Last my selfe."[28]

Spiritual maladies were the reason for other conferences. The Puritan locus classicus, as it were, was Thomas Hooker's ministry in England with Mrs. Joan Drake. New England pastors viewed spiritual counseling of the type successfully undertaken by Hooker as a central part of their ministries. Noadiah Russell of Middletown, Connecticut, for example, noted visits of troubled parishioners in his diary. "Jonothan Higbys wife came to me manifesting many doubts and difficulties about her [spiritual] condition." Another woman, under the ban of excommunication, came for private conference seeking absolution and readmission. "Widdow Hubbard excommunicant came to me at several times before about her [spiritual] condition."[29]

Private conference was not always occasioned by problems, however. "Mr. Torrey here," Sewall entered in 1685, "prays with me and my Wife in the Morning." Spiritual progress or thanksgiving for answered prayer called for a visit with the minister. A parishioner came to Peter Thacher reporting that he "did verily believe [he] was the better for my prayer the day before, for the feaver presently left him and the swelling of his legs was downe; the Lord is the hearer of

---

27. Thacher, "Diary," MS, I, 216. Thomas, ed., *Diary of Samuel Sewall*, I, 33–40.

28. Thacher, "Diary," MS, I, 67–68.

29. For Hooker and Mrs. Drake, see George Hunston Williams, "The Life of Thomas Hooker in England and Holland, 1586–1633," in Williams *et al.*, eds., *Hooker: Writings*, 4–6, and Shuffelton, *Thomas Hooker. Russell Diary for 1687*, 15–16.

prayer." Private conference, in short, was a means by which pastors sought to build and maintain the numbers and spiritual progress of those in church covenant.[30]

Parents were the other primary initiators of private conference, pursuing issues that arose in family devotions or in daily life. The best known cases are Samuel Sewall with his children Betty and Sam and Cotton Mather with his daughter Katy. These exemplify the father's duty to guide his children through conversion. The force behind each of these conferences was the children's anxiety: about their spiritual state; about their own mortality; and about the mortality of their parents. In private conference the father applied the appropriate scriptural passage to the child's fears, explained the theological answer to the problem, gave advice on how to pray effectively, and offered comfort that God would deal faithfully with the child. The father himself prayed with the child. Cotton Mather wrote that at the end of his conference with Katy, "I thereupon made the Child kneel down by mee; and I poured out my Cries unto the Lord, that Hee would lay His Hands upon her, and bless her and save her, and make her a Temple of His Glory. It will be so; It wil be so!"[31]

Other diaries record similar instances of parental prayer with children and servants. Peter Thacher counseled his melancholic maid for months on end, as she repeatedly "came into [his] study and gave an account of her late sore deserted state." When the girl was "ready to draw up deadly conclusions against herself," Thacher "called her in to the study and laboured to Convince her that It was a temptation." When again she was "much over powered with Mallincholly," Thacher recorded, "I had discourse with her in the study about it. She told mee shee was almost weary of life. I told her shee had many times made god waite upon her, now shee must waite for the mercy which shee needed." The Thachers finally were forced to send her home to her parents, who were still primarily responsible for her, until her depression passed. Joseph Green recalled conferences with his father: "In my Infancy (it may be when I was about 4 or 5 years old at most) my father used to tell me I must be a good boy and must serve God, and used to ask me whether I went alone and prayed to God to bless me and to pardon my sins and save my soul from hell; and I sadly remember how my corrupt heart used to hate such motions; I loathed to hear of such things[;] this is that which should humble me before God."[32]

30. Thomas, ed., *Diary of Samuel Sewall*, I, 80. Thacher, "Diary," MS, I, 250.

31. Thomas, ed., *Diary of Samuel Sewall*, I, 249, 349. Ford, ed., *Diary of Cotton Mather*, I, 239–240. Both are cited in Morgan, *Puritan Family*, 137–139.

32. Thacher, "Diary," MS, I, 19, 24, 69, 89–91, 116–119, 235, 237, II, 7–9. Morison,

The father was not always the one who took the child aside. Green also remembered his mother's involvement: "My parents were very careful to instruct me in the principles of religion." A man joining the Cambridge Church testified that in the stage of humiliation, "the Lord seeing me into this case I made use of daily family instructions from my father, mother which did somewhat stay my spirit." Increase Mather wrote in several places of the great influence his mother had on his spiritual development. She frequently took him aside in private conference for prayer and advice, and Mather traced his call to the ministry to her words. One suspects that conferences between parents and children involved mothers as often as fathers.[33]

As the pastor and other church members used the private conference to maintain the church covenant at a personal level, so parents used it within the household to keep the family covenant strong. Formal public worship and general family devotions regularly strengthened the bonds of both church and home. Through private conference New Englanders aimed to strengthen one another in more immediate and personal spiritual crises and to nurture one another in spiritual growth.

ed., "Commonplace Book of Joseph Green," Col. Soc. Mass., *Trans.*, XXXIV (1943), 236.

33. Morison, ed., "Commonplace Book of Joseph Green," Col. Soc. Mass., *Trans.*, XXXIV (1943), 236. Woolley, "Shepard's Cambridge Church Members," 184. Hall, ed., "Autobiography of Increase Mather," Am. Antiq. Soc., *Procs.*, N.S., LXXI (1961), 278–279. Increase Mather, *Awakening Truth's Tending to Conversion* . . . (Boston, 1710), ix.

Chapter Six

Private Devotion

Secret Exercises

 Important as family prayer was in the pattern of Puritan devotional life, a deeper and more intimate practice of devotion lay at the very heart of New England spirituality. "Secret," or "closet," devotions were considered imperative, mandated by Christ Himself: "When thou prayest, enter into thy closet, and when thou hast shut thy door, pray to thy Father which is in secret; and thy Father which seeth in secret shall reward thee openly" (Matthew 6:6). Secret exercises were the most powerful channels through which grace might flow, whereby New Englanders attained their highest reaches of mystical experience. If sleep was emblematic of death, secret devotions performed immediately before retiring and upon waking formed the bridge at either end that connected life with death and death with new life. They provided the crucial point of contact between the believer and God; without them the outward forms of public worship and family devotions could become hollow and hypocritical performances. In John Bunyan's nine stages of apostasy, the first step was the abandonment of "private Duties, as Closet-Prayer, curbing their lusts, watching, sorrow for Sin, and the like." John Cotton wrote, "You say you have been at prayer in the Family, but hast thou been so by thy selfe? if not, I say not that thou wantest grace, but I feare that thou wantest a spirit of prayer . . . it is a suspition of hypocrisie, if a mans gifts be onely Family gifts."[1]

I take exception, therefore, to the commonly held thesis, argued most fully by Horton Davies, that Puritan devotion found its highest expression in family worship. Davies contrasted the active, family-oriented Protestant with the contemplative, monastic Catholic. "It would rarely occur to a Protestant to define prayer as the means of

---

1. Web[be], "Daily Exercise," in Ro[gers] *et al., Spirituall Flowers*, 92, 98. Shepard, "Journal," in McGiffert, ed., *God's Plot*, 88. Bunyan, *Pilgrim's Progress*, ed. Wharey and Sharrock, 153–154. Cotton, *Way of Life*, 94–95.

unity with God as St. John Fisher did so eloquently: 'Prayer is like a certaine golden rope or chaine lett downe to us from heaven and by God himselfe fastened to our hearts . . . soe that att last it is made one spirit with God.'" But Puritans did define prayer in exactly these terms. Secret prayers recorded in New England diaries, in devotional manuals, and in devotional poetry indicate that prayer was a means of union with Christ. Richard Baxter, whose *Saints Everlasting Rest* was as popular in New England as in old, spoke for Puritans throughout the century when he advocated meditation and prayer on the Sabbath: "What fitter day to ascend to heaven, then that on which our Lord did arise from earth."[2]

Three major exercises comprised the practice of secret devotion. In general order of performance they were reading and study of the Bible and other devotional books, meditation, and prayer. Individuals also engaged in occasional psalm singing, and diary keeping and other personal spiritual writing in conjunction with meditative self-examination and prayer. In addition to the two or three regular times ideally set aside daily, "extraordinary" meditation and spontaneous, or "ejaculatory," prayer were possible at any time. For more prolonged exercises believers underwent days, or partial days, of secret fasting and thanksgiving. And weekly, the Sabbath provided special opportunity for individual meditation and prayer.[3]

READING AND STUDY

"To reade the word, and to meditate thereon, is a daily part of a Christian holy life," John Cotton preached. "A man cannot heare it every day, but he may read it most dayes, and if not reade, yet he may meditate upon it in his journies." For New Englanders, who were relatively literate and book-oriented Protestants, reading was an important part of public worship and family devotions. In individual secret devotion, reading was the basis for the deeper exercises of meditation and prayer. The reading and study of religious texts, though an intellectual activity, did not primarily or finally have an intellectual end. The

2. Davies, *Worship and Theology*, I, 422–423. Richard Baxter, *Saints Everlasting Rest: Or A Treatise of the Blessed State of the Saints in Their Enjoyment of God in Glory . . .* (London, 1650), 703.

3. Cotton Mather's diary contains notes on his programs for fast and thanksgiving days as well as other periods of devotional exercise. See, for example, Ford, ed., *Diary of Cotton Mather*, I, 56–58. Mather mentions his use in his private devotions of William Barton's *Select Hymns*, which went through numerous editions in London from 1651 through the 1680s under various titles.

exercise of the rational faculty opened the way to a changed heart. In this way private reading corresponded to the reading of Scripture and explication of text and doctrines in public worship. The vignette of Thomas Shepard in chapter one illustrates how the minister's private intellectual analysis of a biblical text led to his heart's being "sweetly ravished" by Christ. "God requires that you should get knowledge by reading," Cotton wrote, "not of small matters, but of your possession of everlasting life." The Holy Spirit must "stirre up every soule, when you goe about to read the word; I beseech you, if you would not reade the word in vaine, then read it in faith. . . . Therefore, when ever you goe about to reade, lift up your hearts to Heaven, that God would give you a faithfull heart, to looke at all the word as neerely concerning you. Labour so to read, as that you may suck life from it." For Increase Mather and most other ministers in New England reading the Bible and devotional books was a means of conversion. "God has blessed not only the Preaching of Sermons, but the Writing of Books, for the Conversion as well as the Edification of many Readers." As evidence of the efficacy of such reading Mather cited the well-known case of the young Richard Baxter's reading of "Mr. Perkins and some other old Puritan Writers." Richard Mather similarly regarded reading as an ordinance. In one of his last published works he exhorted: "Christian, thou that readest these lines, Lift up thy heart unto God, and pray that he would give thee such an heart that thou mightest in sincerity say, Oh that above all things I might have the enjoyment of God! oh that above all things I might be to the honour of God."[4]

The devotional manuals widely used by New Englanders contained directions for reading Scripture profitably. Lewis Bayly, in his discussion of "How a private man must begin the morning with Piety," laid out a reading plan for going through the entire Bible each year. Other manuals listed various "rules for reading," emphasizing such things as the necessity of daily routine, the techniques for guarding against wandering thoughts, and the importance of seriously applying the

---

4. Cotton, *Way of Life*, 391, 406. Cotton, *Christ the Fountaine*, 192. I. Mather, *Awakening Truth's Tending to Conversion*, vii. Cotton did not view reading as a converting ordinance but as solely for growth in grace already received (Cotton, *Christ the Fountaine*, 181–185), but Increase Mather's view prevailed in New England (R. Mather, *Farewel-Exhortation*, 21). See Rosenmeier, " 'With My Owne Eyes,' " in Bercovitch, ed., *Typology and Early American Literature*, 70–71; Richard Baxter, *Reliquiæ Baxterianæ: Or, Mr. Richard Baxter's Narrative of the Most Memorable Passages of His Life and Times . . .* (London, 1696), 3–4; and John Bunyan, *Grace Abounding to the Chief of Sinners . . .* (1666), ed. Roger Sharrock (London, 1962), 8, 16–17, for the importance of books in each author's conversions.

scriptural passages to one's own life. Many manuals provided a model "Prayer to be used before reading."[5]

The most explicit and complete of the manuals dealing with the private reading of the Bible was by John White, an English Puritan and longtime friend of New England, *A Way to the Tree of Life: Discoursed in Sundry Directions for the Profitable Reading of the Scriptures.* "The reading of Scripture is nothing else but a kind of holy conference with God, wherein we enquire after, and he reveals unto us himself, and his will." The Bible contained "the Word of God himself, who speaks unto us in and by them. . . . We cannot otherwise conceive of our selves, then as standing in Gods presence." Apparently writing from experience, White asserted that "Spirituall Raptures seize on a man, even while he is reading the Scriptures." Devotional reading produced effects "upon the heart and conscience, which are such as cannot possibly be performed by any other then a divine Power." White suggested that God worked in three stages through reading, stages that corresponded precisely to the order of the conversion experience and the redemptive drama. "First, the wounding and terrifying. Secondly, the converting and renuing. Thirdly, the comforting and reviving of the heart." First, as the believer prepares for reading, the heart is "cleansed" and "made pliable." The reader finds out "the true sense" of the passage, applies it to himself or herself, and then "whet[s]" the passage upon the heart till it "warme[s], and quicken[s] the affections." The final stage is the resolution of a changed will. Effective reading, White maintained, then moves naturally into meditation and prayer. "Above all," he wrote, readers must pray, "acknowledging [their] owne blindnesse, and inability, of [them] selves, to search into the deep Mysteries revealed in the Word . . . beg earnestly the assistance of Gods Spirit to open [their] eyes."[6]

The manner of New Englanders' devotional reading yielded emotional and spiritual fruit, as the Shepard vignette shows. Repetition was one important reason for the power of such reading. Going over the same biblical passages, putting oneself through the stages of the redemptive order, rereading favorite manuals again and again, produced a cumulative effect that our twentieth-century desire for novelty fails to comprehend. Robert Keayne throughout his life used

5. Bayly, *Practice of Piety*, 143–145. Bayne, *Briefe Directions*, 162–163. Web[be], "Daily Exercise," in Ro[gers] *et al.*, *Spirituall Flowers*, 110–111.

6. White, *Way to the Tree of Life*, sig. A3–A4, 1, 148, 33, 4, 133, 150–151, 155, 127. On White's relation to New England, see Samuel Eliot Morison, *Builders of the Bay Colony* (Boston, 1930), 21–50.

a eucharistic manual he had copied out himself by hand. He bequeathed to his son "as my special gift to him my little written book in my closet upon 1 Cor. 11[:] 27, 28, which is a treatise on the sacrament of the Lord's Supper per Mr. Briarly. [It is] a little thin pocket book bound in leather, all written with my own hand, which I esteem more precious than gold, and which I have read over I think 100 and 100 times. I hope he will read it over no less [and will] make it his constant companion, and that it may be as precious to him as ever it was and as still it is to me." In describing the place he stored the book as "my closet," Keayne was speaking of the devotional activity associated with that place in his house rather than of an architectural entity. The influence of the book on Keayne, the result of the intensity and repetitive nature of his reading, could only have been second to that of the Bible. As he copied the book out and read it "100 and 100 times," Keayne submitted to and identified his own life with the message of its pages.[7]

Other New Englanders similarly recognized the importance of devotional reading. John Brock recorded that as a child in England, "By Reading through admonitions of Parents in a Book called The Practice of Piety I found some Description, of the Misery of Men in Hell and of Happiness of the Godly which somewhat stirred me." Brock's conversion was gradual, but in 1636 at age sixteen "Encouragement and Light came . . . by a Doctrine of famous Mr Hooker about Gods Drawing a Soul unto Christ that makes a Soul come unto him." He was referring to Thomas Hooker's *The Poor Doubting Christian Drawn unto Christ*, published first as part of *The Saints Cordials* in 1629 and then separately in 1635. Puritans on both sides of the Atlantic also made wide use of Thomas Shepard's *Sincere Convert*, a book so simply and popularly written (published, indeed, without permission from a reader's notes) that anyone who could read would understand its message. According to nineteen-year-old Joseph Green, eucharistic manuals were instrumental in his salvation. "As I was looking over some old books at my Land Lords, I found a paper entitled a preparation for the Lords table, which I took and read from which I had much encouragement; and I read mr Doolittle [*A Treatise Concerning the Lord's Supper*]. And as I was at mrs Lambs I saw a book of Mr Cotton Mathers concerning the Lords supper [*A Companion for Communicants*] which I borrowed, and read, and I think by Gods assistance it so moved me to come to the Lords table that I began to think of closeing wholly with Jesus Christ." Reading was not only prescribed as a useful

7. Bernard Bailyn, ed., *The Apologia of Robert Keayne: The Last Will and Testament of Me, . . . Commonly Called August: The Self-Portrait of a Puritan Merchant* (New York, 1965), 28.

exercise, it was also practiced by a wide range of New Englanders who found it a powerful means of grace.[8]

Cotton Mather, who contributed more to the avalanche of manuals published in late seventeenth-century New England than any other author, himself found devotional manuals useful, and reading formed an important element of his secret exercises. He noted in his diary that "the Lord sent mee a little Book" by John Corbet, *Self-Imployment in Secret* . . . (published in London in 1681 and in Boston in 1684), and that he used Corbet's "excellent Resolutions . . . for my more asiduous Meditation and Imitation." Mather's astoundingly prolific pen was not simply the expression of an author's vanity; his writing was the outgrowth of his sincere desire to flood the towns and homes of New England with pious literature. He worked through Boston booksellers and promoted other traditional methods of distribution in rural areas. In 1683 he noted, "There is an old Hawker, who will fill this Countrey with devout and useful Books, if I will direct him; I will therefore direct Him, and assist him, as far as I can, in doing so." In 1713 when the Massachusetts Assembly passed legislation against "Hawkers, Pedlars and Petty Chapmen," Mather resolved, "I must also assist the Booksellers, in addressing the Assembly, that their late Act against Pedlers, may not hinder their Hawkers from carrying Books of Piety about the Country." Books and Bibles that found their way into New England homes were essential to the secret devotions of individuals.[9]

MEDITATION

In the practice of secret devotion—especially in the early morning, at night just prior to sleep, at midday on the Sabbath or days of fasting, and on Saturday in preparation for the Sabbath—individuals ideally meditated after reading and before prayer. Meditation was the natural outcome of reading in that the substance of the exercise often emerged from the passage read. In meditation the believer applied the written text to the soul. Meditation was linked with prayer, since the saint then slipped inevitably into conversation with God. Theo-

8. Shipton, ed., "Autobiographical Memoranda of John Brock," Am. Antiq. Soc., *Procs.*, N.S., LIII (1943), 97. Williams *et al.*, *Hooker: Writings*, 394. Elizabeth White, *The Experiences of God's Gracious Dealing* . . . (Boston, 1741 [orig. publ. Glasgow, 1696]), 8. Morison, ed., "Commonplace Book of Joseph Green," Col. Soc. Mass., *Trans.*, XXXIV (1943), 240.

9. Ford, ed., *Diary of Cotton Mather*, I, 66. References on book distribution are cited in Hellmut Lehmann-Haupt *et al.*, *The Book in America: A History of the Making, the Selling, and the Collecting of Books in the United States* (New York, 1939), 52.

logically, meditation prepared the heart for prayer and readied the soul for communion with Christ. Meditation was thus not an end in itself, but a door to deeper experience. Edward Taylor's meditative poetry, for example, was preparatory in the sense that it was fulfilled in the prayer that followed and in the Sacrament on the morrow. It is important to note, of course, that not all New Englanders meditated in the advanced and regular manner of Taylor and others for whom spiritual records survive. The degree of observance varied from person to person and according to the stage of one's life. But meditation occurred on many levels, and New Englanders typically practiced it in some manner at least occasionally.[10]

Nocturnal meditation took place after family devotions. The themes were similar to those that were commonly part of family devotions: reviewing the day's activities, giving thanks for the day's blessings, repenting for sin, submitting to the will of God, and being aware that in sleep one rested in God's hands not knowing if morning would come. The physical action of getting into and lying in bed had emblematic value: "Let it put thee in mind of thy grave, which is now the bed of Christ."[11]

In the morning, perhaps while the believer still lay in bed, meditation became the first action of the day. "Awake with God, that is, enter into holy and divine meditation," manuals advised. Lewis Bayly suggested a morning "soliloquy" in which the saint would "offer up to God upon the Altar of a contrite heart, the groans of thy Spirit, and the calves of thy lips as thy morning sacrifice, and the first fruits of the day." His model went: "My soul waitest upon thee, O Lord, more than the morning watch watcheth for the morning. O God, therefore be merciful unto me, and bless me, and cause thy face to shine upon me: fill me with thy mercy this morning, so shall I rejoyce and be glad all my dayes." The themes of morning meditation were, generally, God's love and kindness in providing another day; salvation from sin and death during the night; physical and spiritual refreshment; and the vanity of the world into which one was waking (emblemized by cloth-

---

10. The final movement of most of Taylor's poems pointed to the future, first to the coming Sacrament—"Oh! feed me at thy Table, make Grace grow / Knead in thy Bread, I eate, thy Love to me" (II,13, ll. 43–44)—and ultimately to a vision of life in the Kingdom—"O sweet thought. Lord take this praise though thin. / And when I'm in't Ile tune an higher pin" (I,47, ll. 29–30). See Karl Keller, *The Example of Edward Taylor* (Amherst, Mass., 1975), 91–93.

11. Thomas Watson, *The Saints Delight. To Which Is Annexed a Treatise of Meditation* (London, 1657), 259–275.

ing). Meditation led into secret prayer and, as the person gradually emerged into society, family devotions.[12]

The manuals gave advice on themes for meditation during each part of the day and, especially for the Sabbath, on the proper setting and physical posture. Puritans were undogmatic about these matters and approached them in a utilitarian spirit. "Only these two things are to be observed in our choyce of the place; first that it be free from company and noyse . . . and secondly, this private place must be such, as in our experience we find freest from distraction, and fittest to further us in our devotion." When Richard Baxter promoted "the solitude of contemplative devotion," he wrote: "Though I would not perswade thee to Pythagoras his Cave, nor to the Hermits Wilderness, nor to the Monks Cell; yet I would advise thee to frequent solitariness, that thou mayest sometimes confer with Christ and with thy self, as well as with others." The times for such meditation were to be likewise fitting, well defined, regular, and frequent. The only stipulation for the posture of the body was that it be reverent and conducive to devotion. The body must "be composed to rest and quiet," but this could be accomplished lying down, sitting, standing, or walking. Finally, in preparation for meditation, the faculties must all be "in tune" like a musical instrument. The person must be ready to apply the meditation to the soul, well aware of "how slippery, fickle, and wandering the heart is." With the world "cleared away" and the heart focused on its task, the work could begin. The "matter" for meditation was to be chosen in such a way that it would stir devotion, be appropriate to time and place, and be varied from day to day. It must always be drawn from one's "own wants and infirmities; from Gods benefits, from the changes and mortality of this life, etc." It might be prompted by the reading of a religious book "fit to season" or by the Bible.[13]

Formal, or "ordinary," meditation involved the successive application of the passage or topic to each of the faculties, from cogitation and memory to conscience, affections, and will. The meditative task was "to get these truths from thy head to thy heart." Ordinary meditation was engaged in "at sett times, when as with due deliberation and preparation, setting all other things apart, we settle our selves to spend some time in this religious exercise." Devout New Englanders also practiced "extraordinary," or "occasional," meditation, typically a

12. Web[be], "Daily Exercise," in Ro[gers] *et al.*, *Spirituall Flowers*, 98. Bayly, *Practice of Piety*, 139–142, 185–187, 198, 279.

13. Downame, *Guide to Godlynesse*, 552–570. Bayne, *Briefe Directions*, 137–139. Baxter, *Saints Everlasting Rest*, 712–713, 697–699.

sudden or brief outburst of spiritual insight or reflection during the course of a business day. Occasional meditation is exemplified in many places in Part Two of *The Pilgrim's Progress*, as when the spider reminded Christiana and Mercy that they, too, were venomous creatures in need of grace or when Prudence and Matthew conversed in Palace Beautiful:

> MATT. What should we learn by seeing the Flame of our Fire go upwards? and by seeing the Beams, and sweet Influences of the Sun strike downwards?
>
> PRUD. By the going up of the Fire, we are taught to ascend to Heaven, by fervent and hot desires. And by the Sun sending his Heat, Beams, and sweet Influences downwards; we are taught, that the Saviour of the World, tho' high, reaches down with his Grace and Love to us below.[14]

This technique came to be known as "spiritualizing the creatures" and was most widely popularized by John Flavel in his *Husbandry Spiritualized* (1669) and *Navigation Spiritualized* (1682). As grist for the mill of occasional meditation, Christiana exulted, "God has made nothing in vain." Earlier in the century Puritans were already practicing this type of meditation. Thomas Shepard, for example, recorded, "When I was walking to Roxbury alone I saw it was God alone who gave me a natural life, and I turned the thought into a prayer." At another time he wrote, "I also began to see, nay, feel, God in fire, meat, every providence, and that his many providences and creatures are but God's hands and fingers whereby he takes hold of me." Anne Bradstreet's "Contemplations," the product of her ordinary meditation, contain many instances of occasional meditation that may earlier have suggested themselves to her more spontaneously. Cotton Mather's use of the method is well known. Seeing "a tall Man," he thought of the idea of "heights," and he silently blessed the man: "Lord, give that Man, High Attainments in Christianity; let him fear God, above many."[15]

14. Downame, *Guide to Godlynesse*, 539. Bunyan, *Pilgrim's Progress*, ed. Wharey and Sharrock, 200–201, 231.

15. See Kaufmann, *Pilgrim's Progress and Meditation*, chap. 8. Shepard, "Journal," in McGiffert, ed., *God's Plot*, 128, 137. Anne Bradstreet, "Contemplation 3," in Hutchinson, ed., *Poems of Bradstreet*, 79. Ford, ed., *Diary of Cotton Mather*, I, 63–64, 83. Thomas M. Davis misunderstands the important term "occasional meditation" in his "Edward Taylor's 'Occasional Meditations,'" *Early Am. Lit.*, V (1970–1971), 17–29, using it to describe the irregular intervals between the poems. The term actually means meditation on a naturally occurring and everyday "occasion." Occasional meditation

The common assumption that early seventeenth-century Puritans eschewed meditation as a means of achieving spiritual delight and union with Christ is incorrect, as I have already said. The insistence that dour preachers of repentance such as Thomas Hooker limited meditation to scrutiny of one's own sins and that Puritanism did not begin to follow the more Catholic practice of "formal meditation on the joys of heaven" until the urging of Richard Baxter ignores persisting Catholic meditation on sin and ongoing Puritan meditation on the joy of union with Christ. Thomas Hooker indeed defined meditation as "a serious intention of the mind whereby wee come to search out the truth, and settle it effectually upon the heart." And by "truth" he meant the truth of one's own sinful condition. "Meditation of sins," he wrote, "is a special means to break the heart of a sinner." Meditation "is as it were the register and remembrancer, that looks over the records of our daily corruptions, and keeps them upon file." It was a "beating of the brain" like "the Gouldsmith with his mettal." But what was the Puritan's goal? For Hooker the "Art of Meditation" was not an end in itself but a means to higher spiritual experience. At the throne of grace the sinner would find mercy and the spiritual ability to advance to higher stages through the next act of devotion: the ability to pray for and receive the spirit of Christ. The devotional acts of meditation and prayer corresponded to the two major parts of the order of redemption: preparation and implantation. Through meditation "the Lord prepares the hearts of his people to call upon him, a heart mourning for sinne, and a heart loosened from sinne: when you leave sinne behind you, and send up a prayer from an humbled heart and a broken soule, then God will heare you, and you shall receive an answer from the God of heaven."[16]

The spiritual joy following initial repentance was quite real for some New Englanders at least. In meditation on Saturday night in preparation for the Sabbath, Jonathan Mitchel fixed his mind on his sin. "Lord, It is the Hour and Power of Darkness with me; I feel the Dreadful Rage of Satan, and my vile Heart, now against me, to overturn me . . . but I leave my Woful Soul, and self to thy Disposing, Lord, I am in Hell, wilt thou let me ly there?" Cotton Mather observed that "such passages" from Mitchel's diary "discover the Contrition,

---

was to be engaged in daily and was distinguished from regular meditation by its focus on a creature as subject rather than on a biblical text or spiritual idea.

16. Hooker, *Application of Redemption, Ninth and Tenth Books*, 208–221, 249–251, 271–272. T[homas] H[ooker], *Foure Learned and Godly Treatises . . .* (London, 1638), 102. Downame, *Guide to Godlynesse*, 534.

that laid him exceedingly low" and prepared his soul for the subsequent union with Christ. Thomas Shepard similarly recorded:

> When I was on my bed in Monday morning the Lord let me see
> I was nothing else but a mass of sin and that all I did was very vile,
> which when my heart was somewhat touched with, immediately
> the Lord revealed himself to me in his fullness of goodness with
> much sweet affection. The Lord suddenly appeared and let
> me see there was strength in him to succor me, wisdom to guide,
> mercy in him to pity, spirit to quicken, Christ to satisfy, and so I
> saw all my good was there, as all evil was in myself. . . . and so
> I become his, for him to take care for me and love me, and I to
> pitch my thought and heart on him. . . . An exchange of
> wonderful love.

While meditating on his utter vileness Shepard experienced the "sweet affection" of God's "wonderful love" as He surprisingly "suddenly appeared." The cycle is repeated over and again in his journal. Roger Clap advocated the same pattern when he urged his offspring first to "study to know your own Heart to know the Plague that there is in them" and second to "Come to the Lord Jesus Christ."[17]

The stages that characterized the believer's first conversion—repentance and the experience of grace—also characterized the process of meditation and prayer throughout life. The saint must "go on humbling to be humbled," as Jonathan Mitchel put it. "This is a great thing, not easily and quickly gotten: but sit not down at quiet, till you come to this. . . . This is the work of our lives." Salvation was never considered an attained goal this side of death, but was rather the destination of the pilgrim soul. Yet each journey through the stages might bring progressively more comfort. "Confesse thy sins to God," John Cotton preached to the already converted. "Lay open thy wayes, and set them in order before him, and by this means you will find an unmeasurableness of ease." William Perkins likewise noted the similarity between the stages of devotion and those of first conversion. In meditation after conversion, after the terrors of that first repentance, saints again undertook "a due examination" of their hearts and became repentant. "Spiritual consideration," as Perkins termed it, "must be often used of every man, to move him to repentance, and it is very effectuall thereunto." But if the matter of meditation was "mans misery through his sins," the aim was always higher. Meditation for

17. Cotton Mather, *Ecclesiastes. The Life of the Reverend & Excellent, Jonathan Mitchell* . . . (Boston, 1697), 56–57. Shepard, "Journal," in McGiffert, ed., *God's Plot*, 88. *Clap's Memoirs*, 45.

Perkins was an "action of the minde renewed and sanctified, whereby it doth seriously thinke on those things which may further salvation." By focusing in the self-scrutiny of meditation on their "owne particular temptations" and "present estate towards God," penitents would again be transformed by God into "a cleansed fountaine." Only then could the "sanctified mind" proceed to subsequent devotional stages of "the elevation of the heart to God."[18]

Devotional manuals encouraged believers to move effectively through their spiritual exercises without becoming blocked at any particular point. "Wee are not to bend all our thoughts to meditate and call to mind all our sins" in such a way that "the huge cloud of our sinnes being neere our eyes, will hide from our sight the shining beames of Gods mercy and Christs merit." Rather, said John Downame in a highly significant passage, "as soone as wee cast one eye upon our sins for our humiliation, let us cast the other presently upon Christ Jesus, who hath payd the price for our redemption, and suffered all the punishment which we by our sins have deserved." Richard Rogers made the same point in his "A Direction unto True Happiness." "The first part of diligent meditation, will humble and bring thee low in thine own sight, and raise in thee a true sorrow of heart, seeing thy deadly misery. The second part by the working of Gods Spirit, shall settle thee in most cleare safety and peace, by seeing thy selfe delivered from the same misery." Rogers added a third stage, as the exercise led the saint back into the world renewed. Meditation "will shew thee how to change thy life, and conforme it unto the will of God, and give thee direction how to walke with God daily." Paul Bayne also thought of devotion as a journey through the redemptive stages. Meditation was effective "when we doe on purpose separate our selves from all other things, and consider as we are able, and thinke of some points of instruction necessary to lead us forward to the kingdome of Heaven." The redemptive order was clear in Bayly's organization of *The Practice of Piety*. He began with "Meditations on the miseries of a man not reconciled to God in Christ" and the agony of physical death and punishment in hell. These were, however, preparatory to his "Meditations of the state of a Christian reconciled to God in Christ." While contemplating the "blessed estate . . . in heaven," Bayly wrote, "Here my Meditation dazzleth, and my pen falleth out of

18. Mitchel, "Letter to His Friend," appended to *Discourse of the Glory*, 2d ed., 273–274. Cotton, *Practical Commentary upon the First Epistle Generall of John*, 326. William Perkins, *A Faithful and Plaine Exposition upon the First Two Verses of the Second Chapter of Zephaniah*, in *Works*, III, 412. William Perkins, *A Treatise of Mans Imaginations . . .* , ibid., II, 476–483.

my hand; the one being not able to conceive, nor the other to describe that most excellent bliss." He nevertheless went on to conclude with two model meditations designed to help elevate the soul to God as it was "ravished in contemplation."[19]

At its most rigorous, meditation led to being "possessed" by God. Baxter described the experience as "the soul ravishing exercises of heavenly Contemplation." Downame wrote that this "high and heavenly" meditation was "fit only for such as by long exercise have attained to much perfection." These "great Profitients who by much practice have brought their Art into an habit" were able "to soare (with the Eagle)" daily. Disciplined training such as this was typical in New England of what might be called a spiritual elite including Thomas Shepard, the Mathers, Edward Taylor, perhaps many of the clergy, and many pious women whose inner lives we cannot know in detail. At the more common level, however, meditation involved practices "within the reach of all Christians which will put out their hand unto it." The more elementary form of meditation followed the same spiritual stages as the more advanced variety, an order of redemption that assured the penitent of grace.[20]

The most common type of meditation in New England was probably "self-examination" or "meditation on experience." Based on biblical injunction (1 Corinthians 11:28; 2 Corinthians 13:5; and Psalm 139:23–24), self-examination differed from Hooker's meditation on sin in that it attempted to chart not only repentance but also the further salvific work of God in the soul. The two varieties of meditation are clearly related, however, and Hooker concluded almost every sermon with a "use of self-triall." The classic text for self-examination was William Perkins's *A Case of Conscience, the Greatest That Ever Was; How a Man May Know Whether He Be the Childe of God, or No* (London, 1592). But every preacher in New England gave similar weekly guidance and exhortations to the work. John Higginson in his "Some Help to Self-Examination" defined it as "an enquiry into the inward Acts of our Souls; trying by the Word of God, whether we have the truth of Saving Grace in us or no? and accordingly judging of our spiritual Estates before God." In his personal record of the work of self-

19. Downame, *Christian Warfare*, 56. Ri[chard] Ro[gers], "A Direction unto True Happiness," in Ro[gers] *et al.*, *Spirituall Flowers*, sig. A2. Bayne, *Briefe Directions*, 128. Bayly, *Practice of Piety*, 452–466. See also, Watson, *Saints Delight*, 72–156; Mitchel, "Letter to His Friend," appended to *Discourse of the Glory*, 2d ed., 281–282; Dod and Cleaver, *Ten Sermons*, 17.

20. Baxter, *Saints Everlasting Rest*, 692–693. Downame, *Guide to Godlynesse*, 534–535, 356.

examination John Corbet wrote: "I have no other ordinary way to know my Sincerity in order to the said Peace and Assurance, but to Examine it according to my best understanding by the Marks thereof set down in God's Word. In this Self-Examination it is requisite that I use all Diligence and Impartiality with Constancy; and that I earnestly pray for God's assistance in it, and heartily offer my selfe to His Search, as David did, Psal. 139.23." The exercise was integral to the great Puritan quest for assurance of grace, a quest that dominated the spiritual lives of New Englanders. "Examine now," ministers preached, "and try whether you have the Son or no." Guides were published, such as those by Higginson and Corbet, and Thomas Hooker's "The Character of a Sound Christian in Seventeen Marks." The exercise of self-examination was based on the theory (which prevailed in New England but diverged from mainstream Reformation theology) that sanctification demonstrated justification. As Hooker preached, "There may bee a root, and yet no blossoms, and yet it is certaine, where there are blossoms there is a root." Diligent study of God's Word and rigorous examination of the self enabled the saint to conclude, "I am sanctified, therefore I am justified, therefore called, therefore elected."[21]

New Englanders often examined their souls during moments of spiritual crisis, as the vignette of Roger Clap illustrates. The exercise contained within itself the means of release and resolution. Clap as an old man advised his offspring: "Slight not serious Examination: It is good to commune with your own Hearts upon your Bed." Sometimes, however, a crisis might impede the exercise's effectiveness. When Anne Bradstreet suffered from a fever she discovered that

> Beclouded was my Soul with fear
>   Of thy Displeasure sore,
> Nor could I read my Evidence
>   Which oft I read before.[22]

21. Thomas Hooker, "The Character of a Sound Christian," bound with *Paterne of Perfection*, 376–392. Hooker, *Paterne of Perfection*, 264–265, 192. H[ooker], *Soules Exaltation*, 28. Higginson, "Some Help to Self-Examination," in Higginson, *Our Saviour's Legacy of Peace*, 187–188. John Corbet, *Self-Imployment in Secret . . .* (Boston, 1684 [orig. publ. London, 1681], sig. A5. Cotton, *Christ the Fountaine*, 72. Shepard, *Subjection to Christ*, 94. See also, H[ooker], *Christians Two Chiefe Lessons*; Hooker, *Application of Redemption, First Eight Books*, 272; Hooker, *The Saints Dignitie and Dutie, Together with the Danger of Ignorance and Hardnesse . . .* (London, 1651), 164; Hooker, *Exposition of Religion*, 23; H[ooker], *Foure Learned and Godly Treatises*, 13; and Rom. 8:30.

22. *Clap's Memoirs*, 49. Anne Bradstreet, "For Deliverance from a Feaver," in Hutchinson, ed., *Poems of Bradstreet*, 62.

Self-examination was more commonly a means of grace when it formed part of the believer's regular, especially evening, devotional exercises. Through self-examination, Hooker preached, "We may hence gain certain evidence whether ever the Lord hath made any entrance upon this great work of preparation." Standards of purity and redemption could be brought to bear on every hour of a person's life, through a lifetime of growth in union with Christ. Thomas Shepard's exercise was typical. "When I looked over the day I saw how I fell short of God and Christ, and how I had spent one hour unprofitably. And why? Because though the thing I did was good, yet because I intended not my God in it as my last end, set not my rule before me, and so set myself to please God, therefore I was unprofitable and so desired to be humbled for it, and so I saw the nature of fruitlessness." John Baily's "Watchfulness" in self-examination, according to Cotton Mather, "discovered a singular fear of God, in his whole Conversation." Baily kept a record of the results in his diary, suggesting how closely New Englanders scrutinized their "daily walk." He remarked, for example, "I did not watch my Tongue so as I ought which cost me much Trouble afterwards, and made me walk heavily." Or, "I spoke two unadvised Words to Day." Or, "I was too forgetful of God, and extending in Tobacco. The Lord pardon that, and all other Sins, and heal this Nature, and humble this Heart." Charles Chauncy, too, was described as "very much in meditation, and in that one important kind and part of it, self-examination, especially in his preparations for the Lords table." The extensive outline of Chauncy's "Self-Trials before the Sacrament," including examination of his membership in Christ, his faith, his repentance, his uprightness toward God, and his brotherly love, reveals intense seriousness in the work.[23]

Records show that the exercise of self-examination could lead to positive results. Cotton Mather, for example, noted: "I examined myself by the signs of a State of Nature and a State of Grace, given in Mr. N[athaniel] Vincent's *True Touchstone*; and found joyful course to hope." His father's results were similar. "Prepared for sabbath. examined my selfe by the signs of uprightness in Scudders *dayly walk*. and by the signs of a godly man in Byfield, as also by the marks I am wont to examine by; and I was not without Hope that a work of grace is wrought in my soul, and some growth therein. Lord Jesus perfect

23. H[ooker], *Christians Two Chiefe Lessons*, 278–280. Hooker, *Application of Redemption, Ninth and Tenth Books*, 101. H[ooker], *Soules Vocation*, 195, 202. Higginson, *Our Saviour's Legacy of Peace*, 197–199. Shepard, "Journal," in McGiffert, ed., *God's Plot*, 96. C. Mather, *Magnalia Christi Americana*, I, 621, 470–471.

it." Through self-examination, therefore, New Englanders marked their progress along the way to perfection. They never achieved perfection, for that was impossible this side of the heavenly city, but they discovered successive approximations of perfection.[24]

Examinations that were especially thorough were required at certain times during the year or during a lifetime. One such time was the end of the calendar year. Most of John Corbet's published exercises are dated in February and March, in preparation for the new year (which until 1752 began on March 25 in English-speaking countries). Increase Mather was prompted on New Year's Day to write:

> 1 m. 25 d. 1675. And is it so indeed? Doe I live to write any thing in the year 1675? Who could have thought that it should have bin so, when I was so near death above five years agoe? Providence doth now put me under Humiliation extraordinary; and there is cause for it. 1. particular and private. 1. For the sins of the year past. 2. My old sins. 3. The plagues of Heart that doe still abide in me. 4. of late Times I have found more respect and esteem amongst men, and with the Lords servants than formerly, how should the consideration of that mercy humble me, and break my Heart!

Mather went on to list evidence of sin in "the publick state of things."[25]

The turning of the year was a natural time for self-examination for several reasons. The taking of business inventory at that time suggested the need for a spiritual inventory. John Cotton, for example, examined himself "with Reflections on the *Transactions* of the Day past." He spoke of keeping "exact and particular records," or "Account Books . . . between the Lord, and our souls." Also, winter was traditionally a time for more intense devotional activity than busier agricultural seasons. Samuel Danforth reminded New England in his 1647 *Almanack* verse for January that

> Great bridges shall be made alone
> Without ax, timber, earth or stone,
> Of chrystall metall, like to glass;
> Such wondrous works soon come to passe,
> If you may then have such away,
> The Ferry-man you need not pay.

24. Ford, ed., *Diary of Cotton Mather*, I, 58. Increase Mather, *Diary, March, 1675–December, 1676. Together with Extracts from Another Diary by Him, 1674–1687*, ed. Samuel A. Green (Cambridge, Mass., 1900), 32.

25. Corbet, *Self-Imployment in Secret*, 1, 7, 12, 17. I. Mather, *Diary*, ed. Green, 5.

Danforth's verses for previous months were political; he chose the winter months to make his plea for piety in secret devotion, in his eyes the essence of the New England errand. The "great bridge" was that of devotional practice, especially preparation for death and eternity. It was a bridge made not of earthly materials but of "chrystall"—that is, Christly—materials. Faithful exercise would exempt the saint from the toll taken by the ferryman who conducted souls across the River of Death. Cotton Mather, observing that "Winter, was a Time of Leisure with most of my Neighbors; hereupon I contrived with myself how I might with as charming a Mixture of Religion and Ingenuity, as I could, invite my Neighbours to improve the Leisure of the Winter, for the Glory of God, and their own spiritual and eternal advantage." He published his manual *Winter Meditations* in 1693.[26]

Besides being months for inventory and relative leisure, February and March were times that death seemed especially near. The old year was dying, New England lay in winter's depths, the environment was bleak and cold. By examination of the self the self must die, for the exercise's motivation and plumb line was the God who awaited the soul beyond death. In his explicitly devotional series of verses in the 1676 *Almanack*, John Foster traced the life of an individual over the course of the year from March through February. "A Man, a little world," entered "Lifes Stage" as a youth in the turbulent springtime month of March. The "adverse Blast" of each temptation threatened "to make a Spoil" of "his poor Flame." The summer months brought maturity, by August it was time for the harvest of good works, and September reminded him to prepare for winter, his own years of incapacity, and eventual death. But as "Age is at hand," Foster warned, and larders were stocked, the temptation was "for fear of want" to "covet more." In winter, life by the fireside, symbolic of the devotional life, became more important than life outside. "The good old man needs somewhat to impart/New Life and heat to warm his languid heart." In December "Man now is downward bending/His wearied Course and hasteth to his ending." In January,

> The Tapour's wasted its expiring light
> Death threat the World with never-ending night:

26. Cotton Mather, "Cottonus Redivivus," in *Johannes in Eremo*, 3. Cotton, *Briefe Exposition of Ecclesiastes*, 146. Samuel Danforth, *An Almanack for the Year of Our Lord, 1647* (Cambridge, 1647). See Ziff, *Puritanism in America*, 151–152, for an entirely political interpretation of the poem. Ford, ed., *Diary of Cotton Mather*, I, 169. Cotton Mather, *Winter Meditations: Directions How to Employ the Leisure of the Winter for the Glory of God . . .* (Boston, 1693).

Dim eyes, deaf eares uncertain tidings send:
Hopes and desires of life are at an end.

And in February,

The glimmering flame of life if yet it last
In Danger to go out by every blast
Now swift-winged time which never will return
Our long-liv'd Tapour to an end doth burn.

The key to these verses is that each month was appropriate not only to persons of the particular age; persons of all ages went through the cycle every year. The saint was urged to prepare continually for death, and the "New Life" at the fireside of spiritual exercise was possible for old and young alike. Most significant, New Englanders here used the natural cycle of the seasons to reinforce for devotional purposes the redemptive cycle of Jesus Christ's death and resurrection.[27]

This "religious improvement" of meteorology was in the meditative tradition of "spiritualizing the creatures," but its basis lay in the much older psychological patterns of the seasons, which also underlay the calendar of saints' and holy days in Catholic Europe. New Englanders recognized that emotional changes geared to weather conditions and to the annual work cycle influenced devotional and spiritual habits. This influence had great implications for the exercise of self-examination, for it was in that work that penitents were to "be unbottomed of Self, to dye to Self-advancement, to Self-glorification, and to all Selfish joyes." Self-examination inevitably led to confrontation with one's own death, and by losing the self in that realization, the soul was

27. J[ohn] F[oster], *An Almanack of Cœlestial Motions for the Year . . . 1676 . . .* (Boston, 1676). The significance of the almanac in New England, and for popular culture generally in early modern times, ought not be underestimated. Almanacs since medieval times have been quasi-religious in nature and widely disseminated. The almanac was "*le 'livre des gens qui lisent peu,'*" as a French social historian puts it. In New England the clergy and Harvard College controlled the printing of almanacs through most of the century, but this did not prevent them from being the most popularly written, widely circulated, and intensively used products of the New England press. Cotton Mather, in his rationale for publishing *The Boston Ephemeris: An Almanack . . .* (Boston, 1683), wrote that the "Anniversary Composure comes into almost as many hands, as the best of Books" (p. 16). His aim was evangelical and devotional: "Who knowes, what good may bee done, by such a seemingly trivial, but extensive way, as that of the Almanack" (Ford, ed., *Diary of Cotton Mather*, I, 276). See Marion Barber Stowell, *Early American Almanacs: The Colonial Weekday Bible* (New York, 1977); Charles L. Nichols, "Notes on the Almanacs of Massachusetts," Am. Antiq. Soc., *Procs.*, N.S., XXII (1912), 15–134; Milton Drake, comp., *Almanacs of the United States*, I (New York, 1962), Preface, v–xviii; and Geneviève Bollème, *Les Almanachs populaires aux XVIIe et XVIIIe siècles: Essai d'histoire sociale* (Paris, 1969), quotation on p. 16.

"swallowed up in the love of Him" and resurrected with Christ. A winter verse in the 1679 *Almanack* linked the new birth with New Year's Day and with the New Day of the Kingdom:

> The Seasons cold, but Charity much colder,
> The Year grows old, with Ill Will be not older:
> Let heavenly Influences then allay
> These Brumal blasts, and bring a New-Years day.
> But let Diviner Aspects melt and move
> The hearts of men to Charity and love.

The season at once reflected the harsh reality of sin, the need for self-examination, and spiritual regeneration. From the cold of ill will the penitent could progress to the coming of spring with the new year. March 25 was a symbol of conversion, rebirth, and eschatology. The rebirth of the sinner anticipated the rebirth of the cosmos. Meanwhile, the *Almanack* advised New Englanders not to succumb to the temptations of the world but to let God "melt and move" the heart even while the earth was frozen.[28]

For the same reasons some devout New Englanders celebrated their birthdays as occasions for solemn self-examination and humiliation. John Baily "in the return of every year . . . still took much notice in his diaries" of his birthday "and made his humble and useful reflections thereupon." "This is my Birth-day," Baily wrote, "I am ready to say of it, as Job doth of his: but I forbear any unadvised words about it: only, I have done little for God, and much against him; for which I am sorry." Cotton Mather (whose February birthday lent extra weight to his exercises) and Peter Thacher were others who engaged in annual self-examination, with the same symbolic participation in the death and resurrection of Christ.[29]

Besides these regular calendar exercises, New Englanders might have examined themselves in an unusually thorough manner at any point in the course of a lifetime. Spiritual crisis was sometimes the motivation, as noted above. For John Winthrop, in the exercise already cited, the impetus was the combined political and personal crises that converged on his forty-ninth birthday. Other instances were not necessarily connected with either crisis or calendar. Samuel Newman recorded the results of a special examination in "Notes, or Marks of Grace, I find in my self." He was able to "take ground of

---

28. Corbet, *Self-Imployment in Secret*, 17. J[ohn] F[oster], *An Almanack of Cœlestial Motions for the Year . . . 1679 . . .* (Boston, 1679).

29. C. Mather, *Magnalia Christi Americana*, I, 617. Ford, ed., *Diary of Cotton Mather*, I, 54, 183. Thacher, "Diary," MS, II, 23, Mass. Hist. Soc., Boston.

Assurance, and after our Apostles Rules, To make my Election sure, tho' I find them but in weak Measure."[30]

If any aspect of New England devotional practice was characteristically (though not uniquely) Puritan, it was that of meditative self-examination. U. Milo Kaufmann, commenting on its continual use in *The Pilgrim's Progress*, has stated that Bunyan's book is "a protracted meditation upon experience, the kind of reflection upon one's conversion that occupied an important place in the devotional life of every Puritan." Beginning with "self-trial" to root out sin from the heart, self-examination was in no way limited to meditation on sin or a once-for-all conversion. The aim was to find ongoing evidence of salvation, to mark progress along the pilgrim way. In the highest form of self-examination, as in Thomas Shepard's meditation on the year 1639, the believer was able to list and meditate on "the good things I have received of the Lord" on this latest stage of the journey. Such meditation led the saint into prayers of thanksgiving.[31]

PRAYER

Manuals, sermons, diaries, and autobiographical writings abound with references to secret prayer. With strong scriptural warrant, this discipline was the final and most powerful means by which God might elevate the soul out of sin and into union with Himself. Roger Clap cited the classic text, Matthew 6:6, when he advised his children to "Pray to God in secret; and that often too."

> Our Lord and Saviour bids us, Enter into our Closets, and shut the Door, and Pray to our Father in Secret. . . . I say again, Pray in Secret, though you have not a Closet or Door to shut; you need none: You may Pray alone in the Woods, as Christ did in the Mountain: You may Pray as you walk in the Fields, as Isaac did: When imployed in Business, you may lift up your Hearts in Prayer, as Nehemiah did. And when you are alone at any Time, Think with your self, assuredly God is present tho' none else; I will Confess my Sins, and I will beg God's Favour and Grace, I will Wrestle with God by Faith and Prayer. And you may every one of you prevail, if you Pray sincerely, and persevere in it.

30. C. Mather, *Magnalia Christi Americana*, I, 432–433. The biblical reference by Newman is to 2 Pet. 1:1–10.

31. Kaufmann, *Pilgrim's Progress and Meditation*, chap. 9, esp. 228. Shepard, "Autobiography," in McGiffert, ed., *God's Plot*, 71–74.

Jonathan Mitchel, who defined secret prayer as "the blessed means of getting a poor soul to Heaven" and a source of "happiness" in this life, gave the same advice to a friend. "Besides Family-prayer, get some time for Secret Prayer, daily less or more: Be telling God your heart alone." He admitted that clergymen had more time for secret devotions than did most laity but denied it was a clerical discipline. "I know your occasions and labours . . . would not afford you the liberty that I (wretch) have: But do what you can." Prayer was the culminating devotional act and, as in reading and meditation, New Englanders consciously used traditional techniques in exercising it. John Cotton advised, "As we readily grant the helpe of books and meditation, before prayer, so wee do grant also the helpe of holy and reverent gestures in prayer, as bowing downe the knees, and lifting up the hands, and eyes, and voyce."[32]

Some diaries, notably those of Thomas Shepard and Cotton Mather, are almost entirely spiritual records of secret devotion and provide the most intimate view of closet prayer. Shepard's meditations led him to see "it my duty not only to pray but to live by prayer and begging." His London editors remarked that Shepard would regularly "pray and weep" as he approached God in solitude. Shepard commonly used such phrases as "moved and melted," "precious to me," "ravished," and "a sweet frame" to describe his experiences in prayer. Mather, of a later generation but the same spirit, typically wrote: "This Morning, my Heart was melted, in secret Prayer before the Lord, when I used these Words: 'Lord, I am in thy Hands, a poor, broken, sorry despicable Vessel. But it is with Thee, to make mee a Vessell of Honour. Oh! Do so! . . . Oh! Do these Things in mee, and for mee, and by mee, that upon my Account it may be said, O the Power, the Wisdome, the Grace and the Truth of the great Jehovah!' " Both men, and others for whom records survive, engaged in regular and extraordinary prayer daily, usually in conjunction with the other disciplines of secret devotion, reading and meditation. In addition to these morning and evening prayers, Mather and Shepard kept occasional days of "secret Prayer with Fasting, before the Lord," when prayer was especially intense.[33]

New Englanders believed in the efficacy of prayer. Their faith included belief in its almost magical effects noted by John Brock—"The Worms anoy us; but Prayer chases them away"—as well as in its ability

32. *Clap's Memoirs*, 49. Mitchel, "Letter to His Friend," appended to *Discourse of the Glory*, 2d ed., 282–283. Cotton, *Modest and Cleare Answer*, 36.

33. Shepard, *Subjection to Christ*, sig. A3–A4. Shepard, "Journal," in McGiffert, ed., *God's Plot*, 105, 95, 99–100, 116, 87–88. Ford, ed., *Diary of Cotton Mather*, I, 21–22, 56.

to provide assurance and direction in life—"I seldom pray for any Encouragement about any particular, but the Lord doth some way give me an answer." Thomas Shepard recorded that on his voyage to New England, prayer saved his ship from being swallowed up in a storm. Saints turned to prayer to recover from illness and to survive childbirth. Peter Thacher wrote of the evening when "My dear . . . desired mee to look up to God in prayer with her and for which I pleaded former Experience and gods ability speedily to deliver etc. and with in a quarter of an hour after I had done god answered by giveing mee a liveing daughter and makeing my wife a liveing mother." As stated in a didactic couplet from one of the devotional manuals: "Our prayers do pierce the starrie skie,/And fetch down blessings from on high." Not that every answer came quickly or as expected. "Our praying time is our sowing time, we must not look presently for the harvest," Shepard preached. "The Lord ever gives them their asking in mony or mony-worth, in the same thing or a better. The Lord ever gives his importunate beggars their desires, either in pence by little and little, or by pounds; long he is many times before hee gives, but payeth well for their waiting." If prayers were made in the name of Jesus (as prescribed in John 14:13) and "for his ends," prayers would be answered. "The least groan for Christs ends is ever heard; because it is the groaning of the Spirit, because it is an act of spirituall life."[34]

Regular secret prayer was not only a means of grace but also the primary and most necessary means. New Englanders continually pointed to the dire consequences of the neglect of prayer, making much of the failure, suicide, or criminal conviction of those who "never used Secret Prayer" and "frequently ommitted Family-Prayer too." Thomas Shepard said that the voice of the Lord "singles a man out" and is heard by a divine and newly created "internall spirit of prayer." The other means of grace, both public and private, were preliminary to the awakening of this ability to pray in faith. "Is it not the end of Preaching, that you may learne to pray?" John Cotton demanded. True prayer required faith, so that "a man must not fetch his prayer from his parts, as will, memory, understanding, or ability, but from the Spirit, who is the prayer-maker." In fact, the English Puritan John Preston defined prayer as "the voice of Gods owne Spirit, that is, such as arise from the regenerate part which is within us, which is quick-

34. Shipton, ed., "Autobiographical Memoranda of John Brock," Am. Antiq. Soc., *Procs.*, N.S., LIII (1943), 101–104. Shepard, "Autobiography," in McGiffert, ed., *God's Plot*, 60. Thacher, "Diary," MS, I, 134. Gerhard, *Gerard's Prayers*, 139. Shepard, *Sound Beleever*, 297–302. Shepard, *Sincere Convert*, 9–10.

ened and enlarged to pray from the immediate helpe of the holy Ghost." Believers strove to pray, in the biblical phrase, "in the Spirit" —that is, in the language of the Bible, in tune with God's will, "feelingly," with "fervency, and heat of spirit," and with perseverence. Such prayer needed, first, humility, or "lowlinesse of spirit," a "sense of insufficiency, so much as to thinke a good thought, much lesse to make a good prayer," and submission to God's will. Second, it was built on faith, or "childe-like confidence," that God would make good His promises through prayer. Communion with God was deemed possible through prayer in the Spirit.[35]

Preachers considered the creation of the "internall spirit of prayer" to be the major spiritual accomplishment of the conversion process. The gradual development of the ability to pray followed precisely the redemptive order, with prayers of confession predominating during the preparatory stages and prayers of thanksgiving and petition increasing as the devout made progress. For example, preaching aimed at working preparatory humiliation in the listener's heart concluded with an exhortation: "As you tender your owne good, goe into your private chambers, or else into some fields, and there get downe on your knee, though your hearts will not bow, and say, good Lord, I know and confesse it, to this day, my carnal minde hath not been brought under." Pastors recommended devotional manuals for those who were just learning to pray. John Cotton did "not forbid them to use Books that want other strength" but warned simply, "rest not in thy Book." Model prayers "might give thee matter" and "many good formes of Prayer," but they "cannot give thee humility, and fervencie," which were available only from God. "Use Books as young swimmers use Bladders; the spirit of Grace will help thee beyond what thou wouldst think, and thereby thou wilt more sweetly tell God thy mind, and therefore labour chiefly for a spirit of Grace." As God wrought conversion in the soul, He "encourageth faith for to pray," and the heart "closeth with the Spirit in the promises, sets that on worke, and fetches vertue from thence whereby it may be enabled for to pray." Finally, the Spirit carried the soul to Christ, from whom grace flowed.

35. The first quotes refer to "a most Unparallel'd Wretch, one Potter by Name," who made his confession on the scaffold before being executed for buggery in 1662 (Cotton Mather, "Chrysostomus Nov-Anglorum," in *Johannes in Eremo,* 18–22). See also the widely noted suicide of a well-known merchant in Boston ("Copy of the Diary of Noadiah Russell, Tutor at Harvard College, Beginning Anno Dom. 1682," *NEHGR,* VII [1853], 56. Thacher, "Diary," MS, II, 21). Shepard, *Subjection to Christ,* 94–100, 52. Cotton, *Way of Life,* 420. John Dod, *A Remedy against Private Contentions: A . . . Sermon on James 4, 1 . . .* (London, 1618 [orig. publ. 1609]), 28. Hooker, *Paterne of Perfection,* 321, 328. Preston, *Saints Daily Exercise,* 3. Cotton, *Christ the Fountaine,* 209–219.

As one manual summarized, "When you doe call upon God, he is not changed by your prayers, but the change is wrought in you." Through prayer "the graces of his Spirit may be increased in us." At the same time "prayer brings us to Communion with God." Thomas Shepard wrote, "I have seen God by reason and never been amazed at God. I have seen God himself and have been ravished to behold him." Shepard felt himself "stirred up to pray for the spirit, not only for particular graces of it but for the spirit itself." The immediacy of his communion with the Divine was so intense that he hoped "all this might not be a delusion." Cotton Mather termed the same sensation being "irradiated" with grace. In prayer New Englanders saw most clearly the connection between their own individual spiritual experience and the grandest redemptive design of their God.[36]

Prayer was a human experience, described in psychological terms, though spiritual in nature. One prayed for daily and earthly needs and for outward marks of spiritual progress. But prayer was effectual only if Christ was at work applying grace to the soul, and even more precisely, only if Christ actively interceded with the Father on the praying saint's behalf. Thus Christ's heavenly role was twofold. With the Father He sent the Holy Spirit to believers' hearts, and before the Father He prayed for believers (John 17:9). Christ was seen, as in Hebrews 7–8, as high priest, "set on the right hand of the throne of the Majesty in the heavens." As intercessor for the saints, Christ first "doth present his merits and obedience before the Father as fully performed" for the elect. Then, through the gift of the Holy Spirit, He communicates "all that spiritual good he hath purchased and the Father hath promised to bestow upon them." In the application of redemption, Christ as high priest "intercepts all our prayers, and perfumes them with the sweet Odors of the incense of his own intercession, and so they find acceptance." John 17 set forth the Puritan understanding of Christ as the first cause of efficacious prayer and as the one who conjoined the earthly life of the saints with God in heaven and with the movement of the cosmos toward the eschaton. Thomas Hooker concluded that "the work of Intercession is to act all our affayrs with God the Father, to further our comfort and spiritual welfare here on Earth, until we come to Heaven."[37]

---

36. [Hooker], *Soules Humiliation,* 229. Hooker, *Paterne of Perfection,* 326–329. Shepard, *Saint's Jewel,* 10. Cotton, *Way of Life,* 10–11. Preston, *Saints Daily Exercise,* 44. Bayne, *Briefe Directions,* 160–161. Shepard, "Journal," in McGiffert, ed., *God's Plot,* 136–137, 161. Ford, ed., *Diary of Cotton Mather,* I, 341–345. I. Mather, *Diary,* ed. Green, 19.

37. Thomas Hooker, *A Comment upon Christs Last Prayer in the Seventeenth of John . . .* (London, 1656), 13–16.

The devotional manuals and New England practice recognized two types of secret prayer, which corresponded to ordinary and extraordinary meditation. The most important was "ordinary prayers at set times," and the second type was referred to as "ejaculatory" or "extraordinary prayer."

Regular prayers were to be recited "in a solemne manner, with due preparation, conjoyning together the parts of prayer, confession, petition, and thanksgiving." That is, ordinary prayer was to be lengthy enough to allow the person to move once again through the redemptive cycle. Just as prayer guided the penitent through each stage of conversion, the saint brought the stages of that experience forward and reenacted them in each prayer. Since the disciplines of reading and meditation normally preceded the prayer, the person was already within the redemptive order; but prayer gave that process its fullest expression and completion. For example, the "Prayer to be used at any time, by one alone privately" in one manual opened with confession of sin. "O Lord my God and heavenly Father, I thy most unworthy child doe here in thy sight freely confesse, that I am a most sinful creature, and damnable transgressor of all thy Lawes and Commandments: that as I was borne and bred in sinne, and stained in the womb, so I have continually brought forth the corrupt and ugly fruits of that infection and contagion . . . in thoughts, words and workes. . . . I am a lump of sin, and a masse of all misery." The prayer moved to petitions for the granting of assurance of grace, for the church, and for the advent of the Kingdom.[38]

New Englanders used the same form and phrases as they fell on their knees behind closed doors. When you pray in secret, Roger Clap wrote his children,

> there you may tell God your very Hearts, and lay open to Him your worst Plague-Sore, your vilest Sins, which no Man knoweth, neither is it meet they should know. Yet all Men shall know your vilest, lewdest, most notorious Wickedness, both of Heart and Life that ever was committed by you, tho' never so long ago, or never so secretly done; except you confess them to God, and make your Peace with Him, in and through Jesus Christ, by Repentance and Faith: Then the Blood of Jesus Christ the Righteous cleanseth us, and will you from all your sins.

Through the first stage of secret prayer, confession of sin, the believer renewed his or her repentance for continuing sin. By reenacting the

38. Downame, *Guide to Godlynesse*, 208. Dent, *Plaine Mans Pathway*, sig. Ee2ᵛ–Ee3ᵛ.

first stage of the salvation drama the heart was once again prepared to receive God's grace. When we "abase ourselves," Bayne wrote, we "stand at his mercy . . . our pride abated." The penitent was then able to pray for God's "great mercy towards me, poor sinner, and give me a general pardon." As progress was made in grace, the saint continued to pray for "more and more of [God's] love," as in Arthur Dent's model: "O Lord increase my faith. . . . Enable me to bring forth the sound fruits of faith and repentance. . . . Fill my soul full with joy and peace in believing. Fill me full of inward comfort and spiritual strength against all temptations. . . . Give me victory over those sinnes which thou knowest are strongest in me. Let me once at last make a conquest of the world and the flesh. Mortifie in me whatever is carnall: sanctifie me throughout by thy spirit: Knit my heart to thee for ever. . . . Renue in me the Image of thy Sonne Christ more and more." In New England Thomas Shepard echoed: "Oh Lord imprint this image on me, and give the spirit of this thy Son to me."[39]

Beyond petitions for the salvation of one's own soul, prayers included petition and intercession for blessings in this life, the well-being of neighbors, the commonwealth, the saints in the church, and the sick. The desires expressed in these prayers were expected to be in line with the will of God and based on sound faith. They must, that is, be the "prayer of faith" mentioned in James 5:15 with respect to the healing of the sick. Faithful prayer "carries the heart unto God, and holds it with God" as He bestows His blessing. The heart must be in heaven, not fixed on those things being prayed for. Thomas Shepard recognized in meditation that, "As by Christ I had access to the Father, so by faith and prayer of faith I had access to Christ. . . . The Lord also brought my soul to place all my happiness in being one in and with Christ and to have mind and heart only placed on him. Hence I saw this was heaven on earth." But Shepard resisted the temptation to enjoy selfishly his spiritual delight. "I considered, Why shall I meddle with other matters then? And I considered I must be like to Christ in communicating good to others as well as being united with him." As he prayed for others and sought their welfare, Shepard wrote, "this set my heart right and in a sweet frame." God would reject prayer, John Dod wrote, "when we are more earnest in asking earthly things, which may bee abused, then heavenly and saving graces which cannot bee abused: and aime at serving our own turnes in the requests that we make, rather then at the glorifying of

---

39. *Clap's Memoirs*, 49. Bayne, *Briefe Directions*, 155–161. Dent, *Plaine Mans Pathway*, sig. Ee3ʳ–Ee3ᵛ. Shepard, "Journal," in McGiffert, ed., *God's Plot*, 103.

Gods holy name." John Cotton wrote that "though wee must expresse our selves in words, in our desire for this and that blessing, yet God looks principally at the grounds of our desires. . . . What it is, that moves us to have a desire."[40]

New Englanders were urged particularly to pray for the conversion of others, especially for relatives. Pray for "all those that are in the gall of bitternesse," Hooker preached. "You must use all means to reclaim them." For example, Thomas Shepard once prayed at night for "some godly man's children which wanted clothes, and it was a ghastly spectacle to me." His prayer soon transcended concern about poverty as it came to him that "if these children had God reconciled" to them, then "God might be honored by these wants." When he prayed for their conversion, "the Lord gave me a sweet glimpse of his glory this night upon this occasion to see myself and mine and all his people infinitely happy in having God ours though we had all wants, and so the world was in some measure crucified to me this night." Peter Thacher prayed for the conversion and salvation of his wife and other family members. He kept a day of "private prayer for my dear wife that the Lord would fit her, incline her heart unto, and open an Effectual door unto her in injoyment of, god in his ordinances, that shee might be fat and flowrishing in the Courts of the house of the Lord that her health and life might be Continued: and for the Child that its indisposition of body might be removed, and that its soul might be saved." Increase Mather's prayers for his family during illness reflect the themes of New England's prayers generally.

> In the night my Samuel was taken very ill, and in a feaver this morning, and Nath. seemingly iller today than yesterday. There hath bin much Health in my Family for a long time; and God has spared the lives of all my children, but I have not bin thankfull and humble as I should have bin, and therefore God is righteous in afflicting me. I have nothing to say but to ly down abashed before him, and let him doe with me and mine as seemeth him good. Onely I can not but Trust in him that Hee will be gracious, for his owne Names sake. In prayr not altogether without Hope.

In petitionary prayer believers ultimately threw themselves on the mercy of God and submitted to His will.[41]

Prayers of thanksgiving flowed naturally after the believer felt as-

40. Hooker, *Paterne of Perfection*, 329. Shepard, "Journal," in McGiffert, ed., *God's Plot*, 103. Dod, *Remedy against Private Contentions*, 25. Cotton, *Christ the Fountaine*, 215.

41. [Hooker], *Soules Humiliation*, 275. H[ooker], *Foure Learned and Godly Treatises*, 72.

sured that God had accepted the petitions and intercessions. Thanksgiving was based on knowledge that the benefits that came "to us from God his fatherly love" were real and produced "joy and gladness of heart." The poetry of Edward Taylor and Anne Bradstreet frequently culminated in such thanksgiving, as in Bradstreet's prayer "For Deliverance from a Feaver."

> O, Praises to my mighty God,
>   Praise to my Lord, I say,
> Who hath redeem'd my Soul from pitt;
>   Praises to him for Aye!

Other thanksgivings expressed the limitations of adequate praise. "What shall I render to thy Name. . . . I ow so much, so little can/ Return unto thy Name." By couching thanksgiving in the language of limitation—"How can I sufficiently thank thee, when I can scarce express" all God has done—Puritans carried the experience of humility and spiritual dependence through the entire prayer.[42]

Prayers for secret devotion in manuals followed the same daily cycle as did family prayer and meditation. The entire redemptive cycle of death and resurrection was rehearsed in all secret prayers, but the evening prayers tended to emphasize self-examination, confession of sin, and preparation for death. "Let prayer be the Key to open the Morning; and the Barre to shut in the Evening," for "thou knowest not whether (falne asleepe) thou shalt rise againe alive." The seven themes that Lewis Bayly suggested for evening prayer moved from confession to full submission:

1. Confessing thy sins, especially those which thou hast committed that day.
2. Craving . . . pardon and forgiveness.
3. Requesting the assistance of his Holy Spirit, for amendment of life.
4. Giving thanks for benefits received, especially for thy preservation that day.
5. Praying for rest and protection that night.
6. Remembering the state of the Church . . . Ministers and

Shepard, "Journal," in McGiffert, ed., *God's Plot*, 103–104, 160. Thacher, "Diary," MS, I, 18–19. I. Mather, *Diary*, ed. Green, 7–8.

42. Bayne, *Briefe Directions*, 155. Anne Bradstreet, "For Deliverance from a Feaver," in Hutchinson, ed., *Poems of Bradstreet*, 62–63. See also, for example, her "My Thankful Heart with Glorying Tongue," "For the Restoration of My Dear Husband from a Burning Ague, June, 1661," and "In Thankfull Remembrance for My Dear Husbands Safe Arrival Sept. 3, 1662," *ibid.*, 68, 69, 76. Bayly, *Practice of Piety*, 362.

Magistrates, and our Brethren visited or persecuted.
7. Lastly, commending thy self and all thine to his gracious
   custody.

An evening prayer modeled after this pattern closed with a petition:
"Thy grace O Lord Jesus Christ, thy love, O heavenly Father, thy comfort and consolation, O holy and blessed spirit, be with me, and dwell
in my heart, this night and ever more, Amen." Evening prayers thus
concluded on a significantly more assured note (though the emphasis
was still on confession of sin) than did the meditations because meditation was preparatory to the fulfilling act of prayer. Morning prayers
then even more fully emphasized the soul's resurrection to new life.
They opened with confession—"O Merciful Father, for Jesus Christ
his sake, I beseech thee, forgive me all my known and secret sins"—
but progressed quickly to affirmation of faith and praise for God's
work in the soul. "Sanctifie my heart with thy holy Spirit, that I may
henceforth lead a more godly and Religious life. And here (O Lord) I
praise thy holy name, for that thou hast refreshed me this night with
moderate sleep and rest. . . . Bless me therefore Lord, in my going
out, and coming in." The word "amen," which concluded all prayers,
was a reminder, John Dod wrote, "to end them confidently . . . wee
must say unto our soules; It is so, and it shall be so."[43]
    Besides ordinary prayer at established times on a daily and weekly
schedule, New Englanders practiced extraordinary prayer at irregular
times. Although previous scholarship has not recognized the significance, or even the existence, of ejaculatory prayer within Puritanism,
it was in fact common. This aspect of Puritan spirituality, like several
others, was continuous with Roman Catholic and medieval mystical
practices. Helen C. White described ejaculatory prayer as having "an
ancient and honorable history in the story of religion." She related it
to the Hindu "ᴏᴍ" and cited as Christian examples St. Augustine's "O
Beauty of all things Beautiful!" and St. Francis of Assisi's entire night
of praying simply, "My God, my God!" In post-Tridentine Catholicism
St. Francis de Sales advised spontaneous "aspirations" either "with
your heart or with your lips, those words which love shall suggest to
you at the time." He approved short biblical formulas, especially from
the psalms or "ejaculations of love uttered in the Canticle of Canticles." In the English mystical tradition *The Cloud of Unknowing* advocated prayers of only one syllable: "Short prayer pierces heaven."

---

43. Will[iam] Per[kins], "Directions How to Live Well, and to Dye Well," in Ro[gers] *et
al.*, *Spirituall Flowers*, 24–25. Bayly, *Practice of Piety*, 188, 161–162. Dod, *Exposition on the
Lords Prayer*, 230–231.

White was surprised to find even one seventeenth-century reference to the practice, and that in "one of the most popular of all seventeenth century devotional treatises," Michael Sparke's *The Crums of Comfort* (London, 1628). She had assumed that the seventeenth century "was more intellectual in the discursive sense" in its approach to religion. Sparke's advocacy was typical, however, not unusual. He wrote, "Besides our more special devotions at set times, we may use Ejaculations at all times, upon every good occasion, which are short desires of the heart, lifted up to God with great fervency." Other manuals promoted the practice in very similar wording: "We use sudden and short ejaculations, lifting up our hearts unto God, and as it were darting unto the Throne of grace our fervent desires, which we may doe, without being discerned in the midst of a crowd, and without any distractions from our ordinary affairs." Another said that in worship, "when the Minister prayeth in the behalfe of the whole Congregation, let thine heart joyne with him" with "inward sighes and groanes."[44]

New England diaries and personal writings reveal the actual practice of brief outbursts of prayer. John Eliot's portrait of the "Ancient and Excellent Character of a true Christian" suggested "many scores of Ejaculations in a Day," spontaneously and in various settings. Cotton Mather resolved "to lead a Life of heavenly Ejaculations," by which he meant precisely what the manuals intended: "Every Day, at such Minutes, as I have not Liberty to make my more sett Visits unto the God of Heaven, I would then ty my Desires unto the Arrowes of ejaculatory Prayers, and so shoot them over the Heads of all Interruptions." Mather and others used the same terminology as mystical Catholics, including images of arrows, darts, and piercing. Peter Thacher engaged in ejaculatory prayer continually on some days. In the morning "as soon as I waked I spent a little time in holy Ejaculation." During the day "my heart was often lifted up to god in Ejaculatory prayer for assistance in my preparatory work" for the Sabbath. On a journey he kept his "thoughts . . . upon god by Ejaculation goeing and comeing." And at night "after I was abed I spent some time in Ejaculatory prayer soe went to sleep." Among the laity, both Roger Clap and Anne Bradstreet prayed in this manner at least occasionally, as the vignettes in chapter one show, using phrases from the Song of Songs as St. Francis de Sales had recommended. The outbursts "He is come!" and "Come deare Bridgrome" derive from that

44. White, *English Devotional Literature*, 185–186. St. Francis de Sales, *Introduction to the Devout Life*, trans. and ed. Ryan, 55–56. *Cloud of Unknowing*, 148–149. Downame, *Guide to Godlynesse*, 210. Web[be], "Daily Exercise," in Ro[gers] *et al.*, *Spirituall Flowers*, 104–105.

biblical source. The Bradstreet poem "By Night When Others Soundly Slept" is another instance of her extraordinary devotions that undoubtedly consisted of ejaculatory prayers.

> I sought him whom my Soul did Love,
> With tears I sought him earnestly;
> He bow'd his ear down from Above,
> In vain I did not seek or cry.[45]

The extent to which New Englanders put themselves through these pious exercises, and especially one as private as spontaneous prayer, is, of course, finally impossible to determine. Based on the evidence that does exist, it seems reasonable to conclude that such exercises were practiced widely if unevenly. Anne Bradstreet and the other devout women of whom we know were probably more typical than unusual, and the practice of piety as revealed in clerical and other diaries, and as described in manuals and sermons, was characteristic of many New Englanders' lives.

PERSONAL WRITING

Jonathan Mitchel, in the section on meditation in his "Letter to His Friend," advised not only "reading a good Book" as a means of grace but also writing. Specifically, he recommended "writing of your former and present life: (that is a thing of endless use) gathering up Gods mercies, and your sins in writing sometimes." In their personal spiritual writing Puritans practiced self-examination; recorded ordinary events and "remarkable providences," which taken together could provide clues to God's plan for the soul; kept track of public worship and private devotional activity; and meditated and prayed. Diary entries also included terse notes of entirely secular transactions, of who visited whom or preached on what text. Cotton Mather, writing on "the way of keeping a Diary," advocated brevity; the purpose, after all, was to record time, not to consume inordinate amounts of it. Still, some diaries and journals (including Mather's) contain rather lengthy entries, especially during periods of intense spiritual or political activity. Entries were written mostly at night, in conjunction with the reflective mood of nocturnal secret devotions. In their

45. C. Mather, ed., *Life and Death of J. Eliot*, 20. Ford, ed., *Diary of Cotton Mather*, I, 4, 61. Thacher, "Diary," MS, II, 5, 7, 10, 27. *Clap's Memoirs*, 17–25. Anne Bradstreet, "As Weary Pilgrim," and "By Night When Others Soundly Slept," in Hutchinson, ed., *Poems of Bradstreet*, 77–78, 61–62.

diaries saints recorded and pondered the events of the day and evening. Most clearly in the case of Edward Taylor's poetry, personal writing could be a means of meditation itself.[46]

If not precisely "the Puritan's confessional," as William Haller and others have suggested, diary keeping and other personal writing was certainly an important discipline in the Puritan's devotional life. Scholars have usually paid at least passing attention to this phenomenon, and the popular picture of the seventeenth-century New Englander includes an image of him scrawling a list of overrated sins by candlelight. Edmund S. Morgan has pointed out that the diary of Michael Wigglesworth in fact conforms to the stereotype. It reveals an overwhelming and overweening sense of guilt, especially of a sexual nature, and an anguished, tortuous spirituality. Other diaries, however, demonstrate Puritan ability to experience grace and spiritual delight. Cotton Mather praised his father's diary for its record of "soaring Interviews with Heaven" and "such Flights as his melted Soul was transported to." The journal of the Billerica schoolteacher Joseph Thompson has evoked the appraisal, "it is easy to condemn Calvinism, and to call Puritan introspection morbid, but it is hard to read a narrative like Thompson's without feeling that cant and hypocrisy are foreign to it. His record demands whatever sympathy may be vouchsafed to deep feeling and robust faith." Spiritual autobiography, usually written near the end of one's life in preparation for death and as a legacy for descendants, was also a means of self-examination. The constant theme of Puritan autobiographical narratives was not the mere cataloging of sins but an examination of God's grace in the face of sin. The poetry of Edward Taylor and Anne Bradstreet allowed the poets to rise above the world of sin into a divine embrace. Personal spiritual writing was, in short, a means of grace.[47]

It may be unreasonable to believe that "most" New Englanders kept a diary. But from the large volume of personal writing—diaries and journals, spiritual autobiographies, notes on self-examination exercises, and religious and meditative poetry—that has survived, we may conclude that many of the devout did write extensively. The connec-

---

46. Mitchel, "Letter to His Friend," appended to *Discourse of the Glory*, 2d ed., 282. [Cotton Mather], *Parentator. Memoirs of Remarkables in the Life and the Death of the Ever-Memorable Dr. Increase Mather . . .* (Boston, 1724), 36–48. Shepard, *Certain Select Cases Resolved*, 4.

47. Haller, *Rise of Puritanism*, 38. Watkins, *Puritan Experience*, 18. Wakefield, *Puritan Devotion*, 111, insisted rightly that the office of confessor and spiritual director still belonged to the pastor. Morgan, ed., *Diary of Wigglesworth*, Introduction, v. [C. Mather], *Parentator*, 41, 45. Murdock, ed., *Handkerchiefs from Paul*, xx. McGiffert, ed., *God's Plot*, Introduction, 18. See generally, Shea, *Spiritual Autobiography*.

tion between the diary and self-examination suggests that personal writing was an especially, though again not uniquely, Puritan discipline. Certainly, many people other than those whose writings are extant kept spiritual records. Jonathan Mitchel, for example, said in his "Letter to His Friend" that he kept a diary, but other than excerpts that Cotton Mather included in his life of Mitchel, it has not survived. Many diaries had already disappeared by the end of the seventeenth century. Mather noted that Charles Chauncy "kept a Diary, the loss of which I can't but mention with regret." The meditative poetry of Edward Taylor was not discovered until 1937. Thomas Shepard referred in his autobiography to "a little book" recording his "daily meditations" from university days at Cambridge through the 1630s in New England: "And I so found him in meditation that I was constrained to carry my book into the fields to write down what God poured in." The notebook has not survived. Many of the extant diaries are actually only fragments of a few years at most. Shepard's journal, for example, encompasses only the years 1640 through the beginning of 1644. Virtually complete diaries are exceedingly rare and usually belonged to prominent persons. Cotton Mather's survives because he intended for it to survive, as a source of instruction and inspiration for his descendants and for the writing of his biography. The same motivation drove him to preserve as many diary fragments as possible in his biographies of important New Englanders. The extant personal spiritual writing is but a remnant of what must have been a large body of literature.[48]

Some personal writing did not survive because the writers hid or destroyed it. Edward Taylor's poetry is the best-known example, since it was finally discovered; but Taylor was not the only one whose writing was strictly personal. Joseph Green at age twenty-one included instructions for his manuscript: "And If I should dye before I have commited this book to the flames; I give leave to my nearest relation to look over it; but I give a strict charge to them not to expose it to the view of any; And it is my will that this book be viewed by none unless by one person which is nearest related unto me; and now I pray God to help me to write sincerely humbly, and without ostentation." In his autobiographical notes he meditated on the state of his soul in hope of experiencing God's grace. Green wrote so that he might "be humbled for the sinfulness of my life . . . that so when I look over it I

---

48. Ronald A. Bosco, ed., *Paterna: The Autobiography of Cotton Mather* (Delmar, N.Y., 1976), Introduction, xl. C. Mather, *Magnalia Christi Americana*, I, 470, II, 67, 80–112. Shepard, "Autobiography," in McGiffert, ed., *God's Plot*, 42, 73. Ford, ed., *Diary of Cotton Mather*, I, 41.

may have my heart filled with shame and sorrow, for the disorders of my mispent life." He confessed that "now I desire to return to God, as a poor prodigal." This was business inappropriate for the world's eyes. Cotton Mather found a similar case in Nathaniel Rogers: "He was known to keep a diary; but he kept it with so much reservation, that it is not known that ever any one but himself did read one word of it: and he determined that none ever should; for he ordered a couple of his intimate friends to cast it all into the fire, without looking into the contents of it." Mather lamented "the loss of those experiences, which might in these rich papers have kept him, after a sort, still alive unto us! but as they would have proved him an incarnate seraphim, so the other seraphim, who carried him away with them, were no strangers to the methods, by which he had ripened and winged himself to become one of their society." Even Cotton Mather, as inveterate a diarist as New England produced, allowed only those diaries to survive that he intended as instruction for others. He tended to regard secret diary keeping, which served no social function, as an unwarranted expense of time. More important, as he explained in his quasi-public diary, "all my Services, to my Maker and Master, I desire may bee, as already the most of them have been, both conceled and forgotten, by every one except Him alone, who will not forgett my Labour of Love." Therefore, he wrote, "my Diaries, wherein I had written the Course of my Study and preaching, and the Resolves of Piety upon my Daily course of Meditation, I have thrown, as useless Papers into the Fire."[49]

Edward Taylor did not intend his poetry for public reading for the same reasons. They were the product of secret devotional exercises, the result of "the process of meditating by means of the language of poetry," as Karl Keller has shown, and "we invade his privacy as we read him today." Since Puritans believed that the goal of devotional practices was union with Christ, a union that was expressed in mystically erotic imagery from the Song of Songs and Jesus' parable of the ten virgins, opening the record to the public was as improper as publishing an account of one's sexual experiences in marriage. Just as the experience of tenderness and ecstasy was solely between husband

49. Morison, ed., "Commonplace Book of Joseph Green," Col. Soc. Mass., *Trans.*, XXXIV (1943), 234. C. Mather, *Magnalia Christi Americana*, I, 420–421. Ford, ed., *Diary of Cotton Mather*, I, 73. [C. Mather], *Parentator*, 36–37. Discussion of why Taylor did not want his poetry known includes speculation that he was too modest and that he was a crypto-Catholic. See Keller, *Example of Taylor*, 83–85, 297–298 nn. 7–9 for a discussion of the debate. Keller correctly concludes, "Self-effacing, alarmingly personal, botched, and archaic as his poetry is, there is yet something about Taylor's approach to poetry that justifies its privateness."

and wife, meditation and prayer concerned no one but the individual and God. We have no way of knowing how many New Englanders kept such records and succeeded in suppressing or destroying them.[50]

Notes on the results of self-examination were generally not considered to be confidential. Unlike meditation in its sublime form, self-examination was not designed to lead directly to union with Christ. It was rather a more this-worldly religious exercise, directed toward confession of sin and the search for outward evidence of grace in the Christian life. The results of self-examination were fit material to report to others in private conference, family devotions, and neighborhood meetings. In fact, saints explicitly sought the help of others. John Corbet in England and John Higginson in Massachusetts, therefore, published their self-examination notes for the edification of believers. Diaries such as Samuel Sewall's, of which much is personal but little is secret, could also be shared publicly. Still, Sewall and others who kept a semi-private, semi-public diary that dealt more with current events than with private devotions were motivated at least in part by devotional aims. Sewall believed that God's hand could be discerned in business and political events as well as in meditation and prayer.[51]

The daily record kept as a devotional exercise was related to other ways of marking events over time. New England produced annual almanacs after 1640, a large number of histories, business account books, and travel journals, all of them part of the same mentality that produced diaries and spiritual autobiographies. Puritans were extremely interested in the concept of time and believed (as others had over the centuries) that they were living near the end of it. Time was precious in the New England mind because at the Last Judgment each moment must be accounted for. And now each moment could be the last. By recording time Puritans hoped to redeem time in the Pauline sense: "See then that ye walk circumspectly, not as fools, but as wise, Redeeming the time because the days are evil" (Ephesians 5:15–16). Cotton Mather described his father's as "the Diary of a Time-Saver or time redeemer." In these latter days, New Englanders believed, God would cause catastrophes on earth that would lead to the chiliad and the coming of the Kingdom. These events were prophesied most

50. Keller, *Example of Taylor*, 96, 81. It is perhaps no accident that, aside from the letters of John and Margaret Winthrop, Anne Bradstreet's poems to her husband, Thomas Shepard's lamentation on the death of Joanna, and a few elegiac poems, so few windows into Puritan marital affection exist.

51. Corbet, *Self-Imployment in Secret*. Higginson, "Some Help to Self-Examination," in *Our Saviour's Legacy of Peace*.

clearly by Daniel, Ezekiel, and St. John in the Revelation. Astrology, meteorology, and the course of world political events were taken as clues to the progress of the world to its appointed end.[52]

Almanacs and historiography had apocalyptic as well as everyday practical application. It was their apocalyptic sense that led Puritans to produce such an astounding quantity of time-related literature within so few years of settlement. The *Almanack* was the second item off the Cambridge press in 1639. No society has chronicled its history more thoroughly than did New England. The same forces also moved New Englanders to keep daily personal records. Sometimes their diaries were interleaved with or scrawled tightly onto the pages of the *Almanack*. Cotton Mather noted of John Eliot, for example, "He had always been an Enemy to Idleness; any one that should look into the little Diary that he kept in his Almanacks, would see that there was with him, No day without a Line." Mather's last phrase sounds very much like a seasoned maxim, suggesting again the popular nature of Puritan spirituality. Saint, society, and cosmos were perceived as marching in lockstep toward time's completion.[53]

The relation of the spiritual diary to the entirely secular business and travel diaries reminds us of the complexity of New England society. The most pious men and women still spent more time at business than in devotional exercises. The business and legal records of the non-Puritans William Aspinwall and Thomas Lechford illustrate secular record keeping. Spiritual records were similar to these, however, in that after death and at the Last Judgment each person had to surrender the ledger of one's life to God. Spiritual diaries, and especially records of self-examination, were account books in this sense. But the travel diary especially opens the theological significance of personal spiritual writing. The literature abounds in journals of trips to New England, trips by New Englanders, and trips by outsiders through the colonies. Ships crossing the Atlantic, naturally, kept logs of their voyages, and narratives of voyages did much to stimulate migration in the first place, starting with the prototype of the genre,

52. [C. Mather], *Parentator*, 36.

53. C. Mather, ed., *Life and Death of J. Eliot*, 124. Other examples of personal record keeping include Noadiah Russell's 1687 diary, published by the Connecticut Historical Society in 1934; the 1646 MS "Almanack" owned by the Rev. Samuel Sewall of Burlington, Mass. (American Antiquarian Society microcard); the 1672 MS "Ephemeris of the Cœlestial Motions" (Am. Antiq. Soc. microcard); and the 1673 MS "Almanack" in the possession of the Congregational Library, Boston. See Sacvan Bercovitch, "Horologicals to Chronometricals: The Rhetoric of the Jeremiad," in Eric Rothstein, ed., *Literary Monographs*, III (Madison, Wis., 1970); and Bercovitch, *American Jeremiad*.

Richard Hakluyt's *The Principall Navigations, Voiages, and Discoveries of the English Nation* (London, 1589). Individuals kept private records of the crossing, for example, the entire extant journal of Richard Mather and a large portion of the diary of Edward Taylor. Military officers, such as Captain Joshua Scottow and Colonel Benjamin Church (who composed the popular *Entertaining Passages Relating to King Philip's War* from his diary notes), kept daily journals of expeditions.[54]

The etymological connection between the words "journal" and "journey" reveals a deep relationship between travel and personal record keeping. Both stem from the root meaning "day" ("diary" has the same root). Besides the modern meaning of a trip, in the Middle Ages "journey" denoted a day's travel, twenty miles. The "journal" was, of course, the record of daily events or transactions, but other seventeenth-century meanings included "a day's travel" and "provisions for a journey." Although journals were kept for many reasons, the connotations of the word suggest the idea of the journal as the record of a day's journey. It is no coincidence that even Puritans who may not have kept a journal routinely, such as John Winthrop, Jr., began to keep them when on a journey. Others, such as the senior Winthrop, Richard Mather, and Edward Taylor, began to keep them as their lives became unsettled and they thought of emigration. Mary Rowlandson's stage-by-stage account of her journey through the wilderness as an Indian captive, though written from memory after her redemption, exhibits the characteristics of a journal. "See then that ye walk circumspectly," as Paul had written. When one took to the road, as either a literal or a figurative pilgrim, it was natural to keep a log of events along the way.[55]

The great journey for Puritans was the spiritual one to the heavenly city. Increase Mather began keeping a diary after his youthful travels

54. William Aspinwall, *A Volume Relating to the Early History of Boston, Containing the Aspinwall Notarial Records from 1644 to 1651* (Boston, 1903). Thomas Lechford, *Notebook Kept by Thomas Lechford, Esq., Lawyer, in Boston, Massachusetts Bay, from June 27, 1638, to July 29, 1641* (Am. Antiq. Soc., *Collections*, VII [Cambridge, Mass., 1885]). *Journal of Richard Mather, 1635. His Life and Death. 1670* (Dorchester Antiq. and Hist. Soc., *Colls.*, III [Boston, 1850]), 5–32. "Diary of Edward Taylor," Mass. Hist. Soc., *Procs.*, XVIII (1880), 4–18. Joshua Scottow, "Extracts from a Manuscript Journal of Capt. Scottow," *NEHGR*, XLIII (1889), 68–70. Colonel Benjamin Church, *Diary of King Philip's War, 1675–76*, ed. Alan and Mary Simpson (Chester, Conn., 1975).

55. "Diary of John Winthrop, Jr., Ann. 1645," Mass. Hist. Soc., *Procs.*, 2d Ser., VIII (1892–1894), 4–12. Tobias Payne, "A Short Abstract of the Course of My Life," *ibid.*, 1st Ser., XIII (1873–1875), 405–409. *OED*, s.v. "journal," "journey," "diary." Mary Rowlandson's *The Soveraignty and Goodness of God, Together with the Faithfulness of His Promises Displayed* . . . was originally published in Cambridge, Mass., in 1682, and was an immediate bestseller. The first extant copy is of the Boston 1720 edition.

in Europe were over and when his spiritual pilgrimage as a New England pastor began: "from the time of his return to the New English, to the Time of his withdrawal to the Heavenly World." The theme of the spiritual pilgrimage, as we have seen, was a commanding one in Puritan spirituality and devotional practice. John Bunyan said of *The Pilgrim's Progress*

> This Book will make a Travailer of thee,
> If by its Counsel thou wilt ruled be;
> It will direct thee to the Holy Land,
> If thou wilt its Directions understand.

He believed, as New Englanders had believed long before he wrote it, that every Christian must traverse the same stages as his exemplary Christian. Bunyan's pilgrim traveled the stages once, in archetypal fashion, but the believer progressed through them daily and weekly and over a lifetime in the devotional exercises. *The Pilgrim's Progress* was not written in the form of a journal, but it could well have been. That book and the author's record of his own spiritual journey in *Grace Abounding* are closely related. In both the physical and spiritual worlds travelers kept records of events and landmarks, dangers and narrow escapes. New Englanders who understood life as a pilgrimage were drawn to personal spiritual writing at least partly because of the connection between "journey" and "journal." Diaries, journals, meditative poetry, and spiritual autobiographies are all in this sense travel literature.[56]

56. [C. Mather], *Parentator*, 36–37. Bunyan, *Pilgrim's Progress*, ed. Wharey and Sharrock, 6. Profound expression of these ideas in a non-Western religious culture is found in the work of Matsuo Bashō, Japanese Buddhist pilgrim and master of haiku poetry. In "The Records of a Travel-Worn Satchel" he wrote, "From time immemorial the art of keeping diaries while on the road was popular among the people." Bashō's life (1644–1694) spanned almost precisely the same years as John Bunyan's (1628–1688), and his masterpiece, "The Narrow Road to the Deep North," contains astonishing similarities to *The Pilgrim's Progress*. Bashō, *The Narrow Road to the Deep North and Other Travel Sketches*, trans. Nobuyuki Yuasa (Middlesex, Eng., 1966), 73, 97.

PART III

"Constant Preparation for Glory"

The publick meetings ever did frequent,
And in her Closet constant hours she spent;
Religious in all her words and wayes,
Preparing still for death, till end of dayes.

ANNE BRADSTREET
"An Epitaph on My Dear and Ever Honoured Mother
Mrs. Dorothy Dudley, Who Deceased Decemb. 27. 1643.
and of Her Age, 61."

Chapter Seven

Pilgrimage as Preparation

 The devotional practices of New Englanders are best described as exercises in preparation for salvation. Though God accomplished salvation in conversion, Puritans knew that they would not attain full salvation until the soul was perfectly united with Christ after death. The devout looked toward death as the final barrier. Death was at once a source of anxiety and a source of hope, both impelling and attracting New Englanders to greater piety. If the vignette of Samuel Sewall illustrates the role of anxiety, those of Thomas Shepard and Anne Bradstreet exemplify the importance of hope as a motive. John Cotton preached that saints were those whose faith led them "to prepare and provide for another life." Devotional acts thus were considered "practice" in both senses of the word: as habitual or regular acts, as in the phrase "common practice," and as exercises in preparation for a final performance. The word "exercise" also connotes training or preparation, as an athlete or a soldier, for a future event. Puritans saw confession and meditative self-examination as rehearsals for the Last Judgment. Cotton Mather in *Preparatory Meditations upon the Day of Judgment* even used the surprising metaphor of a theatrical rehearsal. "The most hopeful Preparations for the Day of Judgment, would be attain'd in our Solemn Anticipations of that most Great and Notable Day of the Lord. Let us aforehand Act over the Day of Judgment; not in a Play, Like those Germans, who turned the parable of the Virgins into a Comedy . . . but by Seriously bringing our selves Now to such Trials as will then be pass'd upon us." The practice of devotion prepared the heart for eternal union with Christ on that other side of death. Shepard "began to long to die and think of being with him"; Mrs. Bradstreet could hear the Lord calling her name. Jonathan Mitchel practiced "meditation, yea, daily meditation" because then "Heaven is here begun upon earth: shall I be thinking on and talking with Christ, to all eternity, and not discourse with him one quarter of an hour in a day now?"[1]

1. Cotton, *Briefe Exposition of Ecclesiastes,* 47. Cotton Mather, *Preparatory Meditations*

The ambiguity of being saints and still sinners drove Puritans to perceive devotion as preparation. In "The Ebb and Flow," the title of which suggests the recurrent nature of his experience, Edward Taylor meditated on his dilemma after conversion but before glory.

> When first thou on me Lord wrought'st thy Sweet Print,
>   My heart was made thy tinder box.
>   My 'ffections were thy tinder in 't.
>   Where fell thy Sparkes by drops.
> Those holy Sparks of Heavenly Fire that came
> Did ever catch and often out would flame.

With time the blaze subsided, and Taylor's devotions became a "Censar trim," "Full of thy golden Altars fire." In this state, however, his soul became inured to sensation. "I finde my tinder scarce thy sparks can feel." Even doubts arose, but still, "when the bellows of thy Spirit blow / Away mine ashes, then thy fire doth glow." In "God's Determinations" the saint reminded his own soul:

> You think you might have more: you shall have so,
> But if you'd all at once, you could not grow. . . .
> He'l fill you but by drops that so he may
> Not drown you in't, nor Cast a Drop away.

Salvation was to be prepared for, stage by stage, anticipated, hoped for, worked toward. When Peter Thacher was "exercised about [his] spiritual condition," his appropriation of the blessing of Aaron brought grace: "The Lord lift up upon my soul the light of his Countenance, cause his face to shine upon mee, and I shall be saved." Assurance was always of a future blessed estate, but it calmed the present.[2]

Scholars have limited discussion of preparation for salvation to argument over whether Hooker and his colleagues intended that unregenerate sinners could prepare themselves for conversion. It is clear by now that in conversion God was the actor. But this resolution poses new questions. Since ministers preached for conversion throughout the century, and since both regenerate and unregenerate sat in the meetinghouse, how did saints listen to exhortations to con-

---

upon the Day of Judgment, bound with Samuel Lee, *Great Day of Judgment* (Boston, 1692), 27. Shepard, "Journal," in McGiffert, ed., *God's Plot*, 85–86. Bradstreet, "As Weary Pilgrim," in Hutchinson, ed., *Poems of Bradstreet*, 77–78. C. Mather, *Magnalia Christi Americana*, II, 111. See Stannard, *Puritan Way of Death*, 79.

2. Stanford, ed., *Poems of Taylor*, 470, 441. Thacher, "Diary," MS, I, 199, Mass. Hist. Soc., Boston.

trition and humiliation? John Cotton, for example, called everyone to the preparatory stages:

> How therefore should this awaken the heart
> of every one that heares mee this day,
> call every (thou) every one of your soules by name, and say,
> what thou, whom God hath beene so patient too,
> twenty, thirty, fourty, an hundred yeers
> (Thou) whom hee hath visited with so much sicknesse,
> (Thou) whom God hath brought from a meane condition,
>   to a large measure of estate,
> (Thou) whom God hath beene thus patient too;
> *despiseth thou the patience of God?*
> presse this upon your hearts,
> and abuse his patience no longer.

When preachers cried with Ezekiel, "Make you a new heart and a new spirit," and "Turn ye, turn ye," they were preaching more than preparation for conversion. Conversion was but the point of departure for a life of devotional practice and spiritual progress. Thomas Shepard compared the experience of penitents "at first conversion" with that of mature saints at later stages. There remained "much self in the heart," a remnant of the old Adam, which was gradually, through acts of worship and devotion, driven out. But these later exercises continued to follow the same pattern as conversion—the order of redemption. As with Bunyan's pilgrim who set out after first conversion, salvation was the goal of a life journey rather than an achieved state.[3]

Shepard referred to his own progress in grace with a startling phrase: "renewed conversions." The stages of these deeper experiences followed the original conversion pattern. First "the soul may lie miserable," he wrote, "but Christ may be then had." Just as "at vocation Christ is given first and then sanctification; so in the renewed conversions of the saints, 'tis to be so again." In meditation on his sermon text ("it is in truth, the word of God, which effectually worketh also in you that believe," 1 Thessalonians 2:13), Shepard said, "I did look upon the Lord's call in the gospel to come, repent, and be converted." On another occasion, "In meditation, I saw when Christ was present, all blessings were present" and "mourned for want of this." The exercise then "gave me much light and set my heart in a sweet frame." In

3. Hall, *Faithful Shepherd*, 162. John Cotton, *Gods Mercie Mixed with His Justice, or, His Peoples Deliverance in Times of Danger* (London, 1641), 17. Hooker, *Application of Redemption, First Eight Books*, 132. Shepard, *Ten Virgins*, I, 157, 128, 78–79, II, 167. The classic preparationist texts are Ezekiel 18:31 and 33:11.

prayer, "my heart was much moved and melted to consider of my un-belief past. . . . And so I began that day of fast to believe." The fresh-ness of each successive infusion of grace came in spite of, or because of, Shepard's long and well-assured first conversion.[4]

Others attested to the need for "renewed conversions" as deeper experiences of the stages of redemption. Increase Mather said explic-itly, "There are Second Conversions of the same Christians, though not as to their State, but in respect of Growth in Grace. . . . Further degrees of Mortification and Sanctification are to be endeavoured by true Believers." Solomon Stoddard, Mather's sometime adversary, here took the same position. "It is but an uncomfortable thing to live upon an old work. . . . The best way is to get renewed acts of Love, and Faith and Repentance: and when you feel the workings of them, they will be more discernable." And in Cotton Mather's devotional life, Robert Middlekauff has written, "the most gratifying climax of all occurred when he re-experienced his conversion, an event that was repeated many times in his secret devotions. After humbling himself, he passed through the familiar stages of the conversion process which ended with the assurance that he was one of the Lord's chosen." We have already seen how greatly the salvific cycle determined the form and content of daily private devotions and of public worship. Prepa-ration for salvation, which the preachers called for in their "conver-sion preaching," referred to the means of growth in grace for the converted as well as a means of original grace to the unconverted.[5]

That preparation for salvation involved the continuity of conver-sion and spiritual progress is evident in the relationship between the words "conversion" and "conversation." Conversation was the biblical and traditional term for "the practice of a Christian life" after con-version. William Perkins wrote that "the practice of a Christian life" consisted of "new obedience unto God in our life and conversation." Conversation had to do with life in the covenant, with business and social ethics, with personal morality. Bunyan used the word in this

---

4. Shepard, "Journal," in McGiffert, ed., *God's Plot,* 123, 167, 87–88. McGiffert has pointed to the fact that "his mature piety cyclically re-enacted in abbreviated form that initial trauma." McGiffert's phrase "each fresh conversion," is, however, misleading. Shepard did not fall out of grace periodically and need to undergo the original terrors again. Shepard's own phrase "renewed conversions" is more accurate, since implanta-tion had been accomplished.

5. Increase Mather, *Ichabod or, A Discourse, Shewing What Cause There Is to Fear That the Glory of the Lord Is Departing from New-England* (Boston, 1702), 31. Solomon Stoddard, *The Sufficiency of One Good Sign to Prove a Man to Be in a State of Life* (Boston, 1703), 17. Robert Middlekauff, *The Mathers: Three Generations of Puritan Intellectuals, 1596–1728* (New York, 1971), 206–297.

way to point up hypocrisy. Faithful charged Talkative, "doth your life and conversation testifie the same" as your supposed faith? "Your conversation gives this your Mouth-profession the lye." Conversation flowed from sound conversion, as sanctification from justification. At the Boston Thursday lecture the perennial theme was "first the Affairs of a sincere Conversion, and then the Duties of a pious Conversation." When Joseph Green conferred with his pastor during the final stages of conversion he professed, "I desired a sincere conversion"; and when the pastor asked why, he explained, "that I might lead an holy conversation and do service for God in my generation."[6]

But we must not drive a wedge between conversion and conversation as though the first was a spiritual and the second a social experience. Thomas Merton has shown the inseparability of *conversio morum* and *conversatio morum* in the early history of monasticism and that, indeed, the two were originally synonymous. We might read "covenant" for "monastery" and apply Merton's words to Puritan spirituality: "The two go together, they influence each other, they are, so to speak, two sides of the same coin. One is converted from the *conversatio* of the world to that of the monastery, and by the *conversatio* of monastic life one is gradually 'converted' or 'transformed' in the likeness of Christ." The biblical basis for the words is in St. Paul, who emphasized both the social and the spiritual dimensions of conversation ("in simplicity and godly sincerity, not with fleshly wisdom, but by the grace of God, we have had our conversation in the world," 2 Corinthians 1:12; "For our conversation is in heaven," Philippians 3:20). Conversation was thus above all a spiritual way of life, including the "daily walk" of social intercourse but also the life of private devotion. John Eliot, in fact, identified the system of devotional disciplines that enabled believers to be "in Heaven" in this life as "Holiness in all manner of Conversation." And as an example of conversation as spirituality, Edward Taylor eulogized his wife.

> When in her Fathers house God toucht her Heart,
> That Trembling Frame of Spirit, and that Smart,
> She then was under very, few did know:
> Whereof she somewhat to the Church did show.
> Repentance now's her Work: Sin poyson is:
> Faith, carries her to Christ as one of his.

6. Perkins, *Cases of Conscience*, in *Works*, II, 15–16. Bunyan, *Pilgrim's Progress*, ed. Wharey and Sharrock, 83–84. Cotton Mather, *The Present State of New-England . . .* (Boston, 1690), 1. Morison, ed., "Commonplace Book of Joseph Green," Col. Soc. Mass., *Trans.*, XXXIV (1943), 240.

Fear Temples in her heart; Love flowers apace
To God, Christ, Grace Saints, and the Means of Grace.
She's much in Reading, Pray're, Selfe-Application
Holds humbly up, a pious Conversation.

By conversation Taylor meant the exercises of secret devotion, and in
a few sweeping lines, he demonstrated as well the continuity of subsequent spiritual progress with first conversion.[7]

Conversion and conversation, not simply conversion, was the process by which saints prepared for and progressively came into union
with Christ. The feeling of union with Christ in conversion and the
extension of that in devotional practice were both fulfillment of the
preparatory stages of those specific processes and foretastes of complete union in the Kingdom of God. In the same way Puritans understood that the perfect union with Christ in the future would be the
fulfillment of a lifetime of spiritual preparation. By means of conversion God readied the pilgrim for the journey; as sanctification
enabled the soul to follow God's will increasingly "on its own," through
the life of devotion the saint anticipated arrival at the heavenly destination. Increase Mather spoke specifically in these terms, using
conversation in direct reference to spiritual exercise, in his preface to
John Corbet's manual, *Self-Imployment in Secret.* The aim of Corbet's
meditative exercise was preparation of the soul for death and eternity.

> What blessed and glorious Consolations may they hope for
> who *Exercise themselves unto Godliness in the power of it.* Tho some
> such have their dark hours for the present, yet commonly when
> they are upon their deathbeds their souls are filled with Comfort,
> having this rejoycing, the Testimony of their Consciences, that
> in simplicity and Godly Sincerity they have had their Conversa-
> tion in the world. However they have sowen in tears shall here-
> after reap in joy. We should consider the end of the conversation
> of the Lords faithful servants, especially such as have taught the
> Word of God, and follow their Faith and Holiness.[8]

New England preparationism began with preparation for conversion but stretched out, Sabbath to Sabbath, toward death and beyond.
Preparation for conversion, devotional preparation for the night's

---

7. Middlekauff, *The Mathers,* 241. Thomas Merton, *The Monastic Journey,* ed. Brother
Patrick Hart (Kansas City, Kans., 1977), 107–120. C. Mather, ed., *Life and Death of
J. Eliot,* 19. Stanford, ed., *Poems of Taylor,* 475.

8. Hooker, *Application of Redemption, First Eight Books,* 93–95. Increase Mather, "To
the Reader," in Corbet, *Self-Imployment in Secret,* sig. A3^v.

sleep, preparation for the Sabbath, preparation for the Lord's Supper, preparation for death: In their devotional practice New Englanders ultimately prepared for union with Christ on the other side of death. It is crucial to recognize this breadth and unity in New England preparationism.

PREPARATION FOR THE SABBATH

Weekly preparation for the Sabbath was an exercise in preparation for salvation. We have already seen that Saturday night meditation and prayer were important and that each week's Sabbath rest anticipated eternal rest in heaven. One of the early manuals, Johann Gerhard's *The Soules Watch: Or, a Day-Booke for the Devout Soule*, presented a weekly cycle in which each successive day represented a stage on the pilgrimage to the Sabbath. The scheme was laid out along the borders of the title page; the meditative focus of the day was printed with the name of the day and an emblematic picture. On the left border were Monday ("The evils of man"), Tuesday ("Our confession of sins"), and Wednesday ("Our assurance of salvation"). On the right were Thursday ("The effects and helpes of faith"), Friday ("Christs Passion & our Redemption"), and Saturday ("The willingnesse we have in dying well"). At the top of the page was an emblematic picture of cherubs and the motto "God fore-sees." Along the bottom was Sunday, also with cherubs, with the theme "Our Resurrection and Glorification." Final preparation was actually to be made just "before the publike Exercise doe begin." The purpose of the following prayer, from another manual, was to prepare the heart: "O Most mighty and eternall God, . . . I vile and sinful wretch, . . . doe present my selfe to heare thy holy Word, and to offer up the sacrifice of Prayer and thanksgiving unto thee: . . . sanctifie and prepare my heart, that it may be apt and fit for this Exercise which now we have in hand: enflame my heart with zeal, and teach me how to pray: open mine Eares that I may heare, and mine heart, that I may understand that which shall at this time out of thy holy word bee taught unto mee. Take from me all wandering and by-thoughts."[9]

Preparation for the Sabbath was a common theme in the manuals. An episode from *The Pilgrim's Progress* again demonstrates the climax of the cycle on Saturday night and the denouement on the next day.

9. Gerhard, *Soules Watch*, title page. Web[be], "Daily Exercise," in Ro[gers] *et al.*, *Spirituall Flowers*, 103–104.

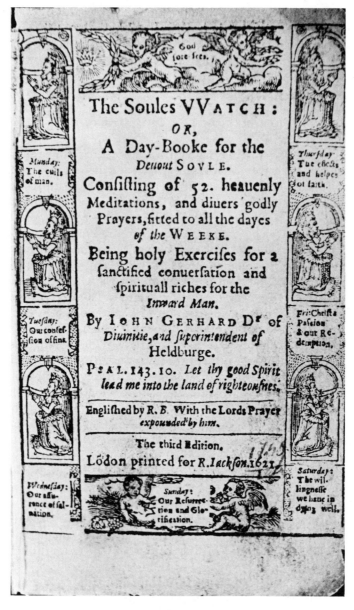

Figure 8. Title page of the English edition of Johann Gerhard's devotional manual The Soules Watch. *The week's calendar traces the order of redemption and the devotional cycle of mortification and vivification. Courtesy the Union Theological Seminary Library, New York City.*

Bunyan has time intrude only once in the essentially timeless dream: when Hopeful and Christian are in Doubting Castle. The Giant Despair "drove them . . . into a very dark Dungeon, nasty and stinking to the spirit of these two men: Here then they lay, from *Wednesday* morning till *Saturday* night." By the end of the week, at the brink of suicide, Christian would have been destroyed without Hopeful's encouragement. But on Saturday night, as the Giant and his wife "were got to bed," the pilgrims "began to *pray*, and continued in Prayer till almost break of day." By the dawn of the Sabbath Christian had his answer: "I have a *Key* in my bosom, called *Promise*, that will, (I am perswaded) open any Lock in *Doubting-Castle*." It did, and on the Sabbath Christian and Hopeful returned to safety and their journey on the King's Highway.[10]

New England practice followed the themes and rhythms of weekly preparation that were presented in the manuals. Jonathan Mitchel advised his friend that "if you could weekly have a piece of an Afternoon (as Saturday in the Afternoon an hour or two, or as God guides) set a part for secret and close converse with God by Meditation and Prayer, thinking, writing, reading, examining, mourning before God, and do this constantly, you will never repent of it." Others, especially ministers, spent the better part of the day in preparation, and Saturday night exercises were the most intense of the week. Their practice corresponded to that of John Cotton, which his grandson presented as exemplary. "The Sabbath, he began, the Evening Before," Mather wrote. "When that Evening arriv'd, he was usually Larger in his Exposition in his Family, than at other times; He then Catechised his Children and Servants, and Prayed with them, and Sang a Psalm." After family duties "he Retired unto Study, and Secret Prayer, till the Time of his going unto his Repose." Thomas Shepard's "renewed conversions" came as he readied himself for Sabbath worship. Saturday night he "gave up myself to the Lord" in hope "he would take me." Saturday night he "saw union to God the greatest good, and my sin in not cleaving wholly to him with all my heart the height of sin." Saturday night "the Lord made himself very precious to me because I might come to him, have access in prayer."[11]

Saturday night was, as Cotton Mather said, not prior to but the beginning of the Sabbath. Just as preparation for conversion was not considered a grace separate from conversion itself but the beginning

10. Bunyan, *Pilgrim's Progress*, ed. Wharey and Sharrock, 114–118.

11. Mitchel, "Letter to His Friend," appended to *Discourse of the Glory*, 2d ed., 283. C. Mather, "Cottonus Redivivus," in *Johannes in Eremo*, 61–62. Shepard, "Journal," in McGiffert, ed., *God's Plot*, 95, 99–100, 116, 135–137, 161.

of conversion, so weekly preparation, and especially Saturday preparation, was the first stage in the redemptive drama that was acted out
on the Sabbath. Worship and private devotion on the day itself offered
assurance of grace that fulfilled the anticipatory prayers of Saturday
night and looked beyond to ultimate fulfillment in the Kingdom.

The cycle of preparation and fulfillment comes across in Increase
Mather's diary entries. On March 27, 1675, he "prepared for Sabbath:" "Examining Heart estate, I was not altogether without Hopes
that the Lord had given me grace, and some growth therein. O for
more of his spirit!" The next day Mather felt "assisted beyond expectation in preaching." When his son Nathaniel was ill Mather saw "a
special hand of God in disappointing me of other help and putting
upon preaching beyond expectation, which caused me to sit up the
night before the sabbath till nigh 2 [o'clock] A.M." In the morning his
son revived, and in worship "God was with my spirit very much." On
the morning of the Sabbath Mather experienced fulfillment in secret
as well as in public worship. "As I was sitting alone in my study, I was
suddenly moved by the spirit of God, and wonderfully melted into
Tears, with a firm perswasion that God would make me his mouth,
and owne the words I should speak, in his name, so as that much good
should be done thereby." He completed his diary entry, "Amen dear
Lord Jesus!" Mather devoted the remainder of the day to public
worship and the exercise of private devotion in all its settings.[12]

PREPARATION FOR THE SACRAMENT

The most intense preparation for the Sabbath was made before the
celebration of the Lord's Supper, which usually took place six to
twelve times a year. The seriousness with which the clergy, at least
those for whom records survive, regarded the discipline was rooted in
the severe biblical injunction: "Let a man examine himself, and so let
him eat of that bread and drink of that cup. For he that eateth and
drinketh unworthily, eateth and drinketh damnation to himself, not
discerning the Lord's body" (1 Corinthians 11:28–29). It is not surprising that Thomas Shepard wrote his longest journal entry when he
was "suddenly surprised by a sin before the sacrament." In meditation
on that sin "the Lord turned [it] to great good to me. . . . Let in a most
glorious light (as I thought) of his gospel and the way of believing for
pardon, more than ever I had." Most directly, "I found my heart

12. I. Mather, *Diary*, ed. Green, 6–8, 19.

drawn more sweetly to close with God thus as my end and to place my happiness in it." Shepard's faith in the efficacy of the Sacrament increased as he became aware that "Christ was here present to prepare and bless the ordinance." He saw that the elements "were not only seals to assure me that Christ's word should be made good to me believing, but also that Christ by sacramental union was given to me." This blessing was "a most sweet thing," both in its immediate spiritual satisfaction and in the final union it anticipated, in "the life of Christ begun, and perfected hereafter."[13]

Gordon S. Wakefield was incorrect in his assessment that "there is none of the more individualistic sacramental piety in Puritanism." The record suggests, on the contrary, that the warmest and most fulfilling moments of Puritan spirituality were achieved in just this setting. Increase Mather wrote that "it has bin my maner constantly to set a day apart in my study, before I administred at the Lords Table. And I would not for all this worlds good, be without the Answer of those prayers." Through his preparatory exercises, Mather believed, "I have often mett with Christ at his Table." He described his experiences with such phrases as "meltings of my soul," being "graciously affected," and spiritually "quicknd." Cotton Mather's methodical "Self-Examination, preparatory to a Communion" adhered to the same form, and in his eucharistic manual *A Companion for Communicants* he made those disciplines widely available. In basic terms the exercises consisted of "The Reflection of our Consciences upon our own motions, Comparing them with the word of God, and Concluding from them, our being either the Heirs of Life, or the Sons of Death." Preparation for the Sacrament once again took the communicant through the stages of the order of redemption. "Our Sins are to be mortifi'd with a Renewed Repentance before our Entertainment" at the Table. The cycle of sin and grace, mortification and vivification, meant that "the more Bitter that Sin has been to us before the Sacrament, the more sweet will Christ be to us in it. When we come to the Lords Table, we come for a General Acquittance of all our Sins; we are therefore to see that we make our Accounts even before we come, that we have Mourn'd for all our sins, that we have Turn'd from all our sins, and that we have thrown away the Spears which gave unto our Lord the wounds that we are now coming to the contemplation of." The aim of the exercise was to come to the Table with "an Heart Prepared." Meditative self-examination blessed believers with "that Preparation and Sanctification which we are to come unto the Feast of

13. Shepard, "Journal," in McGiffert, ed., *God's Plot*, 107–112.

our God withal." The practice of eucharistic preparation, that is, fit into the framework of New England preparationism.[14]

From 1682 to 1725 Edward Taylor used the medium of poetry to prepare his heart for the Eucharist. The 214 "Preparatory Meditations before my Approach to the Lords Supper" have recently been placed in the tradition of European meditative poetry that blossomed in the seventeenth century. Especially close similarities have been noted with the poetry of George Herbert and the meditative method of Richard Baxter. Taylor's method was, however, also typical of Puritan practice from the beginnings of the movement. His Saturday night devotions contained all the themes of New England devotionalism. In his poems the connection of sacramental preparation with the earlier and later phases, preparation for conversion and preparation for death and glory, is clear. Taylor did not simply prepare "for dispensing the Lord's Supper" as though that excluded "preparation for grace" or as though he had fully accomplished his "state of visible sainthood." Taylor's original conversion made his membership in church covenant indisputable, but the saint's devotional life consisted of more than seeking new evidence of saving grace. Through progressive stages of sanctification, in which he was newly infused with grace, Taylor prepared for the perfection of sainthood in eternity. And, as we have seen, the devotional exercises that made up that preparation conformed to the model of preparation and fulfillment first established in conversion. Karl Keller has written in this vein that "Taylor's private poems are themselves for the most part accounts of the process that Taylor went through in preparing himself to be disposed for saving grace. They are not poems *about* the process, but poems showing Taylor *in the process* of preparation. They are miniature dramas in which Taylor is reenacting over and over again that which was to him the most meaningful process of man's life." Meditations I.39 through I.41 have been shown to reflect the commonly accepted morphology of conversion, which Taylor himself outlined in his "Spiritual Relation" and "Profession of Faith."[15]

14. Wakefield, *Puritan Devotion*, 159. Hall, ed., "Autobiography of Increase Mather," Am. Antiq. Soc., *Procs.*, N.S., LXXI (1961), 316–317. Ford, ed., *Diary of Cotton Mather*, I, 44–45. C. Mather, *Companion for Communicants*, 81–100.

15. The first, partial, edition of Taylor's poetry was edited by Thomas H. Johnson as *The Poetical Works of Edward Taylor* (New York, 1939). Donald E. Stanford's definitive edition, *The Poems of Edward Taylor*, was not published until 1960. See Martz, Foreword to Stanford, ed., *Poems of Taylor*, for Taylor's literary debts. Norman S. Grabo, ed., *Edward Taylor's Christographia* (New Haven, Conn., 1962), Introduction, xxix–xxxv. Norman Pettit incorrectly criticized the views of Karl Keller in his review of Sacvan Bercovitch, ed., *The American Puritan Imagination: Essays in Revaluation* (Cambridge,

The more impersonal poems in which Taylor remained close to his text and doctrine, such as Meditation I.8, also exhibit the pattern. After introducing the object of meditation, the first movement was always confession of sin. Confession ranged from the restrained Meditation I.8—

> When that this Bird of Paradise put in
> 　This Wicker Cage (my Corps) to tweedle praise
> Had peckt the Fruite forbad: and so did fling
> 　Away its Food; and lost its golden dayes;
> 　It fell into Celestiall Famine sore:
> 　And never could attain a morsell more (ll. 7–12)

—to the lamenting Meditations I.35 and I.36—"Oh, that I ever felt what I profess" and "What rocky heart is mine?"—to the explosive Meditation I.39—

> My Sin! my Sin, My God, these Cursed Dregs
> 　Green, Yellow, Blew streakt Poyson hellish, ranck,
> Bubs hatcht in natures nest on Serpents Eggs,
> 　Yelp, Cherp and Cry; they set my Soule a Cramp.
> 　I frown, Chide, strik and fight them, mourn and Cry
> 　To Conquor them, but cannot them destroy (ll. 1–6).

During the course of meditation Taylor recognized the atoning work of God already accomplished in Christ:

> But how it came, amazeth all Communion.
> 　Gods onely Son doth hug Humanity,
> Into his very person. By which Union
> 　His Humane Veans its golden gutters ly.
> 　And rather than my Soule should dy by thirst,
> 　These Golden Pipes, to give me drink, did burst
> 　　　　　　(I,10, ll. 13–18).

And he threw himself at Christ's feet for mercy: "Oh! make thy Chrystall Buts of Red Wine bleed / Into my Chrystall Glass this Drink-

---

1974). See Pettit, "The Puritan Legacy," *NEQ*, XLVIII (1975), 290. Keller, *Example of Taylor*, 92. David L. Parker, "Edward Taylor's Preparationism: A New Perspective on the Taylor-Stoddard Controversy," *Early Am. Lit.*, XI (1976–1977), 266–268. Parker, however, treats the poems more as sermons in verse than as Taylor's own preparation. Further, he fails to make the crucial connection between preparation for conversion, preparation for the Sacrament, and preparation for eternity, focusing only on conversion. Taylor was not writing about conversion, but about an experience that followed the same pattern.

Indeed" (I,10, ll. 29–30). When he partook of bread and wine the salvific cycle would be complete.

In meditation during the preparatory stages of conversion Puritans focused on their sinfulness, but Edward Taylor set his eyes on higher realities. Some meditations, to be sure, open with a burst of self-abasement (e.g., I.39 and I.40), but he wrote these during weeks when he was preaching on sin (1 John 2:1 and 2:2). Generally, Taylor opened his poems by establishing his meditative focus from his text and doctrine. Then contrition and humiliation welled up within him in response to that theme. Preaching on Christ as "A Great High Priest" from Hebrews 4:14, for example, he began his meditation:

> Raptures of Love, surprizing Loveliness,
>> That burst through Heavens all, in Rapid Flashes. . . .
> Glory itselfe Heartsick of Love doth ly
> Bleeding our Love o're Loveless mee, and dy
>> (I,14, ll. 1–2, 5–6).

On other occasions, in addition to text and sermon notes, Taylor seems to have held a physical object before him during meditation. On some nights it is likely he meditated on the actual loaf of bread to be used in the Sacrament. The poems make frequent enigmatic reference to a "Silver Chest" (I,4, l. 1), a "Choicest Cabbinet" (I,13, l. 7), a "Wealthy Box," and "A Case more Worth than Gold" (I,27, ll. 13–14). At times the image referred to the "alabaster box of very precious ointment" that the woman poured over Jesus at the Bethany supper just before the Last Supper or at the pharisee's house (Matthew 26:7; Mark 14:3; Luke 7:37). Taylor prayed that he might become like the woman in his own adoration of Jesus (I,2, ll. 19–24; I,3, ll. 7–12). In most cases, however, he appears to have been referring to the bowl or trencher that contained the sacramental bread. Even the ointment box image used in Meditation I.2 prompted him quickly to cry, "Enough! Enough! oh! let me eat my Word" (l. 25). Taylor's "Word" was God's Word made flesh and made present in the bread. One meaning of the word "eucharist" was the box or pyx in which the host was kept. In Catholic devotion this box was as ornate as Taylor's poetic description of his own rude container:

> Oh! Choicest Cabbinet, more Choice than gold
>> Or Wealthist Pearles Wherein all Pearls of Price
> All Treasures of Choice Wisdom manifold
>> Inthroned reign. Thou Cabinet most Choice

Not scant to hold, not staind with cloudy geere
The Shining Sun of Wisdom bowling there (I,13, ll. 7–12).

That the elaborate imagery alluded to the loaf "bowling" in the West-field church's trencher is evident in the concluding stanza:

That little Grain within my golden Bowle,
  Should it attempt to poise thy Talent cleare,
It would inoculate into my Soule,
  As illookt Impudence as ever were.
  But, loe, it stands amaizd, and doth adore,
  Thy Magazeen of Wisdom, and thy Store (ll. 25–30).

Other poems suggest Taylor had before him the sacramental wine:

This Liquor brew'd, thy sparkling Art Divine
  Lord, in thy Chrystall Vessells did up tun,
(Thine Ordinances,) which all Earth o're shine
  Set in thy rich Wine Cellars out to run.
  Lord, make thy Butlar draw, and fill with speed
  My Beaker full: for this is drink indeed

Whole Buts of this blesst Nectar shining stand
  Lockt up with Saph'rine Taps, whose splendid Flame
Too bright do shine for brightest Angells hands
  To touch, my Lord. Do thou untap the same.
  Oh! make thy Chrystall Buts of Red Wine bleed
  Into my Chrystall Glass this Drink-Indeed (I,10, ll. 19–30).

Taylor's "Beaker" may well have been the church's communion cup on his study table. Wine stored in a common flask until brought out in worship became in preparatory meditation the Lord's heavenly "Chrystall Buts of Red Wine"—Christ's own blood.

Taylor and all New Englanders more generally internalized devotional trappings. They did not worship the pyx but prayed, "My Heart . . . Make it thy Box." During one meditation in which Taylor seems to have used the cup as his meditative focus, he quickly moved to the thought of himself as the chalice for the next day's sacramental wine.

Oh! fill my Pipkin with thy Blood red Wine:
  I'l drinke thy Health: To pledge thee is no Crime.
Although I but an Earthen Vessell bee
  Convay some of thy Fulness into mee.
    .   .   .   .   .

Figure 9. Two vessels used for the sacrament of Holy Communion at the First Church in Boston. Left, the silver standing cup or chalice brought by John Winthrop from England in 1630 for use in the church. Above, a cup, one of the earliest dated pieces of American silver, made by John Hull and Robert Sanderson for the church in 1659. Courtesy the First and Second Church in Boston.

> Untap thy Cask, and let my Cup Catch some.
>   Although its in an Earthen Vessells Case
> Let it no Empty Vessell be of Grace.
>
> Let thy Choice Caske, shed, Lord into my Cue
>   A Drop of Juyce presst from thy Noble Vine.
> My Bowl is but an Acorn Cup, I sue
>   But for a Drop: this will not empty thine.
>   Although I'me in an Earthen Vessells place
>   My Vessell make a Vessell, Lord, of Grace (I,28, ll. 9–24).

In the final poem in the first series he prayed similarly: "Make me thy Chrystall Caske: those wines in't tun / That in the Rivers of thy joyes do run" (I,49, ll. 23–24). The inpouring of grace, Taylor concluded, "Twill sweeten me: and all my Love distill / Into thy glass, and me for joy make hop" (ll. 27–28). That is, after Christ's lifeblood had been poured into Taylor, he would then be capable of pouring his own love back into the cup through songs of praise in devotion and worship.

The final movement of Taylor's poems pointed to the future, to the coming Sacrament and life in God's Kingdom. Preparation was, first, for administering and partaking of the Supper. The poems were not complete in themselves; Saturday night was not the whole Sabbath. Meditation on the elements was not the same thing as blessing them and eating them. The poems' fulfillment would come the next morning.

> Oh! feed me at thy Table, make Grace grow
>   Knead in thy Bread, I eate, thy Love to mee,
> And spice thy Cup I take, with rich grace so,
>   That at thy Table I may honour thee (II,13, ll. 43–46).

At the conclusion of meditation he typically prayed, "Then make my life, Lord, to thy praise proceed / For thy rich blood, which is my Drink-Indeed" (I,10, ll. 41–42), referring directly to the morrow's Sacrament. "Eucharist" literally means "thanksgiving," an aspect of praise, and Taylor would "to thy praise proceed" in the Eucharist. The poems look toward singing God's praise in the Sacrament's administration. "Let him in Whom all Fulness Dwells, dwell, Lord / Within my Heart: this Treasure therein lay" (I,27, ll. 45–46). Christ would "dwell" in Taylor when he ingested the elements.

Sacramental preparation looked beyond the morrow, too, for even the Sacrament was not an end in itself but was preparatory in nature. Grace received in the Sacrament nourished the soul as it advanced toward heaven. Taylor concluded Meditation II.13, cited above, with a view to this spiritual growth: "And if thy Banquet fill mee with thy Wealth, / My growing Grace will glorify thyselfe" (ll. 47–48). Taylor's concluding expression was generally one of praise. He sang God's praise for work already accomplished, for preparation achieved, and for his progress toward the heavenly goal. Praise, in fact, put Taylor in mind of the perfect praise he would sing in the Kingdom. His praise now was interim praise, stemming from his prayer that God might "let thy Joy enter mee before / I enter do into my masters joy" in heaven (I,48, ll. 39–40). His poetry, and the Supper itself, were early forms of eternal praise as "thy joyes in mee will make my Pipes to play / For joy thy Praise while teather'd to my clay" (ll. 41–42). Many of the meditations then look beyond interim praise and anticipate and promise the perfect praise Taylor longed to share with the saints in heaven. At the conclusion of the meditation on Revelation 2:10, "A Crown of Life," he wrote that only in glory when "Angels shall set the tune" would his praise be perfect. "Till then I cannot sing, my tongue is tide. / Accept this Lisp till I am glorifide" (I,32, ll. 38, 41–42). In Meditation I.27 Taylor prayed for Christ to dwell in him in the Sacrament, but in the final two lines he turned to the heavenly Sabbath: "I then shall sweetly tune thy Praise, When hee / In whom all Fulness dwells, doth dwell in me" (ll. 47–48). Other poems end similarly: "And when my Clay ball's in thy White robes dresst / My tune perfume thy praise shall with the best" (I,46, ll. 53–54); and "O sweet thought. Lord take this praise though thin. / And when I'm in't Ile tune an higher pin" (I,47, ll. 29–30). Taylor's praise and anticipation of perfect praise are full of confidence. Preparation for the Sacrament was a means of grace that opened to the believer a high order of spiritual experience.

Until the end of the seventeenth century Edward Taylor's poetry reflected the traditional order of redemption. As late as 1700 he still opened his meditations by establishing the theme and then, after the manner of Thomas Hooker's meditation on sin, bringing the heart low. Contemplation of God's love in Christ as "the Head of the Body," for example, evoked the response, "This Wracks my heart, and low my person layes / And rowles mee in the dust at thoughts hereon" (II,38, ll. 13–14). Taylor's continuity with the first generation of New England Puritans is established. He applied the hope of Christ's benefits to his own condition, in words reminiscent of Thomas Shepard's renewed conversions:

But, O my Lord, thou the Beginning art,
   Begin to draw afresh thine Image out
In Shining Colours, on my Life, and Heart

> Begin anew thy foes in mee to route.
> Begin again to breize upon my Soule
> Breize after brieze untill I touch the goale (ll. 31–36).

Renewed, he concluded by praising and promising to praise on the Sabbath and in glory.

> Be ever, Lord beginning till I end,
>   At carrying on thine Interest in my Soule.
> For thy beginning will my marrd minde mende
>   And make it pray Lord, take mee for thy tole.
>   If mee as Wheate thy Tole-Dish doth once greet
>   My tune's to thee Al-tascheth Mictam Sweet (ll. 43–48).

Taylor's use of the Hebrew psalm titles suggests that he thought of his poetry and his praise of God in the Sacrament as being as unassailable and eternal as God's Word itself. His spirituality would carry him on toward the Kingdom. His own preparation for the Supper was one way in which the Lord prepared his soul for that salvation. The prayer that the Lord "Be ever . . . beginning till I end"—one of the clearest expressions of New England preparationism—was his plea that God would continue preparing his heart until his death.[16]

By the beginning of the eighteenth century the preparatory themes in Taylor's poetry had diminished, indicative of the more general changes in New England religion. He increasingly (and after 1713 exclusively) took his texts from the Song of Songs, and the poems became more mystically erotic. The anticipation of perfect praise in glory became more impassioned. Indeed, Taylor frequently opened his meditations at the stage of implantation, where he immediately experienced Christ's mystical love. "When thou, my Lord, mee mad'st, thou madst my heart / A Seate for love, and love enthronedst there" (II,116, ll. 1–2). What had been deep humiliation became in the later period simply an expression of inability. "My Deare-Deare Lord! What shall my speech be dry? / And shall I court thee onely with dull tunes?" (II,120, ll. 1–2). Cotton Mather signaled a similar devotional shift in 1700 when he resolved, seemingly in optimistic pledge to the new century, "That for the Future, my Evening-Prayers both in my Family, and in my Study, every day, shall be mostly made up of Thanksgiving . . . and consist mainly in Praising and Blessing God." On the one hand the trend reflects the breakdown of the old synthesis, which had held the seventeenth century in such unity. But the move

16. John D. Davis and Henry Snyder Gehman, *The Westminster Dictionary of the Bible,* rev. ed. (Philadelphia, 1944), 23, 396–397.

toward increased emphasis on praise and mystical love, if seen within the context of Edward Taylor's religious and poetic development, rather demonstrates his spiritual progress. In fact, New England devotion was not endless repetition of a cycle without progress. Spiritual time was cyclical in that the stages were traversed repeatedly in preparation for Sabbath or Sacrament or sleep, but it was linear as well. New Englanders who persevered in the disciplines could progress in their feeling of unity with God. Cotton Mather, for example, wrote that "in his latter Years, [his father] did not Record so many of [his] Heavenly Afflations, because they grew so frequent with him. And . . . the Flights of a Soul rapt up into a more Intimate Conversation with Heaven, are such as cannot be exactly Remembered."[17]

A dramatic example of spiritual progress in a minister's weekly preparation for the Sabbath is young Peter Thacher, a classmate of Taylor's at Harvard. The external political troubles in contention-ridden Barnstable and an extremely difficult trial pastorate adversely affected Thacher's secret devotional life. His diary entries on Saturdays and Sabbaths while he was at Barnstable are marked by complaints. "This evening and the next morning I was much concerned that I should be able Either to pray or preach. God did much Empty mee of my selfe and caused mee to depend upon him for assistance." And, "my spirits were very low and dejected and not knowing how to goe through the work." The next day he wrote: "This morning I was much concerned how I should goe through the work of the day. 7. Rom. 25., Barnestable, both parts of the day, and god was pleased Exceedingly to Inlarge mee in praying and preaching the after part of the day Especially in closeing that subject. The Lord grant I may not preach unto others and by my selfe a Cast-away but that I may practice as well as preach. I esteem it as an Answer of prayer." The cycle of despair and grace was, of course, characteristic of New England spirituality. Unless the saint was emptied on Saturday night, God's Spirit would not flow through him on the Sabbath. But Thacher's prayer is filled with more than ordinary despondency, and his lack of joy on the Sabbath is uncharacteristic.[18]

After he left Barnstable for Milton, Thacher's spirit was freed, and he made remarkable progress. His experience still followed the redemptive order, so humiliation remained important in his weekly

17. Ford, ed., *Diary of Cotton Mather*, I, 372. [C. Mather], *Parentator*, 36–37, 48. See generally, James W. Jones, *The Shattered Synthesis: New England Puritanism before the Great Awakening* (New Haven, Conn., 1973).

18. Thacher, "Diary," MS, I, 70, 93. The biblical image of the castaway has several sources. See especially Job 8:20, Psalm 51:11, and Luke 9:25.

preparation, but his anticipation of the Sabbath and of heavenly fulfillment was brighter than anything he had known.

> I studied this day in preparation for the Sabbath. My Heart
> was often lifted up to god in Ejaculatory prayer for assistance in
> my preparatory work, I was much Emptied of selfe sufficiency;
> This Evening my soul was Extreordinarily drawn out after god in
> family prayer, in desiring an saveing interest in him, union in
> him, communion with him, universal conformity to him, constant
> preparation for the full injoyment of him in glory; my soul was
> inexpressibly inlarged to god in this duty in (as I thought) a full
> choice of him, and totall resignation of myself unto him, blessed
> be the Lord for it. My meditation was sweet upon god when I lay
> downe to my repose.

Thacher prepared not simply for the task of preaching but "for the
full injoyment of him in glory," the eschatological Sabbath foreshadowed by the weekly Sabbath. The next day he found the ecstasy of
fulfillment. "This morning when I awaked my thoughts were with
and upon God, and when up I went to my closet retirement in family
prayer my soul did greatly breath after god; and just before I went to
meeting I spent a little time in prayer seeking gods presence with mee
that I might worship god in praying, singing, preaching, and that my
heart might bee with god in the dutys lying before mee, then I went to
meeting and the Lord did much inlarge my heart to himself." He now
used the terrible image of the castaway without the fearful overtones.
"When I came from meeting I went into my study and spent some
time in praying that I might not preach unto others and bee myselfe a
cast away, but the word might be saveing to my soul. . . . God grant I
may trust in him as long as I live." He ended the Sabbath with more
secret devotions, which both fulfilled his Saturday preparations and
further prepared his heart for heaven. "When I came home I got into
my study and prayed for a blessing and after supper into my study
where god was pleased againe to warme my heart in secret prayer.
The Lord keep it in the Imaginations of the thoughts of my heart for
ever more to love and live to him, and prepare to live [with] him in the
kingdome of glory." Thacher's final phrase sums up much of Puritan
devotion.[19]

19. Thacher, "Diary," MS, II, 5–6.

PREPARATION FOR DEATH

Between Sabbath and Sacrament in this life and glorification in the next lay death. At its deepest level, preparation for salvation through the means of grace became preparation for death. Cotton Mather's first "counsil on coming to Table," for example, was to "Prepare to Celebrate the Death of the Lord Jesus at his Table, with as much Awfulness and Exactness, as if your own Death, were at the same Time to be prepared for." Preparation for death was also a discipline unto itself, as exemplified in Anne Bradstreet's "weary pilgrim" meditation. Theologically, devout Puritans understood this life of sin and suffering as the preparatory stages of contrition and humiliation; life was to get ready for afterlife, for salvation in its full sense. Saints on earth died to sin in only a preliminary way; the effects of sin would not be fully shaken off until the final death of the body. Saints were implanted into Christ at conversion and grew in union with him through sanctification, but they could only anticipate full implantation and glorification, which would not occur until after death. Preparation for death was the last essential element of New England devotional preparationism.[20]

The message to prepare to die came from so many sides that it was inescapable. Primer, almanac, popular verse, manual, and sermon all urged readiness for death in similar language, reflecting as well as instructing the popular mind. Indeed, the exercise of preparation for death carried with it the weight of traditional and popular religiosity. The roots of the memento mori and *ars moriendi* preparationist traditions reach back centuries before the Puritan movement, into European folk culture. The verses of *The New England Primer* on the one hand inculcated the need to prepare for death, but on the other simply expressed the ancient tradition. "As runs the Glass / Mans life doth pass." "Time cuts down all / Both great and small." "Xerxes the great did die, / And so must you and I." The emblematic pictures for each verse likewise were not original and could be found in the widely appealing iconography of funeral broadsides and gravestones. The same themes were reiterated in the primerlike couplets of Philip Pain's *Daily Meditations*. "This day is past; but tell me, who can say / That I shall surely live another day." "This day is past, God mercy shewed to me, / Who am a Dust-heap of Mortalitie." "Lord, if my Soul this night away thou take, / Let me by morning then in Heav'n awake." The *Almanack* carried the same message. When the printer asked Cotton

20. C. Mather, *Companion for Communicants*, 146.

T *Time* cuts down all
Both great and small.

U *Uriah's* beauteous Wife
Made *David* seek his
Life.

W *Whales* in the Sea
God's Voice obey.

X *Xerxes* the great did
die,
And so must you & I,

Y *Youth* forward slips
Death soonest nips.

Z *Zacheus* he
Did climb the Tree
His Lord to see,

Figure 10. Emblematic pictures and didactic verse in The New England Primer, *the earliest extant edition (Boston, 1727). The selections portray the themes of Original Sin, the trial of the spiritual life, the centrality of the Bible, the preparation for death, and the need for redemption. From Paul Leicester Ford, ed.,* The New England Primer: A History of Its Origin and Development *(New York, 1962 [orig. publ. 1897]). Courtesy the Teachers College Press.*

Mather "to fill the last Leaf of his Almanack," Mather saw it as an "Opportunity, and wrote a few pungent Lines, concerning the Changes, which may bee coming as a snare upon the Earth; and advising every particular Person however, to consider, whether in this Year, there may not come upon himself, the greatest Change that ever befel him; even that of his own mortality." Mather's exhortation was fully within the centuries-old tradition of almanacs and calendars.[21]

Many devotional manuals aided preparation for death, but the Boston reprint of *The Map of Man's Misery* fairly trumpeted the popular themes. The manual's scheme set out the redemptive cycle, progressing through the days of the week in preparation for the Sabbath, but uniquely linked the order with preparation for death by identifying it with stages of life and afterlife. The running subtitle outlines the entire work:

> The Poor Man's Pocket-Book: Being a Perpetual Almanac of Spiritual Meditations: or Compleat Directory for One Endless Week:

Childhood		Monday
Youth		Tuesday
Manhood		Wednesday
Old Age	for	Thursday
Death		Friday
Judgment		Saturday
Eternity		Lords-day

> Containing Many useful instructions, Exhortations and Prayers, with precious Remedies against Satan's Devices; Plainly shewing every Christian so to walk, that he may please God.

The Map of Man's Misery is simultaneously the most ingenious arrangement of the themes of Puritan devotion and New England's most desperate portrayal of the human condition. "Mighty Kings and Monarchs can but have / A stinking Cradle and a rotting Grave."

> Poor wretched man is Born and Cries,
> Lives Sixty Years, falls Sick and Dies,

21. Paul Leicester Ford, ed., *The New England Primer: A History of Its Origin and Development* . . . (New York, 1962 [orig. publ. 1897]). Philip Pain, *Daily Meditations: Or, Quotidian Preparations for and Considerations of Death and Eternity* . . . (San Marino, Calif., 1936 [orig. publ. Cambridge, Mass., 1668]), 19, 20, 24, 33, 34. Ford, ed., *Diary of Cotton Mather*, I, 276. See Philippe Ariès, *Western Attitudes toward Death: From the Middle Ages to the Present*, trans. Patricia M. Ranum (Baltimore, 1974); and Stannard, *Puritan Way of Death*, chap. 1.

And all his Life is but a Scene
Of Sorrow, Sighing, Grief and Pain.

Still, the meditations and the simply written, highly evocative prayers were designed to move the penitent beyond death to glory:

Then lead a Holy Life, Fast, Read, and Pray:
And live content in Faith, from day to day,
That thou may'st sing back from Mount Zion high,
Death Where is thy Sting? Grave where's thy Victory? [22]

The throngs that gathered to hear execution sermons are an index of how deeply rooted the preparation for death theme was in popular mentality. Public executions are always sensational events partly because they dramatically remind the spectators of their own mortality. This was the theme that New England preachers expounded: prepare now for death and judgment. One execution moved the youthful Cotton Mather to meditate, "Alas, I have the Seed of all Corruption in mee. . . . Lett mee bee exceedingly Thankful, for the restraining Grace of God." When he himself preached at an execution he employed popular language to call for general confession and preparation. Church members, congregation, and condemned must all "look unto Jesus Christ for salvation" and prepare to meet "the King of Terrours." Mather led his listeners on a journey to Judgment:

That you would at this hour think of an Interest in Jesus
Christ, as you will quickly at the hour of your Death, and of your
Judgment. Surely, when the Executioner is laying the Cloth of
Death over your eyes, the Look with the shriek of your soul will
then say, O Now a thousand worlds for an Interest in Jesus
Christ! Surely, A few minutes after that, when your naked soul
shall appear before the Judgment seat of the most High, you will
again have it over, An Interest in Jesus Christ, is now worth
whole Mountains of massie gold. O let this be NOW the settled
Opinion of your awakned heart.

"The Cloth of Death" and "the Look with the shriek of your soul" would attend the death not only of the condemned but of onlookers as well. "The Cloth of Death" referred to the hood of the condemned but also evoked the shroud that covered the remains of every deceased person. Mather's phrases speak generally of the anxiety that impelled New Englanders' preparation for death. Public response is

22. [Patrick Ker], *The Map of Man's Misery; . . . Being a Perpetual Almanack of Spiritual Meditations* . . . (Boston, 1692 [orig. publ. London, 1690]), title page.

demonstrated by the size of the crowd that gathered to hear the execution sermon for a woman who had killed her illegitimate baby. "The
greatest Assembly, ever in this Countrey preach'd unto, was now come
together; It may bee four or five thousand Souls. I could not gett into
the Pulpit, but by climbing over Pues and Heads: and there the Spirit
of my dearest Lord came upon mee. I preached with a more than
ordinary Assistence, and enlarged, and uttered the most awakening
Things, for near two Hours together." New England was drawn into
preparation for death almost enthusiastically.[23]

Even *The Pilgrim's Progress*, at one level a guide to conversion and at
another a daily devotional guide, was most truly a manual on how to
die. The spiritual journey had its vertical dimension, but the temporal
journey of life led to death. If life was cut short, as it was with pious
Faithful (in New England Nathaniel Mather comes to mind), the reward was immediate transport "up through the Clouds, with sound of
a Trumpet, the nearest way to the Cœlestial Gate." For most, however, life was long, death natural, preparation protracted. Christiana
began as a young woman with small boys and ended as an "aged ma-
tron" with grandchildren. Part Two concludes with her children's
families encamped on the banks of River Death, waiting in their little
church for their time to cross. In his more frightful journey, Christian's final obstacle was this very river, and his floundering was intended to serve as instruction for others. With the aid of Scripture
and godly conference with friends such as Hopeful the Christian
would shout at last, "Oh I see him again! and he tells me, 'When thou
passest through the waters, I will be with thee, and through the
Rivers, they shall not overflow thee.'" And on the other side "shining
men" would welcome the saint at the gates.[24]

When believers practiced "dying daily" to sin, especially in evening
exercises, the emotional lever was the possibility that one might actually die at any moment. "Think daily of thy death, and that last great

23. Ford, ed., *Diary of Cotton Mather*, I, 30–31. Cotton Mather, *The Call of the Gospel
Applyed unto All Men in General, and unto a Condemned Malefactor in Particular* . . . (Boston,
[1686]), 5–6, 47. Ford, ed., *Diary of Cotton Mather*, I, 279. For other execution sermons,
see S[amuel] D[anforth], *The Cry of Sodom Enquired Into* . . . (Cambridge, Mass., 1674);
Increase Mather, *The Wicked Mans Portion* . . . (Boston, 1675); Joshua Moodey, *An
Exhortation to a Condemned Malefactor Delivered March 7th, 1685/6*, bound with C. Mather,
Call of the Gospel; and John Williams, *Warnings to the Unclean: In a Discourse from Rev.
XXI. 8* (Boston, 1699). Cotton Mather's diary account of the mass gathering anticipates
events of the Great Awakening, especially attending George Whitefield's preaching, to
the extent that Mather used the words "awakned" and "awakening." Ford, ed., *Diary of
Cotton Mather*, I, 279.

24. Bunyan, *Pilgrim's Progress*, ed. Wharey and Sharrock, 97, 305–306, 311, 158.

account," Perkins wrote. When Richard Baxter first began the meditations that led him to write *Saints Everlasting Rest* he was ill, "living in continual expectation of death." The book was written "with one foot in the grave, by a man that was betwixt living and dead." Baxter recommended that every Christian think of himself as such a person and that he look upon illnesses as opportunities for intense devotion. Manual and sermon reminded Puritans of their mortality:

> Whether we sleep or wake, eat or drink, trade or travel, pray
> or play, we are still hastening to the Grave: a dying hour hastens
> upon all; and how fast (pray) does it hasten upon us? faster than
> the Weavers Shuttle does to the end of the Web . . . faster than
> a Post hastens to the end of his Stage . . . or the swift flying Eagle
> to the Prey. . . . So fast, as that, for ought we know, it will be
> upon us before we see the light of another day.

On the other side, depending on how the soul had been prepared, lay either the mercy of salvation or the justice of damnation. "To be ready to live with God for ever in Heaven when we come to die, is the great Work we have to do, the great Concern we have to mind, in our present Pilgrimage." In the seventeenth century one could not possibly take death lightly, as though it were simply the end of life.[25]

Manuals provided advice and model prayers to help the reader face death. Humility and repentance were perennial themes. "Examine thine own heart upon thy bed" when you are sick, *The Practice of Piety* urged, until you find and confess "thy capital sin." Perkins, in "Directions How to Live Well, and to Dye Well," advised reconciliation with neighbors, setting one's estate in order, and devotional preparation. "Yea, endeavour even to die praying," he wrote. "Lastly, when thou feelest death approaching, commend thy departing soule into the holy hands of God: He gave it, to him surrender it againe." With proper preparation the "spiritual sighs" of the dying saint became increasingly sublime. As John Cotton put it, "No growing Christian, but the nearer hee cometh to heaven, the more sweet and spiritual are his meditations." Manuals recommended that believers construct for future use a "Prayer at yielding up of the Ghost," possibly using the traditional Agnus Dei—"O Lamb of God which by thy bloud hast taken away the sins of the world, have mercy upon me a sinner, Lord

25. Per[kins], "Directions How to Live Well, and to Dye Well," in Ro[gers] *et al.*, *Spirituall Flowers*, 30. Baxter, *Saints Everlasting Rest*, sig. A2ᵛ, 707–711. Edward Pearse, *The Great Concern: Or, a Serious Warning to a Timely and Thorough Preparation for Death . . .* (Boston, 1705 [orig. publ. London, 1671]), 38, 1.

Jesus Christ receive my spirit. Amen."—and a meditative sentence as one's last words, such as "The Grave is ready for me."[26]

Manuals also suggested prayers for those who were gathered around "when the sick party is departing," seeking God's mercy for his soul. "O Gracious God and merciful Father, who art the refuge and strength and very present help in trouble: lift up the light of thy favourable countenance at this instant upon thy servant that now cometh to appear in thy presence: wash away, good Lord, all his sins, . . . cause him now to feel that thou art his loving Father, and that he is thy child by Adoption and Grace." Since death was the final stage of life's journey, it was natural that prayers be couched in the language of the preparation of the heart and the pilgrimage of the soul.

> And seeing (O Lord) thou hast smitten thy sicke servant (as wee conceive) irrecoverably, and doest now purpose to put an end to the days of his pilgrimage; we most humbly beseech thee, to prepare him for thine own Kingdome. Weane his mind and affections from the world and earthly vanities, where he is but a stranger, and fix them wholly upon spirituall and heavenly things, as it becommeth a Citizen of thy Kingdome. Let him earnestly desire to bee dissolved and to be with Christ. . . . To this end (O Lord) reveale thy selfe unto him more cleerly then ever heretofore. . . . Give him, even whilst he liveth, an entrance into thy Kingdome, not onely by the assurance of faith and hope, but also by letting him have a lively taste of those heavenly joyes, which thou hast prepared for him.

By making these meditations and prayers available for general use, the manuals sought to systematize preparation for death according to orthodox theology and regular discipline.[27]

The reality of death often served as a powerful stimulus for New Englanders in the preparatory stages of conversion. The sudden death of a friend had the effect of the injunction "prepare *yourself* to die" and its corollary, "Let us search and try our ways, and turn again to the Lord" (Lamentations 3:40). When two Harvard students drowned "scating on fresh pond" in November, for example, Josiah Cotton was a pallbearer and heard his uncle Increase preach "an awful sermon" from Ecclesiastes ("For man also knoweth not his time," 9:2). The event struck dread into Cotton's heart, and he resolved that

26. Bayly, *Practice of Piety*, 365–445. Per[kins], "Directions How to Live Well, and to Dye Well," in Ro[gers] *et al.*, *Spirituall Flowers*, 27–29. Cotton, *Covenant of Gods Free Grace*, 1. Downame, *Guide to Godlynesse*, 959.

27. Bayly, *Practice of Piety*, 444–445. Downame, *Guide to Godlynesse*, 959.

"surely time ought carefully to be redeemed." Jonathan Pierpont dated his conversion to 1682, when "it pleased God to awaken me by the Death of that pious Youth Edward Dudley. I thought it would go ill with me if God should suddenly take me away." Increase Mather linked his conversion to the realization of mortality, first during his own illness but decisively when his mother died, and "the Lord broke in upon my conscience with very terrible convictions and awakenings." Contrition and humiliation were themselves deathlike experiences; the penitent died to sin in order to be reborn in Christ.[28]

The death of a man's father was an important milestone and a serious reminder of the mortality of one's world and oneself. Transferral of family responsibility and property and the son's sudden personal autonomy complicated grief. Peter Thacher began to keep his diary in 1678 when it fell to him, as eldest son, to call "a fast in my family . . . to humble our soules under gods sore bereaving hand in takeing away my Dear Father and Sister." His extended transition to adulthood was not easy. His indecision about whether to accept a call to the Barnstable pulpit was embarrassing; his trial sermon, incredibly, was on Jesus in Gethsemane ("O my Father, if it be possible, let this cup pass from me"). For months Thacher postponed his final departure to Barnstable and embarked at last on the anniversary, to the day, of his father's death! His father's death and the departure from Boston were juxtaposed in his mind. The connection of life changes with death was not uncommon in Puritan devotion. An English devotional manual advised that death "is such a Change, as all other Changes upon the outward Man are but leading and introductory unto, and into which at last they all issue and resolve themselves." Thacher wrote, "This day my heart was inlarged in family duty desiring that by this remove my selfe and family might be fitted for our great remove and that seeing this day twelve moneth father dyed wee might have soe great a losse made up in haveing god for our father and friend." His move was indeed an experience of death: the death of youth, the end of life in Boston. He could postpone his career no longer. The night before departure Thacher fell ill, and the next morning he "lay a bed till ten a Clock."[29]

28. Albert Matthews, ed., "[Extracts from] the Diary of Josiah Cotton," Col. Soc. Mass., *Trans.*, XXVI (1927), 279. "Extracts from Diary of Pierpont," *NEHGR*, XIII (1859), 255. Hall, ed., "Autobiography of Increase Mather," Am. Antiq. Soc., *Procs.*, N.S., LXXI (1961), 279.

29. "Patriarchalism and the Family," in Philip J. Greven, Jr., *Four Generations: Population, Land, and Family in Colonial Andover, Massachusetts* (Ithaca, N.Y., 1970), chap. 4. Thacher, "Diary," MS, I, 1, 42, 54–57. Pearse, *Great Concern*, 74.

Many sons felt the spiritual impact of the father's death. Michael Wigglesworth was filled with guilt feelings that approached neurosis when he even contemplated his father's mortality. "My heart as 'tis asham'd of my self so it swells against my father, and cannot conceiv such things to proceed from love." In meditation he uncovered "want of natural affection to my father, in desiring the continuance of his life," and came to the terrible conclusion that this "ranks among those sins whereto men were given up of God to a reprobate mind." He finally confused God the Father with his own father: "I find an infinite need of the Lord Jesus to reconcile me every day to the father, and I am affraid of my own vile heart that I shall one day fall by the hand of Saul." That is, he feared his bitter relationship with his father, reminiscent of that between David and Saul, would drive him to suicide. Far less emotional and more constructive was John Hull, who accepted his father's death in faith without trauma. "About four in the afternoon, the Lord tried me by calling for my honored father, Robert Hull, home to himself, being two days before taken with a flux, and then with a violent cramp in his legs and burning at his heart, yet bore all with sweet patience and thankfulness; and though I am very loath to part, yet do desire willingly and thankfully to resign him up to his and my good Father's will, and to the bosom of his and my dear Lord Jesus, where I have, through grace, good hope to be again with him (in God's time) for ever." His father's death provided Hull with a spiritual example and an occasion to reflect on his own assurance and hope of glory.[30]

Not only the deaths of fathers but the deaths of family members in general, especially children, strongly marked New England spirituality. Samuel Sewall, we have already seen, was never able to move from under the cloud of his children's deaths. He prayed that his child's death might "prepare [him] and [his] for the coming of our Lord" and that God's "breaking [his] Image in [his] Son would be a means of" humbling his heart. Cotton Mather, also plagued by an extraordinary number of family deaths, collected in *Meat out of the Eater* the funeral sermons and elegiac verse he had written for his family members. The volume was intended for the benefit of "all that are in any Affliction; but very particularly such as are afflicted with the loss of their Consorts or Children." Perhaps the best of the poems accompanied a sermon he preached "the Day after the Funeral of my Daughter Mary, and the Day of my Administring the Eucharist,"

30. Morgan, ed., *Diary of Wigglesworth*, 14, 17, 26. For David and Saul, see 1 Sam. 31:4. Hull, *Diaries*, 156.

entitled "My Resignation." Mather compared himself to Abraham offering up Isaac, in a poignant mixture of pain and hope:

> The Dearest Lord of Heaven gave
> Himself an Offering once for me:
> The Dearest Thing on Earth I have
> Now, Lord, I'll offer unto Thee.

He used conventional *ars moriendi* images: "my best Enjoyments here, / Are Loans, and Flow'rs, and Vanities / . . . Vain Smoke." As firmly fixed as his eyes were on heaven, he surely wrote with great inner hurt:

> I do Believe, That ev'ry Bird
> Of mine, which to the Ground shall fall,
> Does fall at thy kind Will and Word;
> Nor I, nor it, is hurt at all.

The devotional use of grief was preparation for one's own place in heaven. "I will do what I can," Mather wrote, "that the Death of my Children, may promote the Death of my Sins." If he and his family were prepared, he believed, "Afterward there will appear, / Not Grief, but Peace, the End of all."[31]

Preparation for death was the culminating exercise of the entire devotional system. Therefore, the greatest compliment Thomas Shepard paid his deceased and sorely lamented Joanna was that "she was fit to die long before she did die." Not only had she studied his sermon notes each week, but, most important, "she had a spirit of prayer beyond ordinary for her time and experience." She had prepared specifically for death by meditating on its attributes and imminency, especially before the birth of her fourth child. In "the last sacrament before her lying in [she] seemed to be full of Christ and thereby fitted for heaven. She did oft say she should not outlive this child, and when her fever first began (by taking some cold) she told me so, that we should love exceedingly together because we should not live long together." In the depths of fever her preparation had borne fruit. "When she knew none else so as to speak to them, yet she knew Jesus Christ and could speak to him, and therefore as soon as she awakened out of sleep she brake out into a most heavenly, heart-

---

31. Thomas, ed., *Diary of Samuel Sewall*, I, 87–90. Cotton, *Briefe Exposition of Ecclesiastes*, 166–167. Cotton Mather, *Meat out of the Eater. Or, Funeral Discourses Occasioned by the Death of Several Relatives* (Boston, 1703), 31, 68, 27–30. Stannard is wrong when he asserts that "there was simply very little real confidence *possible*" as Puritans faced death. *Puritan Way of Death*, 95.

breaking prayer after Christ, her dear redeemer, for the spirit of life, and so continued praying until the last hour of her death—Lord, though I unworthy; Lord, one word, one word, etc.—and so gave up the ghost."[32]

Anne Bradstreet's picture of her mother was similar. Through public worship and private devotion "in her Closet," Dorothy Dudley was "Religious in all her words and wayes, / Preparing still for death, till end of dayes." Cotton Mather said that his late brother Nathaniel, through "Meditation . . . kept mellowing of his own Soul, and preparing it for the state wherein Faith is turned into Sight." And Jonathan Burr, who experienced a "renewed conversion" in surviving smallpox, wrote a spiritual last will and testament in which he "renewed and applied the Covenant of Grace" to his soul, concluding with the words "*Memento Mori.*" Mather presented Burr's exemplary death as the result of Burr's devotional preparation. With his final words, spoken to his wife, "Hold fast, hold fast!" Burr's preparation was complete. "So he finished his pilgrimage, on August 9, 1641."[33]

Michael Wigglesworth's meditation on mortality during his wife's labor and after her midnight delivery of a daughter was less exemplary. During childbirth, of course, death stood alarmingly near, but more terrible than death was damnation—the possibility of which was quite real to Wigglesworth's disturbed soul. If the pains of childbirth were a curse on womankind, hell, he feared, was God's curse on him. In a manner typical of his spirituality, Wigglesworth meditated not on his wife's possible death but on his own! She endured labor, but Wigglesworth recorded in his diary his own torment. "The nearness of my bed to hers made me hear all the nois. her pangs pained my heart, broke my sleep the most off that night, I lay sighing, sweating, praying, almost fainting through weariness. . . . If the dolours of child-bearing be so bitter (which may be onely a fatherly chastizement) then how dreadful are the pangs of eternal death." His preparations at this stage failed to move him beyond humiliation and fear.[34]

Preparation for death was an important part of Thomas Shepard's regular devotions, as we have already seen. His experience was more spiritually satisfying than was Wigglesworth's. In meditative self-examination Shepard ferreted out the attachments that strapped him to the world and kept his heart from ascending to Christ, his constant

32. Shepard, "Autobiography," in McGiffert, ed., *God's Plot*, 71.
33. Anne Bradstreet, "An Epitaph on My Dear and Ever Honoured Mother Mrs. Dorothy Dudley," in Hutchinson, ed., *Poems of Bradstreet*, 54. Cotton Mather, *Early Piety Exemplified* (London, 1689), 39. C. Mather, *Magnalia Christi Americana*, I, 373–374.
34. Morgan, ed., *Diary of Wigglesworth*, 96.

goal. "I saw my heart was not prepared to die because I had not studied to wean my heart from the world, but I saw and sought (1) the glory of it, (2) the rest and peace of it, (3) the joy of it." He prayed ardently, "Oh Lord, help me so to do and to pray and to study it daily! For what is the glory, peace, rest, joy of world, a creature, a perishing thing, to that of God?" On another occasion, in the wake of illness, mortality so filled his mind that it marked even morning devotions. "When I was sick overnight and in my bed on the morning I saw my life a vapor and bubble, a vanity, and all my righteousness the flower that fades." Shepard found the answer to the problem of death in Christ. After meditating on sin and mortality, "I saw God's deep plot in perfecting the saints' salvation out of themselves in Christ." Over the course of a lifetime of devotion and in a pious death saints would be brought fully "out of themselves"—with the ascent of their souls from the dead body—and brought into Christ. In a highly revealing journal entry Shepard recorded:

> In my meditations at night I found my heart desirous to live
> in this world and do good here and not to die. Hence I asked my
> heart the reason why I should not be desirous to die. And in
> musing on it I saw that Christ was ascended up to heaven [and]
> that not here, but there, all his elect might one day behold his
> glory and love him and glorify him forever. And I saw that this
> was God's main plot and end of all, to make Christ very glorious
> and so beloved in heaven forever, where that which I desired
> most in this world (viz., that Christ might not only be precious but
> very dear and precious) should be perfectly accomplished.

Full union would be experienced "not here, but there," but preparation for the ascent, through spiritual exercise, "was the beginning of that which shall be perfected in heaven, viz., (1) to see and know Christ, though obscurely; (2) to take Christ and receive him and possess him; (3) to love him; (4) to bless him. . . . And I saw it would be glorious."[35]

The ascent of the soul in meditation and prayer was thus practice for the final ascent at death. When "on Saturday night I considered of death and that there would be a separation of soul and body," Shepard wrote, "I did understand what it was to have the soul raised with Jesus Christ." Shepard's foretaste of heaven is evidence that the end of New England devotion was indeed the soul's ascent. He wrote—in phrases startling in their mystical implications—that "when the soul, seeing a

35. Shepard, "Journal," in McGiffert, ed., *God's Plot*, 90–91, 141, 119–120.

certainty of death, believed itself before God as if out of the body, was with God, did rest in him, did suck sweetness out of him, did see and behold him only, made him all in all to him, and felt God all, as if out of the body, and so indeed." As the culminating exercise in Puritan devotion, preparation for death opened the way for the language of mystic ascent. Not everyone, of course, achieved so sublime an experience, but others besides Shepard saw in this life "a glimpse of Christ's glory."[36]

The artifacts of death often played a role in New England practice. To "maintain a frequent and serious remembrance of Death and the Grave," one manual urged, "walke much among the tombs, and con-

36. *Ibid.*, 215, 155.

Figure 11. Emblems of the devotional tradition of preparation for death as they appear on two gravestones from the second half of the seventeenth century. Counterbalancing the reminders of death (skull, coffin, hourglass, bones, shovel) are the cherubs of the immortal soul and the wings of the resurrected body. Left, the John Person gravestone, 1679, Wakefield, Massachusetts. Above, the William Dickson gravestone, 1692, Cambridge, Massachusetts. Photographs copyright Allan I. Ludwig, 1966.

verse much and frequently with the thoughts of a dying hour." Cotton Mather even advised children to "Go into Burying Place. . . . You will there see Graves as short as your selves. Yea, you may be at Play one Hour; Dead, Dead the next." Samuel Sewall at least once used this meditative technique and setting. After burying yet another infant, he wrote, in a well-known but not well-understood passage, "Twas wholly dry, and I went at noon to see in what order things were set; and there I was entertain'd with a view of, and converse with, the Coffins of my dear Father Hull, Mother Hull, Cousin Quinsey, and my Six Children . . . ; Twas an awfull yet pleasing Treat; Having said, The Lord knows who shall be brought hether next, I came away." Sewall was not alone in using physical objects of death in his medita-

tions. Philip Pain, whose existence is known only by his authorship of
Daily Meditations, wrote of the same exercise:

> How often have I view'd the graves, and gone
> Unto that place, and yet returned home
> Again unto my house: The time will bee
> When I must go, but not returning see.
>   Lord, give me so much grace, that I may be
>   Ever-more mindful of Eternitie.

Edward Taylor seems to have had a broadside picture or an emblem
book in hand during at least three of his meditations, though he
turned the conventions of artists, printers, and the *ars moriendi* tradition itself against themselves as he reaffirmed the Christian revelation.

> The Painter lies who pensills death's Face grim
>   With White bare butter Teeth, bare staring bones,
> With Empty Eyeholes, Ghostly Lookes which fling
>   Such Dread to see as raiseth Deadly groans,
>   For thou hast farely Washt Deaths grim grim face
>   And made his Chilly finger-Ends drop Grace
>   (I,34, ll. 25–39).[37]

John Cotton discussed the use of memento mori objects, pointing
to both their value and their danger. "A man passing through a burying place may see a dead mans scalpe cast up, and thereby take occasion from the present object to meditate (for the present) on his
mortality, and to prepare for like change." Such meditation is illustrated in the painting by Georges de la Tour that appears as the frontispiece of Louis L. Martz's *Poetry of Meditation* and in the picture of
the author in Thomas Williamson's anti-Roman tract *The Sword of the
Spirit* (London, 1613). But Cotton rejected as idolatrous regular meditation on a skull kept for devotional purposes. "If he keepe that dead
mans scalpe in his Closet, or Bed-chamber, to be an ordinary helpe to
him to put him in minde dayly of his mortality: Now in so doing he
make an Image of it." It appears that New Englanders regularly, if
occasionally, used death objects in their meditations, even, Cotton
notwithstanding, in their devotional "closets." New Englanders thus
participated in a well-established medieval devotional tradition. The
development of gravestone art, the printing of illustrated broadside

37. Pearse, *Great Concern*, 63–65. Cotton Mather, *Perswasions from the Terror of the
Lord: A Sermon Concerning the Day of Judgment* . . . (Boston, 1711), 35, cited in Stannard,
Puritan Way of Death, 66. Thomas, ed., *Diary of Samuel Sewall*, I, 364. Pain, *Daily Medita-
tions*, 24.

Figure 12. Frontispiece to Thomas Williamson's vigorous attack on the papacy, The Sword of the Spirit *(London, 1613). The illustration is of the author in the act of meditative writing, with skull and hourglass before him as devotional aids. Courtesy the Folger Shakespeare Library, Washington, D.C.*

elegies, and the use of funeral rings gave the public additional opportunities for reflection. Sewall's apparently bizarre behavior, cited
above, must be understood within the context of this devotional
tradition.[38]

Judging from the amount of religious verse that has survived,
poetry was an especially effective way for pious New Englanders to
prepare for death. Edward Taylor concluded meditation on death
with some of his most triumphal personal applications of Christ's
resurrection.

> Say I am thine, My Lord: Make me thy bell
>   To ring thy Praise. Then Death is mine indeed
> A Hift to Grace, a Spur to Duty; Spell
>   To Fear; a Frost to nip each naughty Weede.
>   A Golden doore to Glory. Oh I'le sing
>   This Triumph o're the Grave! Death where's thy Sting?
>   (I,34, ll. 37–42).

In these meditations Taylor moved far beyond the memento mori
images that were his original meditative focus.[39]

For Anne Bradstreet, her poem "As Weary Pilgrim" was actually the
culmination of decades of preparation for death through poetic meditation. Illness, childbirth, and the death of relatives were events that
filled her thoughts with her own mortality. She wrote the first such
poem in 1632, "Upon a Fit of Sickness":

> Twice ten years old, not fully told
>   Since nature gave me breath,
> My race is run, my thread is spun,
>   lo here is fatal Death.

Her poetic images are tritely conventional, coming directly from the
preparation for death tradition—

> All men must dye, and so must I
> For what's this life, but care and strife?
>   since first we came from womb,

---

38. Cotton, *Modest and Cleare Answer*, 20. Ziff, *Career of John Cotton*, 247–248. See
Peter Benes, *The Masks of Orthodoxy: Folk Gravestone Carving in Plymouth County, Massachusetts, 1689–1805* (Amherst, Mass., 1977); Ludwig, *Graven Images*, esp. 90–93, 274–
276; Dickran Tashjian and Ann Tashjian, *Memorials for Children of Change* (Middletown,
Conn., 1974); and Ola Winslow, comp., *American Broadside Verse from Imprints of the 17th
& 18th Centuries* (New Haven, Conn., 1930).

39. See Jeff Hammond and Thomas M. Davis, "Edward Taylor: A Note on Visual
Imagery," *Early Am. Lit.*, VIII (1973), 126–131.

Our strength doth waste, our time doth hast,
  and then we go to th' Tomb

—and she ends with the Christian affirmation that "The race is run, the field is won, / the victory's mine I see." In her poem written "Before the Birth of One of Her Children" she warned her husband that it "may be thy Lot to lose thy friend." And again in a fainting spell she recognized her own mortality and dependence on God.

My life as Spider's webb's cutt off,
  Thus fainting have I said,
And lieving man no more shall see,
  But bee in silence layd.

When God resurrected her so "I here a while might 'bide," she praised God but also concluded on a note of preparation, praying, "O Lord, no longer bee my Dayes, / Than I may fruitfull bee." When near the end of her life her three-year-old granddaughter and namesake died, she consoled herself with the thought, "But yet a while, and I shall go to thee." By this time, the year she wrote "As Weary Pilgrim," she was more than prepared for death; she longed for it.[40]

New Englanders as diverse as governors and tailors turned to verse when they prepared devotionally for death. Eight years before the death of Thomas Dudley, Anne Bradstreet's father, "some nameless author" advised him in an anagrammatic poem, " 'Twill not be long before you turne to dust." Whether it was a political enemy, a political friend lamenting the passing of the first-generation leaders, or a spiritual advisor is unclear. But the poem contains many of the conventions of meditation on death, including the funeral ring:

A death's head on your hand you neede not weare,
A dying head you on your shoulders beare.
You neede not one to mind you, you must dye,
You in your name spell mortalitye.

The shock value of writing an anagrammatic poem for someone still living was deepened by the use put to Dudley's name: "Thomas Dudley / Ah! old must dye." The impact of the poem is impossible to gauge, but Dudley later wrote a poem himself, which was found in his pocket after he passed away. The verses begin with recognition of physical decay—"Dimme eyes, deaf ears, cold stomach shew / My dissolution is in view." Dudley then relied completely on well-worn popular images—

40. Hutchinson, ed., *Poems of Bradstreet*, 50, 45, 64, 16, 58.

My shuttle's shut, my race is run,
My sun is set, my deed is done.
My span is measured, [my] tale is told,
My flower's faded and grown old.
My life is vanished, shadows fled,
My soul's with Christ, my body dead.

His farewell wish, in line with the earlier anagrammatic poem, was that the old ways would continue in New England after his death. Even John Winthrop attempted poetry in old age in his "Epitaphium Meum," once again employing the familiar image of the pilgrim. God "call'd me from my Native place / For to enjoy the Means of Grace," and "In Wilderness he did me guide. . . . As Pilgrim past I to and fro." Winthrop bid

Farewell, dear Children, whom I love,
Your better Father is above:
When I am gone, he can supply;
To him I leave you when I die.

He concluded, as did Dudley, with conventional images. "My dayes are spent, Old Age is come, / My Strength it fails, my Glass near run." Countless others in New England wrote the same phrases. Conventionality produced poor poetry but made the devotional tradition of preparationism universally available.[41]

The most unsophisticated New Englanders were caught up in the need to prepare. John Dane in 1682 wrote "sum poems in waie of preparation for death" in conjunction with his spiritual autobiography, though only the prose has survived. And if we can believe that the obscure Philip Pain, "Who lately suffering Shipwrack, was drowned," was a real young man living in New England, his *Daily Meditations: Or, Quotidian Preparations for and Considerations of Death and Eternity* represents the most systematic preparation by a lay person extant. The book contains sixty-four meditations, dated from July 19 through August 3, 1666. The poems, all composed of six lines, rely heavily on Herbert and Quarles but also on the common images of

41. Meserole, ed., *Seventeenth-Century American Poetry*, 505, 365, 389–390. Harold Jantz has called the poem sent to Dudley "one of the most carefully wrought poems of the period, deeply satisfying aesthetically" ("American Baroque: Three Representative Poets," in Calvin Israel, ed., *Discoveries & Considerations: Essays on Early American Literature & Aesthetics. Presented to Harold Jantz* [Albany, N.Y., 1976], 18). The use of the death's head on a ring in 1645 indicates that it and other funerary symbols were used in the first half of the century and not, as Stannard and others have commonly supposed, only in the second half. See Stannard, *Puritan Way of Death*, 113–114.

dust, the grave, decay, the "King of Terrours," the rose, the hourglass, and so on. In each verse the first four lines establish the meditative theme and the last two are a petitionary prayer, to resolve the problem posed in the theme. Though the language was fully conventional, Pain succeeded in achieving at least ingenuity in his poetry through clever plays on words.

> Man's life is like a Rose, that in the Spring
> Begins to blossome, fragrant smells to bring:
> Within a day or two, behold Death's sent,
> A publick Messenger of discontent.
>> Lord grant, that when my Rose begins to fade,   .
>> I may behold an Everlasting shade.

The dominant mood of preparation for death was self-examination, and Pain identified the "reason 'tis so hard to die" with "the sense / Of guilt and sin." Devotional preparation for death, therefore, entailed repentance and a changed life.

> Alas, what is the World? a Sea of Glass.
> Alas, what's Earth? it's but an Hower-glass.
> The Sea dissolves; the Glass is quickly run:
> Behold, with speed man's Life is quickly done.
>> Let me so swim in this Sea, that I may
>> With thee live happy in another day.

Preparation for death was ultimately preparation for eternity on the other side of death and judgment: "Lord, let me be prepared for that day, / That so with joy (Lord) thee behold I may."[42]

Michael Wigglesworth's poetry was not for the most part personal and meditative. He wrote sermons in ballad form. Still, his verse was almost entirely of the preparation for death genre. Wigglesworth exhorted thousands of New Englanders to prepare for death in *The Day of Doom* and his other poems. His prefatory lines explicitly stated

42. Dane, "Declaration of Remarkabell Prouedenses," *NEHGR*, VIII (1854), 147. Pain, *Daily Meditations*, 17, 21, 33, and *passim*. See Leon Howard's introduction to the 1936 facsimile reprint, esp. pp. 5–12. There is no record of Pain's existence in either England or New England other than this small book. It is tempting to think that "Philip Pain" was the pseudonym of a clergyman or even of Marmaduke Johnson, who published the *Meditations* illegally in 1668 with a second edition in 1670. The circumstances fit almost too neatly: A young man who had piously prepared for death dies at sea. Even his name had emblematic quality: "must I / Go from PAIN here, to pain eternally?" (Meditation 50). However, though books were frequently published anonymously in the 17th century, there was no tradition of writing under a pen name. We may guardedly accept the meditations as the product of an individual's actual spiritual experience.

that the epic's purpose was "That Death and Judgment may not come / And find thee unprepared." His overriding method in *The Day of Doom* was to instill the fear of Christ as terrible Judge and drive penitents to Him for mercy in this life before it was too late. Terror was a means of grace, but the hoped for end was escape from terror. "Oh get a part in Christ," Wigglesworth cried, "And make the Judge thy Friend." His "A Song of Emptiness," bound with *The Day of Doom* "to fill up the Empty Pages following," employed the traditional images of mortality: Man is a wave, a dream, a lifeless picture, a wind, a flower, a bubble, a wheel, dust, and chaff. The things of this world are but "deceitful Toyes."[43]

The Day of Doom was the most popular piece of literature in seventeenth-century New England. An unprecedented eighteen-hundred copies were printed in the first edition in 1662, which sold out in the first year. Thereafter the work was reissued repeatedly. One woman who found the singsong lines echoing through her mind as she approached death was Elizabeth Taylor, wife of the pastor-poet. In his "Funerall Poem" for her, Edward Taylor concluded: "The Doomsday Verses much perfum'de her Breath, / Much in her Thoughts, and yet she fear'd not Death." Wigglesworth's own preparations, as we have them, involved poetic meditation. He wrote,

> Now Farewel WORLD, in which is not my Treasure;
> I have in thee Enjoy'd but little pleasure.
> And now I Leave thee, for a Better Place,
> Where Lasting Pleasures are before CHRIST's Face.

And in "Death Expected and Welcomed" he again wrote in a personal vein:

> Welcome, sweet REST, by me so long Desir'd,
> Who have with Sins and Griefs, so long been tir'd,
> And welcome Death, my Father's Messenger;
> Of my Felicity the Hastener.

His conclusion indicates he had at long last completed the work of preparation. "Into thy Hands I recommend my Sp'rit, / Trusting thro' Thee, Eternal Life to inherit."[44]

---

43. Michael Wigglesworth, *The Day of Doom: Or, a Poetical Description of the Great and Last Judgment* . . . (Boston, 1715 [orig. publ. Cambridge, 1662]), 9.

44. Stanford, ed., *Poems of Taylor*, 476. Wigglesworth, *Day of Doom*, 69–74. Samuel Eliot Morison has written of *The Day of Doom*: "This poem has a social significance far transcending its quality as poetry. For in simple words that everyone could understand, and in a metre that was easily memorized, it carried home to every man, woman, and

Seventeenth-century New England preparationism consisted of the devotional acts of preparation for conversion, preparation for nightly sleep, preparation for the Sabbath and Sacrament, and preparation for death. In each exercise believers could experience grace, the fulfillment of their preparation. The cumulative effect of all the disciplines practiced by the believer was the advancing of God's own preparation of the heart for salvation. Conversion, the Sabbath and Sacrament, and even death were all, ultimately, preparatory stages on the way to the final goal, the eternal life of glory. A lifetime of devotional practice, therefore, made up what Peter Thacher called "constant preparation for the full injoyment of [Christ] in glory." Or as John Cotton preached, "Prepare . . . for an immortall estate. . . . Prepare for a change. Here we have no abiding City, we seeke one to come, Heb. 13.14." At the end of the century his grandson preached in the same manner. "A Sanctifyed Heart, in this World, is a needful Qualification and Preparation for a Glorifyed State in another." Even in a spirituality fueled by anxiety and by constant preparation for a glory not completely attainable in this life, such preparation made contentment and rest possible. A person such as Anne Bradstreet knew this inner joy when she wrote in her autobiographical notes, "I can now say, Return, O my Soul, to thy Rest, upon this Rock of Christ Jesus will I build my faith; and, if I perish, I perish." She knew the anxiety and the joy when she prayed: "O, never let Satan prevail against me, but strengthen my faith in Thee, 'till I shall attain the end of my hopes, even the Salvation of my Soul. Come, Lord Jesus; come quickly."[45]

---

child the essential message of New England's intellectual class. . . . Very seldom in history has an intellectual class succeeded so well in breaking through to the common consciousness." *The Puritan Pronaos: Studies in the Intellectual Life of New England in the Seventeenth Century* (New York, 1936), 209–210.

45. Thacher, "Diary," MS, II, 5–6. Cotton, *Briefe Exposition of Ecclesiastes*, 244. Cotton Mather, *The Everlasting Gospel. The Gospel of Justification by the Righteousness of God . . .* (Boston, 1700), 65. Anne Bradstreet, "Autobiographical Passages," in Hutchinson, ed., *Poems of Bradstreet*, 183–184.

Chapter Eight

"The Travelling Interest of Christ
in This Wilderness"

The Devotional Crisis of the Second Generation

 The problem of continuity and identity that faced the second generation in New England, the children of the founders, was at its base a devotional crisis. With the passing of parents and leaders; with the distinctly American experience of the second generation; with the virtual disappearance of the Exodus-like flight from England, which had been the setting for the spiritual pilgrimage; and with the decline in conversions relative to population growth, the question that troubled New Englanders most deeply was the devotional one. How could people be nurtured in the faith that had motivated their parents? The spiritual images and religious terminology that had been carried over from England needed new referents that would intersect the experience of native New Englanders in the second half of the seventeenth century.

When New Englanders lamented the death of one after another of their emigrant parents and leaders, their grief was more than the natural sense of loss one feels when death occurs. Personal grief was part of the larger social grief, caused by an acute fear of the social change of which each death was emblematic. The very idea of generations as taken from Scripture, David Hall has pointed out, implied declension, and the problem of continuity in the transfer to a second generation is traumatic in any utopian community. When John Hull noted the death in January 1661 of Isaac Heith, the "ruling elder at Roxbury," he used in his prayer the familiar reference to the same transition in the primitive Church (Galatians 2:9). Hull prayed, "The good Lord make us sensible of our pillars falling." His next petition, that God would "raise up others with a double portion of their spirit," was more hopeful than realistic. By "their spirit" he meant not just a godly spirit but the spirit of the Great Migration, a spirit that one born and reared in New England could appropriate only by a leap of faith.[1]

Increase Mather had the spirit perhaps because he, with a number of other Harvard graduates throughout the century, moved to England after completing his studies. Before returning in 1661 to the pulpit of Boston's Second Church, he imbibed the spirit of English nonconformity, persecution, and the international Calvinist movement. Increase was in England during the Restoration, so his experience was in fact similar to what his father had fled, including the dilemma of "conform[ing] to the ceremonies." The zeal of his father became his own when he was able to say, "Thus was I persecuted out of two places, Glocester and Guernsey, before I was 22 years of age." Persecution and migration were important credentials for Mather's ordination in Boston in 1664. But not all second-generation ministers had these experiences.[2]

Church members continued to deem migration from England important, and their desire for continuity is reflected in their tendency to call English-born pastors rather than Harvard graduates. Even when Boston's Third Church sought an associate for Thomas Thacher in 1669, they looked to England and sent John Hull on the search mission. The letter he carried spoke of "much trembling of heart for the ark of God . . . for the travelling interest of Christ in this wilderness, the holy God having, in extraordinary displeasure (even unto astonishment), contended with these churches, by a judicial and successive removal of many eminent and faithful ministers of the gospel, who in their day were principal pillars amongst us."[3]

In the second half of the seventeenth century the geographical exodus as the setting for the spiritual pilgrimage became increasingly unavailable. A few ministers, such as Edward Taylor, emigrated during the Restoration, and Taylor's record of the crossing was virtually identical with those of the first generation. Peter Thacher and others followed the example of Increase Mather years earlier and traveled to England and Europe after graduation. But they were often more like tourists than pilgrims, on holiday before starting their careers. As one English dissenter traveling through New England in 1686 commented, "We are of a Rambling Generation." The Atlantic crossing, no longer a pilgrimage, had declined into a ramble. Most New En-

1. Hall, *Faithful Shepherd*, 176–177. Hull, *Diaries*, 198.

2. Hall, *Faithful Shepherd*, 185. Hall, ed., "Autobiography of Increase Mather," Am. Antiq. Soc., *Procs.*, N.S., LXXI (1961), 281–287.

3. Hull, *Diaries*, 309. See Emory Elliott, *Power and the Pulpit in Puritan New England* (Princeton, N.J., 1975) for a study of the psychological pressures on the second and third generations.

glanders, even the cosmopolitan Cotton Mather, never traveled outside the colonies. The new generation no longer shared one of the basic experiences that had shaped the founders' spirituality.[4]

The acquisition of land and expansion into new territory added another dimension to the spiritual crisis. A pilgrim in the Hebrews 11 tradition was by definition homeless—"our home is nowhere," Robert Cushman had written, "nowhere but in the heavens." The early settlers, of course, believed they owned the land and had the right to apportion it. But they apportioned remarkably small lots and attempted to prohibit movement beyond town center boundaries. Only with the passing of the first generation did expansion become a serious issue. "Outlivers" grew in numbers, and factionalism based on geography became common. As farms spread to outlying areas the location of meetinghouses became hotly disputed. The rise of "contention" in town and church politics was linked directly to the struggle for expansion and acquisition, severely threatening the ideally peaceful village. The clearest statement of the spiritual implications of land hunger came at the Reforming Synod of 1679. "There hath been in many professors an insatiable desire after Land, and worldly Accomodations, yea as to forsake Churches and Ordinances, and to live like Heathen, only that so they might have Elbow-room enough in the world. Farms and merchandising have been preferred before the things of God." In "The Necessity of Reformation" the ministers reminded the people: "We differ from other out-goings of our Nation, in that it was not any worldly consideration that brought our Fathers into this wilderness, but Religion, even so they might build a Sanctuary unto the Lord's Name; Whenas now, Religion is made subservient unto worldly interests."[5]

Individuals who indulged in the covetous sin of outliving were believed to deserve God's judgment, most commonly visited in the form of Indian attack. One outliver, Hannah Swarton, was carried into captivity by Indian and French raiders in 1690. On her return the ministers succeeded in evoking in her a sense of guilt and repen-

---

4. "Diary of Edward Taylor," Mass. Hist. Soc., *Procs.,* XVIII (1880), 4–8. John Langdon Sibley, *Biographical Sketches of Graduates of Harvard University,* II (Cambridge, Mass., 1881), 377. John Dunton, *Letters Written from New-England, A.D. 1686,* ed. W. H. Whitmore (Prince Society, *Publications,* IV [Boston, 1867]), 20.

5. Demos, ed., *Remarkable Providences,* 27. John Winthrop to Sir Nathaniel Rich, May 22, 1634, Emerson, ed., *Letters from New England,* 116. See Sumner Chilton Powell, *Puritan Village: The Formation of a New England Town* (Middletown, Conn., 1963); Lockridge, *New England Town;* Greven, *Four Generations;* and Richard L. Bushman, *From Puritan to Yankee: Character and the Social Order in Connecticut, 1690–1765* (New York, 1967). Walker, *Creeds and Platforms,* 431.

tance. Her besetting sin, which in her moment of repentance she cast at the Lord's feet, was "that I Left the Publick Worship and Ordinances of God, to go to Live in a Remote Place, without the Publick Ministry; depriving our selves and our Children of so great a Benefit for our Souls, and all this, for Worldly advantages." She then "lay hold on the Blood of Christ, to cleanse me." The drama played out in Hannah Swarton's life, the ministers pointed out, was rooted in Scripture. They cited the parable of the marriage feast to demonstrate the relationship of land and violent conflict. Guests who would not come to the wedding because of farming and business responsibilities first killed the king's servants and then were themselves destroyed by his army (Matthew 22:1–7). The elders' comment that "Such iniquity causeth War to be in the Gates, and Cityes to be burnt up" was a direct reference to the devastation of King Philip's War and the continued violence of the frontier. Land acquisition almost necessarily led to conflict. Against fellow settlers the result was contention; against Indians the result was war. But the ultimate result was that possessors of land became possessed by the land. Settlers possessed by land had ceased the spiritual way of life that Puritans thought of as pilgrimage.[6]

Further complications involved the declining conversion rate relative to population growth. The gap between church membership and general population statistics had widened alarmingly by mid-century. Ministers and baptized but unconverted parents were concerned about limiting baptism to children of full communicants. It was a question of continuity: Would the covenant be continued to the next generation? Would it reside with an ever-decreasing group of converts and their children? As early as 1646 at the Cambridge Synod most ministers agreed that an extension of baptism to the children of all baptized parents was advisable, but they waited until the crisis was felt strongly enough to warrant action at the ministerial assembly of 1657 and the Synod of 1662. Even then the churches applied the broader criteria only gradually, and not universally until the crisis years of 1675 to 1690. Both the Halfway Covenant and Solomon Stoddard's attempted elimination of barriers around the Table were ecclesiastical developments that had strong devotional ramifications. They were attempts to keep the population within the devotional structure of

6. "A Narrative of Hannah Swarton, Containing Wonderful Passages, Relating to Her Captivity and Her Deliverance," in [Cotton Mather], *Humiliations Followed with Deliverances* . . . (Boston, 1697), Appendix, 67–68. Walker, *Creeds and Platforms*, 431. See Increase Mather, *A Brief History of the Warr with the Indians in New-England* (Boston, 1676), and W[illiam] Hubbard, *A Narrative of the Troubles with the Indians in New-England, from* . . . *1607, to* . . . *1677* . . . (Boston, 1677).

Puritan spirituality. The opportunity to have one's children baptized brought men and women at least to "own the covenant" intellectually and morally. They, along with their children, then came under the "watch and care" of the church, which included the demand for participation in all aspects of public and private worship and devotion.[7]

Beyond the Halfway Covenant, the ministers attempted to meet the crisis of the second generation by adapting the major themes of Puritan devotion to new circumstances. Three developments, distinct from one another yet pursued simultaneously and toward the same goal of spiritual continuity, may be identified. First, New Englanders sought ways to celebrate and venerate, and thereby to participate in, the pilgrimage of the founders. Second, they reinterpreted the geographical setting in which the pilgrimage took place. Third, they spiritualized the pilgrimage beyond the realm of geography—a task the founders had begun.

THE VENERATION OF THE FOUNDERS' PILGRIMAGE

"The fathers may have founded the colonies," Robert Middlekauff has written, "but the sons invented New England." Belief in the imminent chiliad and worldwide political reign of the saints, which had fired first-generation preaching, did incorporate a vision of New England as the vanguard of the Kingdom. Still, the hope of the founders had not been to be the first generation of Americans but to be the last premillennial generation of saints. Their eyes had been on events in England and Europe and on heaven. Some New Englanders zealous for the Kingdom (Hugh Peter and Henry Vane, for example) had returned to England for the final struggle against Satan and the papacy shaping up in the Civil War. After the failure of the Revolution Puritans had been forced to revise their thinking. For New Englanders revision had meant reworking their self-identity. They had emphasized the idea, present in germ form from Winthrop's *Arbella* sermon, that New England itself was a special place in God's plan for the latter days. Their sense of destiny, we have said, had motivated New Englanders of the first generation to document personal and political history extraordinarily closely.[8]

7. Hall, *Faithful Shepherd*, 201. Walker, *Creeds and Platforms*, 238–239. Robert G. Pope, *The Half-Way Covenant: Church Membership in Puritan New England* (Princeton, N.J., 1969). Thomas M. Davis and Jeff Jeske, eds., Introduction, "Solomon Stoddard's 'Arguments' Concerning Admission to the Lord's Supper," Am. Antiq. Soc., *Procs.*, LXXXVI, Pt. I (1976), 75–111.

8. Middlekauff, *The Mathers*, 98.

The eyes of the second generation, as they continued the historiographical task, were less on the present and future than on the past. They constantly rewrote the story of the early years, transforming it into a golden age. The notion of a golden age helped explain the tarnished quality of contemporary religiosity but, more important, it enabled New Englanders to understand who they were and why they were there. Even when they wrote current history, recounting the horror and final victory of King Philip's War, for example, it was to prove that God had vindicated them against the standard of their deceased parents.

The dominant homiletical style of the second half of the century, the jeremiad, corresponded to the new historiography in its assumption that the founders had established the scale by which all subsequent developments were to be measured. The finest seventeenth-century jeremiad was Increase Mather's 1674 fast day sermon, *The Day of Trouble Is Near*, which sparked the conversion of Sir William Phips. Mather stated the case explicitly: "This is *Immanuels Land.*" What did this designation mean in the last quarter of the century? To be God's country implied the presence of His favor. But Mather's reference was to Isaiah's warning that God, through the Assyrian army, would overrun Judah like the Euphrates! "Gird yourselves, and ye shall be broken in pieces. . . . Speak the word, and it shall not stand: for God is with us" (8:8–10). To be Immanuel's Land—for God to be "with us" in New England—entailed not the outpouring of plenty but similar judgment. The remedy lay in reformation. "Be an humble people," Mather exhorted. "Be a Heavenly people, . . . be a Believing people, . . . be a Reforming people." He elaborated, "Certainly we need Reformation. Where is the old New-England Spirit, that once was amongst us? Where is our first love?" To recover the spirit, he preached, "be a United people." And most of all, "be a Praying people." Mather used "old New-England" as the criterion for spirituality. If the Lord filled the land then with glory and now with judgment, this was a promise that if New England repented and returned, glory too would return.[9]

Thomas Shepard the younger built his sermon *Eye-Salve* around Jeremiah 2:31, "O generation, see ye the Word of the Lord: have I been a wilderness unto Israel? a land of darkness? wherefore say my

9. [Cotton Mather], *Pietas in Patriam: The Life of His Excellency Sir William Phips, Knt.* . . . (London, 1697), 28. I. Mather, *Day of Trouble*, 26–30. Sacvan Bercovitch in *American Jeremiad* shows that New England sermons were jeremiads from the start, but the form took on a new character in the hands of the second and third generations using the 1630s as their standard (pp. 3–30).

people, We are Lords, we will come no more unto thee." And Thomas Thacher's preface to Shepard's sermon captured the essence of the message: "Make haste, return, come unto thy God who is thy strength and glory. Thou shalt be a happy people, O New England, as long as thou art an obedient people." If, as the ministers preached, God had a grand part for New England in His cosmic design, the jeremiad recalled His people to that role. "The Lord intended some great thing," Mather wrote, "when he planted these Heavens, and laid the foundations of this Earth, and said unto New-England (as sometimes to Sion) *Thou art my People*: And what should that be, if not so a Scripture-Pattern of Reformation, as to Civil, but especially in Ecclesiastical respects, might be here erected, as a First Fruits of that which shall in due time be accomplished the whole world throughout, in that day when there shall be one Lord, and his Name one over all the earth." As David Minter has pointed out, "By emphasizing the heights from which they had fallen, they underscored the height at which they yet stood." The sermon was a celebration, and thus a reclaiming, of the original vision. The humiliation that tipped the arrow of the jeremiad was aimed at the heart's rebirth in Christ. If the "Day of Humiliation" could but be "A Day of Reformation," Cotton Mather urged, the "Day of Deliverance" would soon follow.[10]

The widespread institution of covenant-renewal ceremonies in churches and homes was part of the same need for self-identification and self-understanding. Public renewals sprang up seemingly spontaneously throughout New England in connection with the March 1676 fast days during King Philip's War. Increase Mather fixed on the idea as a means to further "reformation." But covenant renewal was not a new practice. In his arguments in 1676–1677 Mather pointed to the continuity with the first generation that such renewals offered. We have already noted that covenant renewal was a long-standing tradition in New England. "Whenever God is worshipped the Covenant is renewed implicitly," Mather said. "Yea, whenever Christians pray unto God in Christ, especially when they Fast and Pray, the Covenant is renewed." Covenant renewal was a renewal of "their Faith and Repentance," a duty that no one could charge was a dangerous innovation. Most important, covenant renewal was intended to promote the same reexperiencing of conversion that Thomas Shepard and others had regularly undergone in their devotions. Mather interpreted Da-

10. Shepard, [Jr.], *Eye-Salve*, 1. Thomas Thacher, Preface, *ibid.* Increase Mather, "To the Reader," in Samuel Torrey, *An Exhortation unto Reformation . . .* (Cambridge, Mass., 1674), sig. A2. David Minter, "The Puritan Jeremiad as a Literary Form," in Bercovitch, ed., *American Puritan Imagination*, 50–52. [C. Mather], *Humiliations*, 7–8, 13.

vid's prayer "Create in me a clean heart O God and RENEW a right spirit within me" (Psalms 51:10) to mean that David "saw that he stood in need of going over the work of Conversion again, and so of Renewing his closure and covenant with God in Jesus Christ."[11]

Mather's great promotion of the ceremony came, significantly, in his sermon on the Day of Humiliation in the last week of 1676, March 21. Covenant renewal was not an innovation but a more specific enactment of what New England had been doing all along. The end of the year was the traditional time for devotional self-examination in preparation for renewal in the new year. Springtime was the occasion for devotional preparation of the heart, the time of planting the seeds of humiliation, the time of fasting as winter stores were depleted. So now Mather preached, on this traditional fast day, "a solemn Renewal of their Covenant, which was a consequent of their Confessions and Humiliations before our Lord." The covenant-renewal ceremony as instituted in the last quarter of the century grew out of, and in most cases continued in conjunction with, the traditional apparatus of the year-end fast day in March.[12]

In the covenant-renewal ceremony, as in all exercises of fasting and self-examination, the penitent reviewed past sins. But in covenant renewal the participants fixed their eyes more directly on the covenant of the parents. In general, they had sinned against God's eternal covenant with His people and thus had fallen like Adam. More immediately, they had sinned against the covenant God had made with their parents in the 1630s. If this covenant was a manifestation of God's great covenant, then in their sin New Englanders had also reenacted Adam's fall. Increase Mather preached that those who "have set this day apart, that so you might humble your selves before the Lord on the account of former breeches of the Covenant, and seek unto him by Fasting and Prayer" might find the "presence and assistance of his Spirit" in their enactment of "that solemn renewal of Covenant." By renewing the covenant ministers hoped that individuals would find their hearts renewed and that society would be reformed. The ceremony was an attempt to reappropriate the spirituality of the founders.[13]

The Synod of 1679, called in response to the manifold "evils" already well rehearsed in countless sermons, became the vehicle for official sanctioning of public covenant-renewal ceremonies in the churches. Three of the eleven remedies for the reformation of society

---

11. Hall, *Faithful Shepherd*, 243–244. I. Mather, *Renewal of Covenant*, 5–7, title page.

12. Mather, *Renewal of Covenant*, title page.

13. *Ibid.*, 15.

justified and outlined the ceremony. The arguments were almost verbatim repetitions of the case Mather had put forth two years earlier in his fast day sermon. "Solemn and explicit Renewal of the Covenant is a Scripture Expedient for Reformation," the Synod proclaimed. A barrage of scriptural citations, almost entirely from the Old Testament, demonstrated the precedents of the practice. These references became the texts for sermons preached at renewal ceremonies throughout New England. The order for carrying out the ceremony followed the familiar pattern of the order of redemption. First, in repentance, "the sins of the Times should be engaged against," and then in a reaffirmed union with Christ "Reformation thereof (in the name and by the help of Christ) promised before the Lord." In anticipation of this desired union with Christ, the ceremony was to emphasize the union of believers in church fellowship. The wording of the renewal statement was to avoid points of controversy. "Such things as are clear and indisputable" ought to be expressed, "that so all the Churches may agree in Covenanting to promote the Interest of holiness, and close walking with God."[14]

The covenant recited on March 17, 1679/1680 by the members of Boston's Second Church makes clear the interrelationship of individual and social renewal. "We do, in humble confidence of his gracious assistance, and acceptance through Christ, each one of us, for our selves, and joyntly as a Church of the living God, explicitly renew our Covenant with God, and one with another." The primary act of devotion was self-surrender: "We do give up our selves unto God" and "We doe give up our selves one unto another, in the Lord." When the members had re-covenanted, Samuel Willard (whose presence in the pulpit was a sign of church unity) preached that they had "by a new and voluntary act chosen you the Lord to serve him." It was voluntary in that participants were church members (nonmembers had yet to make their first covenant) and had experienced conversion. Their wills were free to conform, therefore, to God's will in this "satisfying and contenting act." The act was "new" in the same way that individuals who went through the redemptive drama in their devotions reported reexperiencing grace. Spiritual rebirth, the intention of the covenant-renewal exercises, was effected once but reexperienced repeatedly and continuously.[15]

In the late 1670s the idea of covenant renewal was very much in the

14. Walker, *Creeds and Platforms*, 435–437.

15. "The Covenant Which Was Unanimously Consented unto . . . ," in Increase Mather, *Returning unto God the Great Concernment of a Covenant People . . .* (Boston, 1680), 20–21. Samuel Willard, *The Duty of a People That Have Renewed Their Covenant with God*

air, applied in private as well as in public worship, as a means of maintaining continuity as the generations passed. Thomas Thacher, pastor of Boston's Third Church, prescribed the annual renewal of his family's covenant with God as a way to assure the spiritual well-being of his children and grandchildren after his death. When he died in October 1678, the obligation to carry out the ceremony rested on his son Peter. Within the yearly limit placed by his father, Peter Thacher wrote, "Brother Thomas and his wife, Brother Ralph, my wife and I went to fast wherein we sollemely renewed our Covenant with the Lord and that In answer unto my Father's dying Charge who adviced it might be done once a year at least by us altogether. Otherwise hee told us Religion would dy in our familys if not in our generation yet in the next." In the morning of the daylong exercise Thomas "began . . . with prayer and prayed very sensibly, judiciously and with many tears." Peter wrote, "I confesse it gave mee much satisfaction." Ralph, "who was alsoe much warmed," and then Peter himself prayed. In the afternoon Peter "began with prayer," then preached a sermon to the family on 1 Chronicles 28:9 (the words of David: "And thou, Solomon my son, know thou the God of thy father, and serve him with a perfect heart and a willing mind"), and "Ended with prayer." "The Lord did much to in large my heart both in prayer and preaching, and draw it forth to himself and soe it was alsoe with my Brothers, Sister and wife; I never saw soe much affeckon stirring on a fast day for the Company, Blessed be the holy name of the Lord for it." The fast ended at four in the afternoon, when they supped at the family home.[16]

Others in the late seventeenth century renewed their individual covenant with God in similar private exercises. For young ministers, renewal was often part of preparation for ordination. Cotton Mather wrote and signed his new covenant during a daylong "secret FAST before the Lord" and received assurance from the Lord "that all Controversie between Him and my Soul, was done away." Joseph Green renewed his covenant as the Salem Village Church, which he served on a trial basis, considered whether to ordain him. He addressed his prayers to "Most Glorious Jehovah who art the God of my fathers." He expressed more clearly than did Mather the element of anxiety, but his rehearsal of the redemptive drama was the same. Green had already experienced conversion and union with Christ, of course. Now he once more renounced "Satan, the sinfull vanity of this world,

---

. . . (Boston, 1680), 5–6. See also Willard's *Covenant-Keeping: The Way to Blessedness . . .* and *The Necessity of Sincerity in Renewing Covenant . . .* , bound together (Boston, 1682).
   16. Thacher, "Diary," MS, I, 36–37, Mass. Hist. Soc., Boston.

[1]

Returning unto God the great Concernment of a Covenant People.

Hof. 14. 1.   *O Ifrael ,   Return unto the Lord thy God; for thou haft fallen by thine Iniquity.*

Figure 13. Emblems of death and resurrection at the top of page 1 of Increase Mather, Returning unto God the Great Concernment of a Covenant People *(Boston, 1680). The printer's ornament depicts cherubs with trumpets and a skeleton rising from a coffin. Courtesy the Congregational Library, Boston.*

and all my own hearts lusts" and surrendered himself "soul and body to be thine forever and ever amen." He prayed that God would take "everlasting possession of me for Jesus Christ, altho I am unworthy thou shouldest come into my heart." He asked finally that God would "let this covenant Now be Confirmed in Heaven."[17]

The hope that through covenant renewal dead ideals might live again was expressed visually in the printer's ornament at the top of the first page of Increase Mather's 1679/1680 covenant-renewal sermon, *Returning unto God the Great Concernment of a Covenant People.* Trumpeting cherubs flanked the resurrection motif of a skeleton rising out of a coffin. Although in their desire for a resurrected first-generation spirit New Englanders did not intend to live in the past, but rather to experience anew God's grace, the exercises were nevertheless based on an idealized and venerated past. The way to salvation, in the words

17. Ford, ed., *Diary of Cotton Mather,* I, 96. Mather published an almost identical form as a model for others in *Small Offers towards the Service of the Tabernacle in the Wilderness*

of the oft-used text, was to "Remember therefore from whence thou art fallen, and repent, and do the first works" (Revelation 2:5).[18]

In addition to covenant renewal, developments in the memorialization of the dead enabled the second generation to venerate the founders. These included increasingly elaborate funeral services; elegiac broadsides; the rise of the stonecutter's craft and the use of more iconographic gravestones; great interest in the last words of dead leaders and parents; and the writing of biography.

Memorialization of the dead, however, involved less innovation than extension of early seventeenth-century religious culture. The founders were not lacking in symbolic imagination, nor were they such iconoclasts that they ritually ignored the dead. In the early years, true, the funeral was liturgically bare: "At burials, nothing is read, nor any Funeral Sermon made, but all the neighborhood, or a good company of them, come together by tolling of the bell, and carry the dead solemnly to his grave, and there stand by him while he is buried. The ministers are most commonly present." That clergy attended mourners to the grave indicates a religious significance in even the earliest, supposedly civil, funerals. More important, the funeral was but one part of the total pastoral and ceremonial response to death. The minister was present with the dying and the grieving, and prayers for the dying were offered in public and neighborhood worship. Even the early wooden and stone markers were not devoid of symbolism. It appears that from the start they were fashioned to resemble bedboards, a reminder that the souls of the redeemed "sleep in Jesus" (1 Thessalonians 4:14). The shift from wooden posts and rails to stone made greater iconographic detail possible, and stone carvers portrayed common resurrection emblems and motifs. Peter Benes has concluded that "in the absence of an ecclesiastically authorized representation of the immortal soul, the artistic conventions by which carvers portrayed such spirits were drawn from what we must assume were folk variations and alterations upon traditional English death and resurrection symbols." Artwork at the head of gravestones, broadsides, and published sermons represented "the anticipated, or at the least hoped-for sainthood." Ministers were not hostile to, but shared in this folk tradition.[19]

... (Boston, 1689), 24–25. Morison, ed., "Commonplace Book of Joseph Green," Col. Soc. Mass., *Trans.*, XXXIV (1943), 246–247.

18. I. Mather, *Returning unto God*, 1. Revelation 2:5 was, for example, the text for Michael Wigglesworth's election sermon in the crisis year of 1686, when the Charter was revoked and Sir Edmund Andros arrived. Thacher, "Diary," MS, I, 110.

19. Lechford, *Plain Dealing*, ed. Trumbull, 87–88. Benes, *Masks of Orthodoxy*, 38, 43.

When the passing of the first generation made the question of death crucial, ministers built upon the collective memory of symbolic representation. On the Sabbath following a funeral they preached sermons that eulogized the deceased or focused on the general theme of death. They also wrote elegiac poetry in memory of the departed, using the same images that the stone carver employed.

The elegies were intended on the one hand as memento mori for the living. John Fiske, for example, wrote on John Cotton:

> His soule Embalmd with grace
>   was fit to soare on high
> and to receive its place
>   above the starry skie.
> now grant O G[od that we]
>   may follow afte[r him]
> surviving worlds ocean unto thee
>   our passage safe may swim.

At the same time the elegists sought to memorialize the departed: "A Father in our Israel's ceas'st to be / Even hee that in the Church a pillar was." The memorials were intended to provide a sense that not all ties with the origins had been severed. Edward Johnson in his *Wonder-Working Providence*, published in 1652, included elegies on those who had died by that date. The possibility of a continued presence of the early spirit was the motive behind Nathaniel Morton's 1669 *New Englands Memoriall*, which contained elegies for every major leader from Thomas Hooker (who died in 1647) onward. Morton's commemoration presented the first generation as inspiration, plumb line, and model:

> Now blessed Hooker, thou art set on high,
> Above the thankless world, and cloudy sky;
> Do thou of all thy labor reap the crown,
> Whilst we here reap the seed which thou hast sown.

William Bradford, one of the last survivors of the founding generation, wrote what amounted to an elegy for the entire generation, in "A Word to New England," which incorporated the basic jeremiad message.

> O New England, thou canst not boast;
> Thy former glory thou hast lost.
> When Hooker, Winthrop, Cotton died,
> And many precious ones beside,

Thy beauty then it did decay,
And still doth languish more away. . . .

Repent, amend, and turn to God
That we may prevent his sharp rod,
Time yet thou hast, improve it well,
That God's presence may with you dwell.

The message came from many sources: Repent and return.[20]

The greatest eulogist of all was Cotton Mather. He wrote poetry, but his most successful mode of expression was biography. After the manner of his father's life of Richard Mather, and of John Norton's biography of his predecessor at Boston's First Church, John Cotton, Mather in the last decade of the century wrote a series of biographies of deceased New Englanders. He began with family, with his brother Nathaniel (published 1689), and then collected material on the great ministerial leaders: John Eliot (published 1691), John Cotton, John Norton, John Wilson, John Davenport, and Thomas Hooker (published 1695). His work included civil as well as religious leaders and culminated in the massive historical-biographical volumes of the *Magnalia Christi Americana* (London, 1702). Cotton Mather's drive to save the diaries and other personal writings of the deceased, in addition to contemporary eulogies and other firsthand accounts, was based on his belief that the path to godliness lay in the imitation of the founders' spiritual lives. He hoped that the patterns of their conversions and the methods of their devotional conversation would serve as models for New Englanders at the end of the century. By savoring the earlier generation's experience, later generations might recapture something of their spirit. Biography was devotional literature when the life recorded was the means of grace for the reader.

Second-generation New Englanders did not venerate the founders out of a sense of nostalgia, although many may have felt nostalgic. Their aim was to create a form through which God would work powerfully and popularly. They hoped to engender mass religious feeling, so that the majority of the population would once more know, as they had earlier in the century, God's claim on their lives. David Hall has stated that not until "the preachers of another generation came upon revivalism did the clergy have the weapon that they needed to play upon a fluid, pluralistic culture." But, he suggests, the covenant-renewal ceremony was "a step in that direction." The adap-

20. Meserole, ed., *Seventeenth-Century American Poetry*, 187–188, 387–388. Nathaniel Morton, *New England's Memorial* (Boston, 1855 [orig. publ. 1669]), 155.

tations in worship and devotion that allowed believers to appropriate the spirit of their parents were successful in that they created a religious and cultural identity. The limits of feeding on the experiences of others, however, became apparent by the end of the century. In his famous sermon *The Peril of the Times Displayed*, Samuel Willard recognized the need for an entirely new outpouring of the Holy Spirit. He began to speak the language not of renewal but of revival. "It hath been a frequent observation, that if one Generation begins to decline, the next followeth usually grows worse, and so on, till God poureth out his Spirit again upon them." He concluded: "Pray to God to revive dying Religion . . . and he can revive it in the midst of the days. . . . Pray that he will pour out his spirit upon the dry places, and turn the wilderness into a fruitful field; and thus shall you prove your selves to be Israelites indeed." Continuity was still strong in Willard's exhortation. He called for a fresh experience of the redemptive drama of repentance for sin and the influx of grace, of mortification and vivification, that had characterized New England spirituality from the beginning.[21]

THE RELOCATION OF THE PILGRIMAGE

Puritans always recognized the spiritual pilgrimage as a journey beyond history and geography. But New Englanders had a geographical referent that served as the setting or correlate for the pilgrimage and as an emblem of that greater journey. New England was a way station on the flight from captivity in the Egypt of England to the promised land of heaven. In the second half of the century, since the experience of migration was unavailable to the native born, a new geographical correlate for the pilgrimage emerged. Many of the themes and biblical references remained the same, but the scene was wholly altered.

Hostile relations with the Indians and the French suggested this new interpretation of the pilgrimage, with the drama set entirely in America. New Englanders were held captive at the hands not of Romanizers in the Church of England but of savages and papists. Their journey was no longer across an ocean but into the wilderness of North America. Their destination was no longer a different place from the point of departure but restoration to the point of departure. By 1707 the "Redeemed Captive," John Williams, identified white

21. Hall, *Faithful Shepherd*, 244. Samuel Willard, *The Peril of the Times Displayed. Or, the Danger of Mens Taking Up with a Form of Godliness, but Denying the Power of It* (Boston, 1700), 112–113, 166–167.

New England as Zion, which meant that he defined return to Boston as deliverance.[22]

In the seventeenth century New Englanders had still thought of Zion as existing primarily in the spiritual realm. Return to civilization represented the soul's arrival at the heavenly Zion. In his 1672 election sermon, *Eye-Salve*, Thomas Shepard the younger discussed the physical and spiritual qualities of wilderness. The words of the Lord through Jeremiah, "Have I been a wilderness to Israel" (2:31), referred to the spiritual wilderness in the heart. "The words are Metaphorical," he preached, and meant "have I been that to my People which a Wilderness is unto men that are made to wilder therein, where they meet with nothing but wants, and terrour, and woe." Shepard went on to discuss the physical nature of wilderness, which illumined the plight of those in spiritual wilderness. Wilderness was a place of "confusion and disorder," of chaos in contrast to the ordered cosmos of holy civilization. Wilderness was a place of "suffering hunger and thirst," of "many positive evils," a land "not hedged in, nor fenced about," a land of darkness and "the privation of light." The soul had to make its way through such a spiritual wilderness on its way to salvation. Shepard could not resist pointing out that in New England the Lord had *not* been a wilderness to His people. He had brought about a new Creation through the establishment of towns and social institutions. The created order of Puritan society stood in contrast to the chaos of the wilderness. If in church, commonwealth, and school God "hath granted to us light and salvation," the wilderness was clearly the place of Satan, the master of chaos.[23]

The important development in the second half of the century was that the rise of Indian bitterness toward the English gave these primarily biblical ideas immediate objective referents on the frontier. When one of Peter Thacher's black slaves ran away and was finally found heading out of Concord "in a path that would not have lead him to any towne," Thacher was convinced that, had the slave not been caught, "in an ordinary course of providence hee had perished." It never occurred to Thacher that Ebed the slave did not want to be on a road leading to another town, that he wanted to leave and possibly could have survived outside the white village. For Thacher the wilderness was the place of death. When New Englanders were

---

22. Richard Slotkin traces the development of the captivity narrative, analyzing its emergence from within early American experience, in *Regeneration through Violence* (Middletown, Conn., 1973), 101. John Williams, *The Redeemed Captive, Returning to Zion* . . . (Boston, 1707).

23. Shepard, [Jr.], *Eye-Salve*, 3–6.

forcibly taken into the wilderness by those perceived as Satan's minions, the subsequent journey was both a harrowing physical ordeal in the American wilderness and a transforming spiritual ordeal in which the drama of death and resurrection was once again played out in the soul. The geographical journey that most clearly emblemized the spiritual pilgrimage now took place entirely on American soil.[24]

The first of the great captivity narratives, and the most unaffected in its style, was Mary Rowlandson's *The Soveraignty and Goodness of God*, first published in Cambridge in 1682. Her adventure is noteworthy even apart from her account of it. Increase Mather entered in his diary on February 10, 1676, "A dismal providence this day. Lancaster was set on by Indians. Mr. Rowlandson pastor of the church there. His house was assaulted. They took some of them alive, among whom was Mrs. Rowlandson. The Lord now speaks solemnly to ministers, inasmuch as a minister's family is fallen upon, and his wife and children taken by the enemy." On election day, May 3, Mather was able to write, "This day Mrs. Rowlandson was, by a wonderful hand of Providence, returned to her husband, after she had been absent eleven weeks in the hands of the Indians."[25]

The bare bones of the story are simple: Mary Rowlandson watched as Indians attacked her village and killed many inhabitants, including relatives, before her eyes. She was forced to accompany her captors into the wilderness. She lacked adequate food but gradually adapted remarkably well to Indian ways and the hardships of the journey. The party made twenty "removes" until they joined Metacomet himself. The Massachusetts General Court was finally able to intervene successfully and ransom her. At the end of the account Mrs. Rowlandson is recuperating in Boston and awaiting the return of her surviving children. Her narrative is significant, however, at the spiritual level, and Mrs. Rowlandson's reflections on the personal meaning of her trial are what make it an exceptional piece of writing. As the subtitle implies, she first wrote her story down "for Her Private Use." That is, it was a devotional exercise in the tradition of the journal and the spiritual autobiography, related to the discipline of meditative self-examination. The narrative was "Now Made Publick at the Earnest Desire of Some Friends, and for the Benefit of the Afflicted." This is the same rationale that was commonly given for publication of an individual's secret exercises as a devotional manual. Mary Rowland-

24. Thacher, "Diary," MS, II, 52.
25. I. Mather, "Diary," ed. Green, 319.

son's captivity narrative must be understood, therefore, as devotional literature.[26]

Mrs. Rowlandson was not undergoing first conversion. She was a praying Christian, a saint of the church, before and throughout her captivity. The journey was one of trial and refinement, of reexperiencing the redemptive drama as growth in grace. God stripped away all the supports in her life, all the relationships and comforts that had led her into spiritual complacency. In this preparatory stage of humiliation she found that "All was gone; my husband gone (at least separated from me . . .) . . . my children gone, my relations and friends gone, our house and home and all our comforts within doors and without. All was gone except my life, and I knew not but the next moment that might go too." The town had represented security, first in the positive sense of assurance through the means of grace but also in the sinful sense of carnal security and the delusion of self-security. Humiliation at the hands of Indians brought her once more into absolute dependency on God. The wilderness was literally for her the chaos of life without God's order, the place of temptation (as in Jesus' temptation), and the place of trial (as in Israel's wandering). Two days after her capture the full realization of the journey ahead crashed upon her. "I must turn my back upon the town and travel with them into the vast and desolate wilderness, I knew not whither." The successive removes represented for her not simply the passage of time and distance, but movement farther and farther into the chaos of the wilderness. And, like the stages of *The Pilgrim's Progress*, each remove took her more deeply out of her former self and into a new self. In fact, the very word "remove" denoted far more in the seventeenth century than simply transfer from one location to another. It also meant progress through a series of advancing grades, as in school, and, most significant, through stages in the soul's ascent to God. Mrs. Rowlandson used a traditional devotional form as her interpretive framework.[27]

As she advanced through the first removes Mrs. Rowlandson became disoriented about the meaning and rhythms of white Christian life. Initially, the thought of herself at home humbled her. In the third remove she had nothing to eat "from Wednesday night to Saturday night, except a little cold water" (a surprising correlation to the pil-

26. Rowlandson, *Soveraignty and Goodness of God*, title page.

27. Quotations are from "Narrative of the Captivity and Restoration of Mrs. Mary Rowlandson (1682): Extracts" in Demos, ed., *Remarkable Providences*, 288–289. *OED*, s.v. "remove."

grims in Doubting Castle). On the Sabbath after this forced fast she was brought low with the memory of "how careless I had been of God's holy time, how many Sabbaths I had lost and misspent, and how evilly I had walked in God's sight; which lay so close unto my spirit that it was easy for me to see how righteous it was with God to cut off the thread of my life and cast me out of his presence forever." At that moment she received a word of grace: "He wounded me with one hand, so He healed me with the other." Her contrition was complete when she abandoned herself fully to God after her child, whom she had carried with her, finally died. Mrs. Rowlandson lamented, "There I left that child in the wilderness, and must commit myself also in this wilderness-condition to Him who is above all." The thought of her dead child and of the other two in captivity "overwhelmed" her and drove her to keep "walking from one place to another." In full penitence she was able to ask God for mercy as though for the first time. She "earnestly entreated the Lord that he would consider my lowe estate, and show me a token for good, and if it were His blessed will, some sign and hope of some relief." She received a sign: her son, whom she had not seen since the attack, appeared in her party. A second sign came the next day. An Indian presented her with a plundered Bible. When she read from Deuteronomy 28 of God's curse on the disobedient, a new shadow was cast on her "dark heart." She feared that "there was no mercy for me, that the blessings were gone and the curses come in their room, and that I had lost my opportunity." She persevered to chapter thirty, where penitent Israel was promised return from captivity. Word that God would "return and gather thee from all the nations, whither the Lord thy God hath scattered thee" (30:3) evoked deep assurance. "I do not desire to live to forget this scripture, and what comfort it was to me."[28]

Mrs. Rowlandson was prepared for salvation, but it did not come. She knew she could do or attempt nothing to bring about her own redemption. She discouraged a pregnant woman who desperately wanted to run away, considering the practical matter that the nearest town was twenty miles away. But she was more strongly guided by Psalm 27: "Wait on the Lord." Redemption must be spiritual redemption and not the mere saving of her flesh. In her period of waiting Mary Rowlandson found that Scripture greatly increased her patience in suffering. She also began adapting to life around her. Food that had been "filthy trash" became "sweet and savory." Instead of wholly detesting Indians she began to wonder about them and to appreciate

28. Demos, ed., *Remarkable Providences*, 290–293.

their humanity. When a New England militia company came near, she waited with her captors. "We were not ready for so great a mercy as victory and deliverance—if we had been, God would have found out a way for the English to have passed this river." She demonstrated no anxiety about escape or rescue but relied entirely on God's timetable. Perhaps her greatest discovery was that God's hand reached even into the wilderness. Indeed, it is doubtful that by the end of her journey Mrs. Rowlandson thought of the land beyond the towns as wilderness at all. It was no longer the place of the devil, but another place of God, as the psalmist had written: "If I ascend up into heaven, thou art there: if I make my bed in hell, behold, thou art there" (139:8). She remarked, "I can but stand in admiration to see the wonderful power of God in providing for such a vast number of our enemies in the wilderness, where there was nothing to be seen but from hand to mouth." In the wilderness she found grace to persevere and even flourish in a situation that New England townsfolk could hardly imagine. The wilderness was regenerative, but it was a hard regeneration.[29]

The peacefulness of Mrs. Rowlandson's redemption testified to her that it was God's doing. "Oh, the wonderful power of God that I have seen and the experience that I have had. I have been in the midst of those roaring lions and savage bears." She gave thanks that she was one "whom He hath redeemed from the hand of the enemy, especially that I should come away in the midst of so many hundreds of enemies quietly and peaceably, and not a dog moving his tongue." Her final phrase refers to the survival of Israelite children when God killed the Egyptian firstborn (Exodus 11:7). Mrs. Rowlandson's redemption was an experience of salvation from the bondage of sin; she was a child of Israel, one of the chosen. As patient as she had been in waiting on the Lord, when she walked into freedom she was all but ecstatic. "In coming along my heart melted into tears, more than all the while I was with them; and I was almost swallowed up with the thoughts that ever I should go home again." But return to the freedom of Boston had a surprising effect on her. She was incapable of feeling simple joy in her reborn life. She had seen too much; the thought of her child's slow death in the wilderness plagued her.

> I can remember the time when I used to sleep quietly, without workings in my thoughts, whole nights together; but now it is otherwise with me. When all are fast [asleep] about me, and no eye open but His who ever waketh, my thoughts are upon things

29. *Ibid.*, 294–305.

past, upon the awful dispensation of the Lord towards us, upon
His wonderful power and might, in carrying of us through so
many difficulties, in returning us in safety, and [in] suffering
none to hurt us. I remember, in the night season, how the other
day I was in the midst of thousands of enemies, and nothing but
death before me. It is then hard work to persuade myself that
ever I should be satisfied with bread again.

She remained uncomfortable with the "extreme vanity of this world,"
which she knew to be a "bubble." She was redeemed from sin and on
her way to Zion. But Boston was not Zion; once more she had to "wait
upon the Lord."[30]

The impact of Mary Rowlandson's narrative upon the New England
religious consciousness was so great that the clergy began to capitalize
on the theme of captivity and redemption. It was emotionally compelling because of the horror of King Philip's War and because a large
number of persons, especially women and children, were actually
taken captive (men were killed). Since it played on an elemental fear
of the wilderness and of Indians, the narrative could be generalized
and applied to the entire population. King William's War in 1688, according to Richard Slotkin, finally "compelled the Puritans to look to
the captivity narrative for their mythological sustenance." The alliance
of demonic Indians and papist French compounded New Englanders'
fears and posed a threat that crystallized many of the negative referents of Puritan spirituality.[31]

Cotton Mather recorded, incorporated into sermons, and published
the narratives of two women who returned from captivity in this later
period. Except for two major details, Hannah Dustan's story adhered
to the pattern that Mary Rowlandson had established. The initial car-
nage and white heroism were similar, as was the jeremiad-like judgment of white society. Hannah Dustan (or Cotton Mather) pointed
to the Indians' prayers under French Catholic tutelage as an indictment of New England's apostasy. But altogether missing was the self-
indictment of Mrs. Rowlandson's devotional approach to captivity
and redemption. Dustan's tale degenerated into sensationalism. The
crucial difference in her restoration was that she failed to wait for the
Lord to act on her behalf. She took matters into her own hands, albeit
with biblical precedent (Judges 4:17–24), killed ten of her captors
with a hatchet while they slept, and scalped them for the bounty. Hannah and two others who escaped with her were in the congregation

30. *Ibid.*, 306–310.
31. Slotkin, *Regeneration through Violence*, 116.

when Cotton Mather recited her story from the pulpit and then "improved" the narrative with a few words of application. He may well have shocked his listeners, especially the redeemed captives themselves, because instead of praising God for their restoration he vigorously exhorted the returnees to "make a right use of the Deliverance." He turned Hannah Dustan's words against her: "You are not now the Slaves of Indians, as you were a few Dayes ago; but if you continue Unhumbled, in your Sins, you will be the Slaves of Devils. . . . Become the sincere Servants of that Lord, who by His Blood has brought you out of the Dungeon, wherein you were lately Languishing. Oh! Deny not the Lord, who has thus Brought you, out of your Captivity." His application was not aimed only at the returned captives.[32]

The second narrative Cotton Mather published, which more closely resembles the Rowlandson prototype, is that of Hannah Swarton, who was captured in May 1690. Hannah Swarton underwent conversion or renewed conversion during the course of her wilderness journey, beginning with her humiliation in facing Indian food. A maggot-filled moose bladder was her only available nourishment from her first Sabbath to the following Saturday. Judgments against New England pierced her own heart. The Indians prayed more than she had, she confessed, and she came to see her captivity as God's judgment for her land hunger and Sabbath neglect. The entire ordeal was "for my Humiliation, and put me upon Prayer to God, for His Pardoning Mercy in Christ." She made the prayer of David her own: "How long wilt thou forget me, O Lord for ever! How long wilt thou hide thy face from me?" (Psalm 13:1). Then, she recounted, "I made my Vows to the Lord, that I would give up my self to Him, if He would accept me in Jesus Christ, and pardon my Sins." But this was early on in the journey; many more spiritual trials awaited her on the road ahead. The narrative, indeed, reads like *The Pilgrim's Progress* set in North America, with the Indians and Frenchmen in the roles of the giants and citizens of Vanity Fair. Swarton used the traditional pilgrimage language: "Thus I continued with them, hurried up and down the Wilderness." "My Feet were pricked with sharp Stones, and prickly Bushes sometimes; and other times Pinched with Snow, Cold, and Ice, that I travelled upon, ready to be frozen, and faint for want of Food; so that many times I thought I could go no further, but must ly down, and if they would kill me, let them kill me. Yet then, the Lord did so Renew my Strength, that I went on still further." The parallels with Bunyan's allegory are so close as to suggest direct borrowing. "I Trav-

32. [C. Mather], *Humiliations*, 41–50. For a different interpretation of Hannah Dustan's story, see Slotkin, *Regeneration through Violence*, 112–114.

elled over steep and hideous Mountains" and "over Swamps and Thickets of Fallen Trees," all the while "carrying a great Burden on my Back." In the march through the wilderness the "burden" was no doubt a real load that she was forced to carry. Later in the narrative, however, Hannah Swarton identified her burden in spiritual terms: "My Sins have been a Burden to me." After much more progress on the journey, in which she received aid from Englishmen identified as "Fellow Travellers" and was tempted by the false safety of Catholicism in Quebec, she was finally free of her burden of sin. In meditation on "the Prayer of Jonah" ("I am cast out of thy sight; yet I will look again toward thy holy temple," 2:4), "the Lord was pleased, by His Spirit, to come into my Soul, and so fill me with Ravishing Comfort, that I cannot express it. . . . I was so full of Comfort and Joy, I even Wished I could be so alwayes, and never sleep; or else Dy in that Rapture of Joy, and never Live to Sin any more against the Lord. Now I thought God was my God, and my Sins were pardoned in Christ; and now I thought I could Suffer for Christ, yea, Dye for Christ, or do any thing for Him."[33]

Hannah Swarton's longing for deliverance was not a selfish desire for freedom but a spiritual desire to enter into covenant with God and His people in the church. Her ransom and liberation, like Mary Rowlandson's but unlike Hannah Dustan's, were anticlimactic. The negotiations and her return to New England were not the important moments in the story. Hannah Swarton was freed from sin before she was freed from her French masters.

The tremendous popularity of the captivity narrative furnished New England with a suitable geographical correlate for the spiritual pilgrimage. The journey into the wilderness at the hands of Indians and the safe return was an actual experience that contained within it all the elements of the redemptive drama. It could serve native-born New Englanders as the voyage from old to New England had served the founders. Michael Wigglesworth anticipated this as early as 1670 in his devotional manual, *Meat out of the Eater.* He enunciated in precise terms the devotional and spiritual implications of the captivity theme.

> God hedges up with thorns
>   The Path of Wanderers,
> That have of Creature-comforts been
>   Too eager Followers,

33. [C. Mather], *Humiliations,* 51–72.

Stops their pursuit, them brings
    Into a Wilderness,
That thereunto their humble Souls
    He may more Love express.

Captivity and affliction became means of grace as God "by these Bands, unto their Souls / More Libertie affords." And in meditation on 2 Chronicles 33:11–13 Wigglesworth explicitly stated how the pilgrimage of the soul was related to the preparation of the heart through captivity and redemption.

Manasseh was a slave
    To Sin and never free;
Until his Foes had carried him
    Into Captivitie:
But being bound in Chains,
    He calls to mind his sins,
Humbleth himself, and to bewail
    His former life begins.

His Prison was a place
    Of greatest Libertie:
For from the bondage of his sins
    It helpt to set him free.
As Liberty abus'd
    Procur'd his Misery:
So Bonds him humble and prepar'd
    For blessed Liberty.

The only freedom that really counted was spiritual salvation. The captivity narratives provided a literary and geographical framework within which the drama could be told.[34]

THE SPIRITUALIZATION OF THE PILGRIMAGE

The third way New England attempted to appropriate the spirituality of the first generation was to emphasize the personal and spiritual nature of the pilgrimage. The entire drama was played out in the heart of the believer and did not depend on the mythology of flight from England. The biblical paradigm of Egypt, wilderness, and Promised

34. Michael Wigglesworth, *Meat out of the Eater: Or Meditations Concerning the Necessity, End, and Usefulness of Afflictions unto Gods Children* . . . , 4th ed. (Boston, 1689 [orig. publ. Cambridge, Mass., 1670]), 140–144.

Land, after all, was a spiritual rather than a geographical reality. As
Increase Mather preached, "We must through much tribulation enter
into the kingdome of God. As the children of Israel went through the
Red Sea, and through the Wilderness, before they could enter into
Canaan, so must we wade through a Red Sea of Troubles, and pass
through a Wilderness of Miseries, e're we can arrive at the heavenly
Canaan. Here is the difference between this world and that which is
to come." This emphasis was by no means an innovation. Devotional
manuals for one hundred years had contained no references to other
than the spiritual journey, and they had guided saints along the
"pathway to heaven." In the second half of the century the clergy
placed renewed emphasis on the use of manuals in an attempt to
rekindle the kind of devotional life that had prevailed in the early
years.[35]

The manuals that had been used in New England since the earliest
days of settlement continued to be important, but the new generation
of Puritans in both old and New England produced a burst of their
own devotional literature. English manuals by Restoration writers
such as Flavel, Baxter, and Bunyan (and earlier Anglican writers,
notably Joseph Hall) were imported in large numbers into New England. John Bunyan played with his chief metaphor in the introduction to volume two of *The Pilgrim's Progress*: "My Pilgrims book
has travel'd Sea and Land," he was pleased to write. It had been distributed throughout Europe and America. Referring to both its im-
portation and local publication (Boston, 1681), he reported that

> 'Tis in New-England under such advance,
> Receives there so much loving Countenance,

35. I. Mather, *Day of Trouble*, 3. See also his *Pray for the Rising Generation, or, a Sermon
Wherein Godly Parents Are Encouraged to Pray and Believe for Their Children* . . . (Cambridge, Mass., 1678), 172. Perry Miller in *New England Mind: From Colony to Province*,
407, noted the fresh outpouring of "many handbooks of practical piety," but he
mistakenly viewed it as a late 17th-century innovation. "Hundreds of manuals produced for their purpose [the supposedly desperate attempt to simplify religion] were
reprinted in Boston, to join the domestic flow." Miller is then forced to account for the
connection between the New England and English manuals. He saw it as accidental:
"What had commenced in New England as a furtive maneuver, a timid endeavor to
rescue religion from sterility, by methods which in the canons of the founders seemed
tawdry, proved to be a providential falling in step with the progressive march of the
century." Miller failed to recognize the importance of devotional manuals throughout
the century. The methods of meditation and prayer outlined in the new manuals were,
far from being "tawdry" in comparison, identical with those put forth by the first
generation. Nor did the New England press produce "hundreds" of manuals. Miller's
hyperbole vastly overestimates the capacity of the press even by late century.

As to be Trim'd, new Cloth'd, & Deckt with Gems,
That it might shew its Features, and its Limbs,
Yet more; so comely doth my Pilgrim walk,
That of him thousands daily Sing and talk.

Other English works also came out in American editions. The first was actually published for the Christian Indians in 1665, John Eliot's translation and abridgment of Lewis Bayly's influential *The Practice of Piety, Manitowompae Pomantamoonk*. Manuals by New England authors began to issue from the Cambridge and then the Boston press in the late 1660s. This new flood of devotional literature helped spiritualize the pilgrimage for the second and third generations.[36]

From the beginning of the Puritan movement devotional manuals were written for a popular market, and this was true of the new material. The late-century manuals presented the traditional devotional apparatus: brief numbered directions for meditation and prayer, appropriate themes for daily use, and meditative poetry. The manuals in their pure form were distinguished from the many published sermons on devotional themes, although the two genres were sometimes combined and the line between them often blurred. The first products of the Cambridge press were tried and true English manuals. Even publication of the Protestant version of *The Imitation of Christ* was attempted in 1667. It was licensed for publication, but the General Court halted its printing until "the more full revisale" of Catholic remnants was completed. The classic, though widely read in English versions, was never published in New England.[37]

Samuel Green was more successful, in the same year, with his publication of Edward Reyner's *Precepts for Christian Practice: Or, the Rule of the New Creature: Containing Duties to Be Daily Observed by Every Believer*. The manual was a known quantity, having already appeared in twelve London editions. *Precepts* was organized around ten chief devotional duties of an entirely conventional nature. The first two corresponded to the major parts of the order of redemption: (1) "Bee always sensible of thy original corruption" and daily "endeavour to

36. See Ford, *Boston Book Market*. The inventories published by Ford contain 18 orders for shipments of books by Flavel, 6 for works of Bunyan, and 2 each for Baxter and Hall. Bunyan, *Pilgrim's Progress*, ed. Wharey and Sharrock, 169.

37. Charles Evans, *American Bibliography* . . . (Worcester, Mass., 1903–1959), I, 25. For possession of *Imitation of Christ* see Ford, *Boston Book Market*, 48. For its ownership and use by Cotton Mather, see Bercovitch, *Puritan Origins*, 34, 214 n. 49. Bercovitch suggests that the book was published in New England but suppressed; David Hall says it was published ("World of Print," in Higham and Conkin, eds., *New Directions in American Intellectual History*, 170–171), but this was not the case.

make your peace with God before you go to bed" by "repenting and confessing your sins to God; working your hearts to grief and sorrow for them . . . for reconciliation with God." (2) "Get your union with Christ . . . cleared and confirmed to you daily more and more" by a "daily renewal of your faith" through meditative self-examination. The remaining duties concerned the daily conversation of the believer in the world and the various exercises "in Family and Closet, especially . . . Prayer, Meditation, and Reading." The final duty looked toward death and judgment: "Get your heart daily weaned from the World, and from those creatures and comforts in it, which are dearest and sweetest to you." *Precepts for Christian Practice* was a sound primer on the essential acts and attitudes of the devotional life.[38]

Other English manuals published in the late 1660s in Cambridge have not survived, which suggests that the books were used intensively. Among these were the anonymous *The Way to a Blessed Estate in This Life* (1667), Thomas Wilcocks's *A Choice Drop of Honey from the Rock Christ . . .* (1667), Timothy Rogers's *The Righteous Man's Evidence for Heaven . . .* , first published in 1619, with thirteen editions by 1643, and the anonymous *The Young Man's Monitor* (1668). Philip Pain's *Daily Meditations*, never published in England, went through three New England editions, in 1668, 1670, and 1682.

Of even greater importance, Michael Wigglesworth, whose 1662 epic, *The Day of Doom*, had established him as a devotional writer, published a large collection of meditative poetry, *Meat out of the Eater: Or Meditations Concerning the Necessity, End, and Usefulness of Afflictions unto Gods Children*, in 1670. The work went through four editions by 1689. It was essentially a devotional manual, not a book of poetry in the modern sense, in that the poems were intended as models for the reader's own meditation and were arranged according to the order of redemption. Wigglesworth opened with ten meditations on the theme "All Christians must be Cross-bearers," including the famous autobiographical lines:

> The Christian that expects
> An Earthly Paradise
> When Christ bids him take up the cross
> And bear it, is unwise.
> We must not on the knee
> Be alway dandled,
> Nor must we think to ride to Heaven
> Upon a Feather-bed.

38. [Edward Reyner], *Precepts for Christian Practice* . . . (Cambridge, Mass., 1667).

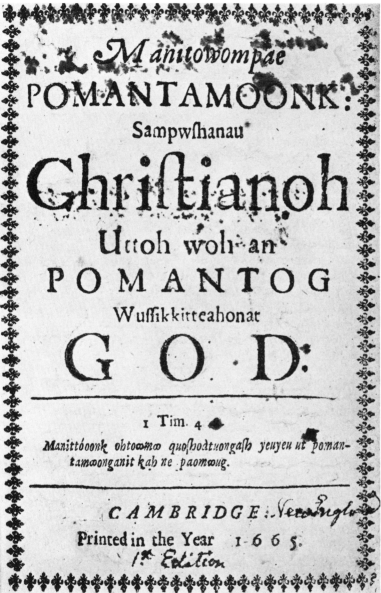

Figure 14. Title page of Lewis Bayly, Manitowompae Pomantamoonk
(The Practice of Piety), *translated and abridged by John Eliot (Cambridge,
1665). The appearance of this edition underscores the central importance of
Bayly's work in particular and of devotional manuals in general for Puritan
piety. Courtesy the American Antiquarian Society, Worcester, Massachusetts.*

He urged meditation on the idea that "Affliction is Christ's School." The remainder of the book consists of a series of poems on "Christian Paradoxes," conundrums for sharpening the faithful mind in meditation. The believer could find

> Light in Darkness
>   Sick mens Health,
> Strength in Weakness,
>   Poor mens Wealth.
> In Confinement, Liberty,
>   In Sollitude, Good Company.
> Joy in Sorrow,
>   Life in Deaths,
> Heavenly Crowns for
>   Thorny Wreaths.

Each paradox elicited about ten "songs," some in the form of a dialogue—between the flesh and the spirit, the believing soul and "her Saviour," fear and death, "Distressed Conscience and Rectified Judgment"—others in the form of meditation on a biblical figure such as Job or Lazarus the beggar.[39]

The mood of *Meat out of the Eater* is overwhelmingly of repentance and sorrow for sin, but Wigglesworth presented Christ as the reward of a broken heart.

> Well, let it humble thee
>   To feel a treacherous part
> A sinful Self; a wicked Flesh
>   Remaining in thy heart.
> Yet for thy comfort know,
>   Thou hast not lost the field,
> So long as thou do'st sin resist,
>   And strivest not to yield.
>
> If by Repentance from thy Falls
>   God helps thee to arise;
> Fear not, all turns to gain;
>   For God is purify'd,
> And loseth nothing, but its dross,
>   By being often try'd.

The means of salvation, as always, were the traditional devotional exercises:

39. Wigglesworth, *Meat out of the Eater*, 3–9, 52.

Follow thy Calling close.
   Love not to be alone;
Save only when by secret Prayer,
   Thou makes to God thy moan.
Omit not secret Prayer,
   Nor other Means neglect:
The Tempter hath thee where he would,
   If once he that effect.

Wigglesworth was bold to speak in the name of Christ when he wrote that meditation on sin should produce repentance and "a broken heart, / That may both bleed and smart."

Behold at thy request
   I'm here full ready prest
To save and succour thee;
   Fear not to come to me.

He proceeded to a series of poems on affliction and sorrow, preparation for death—

Read on, and thou shalt see
Both many Deaths in one short Life,
And life in Deaths to be

—and finally meditation on Glory, on Christ Triumphant and the union of saints with Him in heaven. "Every saint shall be," he wrote, "A Diamond in Christ's Crown." He delighted in the thought of "happy, happy Souls / That in God's bosome rest!"[40]

The pilgrim metaphor had introduced the first section,

Thou art a Pilgrim here;
   This world is not thy home:
Then be content with Pilgrims fare,
   Till thou to Heaven come.

And the metaphor's promise was assured in the final section of the book.

By chearful Suffering Saint,
   Let nothing cast thee down:
Our Saviour Christ e're long will turn
   Thy Cross into a Crown.

40. *Ibid.*, 78–80, 87–88, 181, 190–203.

The meditative program modeled in Wigglesworth's poems played continually on the juxtaposition of opposites, moving generally from concentration on the suffering of the cross to the glory of the crown. Meditation and prayer, he believed, resolved the opposites in a vision of heaven.[41]

The most homespun of the local products, which at the same time linked New Englanders in 1673 with their early seventeenth-century English roots, was a collection of advice by the English devotional author John Dod, *Old Mr. Dod's Sayings,* published by Marmaduke Johnson. While the thrust of Johnson's earlier publication, Pain's *Daily Meditations,* was preparation for death, the *Sayings* focused on the daily conversation of the saint at mid-journey. The book consists of forty-two aphoristic thoughts suitable for meditation, with a rough alternation between doctrinal statements and short inspirational thoughts such as "So much Sin, so much Sorrow; so much Holiness, so much Happiness" and "Brown bread with the Gospel is good Fare." Dod also offered plain advice on carrying out the devotional life: "Make the Sabbath the market-day for thy soul. Lose not one hour, but be either praying, conferring, or meditating; think not thy own thoughts; let every day have its duties; turn the Sermon heard into matter of prayer; Instruction into petition, Reproof into confession, Consolation into Thanksgiving: Think much of the Sermon heard, and make something of it all week long." The "Directions for every day" outlined once again the familiar themes for morning and evening devotions.[42]

Other manuals, including the Boston edition of *The Pilgrim's Progress* (1681) and John Corbet's *Self-Imployment in Secret* (1684), were also by English authors. John Higginson, one of the last survivors from the first generation, appended his guide, "Some Help to Self-Examination," to a collection of sermons published in his old age, *Our Dying Saviour's Legacy of Peace* (Boston, 1686). As Samuel Willard stated in the preface, Higginson was "an Old Disciple," a living reminder of the Good Old Way. Higginson explained that he published his work "as a due acknowledgement unto the memory" of John Cotton, Thomas Hooker, and Samuel Stone, who had trained him for the ministry. He prayed "that New-England may never want such men (like those in the first times)." It is no coincidence that so much devotional publication through the 1680s was comprised of English reprints and the work of men who had ties to the first generation. New

41. *Ibid.,* 20, 208.
42. [John] Dod, *Old Mr. Dod's Sayings* . . . (Cambridge, Mass., 1673), 3, 6–7, 13.

Englanders hoped that by practicing the disciplines of the founders they might regain the original spiritual quality and experience.[43]

The new manuals followed the same spiritual patterns that had characterized New England practice from the start. A manual attributed to English author Christopher Nesse entitled *The Crown and Glory of a Christian*, for example, was subtitled *Consisting in a Sound Conversion and Well Ordered Conversation*. In the usual format of numbered directions under topical headings, Nesse instructed a Christian how he ought "to carry himself in Natural, Civil, and Religious Duties." The first two parts of the book deal with the social and moral aspects of the saint's conversation, and the final section discusses the two major "Religious Actions" of meditation and prayer. The manual emphasized the affirmative way of meditation, rather than meditation on sin, as the preparatory work of devotion and defined meditation as "your spiritual Ladder (as Jacob had his) whereon you ascend in divine Contemplations of the excellency of your blessed and bleeding Saviour, till your heart be ravished therewithal." Reflecting trends characteristic of the second half of the century, *The Crown and Glory* also prescribed "occasional meditation" on "the Book of Nature" rather than sole emphasis on the Bible. The relationship between prayer and meditation was that which had prevailed throughout the century. Prayer, "which well follows Meditation," was the action of "pouring out of the heart to God." "As Meditation is a blessed beginning to prayer, so prayer is a blessed conclusion of meditation." At the same time, the wording of the manual's advice—"when your heart is well warmed with the Angelical duty of Meditation, then fall upon the Evangelical duty of Prayer"—demonstrates that New England published a work thoroughly in tune with the Restoration spirit of Richard Baxter.[44]

Samuel Hardy's *A Guide to Heaven from the Word*, published in Boston in 1689, was an important work because it presented the major themes of Puritan devotion under four simple headings: "Twelve Rules to prepare you for closing with Christ," morning devotions, evening devotions, and Sabbath devotions. Hardy's preparation entailed not only preparation for conversion but also continual preparation for union with Christ in heaven through devotional exercises. In keeping with the language of preparationism, Hardy directed be-

43. Higginson, *Our Saviour's Legacy of Peace*, sig. A2–A6ᵛ.
44. [Christopher Nesse], *The Crown and Glory of a Christian* (Boston, 1684 [orig. publ. London, 1676]), sig. A2, 62–73.

lievers to "Come to Christ, a poor, lost, and undone Wretch, hopeless and helpless," through morning and evening devotions. "Every morning set your self solemnly as in the presence of God Omniscient" and answer a set of meditative questions: "How did I lie down and rise up? was God in my thoughts? and if so, were the thoughts of him sweet and precious to my Soul?" And: "In what frame is my heart at present? do I admire Gods goodness for the last nights sleep, for adding more time to my life: and am I heartily thankful?" At the end of the day, Hardy advised, "Separate your self every evening from all Company" and again engage in self-examination. "Wherein you have been guilty, be heartily sorrowful and beg pardon: and wherein God has enabled you to be in any measure faithful, bless God and be thankful." The questions were of the type common for evening exercises and concluded with preparation for death. "Have I really set death before me? My life is as a vapour a shadow; if I should die daily what preparation have I made for it? am I sure, but this is my last night? If God should shut mine eyes by death, how is it like to be with my Soul?" Finally, a "strict Observation of the Lords Day" depended fully on preparatory meditation and prayer on Saturday night and the Sabbath morning. The manual summarized: "Prepare with all your might."[45]

Cotton Mather, whose link with the founders was ever apparent in his name, launched his manual-writing career in 1689 with a work that incorporated sermon material and devotional guidance from his own experience. *Small Offers towards the Service of the Tabernacle* presented models and advice on secret meditation, prayer, covenant making, and family prayer. The next year he brought out his eucharistic manual, New England's first, *A Companion for Communicants.* Again, Mather combined sermons on approaching the Sacrament with guidance in manual form. The key work was self-examination, using Mather's "Signs of a Good State" or a similar rubric, to cultivate increasingly "an Heart Prepared."[46]

Besides manuals that dealt with the general and lifelong disciplines of meditation and prayer, other books were directed toward age and occupational groups and toward each of the sexes. The appearance of these books coincided with the development of the specialized private

45. Samuel Hardy, *A Guide to Heaven from the Word: Or, Good Counsel How to Close Savingly with Christ . . .* (Boston, 1689), 1–26. Quotations on pp. 1, 6, 14–23.

46. C. Mather, *Small Offers,* 6–35. Some of the English precedents of Cotton Mather's *Companion for Communicants* are discussed by Biggs, "Preparation for Communion," *Congregational Qtly.,* XXXII (1954), 17–27.

meetings. That one's natural life was a journey through time was a commonplace. John Higginson published his sermons and manual in "thankful Rememberance of the gracious dealings of God with me, in the midst of all the changes of times that have passed over me, in this my Pilgrimage upon Earth." Psychological and spiritual characteristics marked each stage of life, as Anne Bradstreet recognized in her poetic "Quaternion," "Of the four Ages of Man." Many sermons aimed their exhortations at the special problems of "the rising generation," and Cotton Mather's first published biography praised teenage "early piety." Yet devotional writers also addressed themselves to the elderly. Most notable was an English manual that James Allen saw through the Boston press in 1679, William Bridge's *A Word to the Aged*. Bridge began, of course, with "The Old Mans Weakness," ten common sins of which older persons must repent. The word of grace, in the language of pilgrimage, came as "The Old Mans Staff." In his chapter on "The Old Mans Guide," Bridge discussed familiar topics: reading, meditation, and prayer in preparation for death and eternal life. Finally, "The Old Mans Will and Legacies" must consist primarily of leaving his soul to God and a good example to posterity. He advised writing down "some good exhortations and admonitions" for one's offspring.[47]

The greatest devotional writer for occupational groups was the Englishman John Flavel. His works did not appear in American editions until the early eighteenth century, but they were enthusiastically imported in the closing decades of the seventeenth. *Husbandry Spiritualized* (London, 1669) and its sequel, *Navigation Spiritualized* (1671), contained meditations in poetry and prose directing men "to the most Excellent Improvements of their common Imployments." Flavel cast the message of salvation in the language of working people, as "occasional meditations" on the "creatures."

Seas purge themselves, and cast their filth ashore
But graceless Souls retain and suck in more.

Lord turn into my Soul that cleansing Blood,
Which from my Saviour's side flow'd as a Flood.
Flow sacred Fountain, brim my Banks; yea, flow
Till you have made my Soul as white as Snow.[48]

47. Higginson, "Epistle Dedicatory," in *Our Saviour's Legacy of Peace*. Hutchinson, ed., *Poems of Bradstreet*, 153–167. Will[iam] Bridge, *A Word to the Aged* (Boston, 1679).

48. John Flavel, *Navigation Spiritualized: Or a New Compass for Sea-Men . . .* (Boston, 1726 [orig. publ. London, 1671]), 19, 21.

Cotton Mather used the same spiritualizing technique in 1692 when he wrote the best example of a manual for a special group in New England, *Ornaments for the Daughters of Zion*, the last book to issue from the Cambridge press. Mather set out to "direct the Female Sex how to express the Fear of God in every Age and State of their Life; and obtain both Temporal and Eternal Blessedness." He composed themes for meditation and sample prayers for "the virtuous maid, wife, mother, and widow." In the following year Mather published his collection of *Winter Meditations*, in which he used the method of spiritualizing the seasonal traits of winter as matter for meditation.[49]

The 1690s saw the publication in Boston of Richard Standfast's popularly written manual, *A Little Handful of Cordial Comforts . . . for the Good of Those That Walk Mournfully with God* (1690), which had already appeared in at least five London editions. *The Map of Man's Misery*, attributed to Patrick Ker, came out in 1692, only two years after its original English edition. Increase Mather's *Solemn Advice to Young Men . . .* (Boston, 1695) and Samuel Lee's *Contemplations on Mortality . . .* (Boston, 1698 [orig. publ. London, 1669]) were books of devotional guidance but were primarily sermonic in form.

After the turn of the new century Cotton Mather and his father published many more books of devotion, building on a trend that was by then well established. Little was new in these late-century manuals, although the technique of spiritualizing that Flavel, Mather, and others had popularized was taken beyond earlier usage and emphasized more than before. The sheer volume of new manuals suggests a renewed interest and vitality in devotional practice. By encouraging the production and use of devotional manuals, the ministers hoped they could engender the same sense of spiritual pilgrimage that had marked the devotion of the founders of the colonies. The popularity of the manuals indicates something of the ministers' success in preserving the continuity of Puritan spirituality over the course of the century.[50]

49. C. Mather, *Ornaments for the Daughters of Zion*. C. Mather, *Winter Meditations*.

50. Books on devotional themes by Cotton Mather that were published after the turn of the century include: *A Companion for the Afflicted. The Duties and the Comforts, of Good Men, under Their Afflictions* (Boston, 1701); *Christianus per Ignem. Or, a Disciple Warming of Himself and Owning of His Lord* (Boston, 1702); *A Family-Sacrifice. A Brief Essay to Direct and Excite Family-Religion . . .* (Boston, 1703); *The Sailour's Companion and Counsellour. . . . Awakening the Mariner to Think and to Do Those Things That May Render His Voyage Prosperous* (Boston, 1709); *A Christian Funeral . . .* (Boston, 1713); *Death Approaching: A Very Brief Essay on a Life Drawing Nigh unto the Grave* (Boston, 1714); and *Genethlia Pia; or, Thoughts for a B.rth-Day . . .* (Boston, 1719). Increase Mather published seven medita-

tive pieces between 1704 and 1712, all of which, however, retained their sermonic form: *The Voice of God, in Stormy Winds* (Boston, 1704); *A Brief Discourse Concerning the Prayse Due to God, for His Mercy in Giving Snow Like Wool* (Boston, 1704); *Meditations on the Glory of the Lord Jesus Christ . . .* (Boston, 1705); *Meditations on Death . . .* (Boston, 1707); *Meditations on the Glory of the Heavenly World . . .* (Boston, 1711); *Meditations on the Sanctification of the Lord's Day: And the Judgments Which Attend the Profanation of It* (Boston, 1712); *Seasonable Meditations both for Winter & Summer . . .* (Boston, 1712).

Chapter Nine

The Puritan Contemplative

 The passage from John Eliot's sermon that forms the epigraph of this book delineates the essentials of Puritan devotional life. Eliot (and Mather, who wrote about him) was concerned with spiritual conversation beyond conversion, what Hooker and Shepard referred to as growth in grace after implantation into Christ. The ministers presented spirituality in dynamic terms, most characteristically as the soul's progress on a pilgrimage to heaven. Puritans understood the pilgrimage of life as the way of the soul's preparation for glorification. But the various acts of devotional preparation brought their own penultimate rewards. Union with Christ in heaven might be anticipated even in this life through the experience of death that one underwent in the devotional act of repentance. As St. Paul put it, "If we be dead with Christ, we believe that we shall also live with him" (Romans 6:8). Life lived in the Spirit was set against life in the world of sin. Mather recorded Eliot preaching: "We have our spiritual warfare. We are always encountring the enemies of our souls, which continually raises our hearts unto our Helper and Leader in the heavens." Separation from sin was requisite for the subsequent and continually repeated raising (resurrection) of the heart in union with Christ. For Eliot and Mather conversation meant more than moral behavior in everyday life. Glorifying God "in our civil callings" formed only one small part of "the way of godly conversation." Conversation encompassed the activities of public worship and private devotion, which the sermon outlined so fully. Saints were "strangers and pilgrims" on earth, but through the range of exercises that made up Puritan devotional life they could be "no stranger to heaven" in this life. Saints were thus fully prepared for judgment and eternal glory after death. "When thou dyest," Eliot and his distinguished amanuensis preached, "heaven will be no strange place to thee; no, thou hast been there a thousand times before." Both men insisted it was not "impossible to live at this rate" because they were personally acquainted with such devout souls. Further, "others

that have written of such a life" in devotional manuals "have but spun a web out of their own blessed experiences." In spite of its increasing worldliness over the course of the century, "New England has examples of this life."[1]

New England changed much between the 1630s and the 1690s, but an essential continuity underlay its practice of piety. Cotton Mather and John Eliot spoke with one voice in the sermon portion Mather published. One of Mather's motives in his massive fin de siècle undertaking of compiling the biographies of Eliot and every other public figure of the preceding century was to remind his contemporaries of the devotional origins of their society and of the New England self. His method of writing history as biography was calculated to allow him to focus not only on the civic but also—and in many cases, principally—on the spiritual life of his subjects. Mather's biographies are well documented, so much so that the term "compiler" often better identifies his task than does the term "author." In contrast to the work of modern historians of New England, his accounts of the contemplative life are at least as full as are those of the active life of politics, war, social organization, and theological debate. Writing within a half century of the death of his oldest subjects, he had access to diaries, personal papers, and oral accounts that quickly passed out of existence. They were disappearing even as Mather planned his work. He rushed to find and preserve fragments of these records of spiritual exercises and experiences, and the results form the backbone of his narratives. Collected in the monumental *Magnalia Christi Americana*, the lives of ministers and magistrates were both an elegiac century-in-review and an intended map for the future. Mather presented his biographies as "the rock whence ye are hewn" (Isaiah 51:1), or as it has been put more recently, "*exemplum fidei*."[2]

Cotton Mather, the compiler and spokesman for the first generation, was also among the most thoroughgoing practitioners of devotional exercises. The caricature of Mather as the trivializer of faith into merely "doing good" and as the desperate innovator of "tawdry" devotional gimmicks to stem the tide of social change has been effectively corrected. As David Levin has shown, Mather established his interest in practicing and promoting the "Methods of Religion" "be-

1. Eliot, "Sermon," in C. Mather, ed., *Life and Death of J. Eliot*, 19–21.
2. For diaries and personal papers salvaged by Cotton Mather, see, for example, the lives of Jonathan Burr, in *Magnalia Christi Americana*, I, 368–375; Nathaniel Rogers, *ibid.*, 414–428; Samuel Newman, *ibid.*, 428–433; Charles Chauncey, *ibid.*, 463–476; John Oxenbridge, *ibid.*, 597–599; and John Baily, *ibid.*, 602–626. Bercovitch, *Puritan Origins*, 8.

fore he was twenty and before the original charter of Massachusetts Bay had been revoked." Indeed, Mather built his own exercises on the firm foundation of the inherited devotional traditions of English and early New England Puritanism. These traditions, expressed in the very origins of the movement, came to Mather through observation of and participation in family devotions as a child, hundreds of sermons he heard as a youth, devotional manuals, and conversations and conferences with others. He consciously emulated the methods practiced earlier in the century, especially those of his father, Increase Mather, and his grandfather, John Cotton. As a collector of the experiences of others he took his own advice and used those experiences as models. Mather's continuity with earlier American Puritans thus also corrects those scholars who portray ecstatic prayer and the more sublime meditation on heaven as a late-century development initiated by Richard Baxter. Still, as his diary reveals, Mather was always experimenting and improving his methods, based on some new refinement or set of criteria that he had read or heard about. Cotton Mather is a crucial figure in the study of New England devotion precisely because he collected and experimented with every method that came to his attention. He embodied the distillation of the devotional practice of the century and was a mirror image of the composite of his predecessors. If he seems to have risen above most of them in the intensity and thoroughness of his exercises, it is perhaps because no one, not even Edward Taylor, left as complete a personal record of so many aspects of the practice of piety. The breadth and depth of the exercises Mather recorded in his lives of the ministers and in his own diary suggest that we can now accurately speak of the Puritan "contemplative" as well as the Puritan "active."[3]

It was in Cotton Mather's childhood, as David Levin has shown, that "he confirmed his lifelong habit of filling his days with study and meditation." The earliest evidence of a daily program, however, is from 1681 when Mather was eighteen and just finishing his years at Harvard. He resolved to "pray at least thrice" every day and to "meditate once a Day" following the traditional method of probing a question of doctrine and applying the results to his own soul. He also pledged to put three questions to his soul before retiring at night, in

3. Miller, *New England Mind: From Colony to Province*, 406–407. Cotton Mather, *Bonifacius: An Essay upon the Good*, ed. David Levin (Cambridge, Mass., 1966), Introduction, xi–xiv. "The Psychology of Abasement," in Middlekauff, *The Mathers*, chap. 13. Ford, ed., *Diary of Cotton Mather*, I, 18–19. Richard F. Lovelace, *The American Pietism of Cotton Mather: Origins of American Evangelicalism* (Grand Rapids, Mich., 1979), esp. chaps. 4 and 5.

the traditional mode of self-examination: "What hath been the Mercy of God unto mee, in the Day past?" "What hath been my carriage before God, in the Day past?" And, typically, "If I dy this Night is my immortal Spirit safe?" Besides praying at these set times, he added the resolution to "lead a life of heavenly Ejaculations" and to "bee diligent in observing and recording of illustrious Providences." His lifelong aim was "in all, to bee continually going unto the Lord Jesus Christ, as the only Physician, and Redeemer, of my Soul." He had hopes that the "Flights of my Soul" that he was beginning to experience would "ere long proceed unto a Mounting up with the Wings of Eagles." Early in his life, therefore, Mather set himself the goal of the contemplative.[4]

Mather's devotions on the Sabbath and on days of secret humiliation and thanksgiving in the early 1680s adhered to the cycle of self-abasement and ecstasy. Abasement was most agonizing psychologically when it accompanied a period in which he seemed "not able to pray as formerly." Sometimes he was "full of Darkness, Horrour, and Confusion" over the state of his soul. He meditated on his "unsuitable and unsanctified Frames . . . and the Desertions which had lately darkened my Soul." The results of these meditations were as difficult to bear as the throes of first conversion, and he made that connection himself, reflecting that he was "strangely led by the Spirit of the most High, to go the whole work of conversion often over and over again." "Horrible Agonies and Amazements took hold of my Soul this Day, when I was, as in the Beginning of such Dayes I ever use[d] to bee, entertaining myself with the manifold Instances of my Sinfulness and Wretchedness." The most desperate moment was the one in which "essaying to go unto the Lord Jesus Christ, I found that I could not beleeve on Him." Mather cried out, "Even as for my Life," and a new assurance of grace flowed within. "Oh! Blessed bee His Name! Hee did help mee; with a moved, melted, raised Soul, I laid hold on the Lord Jesus Christ." The extreme emotion of these early sessions is partly characteristic of the trauma of early adulthood that we have observed in Peter Thacher and others. But the pattern was one that Mather would repeat countless times throughout his life. Most important, he entered into the experience intentionally, as a devotional exercise. He could not control the Lord's dealings, of course, but the decision to put himself through days of humiliation in which he might meet with the Lord was his own.[5]

On a typical day of "secret Prayer with Fasting, before the Lord,"

4. David Levin, *Cotton Mather: The Young Life of the Lord's Remembrancer, 1663–1703* (Cambridge, Mass., 1978), 22. Ford, ed., *Diary of Cotton Mather*, I, 3–5.
5. Levin, *Cotton Mather*, 61. Ford, ed., *Diary of Cotton Mather*, I, 7–10.

Cotton Mather recorded fourteen stages of devotional activity in three major phases. The three phases corresponded to the redemptive cycle of confession, grace, and new life. The details of his exercise summarize so much of the devotional ideal that they are worth outlining here. Mather "Began the Day, with expressing before the Lord, my Beleef, of His being a Rewarder of them which diligently seek Him, and my Request, that Hee would now strengthen mee to seek Him." After this opening prayer he progressed through the classic order of reading, meditation, and prayer. Mather read and studied those chapters of Scripture scheduled in his "Course of Reading," turning their message into brief prayers. He then "essayed in Meditation, to affect my own Heart, with a Sense of the manifold Vileness wherewith I have provoked God." Meditation led to prayer, and especially on fast days, to prayers of confession in which he "bewayled" his sins "before God." He concluded the first phase and marked the transition to the second by singing "that Hymn of Barton's, which is called *Confession of Sin.*"[6]

In the second phase Mather meditated again, this time not on sin but on "a profitable and seasonable Quaestion" of doctrine. The stage of confession past, he moved into petitionary prayer. He knew that "after all my Vileness, the Lord is willing to deal with mee, in the way of the Covenant of Grace." In prayer, "I now stirr'd up myself, to take hold of Him, earnestly putting my Soul, into the Hands of the Mediator, and crying to Him that Hee would convey unto mee, not only Pardon of Sin, but also Power against it, and make mee an happy Subject of all His redeeming Works." He marked the transition to the third phase of the day's exercises by singing William Barton's hymn "Humble Confessions and Supplications."[7]

From confession of sin and assurance of grace Mather turned to his responsibilities as a saint in the world. He meditated on his role as a spokesman for the Lord, that even casual verbal exchanges might be godly. "I sett myself, by further Meditation, to establish myself, in the use of such Rules of Speech, as might render mee a perfect Man." He petitioned the Lord in prayer for a new "Door of Utterance" or means by which he could proclaim the Word. "I had a full Assurance," Mather wrote, "that I was heard in this Petition." He sang the fifty-first psalm, prayed for wisdom and "the Presence of God with mee," sang Psalm 103, and, with evening approaching, examined his soul

6. Ford, ed., *Diary of Cotton Mather*, I, 56–57. For William Barton's hymn "Confession of Sin," see his *Six Centuries of Select Hymns and Spiritual Songs Collected Out of the Holy Bible . . .* , 4th ed. (London, 1688), 38–39.

7. Ford, ed., *Diary of Cotton Mather*, I, 57.

"by the signs of a State of Nature, and a State of Grace, given in Mr N[athaniel] Vincent's True Touchstone; and found Joyful cause to hope." Even then the day was not finished; Mather prayed for his congregation and went to a neighborhood meeting of "Christians, that were praeparing for the Communion tomorrow." He "pray'd and preach'd with them." After the meeting he visited a sick neighbor and prayed with him. Finally, in secret devotion he "shutt up the Day" by throwing himself fully "upon the Lord Jesus Christ alone, for Acceptance and Salvation."[8]

On days of secret thanksgiving Mather subjected himself to the same redemptive cycle but emphasized the renewed experience of grace and spiritual joy. He recollected "the merciful Dispensations of God unto mee" and the freeness with which God granted them. He registered them "in my Memorials," acknowledged them "in my Devotions," and resolved on a course of action to express his "Gratitude unto the Lord." In his daylong praisings of God Mather charged himself, "Think on these Things, O my Soul. Soak thyself in the Meditation of them." As a result, his "Heart was melted, in secret Prayer before the Lord."[9]

From the fall of 1681 onward Mather was meditating on a scriptural text in both the morning and the evening; in 1683 he further "methodized" his "nocturnal Recollections," or self-examination. He nightly questioned if he lived "under a deep Sense of Mortalitie and Eternitie; and as a Stranger in the World." He evaluated the effectiveness of his daily "Meditations upon heavenly Things" and his practice of ejaculatory prayer. He examined his usefulness to others and finally questioned himself: "Am I in a fitt State and Frame, to dy this Night if called thereunto?" At the turn of the new year, in March 1685, Mather added a midday period of devotion. For "at least Half an Hour" between twelve and one, he made "large Supplications to God, for myself, and my Flock, and my Countrey." When particular crises arose, Mather squeezed in additional hours for prayer by getting up earlier, as he did in the summer of 1685 to pray for "the distress'd Churches" in Europe. And Cotton Mather was master of the technique of spiritualizing common daily occurrences in occasional meditation and ejaculatory prayer in order "to redeem the silent, and otherwise thoughtless minutes of time."[10]

Preparation for the Sabbath was an important part of Cotton Mather's devotional life, as it was typically in New England. Even the

---

8. *Ibid.*, 58. Mather may have been using the 1681 London edition of Nathaniel Vincent's manual, *True Touchstone.*

9. *Ibid.*, 21–22.

composition of his sermons became not a rational but a devotional activity as he studied for "a great Part of my Sermons, kneeling" with his "Table-Book of Slate" before him on a chair. Mather would "intermingle" prayer, study, and writing. His final study of completed sermons on Saturday was also "an Exercise of Devotion." His technique was identical with his method of listening to another minister preach, and similar to the way he read and sang in private. As in reading and singing he strove to "fetch at least one Observation, and one Supplication, a Note and a Wish, out of every verse," so in going over his sermons he tried "to fetch an Ejaculation, out of every Head, and every Text." In the system of devotion Mather developed for his preparatory devotions on Saturday afternoon and evening, he engaged in the familiar exercises of reading, singing, meditation, and prayer, with specific focus on his congregation's needs, his pastoral vocation, and his message for the next day. Week after week Mather exulted in "the rare Experiences, which the Devotions of my Saturday-afternoons have brought unto mee."[11]

Mather's intense awareness of his own sinfulness continued, as Robert Middlekauff has said, throughout his life. But it would be a mistake to stop with an analysis of "the massive anxiety he endured so long," for Puritan anxiety was not spiritually crippling. By the final years of the seventeenth century Mather also commonly felt his soul lifted up into union with Christ and "exceedingly ravished." Nor is it correct to view spiritual discipline as dull routine, as does the recent editor of Mather's diary, who complains, "It never seems to occur to him that pursuing a given routine over and over, day after day, year after year, might result in a 'piety' more mechanical and formal than spiritually meaningful." Even at the superficial level, Mather continued to experiment and develop his methods, albeit along traditional lines. More important, however, Mather's exercises were, in the manner of contemplatives throughout religious history, a lifelong and habitual activity that led to an ever-deeper relationship with God. The unfathomable depths of his God prevented the "routine" from running dry. And Mather continually moved far beyond the awareness of sin that marked not only Puritan but early modern European sensibilities in general by channeling it into the constructive exercises of meditation and prayer. The order of redemption to which Mather and New Englanders submitted was a dynamic spiritual drama capable of filling the soul with delight and elevating it to ecstatic heights. The words Mather used to describe his experiences are similar to

10. *Ibid.*, 29, 74–75, 88, 104, 81–83.
11. *Ibid.*, 100–101, 108–109, 103, 88–89, 91.

those used by other, non-Puritan contemplatives, and they have mystical connotations: "inexpressibly irradiated from on High," "exceedingly ravished," "wondrously irradiated," "raised up into Heaven," "delights and raptures," and "afflatus." Cotton Mather was frequently lifted into a spiritual state in which he felt God was speaking to him either directly or through an angel.[12]

The contemplative is distinguished from the common practicing believer by the regularity, protractedness, and continuing intensity of the exercises. Early in his life Cotton Mather developed the traditional methods of piety to the point where he was capable of entering and persevering in the cycle of humiliation and thanksgiving over the period of a full week. He would "manage" a day of secret fasting and prayer one week, carry the results through to his preparation for the Sabbath, then keep a day of secret thanksgiving the next week. Confession of his own "Sinfulness and Filthiness" as he lay prostrate on the floor "with [his] mouth in the Dust" was the basis for prayers praising God a full week later. "In these Exercises," Mather wrote, his heart was rapt into "heavenly Frames, which would have turned a Dungeon into a Paradise." As he progressed in faith, Mather yearned increasingly for the ecstasy of being "possessed" by God and actually entering into complete union with Christ. His devotions became more and more emotional until by the mid-1690s he was commonly overcome by "a Flood of Tears" as they reached their climax. He wrote of "my weeping Faith" and of God renewing "my weeping Assurances and Evidences," outbursts that expressed his longing that the "Holy Spirit would yett more gloriously take possession of mee." He soon found at least an approximation of this mystic absorption of the self into God in moments that were finally and repeatedly ineffable. Most significant, Mather wrote not only of the Spirit and God's angel coming down but also of his soul being "raised up into Heaven." In November 1698, for example, he recorded that while using his traditional "Methods of Devotion" the "Delights and Raptures, whereto the Lord raised my Soul . . . were beyond, what I ordinarily enjoy'd." He reached the limit of his profound vocabulary: "I have this Day gone into the Suburbs of Heaven; the Spirit of my Lord has carried me thither, and has told mee glorious things; yea, Heaven has come near unto mee, and fill'd mee with Joy unspeakable and Full of Glory. I cannot utter, I may not utter, the Communications of Heaven,

12. Middlekauff, "Piety and Intellect," *WMQ*, 3d Ser., XXII (1965), 461. William R. Manierre II, ed., *The Diary of Cotton Mather, D.D., F.R.S. for the Year 1712* (Charlottesville, Va., 1964), xix. Ford, ed., *Diary of Cotton Mather*, I, 98, 37, 234, 241, 278, 355. See Thomas Merton, *New Seeds of Contemplation* (New York, 1961), e.g., 227.

whereto I have been this Day admitted: but this I will say, I have tasted that the Lord is gracious." Mather's use of the word "taste" did justice to the ultimately sensual nature of his experience even as it kept his devotions rooted in Scripture (1 Peter 2:3). He concluded, "My Exercises and Enjoyments, left mee very faint."[13]

Puritan theology and much of the preaching was rational in nature. But the devotional exercises, when pursued by the contemplative, led to experiences quite beyond the realm of reason. This ultimate non-rationality of religious experience linked Cotton Mather to Puritan contemplatives of the first half of the century. Thomas Shepard and Anne Bradstreet had engaged in the same devotional practices as did Cotton Mather, and they recorded their experiences in the same language of rapture, ravishment, and ecstasy. Near the end of the century Mather wrote: "Thus did I try to argue myself into the Faith, and Hope of my justification. But I must say, that I found no Spirit in all this rational way of Arguing: None of the Argument brought unto my Soul, that joyful Peace which I wanted. At last, the Spirit of God powerfully came in upon my Heart, and enabled mee to receive the Pardon of my Sin." Two generations earlier, Thomas Shepard had written of the same phenomenon. "A man's discourse about spiritual things is like philosophical discourse about the inward forms of things which they see not, yet see that they be. But by the light of the spirit of faith I see the thing presented as it is. I have seen a God by reason and never been amazed at God. I have seen God himself and have been ravished to behold him." In Puritan devotion the highest relationship of the soul to Christ was that of the lover.[14]

The cycle of anxiety and assurance and the availability of perfect union with Christ only after death, which some scholars have seen as signs of the limitation and neurosis of Puritanism, spawned the con-

13. Ford, ed., *Diary of Cotton Mather*, I, 109–112, 205, 207, 213, 241, 278.

14. *Ibid.*, 39. Shepard, "Journal," in McGiffert, ed., *God's Plot*, 136. Sacvan Bercovitch in *Puritan Origins*, 13, underestimates the extent and range of New England devotional practice by adopting the conventional understanding of Puritan spirituality. "Puritans stressed activism and experience" in the world and did not engage in "the contemplative life." He cites with approval Gordon Wakefield: "*Union with Christ is not the end but the beginning of the Christian Life.* It is not the result of a mystical technique, but of justification" (Wakefield, *Puritan Devotion*, 160). Bercovitch and Wakefield are correct at the level of theology, but at the level of spiritual experience they are incorrect. Conversion and knowledge of justification awakened in New Englanders the desire for *experience* of union with Christ. Even in the most common practice, preparationist devotions led believers into the realm of ever-nearer union with Christ and anticipation of full union with Him in the Kingdom.

templative side of the Puritan religious character. Those who took seriously the charge to prepare for meeting God on the Sabbath, in the Sacrament, and in death were perforce brought into contact with the ultimate realities of the soul and God. Though many devout New Englanders who participated fully in the life of worship and devotion seem to have limited their expectations to the knowledge of assurance of grace and an ongoing life of prayer (one thinks of Roger Clap and John Hull), assurance of grace was not the final goal of New England piety. The cycle of anxiety and assurance was the mirror image of Christ's death and resurrection. Puritan theology translated into devotional disciplines of repentance for sin and meditation on the glory of heaven, which, over months and years of continual practice, intensified into a higher contemplation of the Divine. It would be a mistake to underestimate the number of men—perhaps most of the clergy— and women who might be described by the phrase "Puritan contemplative." At the same time, the most advanced level of devotional practice was not generically different from the devotions of men and women of common piety. The Puritan contemplative demonstrates the rigorous culmination of a pervasive spirituality in which the entire populace participated.

Index

Index of Biblical References

NEW TESTAMENT